A Question of Priorities

The German Länder under the Occupation Powers until 1949.

A QUESTION OF PRIORITIES

Democratic Reforms and Economic Recovery in Postwar Germany

Frankfurt, Munich, and Stuttgart under U.S. Occupation 1945–1949

Volume 2: Monographs in German History

Rebecca L. Boehling

Berghahn Books
NEW YORK • OXFORD

First published in 1996 by
Berghahn Books

Editorial offices:
55 John Street, 3rd floor, New York, NY 10038, USA
3, NewTec Place, Magdalen Road, Oxford, OX 4 1RE, UK

© 1996, 1998 Rebecca L. Boehling

Boehling, Rebecca L., 1955-
   A question of priorities: democratic reforms and economic recovery in postwar Germany:
Frankfurt, Munich, and Stuttgart under U.S. occupation 1945-1949 / Rebecca L. Boehling.
   p.   cm. -- (Monographs in German History : v. 2)
   Includes bibliographical references.
   ISBN 1-57181-035-8 (alk. paper). -- ISBN 1-57181-159-1 (pbk. : alk. paper)
   1. Frankfurt am Main (Germany)--Politics and government. 2. Munich (Germany)--Politics
and government. 3. Stuttgart (Germany)--Politics and government. 4. Military government--
Germany--Frankfurt am Main. 5. Military government--Germany--Munich. 6. Military govern-
ment--Germany--Stuttgart. 7. Reconstruction (1939-1951)--Germany--Frankfurt am Main. 8.
Reconstruction (1939-1951)--Germany--Munich. 9. Reconstruction (1939-1951)--Germany--
Stuttgart. I. Title. II. Series.
DD901.F78B64 1996
352.043' 09' 044--dc20   96-24204
                                                             CIP

Library of Congress Cataloging-in-Publication Data
British Library Cataloguing in Publication Data
A catalogue record for this book is available from the British Library.

Printed in the USA on acid-free paper.

community
DL
90
F 8
6 4
a 96

CONTENTS

ABBREVIATIONS

ACC	Allied Control Council
AG	Adjutant General
ASTP	Army Specialized Training Program
BHKP	Bayerische Heimats- und Königspartei
BuR	Bürgermeister und Rat
BVP	Bayerische Volkspartei
CAD	Civil Affairs Division (also known as G-5)
CATS	Civil Affairs Training Schools
CCS	Combined Chiefs of Staff
CDU	Christian Democratic Union
CIC	Counter Intelligence Corps
CSU	Christian Social Union
DAF	Deutsche Arbeiterfront (German Labor Front)
DDP	Deutsche Demokratische Partei
DISCC	District Information Services Control Command
DMGO	Deputy Military Government Officer
DNVP	Deutsche Nationale Volkspartei
DPs	Displaced Persons
DVP	Deutsche Volkspartei
EAC	European Advisory Commission
ETO	European Theater of Operations
ETOUSA	European Theater of Operations U.S. Army
FAB	Freiheits-Aktion-Bayern
FDP	Freie Demokratische Partei
FDR	Franklin D. Roosevelt
FIS	Field Intelligence Study
HICOG	High Commission for Germany
ICD	Information Control Division
IfZ	Institut für Zeitgeschichte in Munich
ISD	Information Services Division

JCS	Joint Chiefs of Staff
KPD	Kommunistische Partei Deutschlands
L&S	Liaison and Security
LDP	Liberal Demokratische Partei
Mag	Magistratsakten
MG	Military Government
MGO	Military Government Officer (detachment commander)
MSo	Ministerium für Sonderaufgaben
NARA	National Archives Records Administration (U.S.)
NSV	Nationalsozialistische Volkswohlfahrt
OB	Oberbürgermeister (lord mayor)
ODI	Office of the Director of Intelligence
OMGBY	Office of Military Government – Bayern
OMGH	Office of Military Government – Hessen
OMGUS	Office of Military Government – U.S. Zone
OMGWB	Office of Military Government- Württemberg-Baden
OSS	Office of Strategic Services
OWI	Office of War Information
Pg	Parteigenosse (member of the Nazi [NSDAP] Party)
PMGO	Provost Marshall General's Office
POLAD	Office of the Political Advisor (of the U.S.)
POLAD/TS	Office of the Political Advisor – Top Secret
PWD	Psychological Warfare Division
R&A	Research and Analysis Branch (of the OSS)
RB	Regierungsbezirk
RG	Record Group
RP	Ratssitzungsprotokoll
SCAEF	Supreme Command Allied Expeditionary Forces
SED	Sozialistische Einheitspartei Deutschlands
SHAEF	Supreme Headquarters Allied Expeditionary Forces
SPD	Sozialdemokratische Partei Deutschlands
SSU	Special Services Unit
StA Ffm	Stadtarchiv Frankfurt m Main (now renamed Institut für Stadtgeschichte)
StA Mü	Stadtarchiv München
StA St	Stadtarchiv Stuttgart
USFET	United States Forces European Theater
USGCC	U.S. Group(Allied) Control Council
VVN	Vereinigung der Verfolgten des Naziregimes
VVW	Vorläufige Württembergische Wirtschaftsrat
WAV	Wirtschaftliche-Aufbau-Vereinigung

PREFACE

More than a decade ago my attention was drawn to the occupation of Germany after World War II because of an interest in the different national perspectives on modern German history. I thought I had finally found an actual case where historical interpretations about a country's past were used to develop real plans for its future. Much of the early planning for postwar Germany in the United States, in fact, involved prominent historians and social scientists like William Langer and Herbert Marcuse. I did write an M.A. thesis on U.S. planning for postwar Germany, but found myself still wanting to know what happened to those plans when – and if – they were implemented.

As a historian of Germany, I was also curious about the German side of the story. I felt certain that there was more to German expectations for Germany after the defeat of the Nazis than the plans of those Germans involved in the conspiracy of 20 July 1944 to assassinate Hitler. I suspected that other anti-Nazi Germans, who were less well-known than the July 20th conspirators, had offered their services to the conquering Allies, whom they would have considered liberators. But I also suspected that German opponents of the Nazi regime, many of whom were far to the Left of most of the July 20th group, may well have had political views and sociocultural orientations that differed considerably from those of the American planners, let alone from the military men of the U.S. occupation authorities. It was thus this interplay of expectations, plans, and hopes on the one hand, and political and cultural contrasts, on the other, which first drew me to the topic of the development of German self-government under U.S. occupation.

I chose the local level to explore this interplay, because this was the first place that military government was actually set up and the only level of German social organization to remain in any way intact after hostilities ceased. To learn about this interplay, one has to capture the personal interactions which can be discovered best on the local level. Although a few regional studies and single city studies do exist, no one has ventured to examine two or even three cities from a comparative perspective. Yet it is necessary to move beyond a single sample to avoid the danger of regional or personal anomalies. I have thus taken a comparative approach to a sample of what were arguably the three most important cities in the U.S. Zone of occupation: Frankfurt am Main, Munich, and Stuttgart.

My approach shows that both German and American motives and activities on the local level were often quite different from those of the Americans in Washington or Berlin, and those of the Germans at the state (Land) government level and zonal or "national" political leadership level. Although in some cases local developments did eventually mesh well with some top-level plans, this does not mean that either the motives or the intentions were the same. I explore not only what ultimately occurred, but also what initiatives were taken and why some worked out while others did not. My extensive use of both U.S. occupation materials and German municipal records from the three cities, as well as numerous interviews and correspondence with Germans and Americans from either municipal government or Military Government, provided me with a broad data base. I was then able to explore both the German and the American initiatives and each side's perspective of the other, as well as the interactions between the occupiers and the occupied. Even more importantly, in these interactions I found that there was often just as much cooperation as conflict. The German-American cooperation was often based on the pursuit of similar goals, sometimes ideological and sometimes pragmatic. Here, there were losers as well as winners, as one German-American shared interest lost out to another, especially when the goals of one shared interest meshed well with what eventually became the goal of the upper echelons of the U.S. authorities, namely, an expeditious German economic recovery.

This book would not have been possible without the support of a number of people and institutions. In graduate school at the University of Wisconsin, Professors David Bathrick, Gerhard Bauer, Jost Hermand, and Jim Steakley in the German department indirectly helped lead me to this topic when they allowed me to combine my interest in German literature and culture with sociopolitical historical concerns in my choice of seminar paper topics for my Ph.D. minor. In the history department, course work in British,

French, German, and European intellectual and cultural history with Professors James Donnelley, the late Edward Gargan, Theodore S. Hamerow, and George Mosse aided me in developing a comparative approach to history, which was particularly useful in my selection of a dissertation topic that involved both U.S. and German history.

The German Academic Exchange Service (Deutscher Akademische Austauschdienst or DAAD) provided me with two dissertation research grants in order to visit West German archives over an eighteen-month period between 1981 and 1983. The financial support provided by the colleges and universities where I have studied and taught was crucial to my completion of the dissertation and the research I have done for this book since then. Franklin and Marshall College and the University of Maryland Baltimore County have helped to finance my travel to conferences in the Federal Republic of Germany and the United States, where I have presented papers on themes that have helped me expand my dissertation on the development of German self-government under U.S. occupation. I often benefited greatly from the feedback of other conference participants. My 1993-94 Volkswagen Foundation Fellowship in Postwar German History at the American Institute for Contemporary German Studies (AICGS) and the German Historical Institute in Washington, D.C. provided me with the facilities and time to finish up some secondary research for this project, as well as to initiate my next project on postwar German women city councilors. Lily Gardner Feldman, the research director at AICGS, inspired me with her thoughtful scholarly reflections, her administrative know-how, her open-mindedness, and her personal warmth. My East German colleague at AICGS, Bernhard Maleck, provided me with both provocative insights into the early postwar period and genuine camaraderie.

In terms of the research itself, I would like to express my gratitude to a number of archivists and research staff whose help in pointing me in the right direction and in allowing me access to as many documents as I could order made this project possible. Robert Wolfe of the U.S. National Archives, Modern Military Branch, was helpful both with the use of documents and with his sharing of experiences with Military Government in Heidelberg. At the Institut für Zeitgeschichte in Munich, Hermann Weiss and Dr. Christoph Weisz were especially helpful with the OMGUS (Office of Military Government – U.S. Zone) files on microfiche and various collections pertaining to postwar political figures. Dr. Paul Sauer at the Hauptstaatsarchiv Stuttgart and Dr. Wolf-Arno Kropat at the Hessisches Hauptstaatsarchiv, along with Dr. Busli and Herr Saupe at the Bayerisches Hauptstaatsarchiv, made all the pertinent documents and archival finding aids, as well as their own expertise, available to me. The staffs of the city archives of Frankfurt, Munich, and Stuttgart showed great patience with my months-long period of daily visits and tall piles of document order forms. In particular, I would like to thank Frau Elke Weiss Weber and Frau Bayer of the Stadtarchiv Stuttgart; Dr. Stahleder and the Archivdirektor, Dr. Richard Bauer, of the Stadtarchiv München; the two now retired directors of the Stadtarchiv Frankfurt, Dr. Andernach and Dr. Wolfgang Klötzer; and Frau Karla Ihlde for their friendly cooperation, helpful suggestions, and encouragement. The current directors of all three of these city archives, Dr. Richard Bauer (Munich), Dr. Paul Sauer (Stuttgart), and Professor Dr. Dieter Rebentisch (Frankfurt am Main) have been most generous in granting me permission to use photographs from the archival collections for this book.

The many individuals I interviewed and corresponded with in (West) Germany and the United States were extremely helpful to me in terms of filling in research gaps and providing a more personal side to the occupation experience. The number of homes in which I was welcomed as a guest to meals and even sometimes on weekend visits, as in the case of Mr. Henry Walter and his wife, was overwhelming. The hospitality shown to me was especially appreciated because it carried with it no strings in the form of restrictions on how I interpreted the information provided me in the interviews or on my scholarly independence.

Although the responsibility for the contents of this book is mine alone, I have received support and encouragement at various stages of research and writing from a number of friends and colleagues whom I would like to acknowledge. The list is much too long to include them all, but I would like to single out Carole Fink for her steady encouragement and intellectual stimulation over many years, particularly for her very welcome suggestions on earlier versions of chapters 1 through 5. Frances Gouda provided me with helpful suggestions for strengthening my introduction and conclusion. She and her husband, Gary Price, and my friends, Whitney Walton, Sandra Marquardt, Annette Aronowicz, and Sol and Barbara Wank, provided me with solace and nurturing more than once when I was forced to postpone work to recover from surgery four times over the last six years. Most recently I owe my gratitude to Maria Höhn, who took out precious time from writing her own dissertation to read this entire manuscript. Thomas Schwartz, my former Volkswagen Fellowship colleague, graciously read the full manuscript and provided very helpful comments. Other Central European history colleagues who have shared with me their expertise, as well as my trials and tribulations in researching and writing, include Solomon Wank, Michael Fichter, Lawrence Flockerzie, James Diehl, and Günther Gerstenberg. Friends with other academic and nonacademic specialties have also contributed in various ways to the successful completion of this book. Of these, I would like to thank in particular Jean Soderlund, JoAnn and Peter Argersinger, Ed and Uta Larkey, Flo Martin, Margaret Knapke, and my German friends: Vera Neugebauer Rossner, Hans and Ursula Heitmeier, Peter Pischke and Hiltrud Pischke-Thelen, and Elke Weber, who so graciously opened their homes to me during my research trips. At the University of Maryland Baltimore County Nafi Shahegh and Faye Adams volunteered their invaluable clerical assistance, always showing me patience and understanding, especially when the deadlines approached and my nerves began to fray.

Last, but not least, I would like to dedicate this book to my family: my parents, who were the first to encourage me in my educational endeavors, my relatives in Germany, whom I got to know as a result of my interest in German history, and the most recent addition to my family, my husband Mark Lipkus, who has so graciously accepted my focus on the completion of this book both during our courtship and these first months of our marriage.

INTRODUCTION

*U*nlike the situation in 1918, the end of World War II in Germany resulted in complete military occupation and, in just over a year, a commitment from the United States to help rebuild Germany economically. Economic reconstruction brought with it political stability. The conditions under which the parliamentary democracy of the Bonn Republic was created differed fundamentally from those of the Weimar Republic. Yet there were certain characteristics of both the Weimar and the early Bonn Republic's governmental and societal infrastructures, including aspects of the civil service, the political party system, and economic structures, that did little to promote civic involvement and democratic responsibility. Although some very important changes were implemented by the Allies in order to make post-World War II Germany more democratic than any of its predecessor regimes, there were also numerous unsuccessful attempts by individuals and groups within the United States Military Government, and by German individuals and groups to push through even more sweeping changes. Such changes included a thorough denazification of German society, both in terms of individuals and structures. This involved compensation and "affirmative action" for victims of the Nazis; the redistribution of social and economic resources via decartellization and demilitarization; new, stronger roles for unions; either the nationalization of, or more cooperatively run and owned, housing and businesses; and codetermination (*Mitbestimmung*) by workers and management in all industrial decision making; the promotion of democratic civic involvement and accountability for elected and administrative officials; and less bureaucratic and authoritarian behavior in politics and government at all levels. The inability of reformers to facilitate these developments had little to do with the level of popular support for these changes in German society or with opposition, at the time, from U.S.

occupation policy makers. Rather, it can be traced back to the jurisdictional rivalries within the U.S. government during the war, which
resulted in the problematic training and selection of Military Government personnel and ambiguous instructions to them. These, in
turn, allowed numerous local-level German administrators and the
U.S. Military Government officials, who appointed or approved
them, to grant priority to material reconstruction over political and
social democratization. This prioritization ultimately meshed well
with the growing U.S. and Western concern with Communism, and
with the concurrent declining concern with Nazism in the midst of
the heightening tensions of the Cold War.

German municipalities constituted the first level of administration
and occupation for the Allies when hostilities ceased. In the U.S.
Zone of occupation, they were often the only level of organized
administration to exist for months. Both the U.S. Military Government detachment officers and the German local administrations and
bureaucracies, which the Americans filled with appointed personnel, agreed about the primacy of material recovery in stabilizing
postwar German communities. They felt that material recovery
required, first and foremost, order, efficiency, and an avoidance of
politics. Granting top priority to these prerequisites for material
recovery allowed, however, little if any room for many of the
changes required for a thorough democratization of German society
– one of the official goals of the U.S. occupation. Change, in its
capacity to upset routine, represented anathema to many bureaucrats and administrators. But it was often precisely these experienced bureaucrats and administrators who were in a position, on
the local level, to implement changes or to retain or revive old structures. The Third Reich had transformed some structures, and its
defeat certainly brought change again, but retaining unchanged
structures and returning to still-familiar pre-1933 forms of organization was a natural predilection for experienced bureaucrats and
administrators. Deep political and socioeconomic changes, such as
those called for in various Allied agreements, would transform what
was left of many familiar structures and could hinder material recovery. Until the kinks of new operating procedures and organizations
could be worked out, efficiency was bound to be affected.

The early emphasis on efficiency and material recovery, above all
else, of the local-level Military Government authorities and their German appointees meshed well with the later, higher-level decisions that
began in occupation policy in late 1946 as a result of growing Cold
War tensions. The original official U.S. occupation policy, which

stressed sociopolitical transformation through denazification and democratization programs, was replaced with a form of anti-Communism that saw economic reconstruction along capitalist lines as the means to revive the German economy and normalize German social and political life. The early efficiency-oriented local-level German developments under U.S. occupation facilitated economic recovery in a manner that allowed it not only to take precedence over more far reaching political and socioeconomic democratization, but also to discourage the participation of numerous Germans who were anxious to cooperate with the Allies in implementing democratization and denazification. This meant the loss of potentially widespread civic support for a new, democratic Germany and thus diminished the opportunity that 1945 represented as a major watershed in German history.

I will develop the arguments behind this assertion both chronologically and thematically in the seven chapters that follow. Chapter 1 will set the stage for the U.S. occupation of Germany and describe the various plans, personnel training, and administrative agencies involved in preparing for the occupation. Chapter 2 will outline the structure and jurisdiction of local Military Government and the guidelines for the appointment and election of German local officials that the Military Government detachments received from their superiors. Chapter 3 will delineate the actual "Zero Hour" situation in all three cities. It will discuss who the representatives of the U.S. occupation were in the three cities, and what kind of appointments they made upon their arrival. Chapter 4 will explore who the German appointees were, and who else was qualified or actually prepared to fill these key municipal posts. Chapter 5 will portray the early forms of German semi-self-government, including the various bureaucratic, political, and socioeconomic structures and democratic initiatives. This will be shown within the framework of conflict and/or cooperation with the U.S. occupation authorities and their German appointees. Chapter 6 will sketch the ways in which democratic self-government was restored over time (for example, through elections), and at what points Military Government intervened in this process. It will also explore how certain political and socioeconomic reforms that were related to denazification and democratization were either safeguarded or stymied by those individual German officials and American occupiers who were in positions of power. I will place these developments in the context of the goals of the U.S. occupation as they changed from the prevention of a survival or revival of Nazism in Germany to the reconstruction of Germany into an economically strong bulwark against Communism.

In the final chapter, "The Legacy of the Occupation,"I will draw conclusions about the tension between the apparent potential for reform in the interregnum between the Third Reich and the division of Germany and the limitations caused by unclear Military Government instructions, inadequate personnel, and the distrust of unfamiliar and/or radical politics. I will also discuss the natural desire to restore order and normalcy on the part of Germans and Americans alike in the midst of overwhelming wartime destruction. Then I will consider the larger question regarding the extent to which the pursuit of certain occupation goals and the abandonment of others affected the long-term development of West German political and socioeconomic tendencies.

I have chosen major cities in the U.S. Zone as case studies for the influence of U.S. Military Government on the development of German self-government because of the importance of urban centers for what eventually became the primary goal of the U.S. occupation: economic reconstruction. Although urban developments may have a local flair and flavor to them, they are less likely to depend on individual relationships than developments in rural areas. In addition, studies of major metropolitan centers can provide insights into relations between labor and management, relatively complex government structures, and elite formation, as well as into party politics, which transcend anecdotal evidence. Local politics in major cities and state capitals such as Frankfurt am Main, Munich, and Stuttgart were more likely to influence regional, zonal, and national political and socioeconomic developments than those in smaller towns and rural counties. Cities, with their more complex level of municipal administration, were also occupied by larger Military Government detachments than towns or rural counties, so that a larger sample of Military Government personnel from which to draw conclusions is available and individual anomalies can be recognized as such.

Cities that were either Länder capitals, such as Munich and Stuttgart, or the headquarters of U.S. Military Government and the U.S. Forces-European Theater (USFET), such as Frankfurt, provide additional advantages for this kind of socio-political focus. In the former case, these capitals were seats of the German Länder governments and of the Land-level Military Government detachments. As such, they received special attention from both levels of Military Government, and their local German leaders were likely to have special contacts with the Land leaders and to play special roles beyond their municipal affairs. In fact, Land officials were often recruited by Military Government and the Germans from these local municipal elites. Frankfurt would have been the capital of Hesse if the Americans had not seized so many of its available, intact buildings for their headquarters and housing. Its near-capital status, and the fact that it was looked upon as the role model of the U.S. Zone while USFET and OMGUS headquarters were located there, made it an appropriate choice; certainly more appropriate than the spa resort of Wiesbaden, which became the Hessian capital. The importance of these three cities for the three Länder of the U.S. Zone, and for the Zone as a whole, justifies their selection for this study.

Rather than just one, I scrutinize three cities so that I can exclude peculiarities and facilitate generalizations about U.S. occupation policies and their implementation in postwar Germany. This comparative approach allows me to identify those traits unique to a particular city because of its sociological make-up; its political, cultural, and religious traditions; and its economic base; and conversely, those tendencies which could be considered more universal. Although these three cities share the attribute of being the most important in each of the three Länder of the U.S. Zone, there are also some significant differences among them; differences that should enhance the validity of the generalizations made about the impact of the U.S. occupation on the development of German self-government. The recognition of critically different variables in otherwise similar situations can help explain disparate outcomes and identify relationships that might otherwise remain obscure. The particular nature of the immediate postwar circumstances in Frankfurt, Munich, and Stuttgart must be understood in order to bring together a range of social and political phenomena under some common rubric that can illustrate similarities and differences.

Frankfurt, Munich, and Stuttgart provide sufficient diversity in terms of religious, cultural, sociological, economic, and political structures to merit comparison and to allow for generalizations. In Hesse, the predominantly Protestant city of Frankfurt am Main served as the commercial and trade center of pre-1945 Germany and continues to do so in the postwar Federal Republic. Frankfurt, long known as a cosmopolitian city with tolerance for diversity, had one of the largest Jewish communities in Germany before World War II. Its nickname during the Weimar Republic was "Rote Frankfurt" because of its history as a stronghold of the Social Democratic Party (SPD). Because of the city's forced annexation into Prussia in the 1860s, Frankfurt's governmental structures, with both an elected lord mayor and a professional city administrator, are based on the Prussian model of municipal administration.

Munich, the capital of Bavaria, was the cultural center of southern Germany and the former so-called "Hauptstadt der Bewegung" (capital of the Nazi movement). Traditionally, Munich exhibited political extremes: it experienced the only soviet-style (*Räte*) republic during the 1918/19 German Revolution and became the birthplace of the Nazi Party in 1920. Munich, like almost all of Bavaria, was (and still is) very strongly Catholic, although its Bavarian regionalism and antifederalist tendencies were stronger than any internationalist Catholic ones. This is evidenced in the post World War I formation of the Bavarian People's Party (BVP), an organization separate from the Center Party, and in the continued existence of the postwar Christian Social Union (CSU) (distinct from the Christian Democratic Union [CDU]). This Bavarian particularism can also be found among the other political parties, whether the SPD, the Free Democatic Party (FDP), or other postwar small parties and social groups, and fostered a certain amount of provincial xenophobia and anticentralism. The traditional local particularism, in turn, inculcated an independence in Bavarian political figures, who were less likely to follow political party discipline if it was ordered from outside Bavaria. Bavarians in general were and continue to be more likely to be skeptical of parties that have strong allegiances outside of Bavaria.

Württemberg-Baden, as the Land was called at the time, was divided among the French and the U.S. Zones of occupation, with the south going to the former and the north to the latter. Located in North Württemberg-Baden, Stuttgart has been the industrial hub of southern Germany in the twentieth century. Its population included a very large industrial working class as well as a very wealthy industrial elite. The vast majority of the population of Stuttgart was and is Protestant. Its Swabian ties give Stuttgart's people a reputation for being very hard-working and industrious, while its proximity to France has nurtured certain Francophile aspects of its culture. Stuttgart, in fact, was initially occupied in 1945 by the French, although it was, according to wartime Allied agreements, supposed to fall under U.S. control. After several months, the French gave in to U.S. pressure and relinquished control of the city to the Americans. The city's geography resembles a kettle, with the inner city at the bottom and various outlying districts, segregated on the basis of class, along the walls. Stuttgart's geography promoted strong neighborhood allegiances, especially during the war when bombing often cut off one area from another.

My three-city approach fills a research gap in numerous ways. It combines social with political history and merges American with

German history in order to explore the impact of the U.S. occupation on the development of German self-government. By analyzing three locales, this book sheds light on the reciprocal influence and interaction between and among various Germans and Americans. Being primarily concerned with the complicated question of continuity and change in postwar Germany, this book focuses on the political and administrative elite, and explores personnel continuity in municipal government in these three cities from the Weimar Republic until 1949. I examine the German personnel policies of the U.S. Military Government detachments starting with the first year of the occupation, when all city officials and provisional city council members were appointed either directly by Military Government or approved by it upon the recommendation of its German appointees. My analysis of personnel policies continues through the first postwar municipal elections in 1946 and 1948, when democratic local self-government was gradually restored. This study also examines the occupation of these three cities to assess the extent to which U.S. Military Government accomplished, or even pursued, the occupation goals proclaimed by the United States. In this context, I examine the background of the members of the Military Government detachments, whose assignment it was to implement these goals on the most basic level of German administrative organization, i.e., the municipality. I also investigate the personal profiles of the Germans whom the Military Government officers selected to restore German self-government as a way of comprehending motives and priorities. By exploring which other Germans Military Government detachments could have chosen, and whether different choices would have made a difference in the pursuit of the original occupation goals or in the results of German elections, I hope to illuminate how the interaction between Americans and Germans affected subsequent political and socioeconomic developments.

My primary chronological focus is on the first year of the occupation, the potential Zero Hour or *Stunde Null* – the time most conducive to change – precisely because Germans had less autonomy and self-government, and Military Government had more influence on German developments at this time than at any other during the occupation period. But this study is not limited to the first year of the occupation. In order to show the influence of the decisions made in this first year, I cover the entire OMGUS, or military phase, of the occupation, which ended in 1949. At that point, a switch occurred from military control to civilian supervision by the High Command for Germany (HICOG) under the State Department. This transition reflected the growing autonomy of the Germans as manifested in the 1949 proclamation of the Basic Law and the founding of the Federal Republic of Germany.

Unlike previous research on the U.S. occupation of Germany, this study uses a comparative sociopolitical case-study approach, in order to explore a series of questions: What goals were given the top priority by those Americans and Germans with the most influence in that first year? What kind of pattern did the pursuit of these priorities, on the local level, establish for the rest of the occupation period and the early years of the Federal Republic? Where did these local developments intersect with international ones, such as the growing Cold War tensions? When and why did economic recovery take precedence over political and social democratization? What was the legacy of the occupation for the development of the Federal Republic?

I use both quantitative and qualitative methodologies to explore questions of continuity and change with regard to the Weimar Republic and the Third Reich. Quantitatively, the political and social backgrounds of the 1945 German appointees to the municipal offices of the lord mayor or *Oberbürgermeister* (OB), the deputy mayor or 2. *Bürgermeister*, and the advisory city councils are compared with those of the 1946 and 1948 elected officials. I also compare these data with similar data I have collected on the municipal officials of the Third Reich and the Weimar Republic in order to have a broader historical perspective. But my approach is qualitative in its in-depth inquiry into the biographies of the mayors, police chiefs, and other key German officials. Here I use personnel documents and oral interviews with former city councilors and department heads. I have also conducted oral interviews and surveys by mail of U.S. Military Government officers in order to determine the social and educational background, as well as the specific civil affairs training, of the detachment officers.

I use primary sources from both American and German archives. The majority of the historical documents of the immediate postwar period have only recently been made accessible to the public, because most documents remain closed to researchers for thirty years after the documented event, or in some cases, thirty years after the death of the individual(s) involved. When I began this research the documents were in the same disarray as they had been when they were sent to the city and state archives from the city halls and municipal department offices. German municipal and state archivists are still busy reordering materials from as far back as the Middle Ages because of the great extent to which they were shuffled about and/or partially destroyed during the war. This means that very few of the postwar materials had been perused by archivists even for classification or declassification purposes at the time I conducted this research. In the meantime, many of the materials I used for this book have been organized by the archivists and access has been restricted. Although future researchers will have a less time-consuming task ahead of them due to the better organization of the sources, they will also have more limited access to materials. This is also true for some of the American documents in the OMGUS files and the Office of Strategic Services (OSS) and State Department files in the United States National Archives Record Administration, some of which were reclassified during the Reagan administration, after previously having been declassified. These recent restrictions on access to some of the sources cited in this book, also, will affect the content and analysis of future related research. I can only hope that the publication of my book will place pressure on government and archival authorities to open scholarly access to these documents once again.

The period following the collapse of the Third Reich has been a topic of great interest to political scientists and scholars of contemporary German history (*Zeitgeschichte*). Many more authors have focused their attention on the U.S. occupation than on the other three Allies. This preoccupation with the role of the United States in Germany was partly due to the earlier public access to archival documents in the United States as compared to access to the British and French, and especially the Soviet documents. The emphasis on the U.S. occupation can also be attributed to the political and economic hegemony of the United States at the time, resulting in the stronger impact of the American occupation than that of the British and particularly the French on the founding of the Federal Republic.

Actual participants in the American occupation, in particular academics who served as temporary advisors, rendered the first accounts of the occupation of Germany.[1] Their motives ranged from

---

1. See for example Carl J. Friedrich (ed.), *American Experiences in Military Government in World War II* (New York, 1948), Hajo Holborn, *American Military Government. Its Organizations and Policies* (Washington, 1947), Harold Zink, *American Military Government in Germany* (New York, 1947), and *The United States in Germany, 1944 –1955* (Princeton, 1957). See also various articles by other academics who had worked with MG which appeared in the late 1940s and early 1950s in journals such as the *Political Science Quarterly* and the *Annals of the American Academy of Political and Social Sciences*. Several are cited in the early chapters of this manuscript and are included in the bibliography. A somewhat less academic account of the U.S. Army's occupation of Germany, stressing material and social condi-

purely scholarly ones, to a desire to criticize decisions that were made against their better judgment in the hope of promoting policy changes while it was still possible. The U.S. Army itself commissioned a number of studies on various aspects of the occupation,[2] although most of those were not published until quite some time after they were written.[3] The Army's interest was in the planning of the occupation and the military's role in carrying out those plans. In the first postwar decades, nonmilitary historians and political scientists focused their analyses on tracing the division of Germany back to conflicts between the Allies during the quadripartite occupation of Germany. Over time, this Cold War focus[4] was broadened to include relations between the Germans and the various Allied powers during the occupation period. The inclusion of the vanquished alongside the victors stemmed from the desire, especially on the part of German scholars, to know how much leeway the Germans had had in determining their future,[5] and to see how they had reacted to various international and domestic developments.[6] But this was still more of a traditional approach to political history.

By the early 1970s, however, a number of scholars began examining the economy and culture of German society, under the occupation in order to explore how much of a legacy these early trends had left for the development of West Germany.[7] This stress on Ger-

---

tions in Germany from the occupier's perspective is Franklin M. Davis, Jr.'s *Come as a Conqueror: The United States Army's Occupation of Germany 1945–1949* (New York, 1967).

2. Probably the most famous military history is that by Earl F. Ziemke, *The U.S. Army in the Occupation of Germany 1944–46*, Army Historical Series (Washington, 1975).

3. Joseph R. Starr was commissioned to write a history of denazification by HICOG, which he completed in 1950. It was not published until 1977, and then it was done by a private company. Whether this was due to the critical conclusions of the study or whether the subject was simply classified until 1977 is unclear. See Joseph R. Starr, *Denazification, Occupation and Control of Germany* (Salisbury, N.C., 1977).

4. See in particular Josef Foschepoth (ed.), *Kalter Krieg und deutsche Frage. Deutschland im Widerstreit der Mächte 1945–1952* (Göttingen, 1985) and Bruce Kuklick, *American Policy and the Division of Germany* (Ithaca, N.Y., 1972).

5. See especially the various essays in Heinrich A. Winkler (ed.), *Politische Weichenstellungen im Nachkriegsdeutschland* (Göttingen, 1979).

6. For example, see Hans-Peter Schwarz, *Vom Reich zur Bundesrepublik. Deutschland im Widerstreit der aussenpolitischen Konzeptionen in den Jahren der Besatzungsherrschaft 1945–1949*, 2nd ed. (Stuttgart, 1980).

7. A few examples include Wilhelm Abelshauser, *Wirtschaft in Westdeutschland, 1945–1948. Rekonstruktion und Wachstumsbedingungen in der amerikansichen und*

man domestic developments led to a new focus of historiography in the 1970s and early 1980s on the issue of whether U.S. Military Government and the western German occupation, as a whole, had either reinforced continuity or forged change in German history.[8] Some of the authors tended to place the responsibility for what they considered, falsely in my opinion, a restoration of pre-1945 Germany, minus Hitler and the Nazi elite, exclusively on the shoulders of the Americans while presenting the Germans as victims. Others saw German conservative forces, with the acquiescence of the American occupiers, as actively preventing change. Although scholars recognized that there were different political and socioeconomic forces at work on the German side, few historians differentiated among the American occupiers or their motives, or explored how Military Government's influence sometimes intensified and sometimes subverted German intentions. U.S.-German interactions were neglected because many early studies were either issue-oriented (such as the case of the socialization of industry, when a top-level figure in U.S. Military Government, General Lucius D. Clay, played

---

britischen Zone (Stuttgart, 1975); Karl-Ernst Bungenstab, *Umerziehung zur Demokratie? Re-education Politik im Bildungswesen der US-Zone 1945–49* (Düsseldorf, 1970); Jutta-B. Lange-Quassowski, *Neuordnung oder Restauration. Das Demokratiekonzept der amerikanischen Besatzungsmacht und die politische Sozialisation der Westdeutschen* (Opladen, 1979); Wolfgang Rudzio, "Die ausgebliebene Sozialisierung an Rhein und Ruhr," *Archiv für Sozialgeschichte,* 18 (1978), pp. 1–39; Volker Christian Wehdeking, *Der Nullpunkt. Über die Konstituierung der deutschen Nachkriegsliteratur (1945–48) in den amerikanischen Kriegsgefangenenlagern* (Stuttgart, 1971); Gerhard Wettig, *Entmilitarisierung und Wiederbewaffnung in Deutschland 1943–1955* (München, 1967).

8. See Jürgen W. Falter, "Kontinuität und Neubeginn. Die Bundestagswahl 1949 zwischen Weimar und Bonn," *Politische Vierteljahresschrift* 22 (1981), pp. 236–63; Ernst-Ulrich Huster, et al., *Determinanten der westdeutschen Restauration 1945–1949* (Frankfurt a. M., 1972); Jürgen Kocka, "1945: Neubeginn oder Restauration?" in: Carola Stern und Heinrich A. Winkler (eds.),*Wendepunkte deutscher Geschichte 1848–1945* (Frankfurt a. M., 1979); Horst Lademacher, "Aufbruch oder Restauration – Einige Bemerkungen zur Interdependenz von Innen – und Aussenpolitik in der Gründungsphase der Bundesrepublik Deutschland," in: Immanuel Geiss and Bernd J. Wendt (eds.), *Deutschland in der Weltpolitik des 19. und 20. Jahrhunderts* (Düsseldorf, 1973), pp. 563–84; Karlheinz Niclauss, *Restauration oder Renaissance der Demokratie? Die Entstehung der Bundesrepublik 1945–1949* (Berlin, 1982); Lutz Niethammer, et al, *Arbeiterinitiative 1945: Antifaschistische Ausschüsse und Reorganisation der Arbeiterbewegung von Deutschland* (Wuppertal, 1976); Eberhard Schmidt, *Die verhinderte Neuordnung 1945–1952* (Frankfurt a. M., 1970). An even earlier regional study is Lutz Niethammer, "Die amerikanische Besatzungspolitik zwischen Verwaltungstradition und politischen Parteien in Bayern 1945," *Vierteljahrshefte für Zeitgeschichte* 15 (1967), pp. 153–210.

the major role in the final outcome), or they attempted to give broad macrocosmic analyses, which were not sensitive to geographic or individual differences.[9] Few delved deeply into the relationships between the Germans and the Americans on any level below that of the top Military Government leadership and minister presidents (heads of the states or Länder) and their cabinet members. The OMGUS public opinion surveys, which were published with editorial comments in 1970, provide helpful insights into German reaction to the U.S. occupation.[10] But they possess the limitations of all surveys in terms of the quantity and quality of the questions posed and the reliability and representativeness of the responses. The surveys also fail to explore the relationships between Germans and U.S. personnel beyond German reaction to Military Government policies.

Several historians have explored the relations between Germans and their occupiers in a few local histories of individual towns, counties, or cities, but these studies are often narrowly focused on concerns of interest to native residents. Although these local histories chronicle interesting anecdotes, their authors rarely have addressed the broader political and socioeconomic issues, such as those of structural change in the context of the development of German self-government. Very few of these studies include materials from the OMGUS files or other American documents, but, because of restricted access or language barriers, or perhaps even owing to a lack of interest, were limited to German sources.[11] On the other

---

9.   One might have expected these works to have generated more narrowly focused monographs to test the continuity/change analysis in more detailed ways. But this focus was perceived by a number of more traditional scholars and contemporaries of the period to be so ideologically laden that more junior historians and graduate students were discouraged from giving a number of the core issues that were brought up in these works the scholarly attention that they deserved. As a result, the general issues often were not pursued further by more narrowly focused monographs such as doctoral dissertations. As experienced by this author at a number of West German scholarly conferences in the 1980s, this research direction often was relegated to a leftist ghetto that was considered polemical and labeled with the red herring of Marxism.

10.   Anna J. and Richard L. Merritt (eds.), *Public Opinion in Occupied Germany. The OMGUS Surveys 1945–1949* (Chicago, 1970).

11.   In 1966 Peter Beyersdorf published his dissertation at the University of Nürnberg/Erlangen on U.S. occupation policies on the local level from 1945 to 1948 by looking at the town and county (Landkreis) of Coburg. The U.S. Military Government files were not yet available to researchers when Beyersdorf did his research. His research relied somewhat uncritically on German sources and a few published U.S. sources with the result that his interpretations come across as impressionistic. His analysis never really considers issues of continuity and change. See Peter Beyersdorf, *Militärregierung und Selbstverwaltung: Eine Studie zur*

hand, one of the two studies of the military occupation of cities in the U.S. Zone, Nuremberg and Würzburg, relies almost exclusively on American sources without any apparent awareness of the short-comings resulting from the lack of German documents. The Nurem-berg study does not even concern itself with the development of German self-government.[12] Yet a case study of a German munici-pality could reveal the development of German self-government, because the municipality was the first level to receive any semblance of German self-government after the occupation began.

Two sophisticated case studies of the effects of the U.S. occupa-tion with broader analyses do exist. By venturing to transcend the microcosm, John Gimbel and Hans Woller present their local stud-ies as case studies of the larger question of the impact of the U.S. occupation on general German developments. As early as 1961, John Gimbel published a groundbreaking sociopolitical case study of the Hessian town, Marburg, under American occupation in order to examine the impact of U.S. Military Government on one particular town and to speculate about the influence of the occupation on Ger-man developments.[13] More recently, Hans Woller, a researcher at the Institute for Contemporary History in Munich, published a detailed study of politics, society, and the economy in the rural counties (*Landkreise*) of Ansbach and Fürth in Franconia in Bavaria under the American occupation.[14] Gimbel's work was not able to

---

amerikanischen Besatzungspolitik auf der Stufe einer Gemeinde in den Jahren 1945–1948, dargestellt an Beispiele aus dem Stadt – und Landkreis Coburg, Diss. University of Erlangen/Nürnberg, 1966.

12. Boyd L. Dastrup, *Crusade in Nuremberg: Military Occupation, 1945–1949* (Westport, Conn., 1985). The other study of a major city in the U.S. Zone is Herbert Schott's 1984 dissertation on Würzburg, which reflects detailed research but is sorely lacking in solid analysis. His tendency to overgeneralize may issue from his extreme reliance on newspapers as primary sources. Schott extrapolates wildly on the basis of examples from other cities when he has no information about Würzburg. He also displays little knowledge of international relations at the time. His exclamatory remarks about MG's power denotes a nationalistic defensive-ness, on the one hand, and a lack of understanding of unconditional surrender and total occupation, on the other. This case study suffers from a lack of famil-iarity with the overarching political, social, and economic circumstances of the occupation period as a whole. See Herbert Schott, *Die Amerikaner als Besatzungs-macht in Würzburg (1945–1949)*, Mainfränkische Studien (Würzburg, 1985).

13. John Gimbel, *A German Community under American Occupation* (Stanford, 1961). A few years later, Gimbel published a history of the U.S. occupation of Germany, which remains a standard work on the topic: *The American Occupation of Ger-many. Politics and the Military, 1945–49* (Stanford, 1968).

14. Hans Woller, *Gesellschaft und Politik in der amerikanischen Besatzungszone: Die Region Ansbach und Fürth* (München, 1986).

incorporate many of the archival sources which are, after thirty years, now accessible to researchers. Woller's study reflects extensive use of both American and German sources; although its rural focus is enlightening, it tells us little about urban experiences under the occupation.

Besides the 1985 studies of Nuremberg and Würzburg, which are not in any way comparable to the works of Woller and Gimbel, no one else has ventured to examine a major urban center in the U.S. Zone of occupation as a case study of the impact of the occupation on German developments. Both Gimbel's and Woller's works touched upon the issue of continuity and change, but this was not their primary concern. A comparative urban case study, with a focus on continuity and change as well as on individual decisions and interactions, is needed in order to examine more thoroughly the impact of U.S. Military Government on the development of German self-government and thus its influence on German political and socioeconomic developments. In this book, I hope to fill this need.

Chapter 1

AMERICAN PREPARATIONS FOR POSTWAR GERMAN SELF-GOVERNMENT

Introduction

*T*he purpose and goals of the U.S. occupation of Germany were rid-
dled with both ambiguity and controversy. There were two levels of
planning for postwar Germany: the actual departmental level in the
U.S. government and that of the more abstract, public opinion-ori-
ented schools of thought. Only when a school of thought had support in high-level decision-making posts did the two levels intersect,
and only then did such schools have any real impact upon policy.

Historians and political scientists have generally examined the
departmental level of planning for the treatment of postwar Germany. Was Germany to become an agrarian pastureland, as Secretary of the Treasury Morgenthau's "Program to Prevent Germany
from Starting a World War III" proposed, or was it to play an indispensable international role as an economically and politically strong
capitalist nation between East and West, an approach which the
State Department came to advocate? Adopted by American historiography since 1945 and by numerous West German scholars,[1] this

---

1. The American literature tends to group the State and War Departments together
    as Cold War reconstructionists and the Treasury and FDR together as
    vengeance-seeking Morgenthau Plan supporters. See Edward N. Peterson's *The
    American Occupation of Germany* (Detroit, 1978). The German political scientists,
    Karl-Ernst Bungenstab and Jutta-B. Lange-Quassowski use the terminology
    "Linke-Realpolitiker" for the two groups. In his 1970 *Umerziehung zur Demokratie*
    and her 1979 book, *Neuordnung oder Restauration*, they associate the Left-
    oriented politics of the New Deal with Roosevelt and the Morgenthau Plan

characterization into two schools not only oversimplifies the departmental rivalries, but also ignores a school of thought outside the neat categories of retribution and reconstruction. The "Other Germany" school[2] was concerned with structural political and economic changes in postwar Germany and with the question of who would implement them. Paralleling the hopes of many anti-Nazis in Germany, the "Other Germany" school was more or less detached from both the Treasury-State conflict over industrial emasculation versus economic reconstruction, and from the controversy between War and State over short-term military occupation versus long-term civilian control. The "Other Germany" school was oriented seemingly more toward German interests than American ones; it hoped to revive and foster Germany's own democratic traditions so that the Germans themselves could create a denazified, demilitarized, and decartellized new order.

The rivalry in the planning stage was reflected in the ambiguity of occupation directives that the actual on-the-scene Military Government (MG) detachments were obligated to implement in the towns, cities, and counties they occupied. The pragmatism and individualism which characterized most detachment officers' approach to MG was exacerbated by the absence of clear-cut directives expressing the policies and goals of the U.S. occupation. By the time Secretary of State Byrnes emphasized the positive goal of economic reconstruction and the reintegration of Germany into the international community of nations in Stuttgart in September 1946, the practice of U.S. MG had already been firmly established. Policy as implemented was pragmatic and practical: getting German cities and towns running again as expeditiously as possible and resuming "business as usual." Although feeding and housing the German population was indisputably crucial, the often singular emphasis on the clear and seemingly less controversial policy of material reconstruction and efficient administration resulted not just in a postponement of numerous political and socioeconomic reforms, but in the loss of a potential Stunde Null, when the exploration of structural renovation

---

advocates, and therefore label this group the Linke. They designate the ardent anti-Communists, predominantly in the State Department, who advocated a speedy economic reconstruction, the "Realpolitiker."

2. *Das andere Deutschland* was a newspaper in the Weimar Republic advocating an end to so-called Prussian militaristic traditions and promoting international peace and disarmament. It seems probable that the expression, the "Other Germany," dates back to this publication, or at least to the association with the interwar peace movement.

was so opportune. This development, irrespective of intention, facilitated the realization of many of the plans of the State and War Departments, yet spelled defeat for many of the goals of both the Treasury Department and the "Other Germany" school.

Government Departmental Rivalries over Planning for Postwar Germany

President Franklin D. Roosevelt fanned the flames of interdepartmental rivalry by assigning occupation planning tasks to both the State and War Departments and by allowing the Treasury Department under Henry Morgenthau to advise him on policy, without clearly defining the limits of the departments' respective jurisdictions or the distinction between civilian and military roles. According to army doctrine, the theater commander had to be the military governor, at least until hostilities ceased. In Novermber 1942, FDR granted Secretary of State Hull full authority over economic and political questions in all liberated territories, including Germany.[3] Because Germany would not be defeated in a single battle or by the United States alone, hostilities would continue in some regions while other regions would be conquered, occupied, and subject to specific economic and political policies. Without agreement over the distinction between military factors and political considerations, jurisdictional conflicts seemed inevitable.

In early 1943 the Civil Affairs Division (CAD) was created within the War Department as a staff division limited to the planning and supervision of MG wherever needed, anywhere in the world.[4] In November 1943 the president assigned the Army (i.e., War Department) the primary role in running MG and training its personnel.[5] But while the War Department seemed to have gained control over the training of MG personnel, jurisdiction over occupation policies and goals remained an area of contention, not only by the State and War Departments, but, as of mid-1944, by the Treasury Department as well.

In the State Department, Secretary Cordell Hull supported the long-term economic reconstruction of Germany[6] as a prerequisite to

---

3. Peterson, *American Occupation*, p. 31f.
4. Zink, *American*, p. 2.
5. Peterson, p. 31f.
6. John L. Snell, *Wartime Origins of the East-West Dilemma over Germany* (New Orleans, 1959), p. 24.

a "broadly based democracy" and as an assimilation of the Germans into the international order.[7] But it was not until the fall of 1943 that a State Department consensus emerged on the necessity of demobilization, demilitarization, denazification, and restitution. There was also concensus on a long-term occupation policy aimed at creating postwar German living conditions that would be "attractive enough to endear the new regime to the Germans."[8] On the other hand, Secretary of War Henry Stimson and his Assistant Secretary John J. McCloy preferred a short military occupation with minimal political responsibilities. Emphasizing "military necessity," the War Department's "theory of limited liability" reduced MG to the basic, essential tasks related directly to the war and its physical consequences.[9] Although Secretaries Hull and Stimson were both haunted by the fear that too drastic a weakening of Germany would allow the ascendancy of the Soviet Union in Europe,[10] the War Department was not in agreement with the State Department's long-term commitment to reconstruct Germany, and wanted, rather, to avoid a harsh peace in order to "get the hell out of Dodge" as quickly as possible. The War Department hoped both to avoid establishing its own occupation policy and to prevent civilians from interfering in MG planning. When its CAD refused in 1943 to cooperate with the State Department in drafting a long-term occupation program,[11] the prospect of harmonious interdepartmental cooperation, essential for concrete policy formulation, appeared rather remote. In this strife-ridden atmosphere the Morgenthau Plan was conceived and, at least temporarily, well received by the President.

The Morgenthau Plan originated with the treasury secretary's discovery that the policies proposed in the European Advisory Commission (EAC), SHAEF (Supreme Headquarters Allied Expeditionary Forces) in London, and in the State Department in Washington were all based on the economic reconstruction and general rehabilitation of Germany. The three men who assisted John G. Winant, the U.S. representative in the EAC, governed their views toward Germany by

---

7. Harley A. Notter, *Postwar Foreign Policy Preparation 1939–1945*. Department of State Publication 3580, General Foreign Policy Series 15 (Washington, 1950), p. 558f.

8. Hammond, p. 324.

9. IfZ Munich, Walter Dorn, *The Unfinished Purge*, Unfinished MS, p. 73.

10. Hans W. Gatzke, *Germany and the United States: "A Special Relationship?"* (Cambridge, Mass., 1980), p. 146.

11. Henry L. Stimson and McGeorge Bundy, *On Active Service in Peace and War* (New York, 1947), p. 25f. See also John Lewis Gaddis, *The United States and the Origins of the Cold War* (New York, 1972), p. 104f.

their abiding suspicion of the Soviet Union.[12] One of them, George F. Kennan, was even wary of denazification because of the time that would be lost in finding new German leadership.[13] By early 1943 the State Department had already altered its view of the permanent threat to European peace and stability from considering it to be the adversary, Germany, to the ally of convenience, the Soviet Union.[14] It therefore wished to limit German economic self-sufficiency only to the point at which Germany would become dependent upon western markets.[15] The State Department foresaw the resolute application of American political, economic, and social principles and the gradual removal of controls once the Germans conformed to what it conceived of as the American model of democracy and free enterprise.[16]

Henry Morgenthau perceived this to be a politically irresponsible and naive policy; simply disarming or rehabilitating Germany provided insufficient safeguards against a revival of Germany's economic potential for military aggression. He therefore proposed his "Program to Prevent Germany from Starting a World War III," which came to be associated with a policy of anti-German revenge and an acceptance of an assumption of German collective guilt.[17] It was also labeled a plan of the Left, because of its alleged lack of concern with the East-West implications of not rebuilding Germany as a bulwark against Communism.[18] Both characterizations were quite convenient for the State and War Departments because they could try to argue against it as either too leftist or as too emotionally charged.[19]

The plans of these three departments had important political implications. The State Department desired to rehabilitate Germany as an economically strong bastion of anti-Communist capitalism. The Treasury Department had a more punitive goal of reducing Germany's future political and economic role internationally. The War Department's short-term military occupation plans facilitated the retaining of or appointing of Germans who had expertise and expe-

12. Blum, p. 329.
13. George F. Kennan, *Memoirs, 1925–50* (Boston, 1967), p. 175.
14. Warren F. Kimball, *Swords or Ploughshares? The Morgenthau Plan for Defeated Nazi Germany* (Philadelphia, 1976), p. 10.
15. Ibid., p. 45.
16. Ibid., p. 22f.
17. Albert Norman, *Our German Policy: Propaganda and Culture* (New York, 1951), p. 11. Norman was the head of the Historical Division of the Information Control Division of USFET, later under OMGUS.
18. See Bungenstab, *Umerziehung*.
19. Hammond, p. 348.

rience, rather than seeking out those with democratic political credentials in order to be able to restore order quickly once the Nazis were defeated.

The "Other Germany" School and its Impact on U.S. Planning for Postwar Germany

The views of the State, War,and Treasury Departments do not alone reflect the diversity of opinion in the United States about the future of postwar Germany. A school of thought, located primarily in academic and emigré circles, promoted the cause of democratic structural change to be implemented by anti-Fascist Germans who would survive the Third Reich in Germany or in exile, and who would need the active support of Allied occupation authorities. The goals of this "Other Germany" school had elements in common with the plans of the State and Treasury Departments. They included stringent denazification and demilitarization, as did Morgenthau's plan, and a long-term occupation with an eventual economic recovery, somewhat like the State Department plan. But these were means rather than ends. The essential goal, however abstract and idealistic, was a new political and socioeconomic order based on what they considered to be pre-1933 German democratic traditions. Denazification, demilitarization, decartelization, material reconstruction with a certain degree of socialization of industry, and the positioning of active democratic anti-Nazis in key administrative posts prior to elections were all preconditions to the democratic and frequently socialist reforms which this school propagated. It did not, however, advocate a reintegration of Germany into the Western capitalist system or an agrarianization of the economy, nor did it conceive of postwar Germany as an anti-Communist bulwark.[20]

The "Other Germany" school was not represented in any of the governmental planning agencies nor did it have direct access to government policy making. It was able to make its views on the future of postwar Germany known in various publications of emigré and German-American organizations, such as the American Friends of German Freedom and the Association of Free Germans. But little

20. For an elaboration of the American schools of thought on the treatment and future of post-WWII Germany, see Rebecca L. Boehling, *The Effects of American Anti-German Sentiment on Planning and Policy-Making for Postwar Germany, 1943–1947*, M.A. thesis, University of Wisconsin-Madison, 1980, chapter 3.

unity existed among these unorganized individual emigrés, a majority of whom were on the Left politically.[21] These individuals had left their homeland for political reasons and had sought refuge in the United States, where they were met with neither open arms nor open minds. They were unlikely to rally political support for the cause of a postwar German democracy during the peak of wartime anti-German sentiment in the United States. Those Americans "consorting with" these emigrés and advocating a temporary occupation conducive to the renewed development of native German social reformist and democratic traditions were frequently suspected of pro-German/pro-Nazi sympathies.[22]

These Americans and emigrés, who would have liked to instill American confidence in the postwar potential of native German anti-Nazi democratic elements, sought to counter the thesis of collective German guilt that was implicit in plans like that of Morgenthau. They had to deal with a "From Luther to Hitler" interpretation of German history, which was widely accepted in the United States and Great Britain at the time.[23]

The American Friends of German Freedom, a group formed in 1936 in New York "with the purpose of supporting the underground anti-Nazi movement in Germany," included such prominent intellectuals as Dr. Reinhold Niebuhr (chair), Paul Hagen, pseudonym for Dr. Karl Frank (research director), Lewis Mumford, and Paul Tillich.[24] In its book, *Germany Tomorrow*, this group conceded that they could well understand how "the barbaric warfare of the Nazis" had biased a large segment of American public opinion against the Germans. But they could not help but deplore the reversed racist contention "that the German people are different from all others, that there is a

21. Gatzke, p. 112.

22. The Hunter College president during World War II, George Shuster, who was of German heritage and had close ties to reform-oriented exiles from the Nazi regime, wrote that even a German-American anti-Nazi group like the one to which he had belonged, the Loyal Americans of German Descent, dissolved themselves during the war because "[they] felt that [they] could not put [themselves] so blatantly into the political arena." See George Shuster, *The Ground I walked On: Reflections of a College President* (New York, 1961), p. 70.

23. See James Kerr Pollock, *What Shall Be Done With Germany?* (Northfield, Minn., 1944), p. 8. Wartime public opinion polls also indicated very strong anti-German sentiment that generally did not differentiate between Nazi and non-Nazi Germans. See Hadley Cantril and Mildred Strunk, *Public Opinion 1935-1946* (Princeton, N. J., 1951), pp. 268, 1115, 1153f. See also Jerome S. Bruner, *Mandate from the People* (New York, 1944), chapter 7.

24. American Friends of German Freedom, *Germany Tomorrow* (New York, 1944), p. 17.

thousand-year history to prove the eternal evil residing in the blood and bones of the Teutonic race."[25]

Two members of the Association of Free Germans, an organization of German political exiles founded in 1941 in New York under the sponsorship of a U.S. committee headed by William Green (the president of the American Federation of Labor),[26] asserted in 1943 that "democracy, though temporarily defeated, is by no means dead in Germany."[27] James K. Pollock, a political scientist from the University of Michigan (who later served as a political advisor to the U.S. Zone's military governor and as the American liaison officer to the *Länderrat* [Council of the States] in Stuttgart), promoted a belief in German democratic potential in his book, *What Shall Be Done with Germany?* In it he denied "that the democratic and liberal traditions which were developed in local and state governments, and in labor unions, farmers' organizations and consumers' cooperatives had been destroyed during the period of Nazi rule."[28]

Emigrés like the political scientist, Sigmund Neumann, and the psychologist, Paul Hagen, who had great hopes for a revived German Social Democratic Party, feared that exclusively vindictive postwar programs for Germany would discourage potential anti-Nazi leadership and the early recovery of trade unionism, which would be needed for a strong social democratic revival.[29] As will be shown in a later chapter, the lack of encouragement of potential anti-Nazi leadership and the revival of Chambers of Commerce and Industry prior to the formation of trade unions and political parties did limit the possibilities for new democratic political and economic structures. But this development was not caused by vindictive postwar programs. The possible exception to this was during the early phase of the occupation, when the nonfraternization policy was in effect and the help and advice of anti-Nazis were often rejected. Otherwise, the reason behind this frequent lack of support for anti-Nazis and trade unionists was the desire to expedite the recovery of Germany's economy and administrative efficiency. In doing so, the U.S. MG sought to work with those Germans who shared such priorities and seemed more pragmatic, rather than those seeking major struc-

25. Ibid., p.1.
26. Gerhart H. Seger and Siegfried K. Marck, *Germany: To Be or Not To Be?* (New York, 1943), p. 177f.
27. Ibid., p. 51.
28. Pollock, p. 35.
29. Paul Hagen, *Germany after Hitler* (New York, 1944), p. 104f. and Sigmund Neumann, "Democracy in Germany," *Political Science Quarterly*, 59 (1944), p. 351f.

tural, political, and social transformations. Such changes usually involved considerable government control and thus were often unfamiliar and at times seemed revolutionary to these Americans, not to mention the fact that the amount of time such reforms would have required conflicted with their goals of expediency.

During the last years of the war, this "Other Germany" school felt compelled to counter the propagation of anti-German sentiments that did not differentiate among individuals or groups, sentiments it felt were reflected in the Morgenthau Plan. It was also diametrically opposed to a "soft peace" in the form of an expedient restoration of the economy and the state as a means of building up postwar Germany as a capitalist bulwark in Central Europe. On a certain level, these forces were rallying behind the cause of German self-determination in their warnings against attempts to impose a foreign political and socioeconomic structure upon the Germans. As an insightful anti-Fascist German prisoner of war in the United States wrote while observing the postwar planning developments: "We want to be neither Americans nor Russians ... We want to remain Germans."[30] In his article, "Democracy in Germany," Sigmund Neumann censured those Americans wishing to force upon Germany a government, "which the Allies might regard as the most comfortable partner in the future peace."[31]

Already aware of the growth of anti-Communism in the United States, the Association of Free Germans warned in 1943 against the repercussions of making Germany "an object or subject of imperialistic intrigues between the East and the West [because] every new tension between Russia and the West would have a fateful influence upon Germany's politics."[32] They went on further to say: "We feel ourselves opposed to all those reactionary forces that would endanger cooperation among the United Nations during or after the war because they are opposed to Communism. We have no desire to see Germany remain an object of strife between the interests of the West and the East."[33]

The potential effect that "Other Germany" proposals might have had on U.S. public opinion and on policymakers was minimized by the German collective guilt propaganda put out by other European

30. Hans Werner Richter, "Ost und West – Die ausgleichende Aufgabe Mitteleuropas," *Der Ruf*, No. 12, 1 Sept. 1945, p. 2. In the original: Wir wollen weder Amerikaner noch Russen werden ... . Wir wollen Deutsche bleiben."
31. Neumann, p. 343.
32. Seger and Marck, p. 137.
33. Ibid.

exiles. Emigré Germans speaking out for this "Other Germany" were frequently denounced as pan-German militarists by fellow refugees. An emigré, Emil Ludwig, worked with U.S. government officials in compiling information for the occupation troops on how to behave toward and treat all Germans. Ludwig also influenced future U.S. MG officers through his guest lectures at the training school for MG officers in Charlottesville, Virginia.[34] He publicly accused the emigré proponents of a democratic "Other Germany" of being motivated by the ambition to be powerful in postwar Germany: "These exiles seek to make people in this country believe ... that the good, democratic Germany whose spokesmen they used to be is still extant, impatient to call them home in a triumph matching Victor Hugo's return to Paris, Mazzini's to Rome, or Lenin's to Russia. (...) These emigrés have surrounded themselves with gullible American citizens, have set up committees, and published manifestoes asserting that the Nazis, far from representing the whole nation, are but a tough gang which held up the German people and for eleven long years kept them gagged and bound. Once these gangsters are done away with, the 'other Germany' will rise again, as the Liberals did in 1918."[35]

Given the widespread acceptance of the collective-guilt thesis and fears of a fifth column, many potential public supporters of the "Other Germany" school of thought kept their mouths shut and concentrated on dispelling doubts about their own loyalty to the United States. Politically, the groups that comprised this school were neither cohesive nor credible enough in the eyes of U. S. government occupation planners to exert any real influence. They were suspect on the grounds of their national origins and because of their leftist leanings, particularly in the eyes of the State Department.[36]

34. Karl-Ernst Bungenstab, "Die Ausbildung der amerikanischen Offiziere für die Militärregierungen nach 1945," *Jahrbuch für Amerika-Studien*, 18 (1973), p. 204.
35. Emil Ludwig, *The Moral Conquest of Germany* (Garden City, N.Y., 1945), p. 135f.
36. Gatzke, p. 112. As late as spring 1947, Paul Hagen was still trying to return to Germany to work with SPD leaders to rebuild Germany, but the State and War Departments fought his return because of his associations with the Austrian and German Communist Parties after World War I and thus, as they put it, his reputation as a "fellow traveler." Paul Tillich was also suspected of "'not be(ing) independent of the Communists,'" according to a State Department compilation. 26 March 1947 memorandum from Perry Laukhuff of the Office of the Political Advisor to Mr. Heath and Mr. Chase, RG (Record Group) 84, POLAD/773/1, 1 of 1, Institut für Zeitgeschichte-Munich (Hereafter cited as IfZ). I chose to use these U.S. MG records in West German archives, where they are on microfilm. The IfZ, which went through the multitudinous records and selected appropriate ones for filming, provided a useful finding guide for them. In the meantime,these original OMGUS files (RG 260) and POLAD files(RG84) have been

At most, the voices of the "Other Germany" were to be heard in intelligence reports such as those of the Research and Analysis Branch (R&A) of the OSS, which "harbored" many emigré and German-American academics such as Franz Neumann, Herbert Marcuse, and Walter Dorn.[37] The OSS proposed the idea of officially recognizing a German exile committee in the United States, but the State Department opposed any such sanctioning. Moreover, the State Department even opposed the employment of German emigrés for research work by the OSS, although unsuccessfully. Many of the German refugees working for the OSS had been recruited from the Institute (New School) for Social Research, whose studies focused on the growth and nature of German Fascism, and which had moved from Frankfurt after the Nazis came to power, and eventually to New York. Many from this same group of emigrés, including Paul Hagen, had informal ties to the American Friends of German Freedom.[38] As researchers and analysts, these emigrés and scholars in the OSS played an information-gathering and educational role in terms of providing historical background and sophisticated analyses of Germany's past and present. They, however, had no control over whether and how this information would be used by U.S. occupation planners and later, MG officers. These extremely informative OSS reports rarely filtered down to those Americans in MG who interpreted and implemented vague MG directives on the regional and municipal level of occupation.[39]

---

moved from their original repository in Suitland, Md. to the new National Archives repository in College Park, Md. and are now much more accessible.

37. Analyses of emigrés working for the OSS are presented and commented upon by Alfons Söllner (ed.), *Zur Archäologie der Demokratie in Deutschland: Analysen politischer Emigranten im amerikanischen Geheimdienst*, 2 vol. (Frankfurt, 1982) and in the Introduction to Ulrich Borsdorf and Lutz Niethammer(eds.), *Zwischen Befreiung und Besatzung* (Wuppertal, 1976). For histories of the OSS, see Richard Harris Smith, *OSS: The Secret History of America's First Central Intelligence Agency* (Berkeley, 1972) and Bradley F. Smith, *The Shadow Warriors: OSS and the Origins of the CIA* (New York, 1983). These OSS R&A reports are housed in the U.S. National Archives, Modern Military Branch in Washington, Record Group (RG) 59 and RG 226.

38. Richard Harris Smith, p. 217.

39. This information is based on interviews held with Henry Walter, deputy detachment commander in Stuttgart and Kal Oravetz, legal advisor to G-5, USFET Headquarters from 17 to 19 Oct.1986 in Plymouth, N.H., Professor James Aronson, chief of press, District Information Services Control Command (DISCC)-Western Military District on 27 Dec. 1985 in New York, Ernest Langendorf, DISCC Press Control officer in Munich, on 25 Feb.1982 in Munich; correspondence from Cedric Belfrage, Press Control officer in Frankfurt, 22 Nov. 1984 and

The director of the OSS, William J. Donovan, sought out left-wing intellectuals and activists for both the operational and the research and analysis branches, while appointing corporate attorneys and business executives as the administrators in charge. While the former group ranged from New Deal liberals to leftists politically, the latter group was more likely to include registered Republicans and anti-New Dealers.[40] This dichotomy between more conservative, administrative types as superiors and more progressive, intellectual types as subordinates also frequently occurred in the MG hierarchy. This meant that those generally most informed and most reform oriented were rarely in a position to implement reforms or provide effective support to anti-Nazi Germans trying to introduce political and socioeconomic changes.[41]

President Roosevelt and Official Policy for Postwar Germany

In 1944 in the midst of the departmental conflicts and with the "Other Germany" orientation filtering through in OSS reports and recommendations, President Roosevelt seemed to be leaning toward approval of Secretary Morgenthau's program of dismemberment, deindustrialization, demilitarization, and denazification – at least until shortly before the presidential election of 1944, when he postponed all postwar planning.[42] Then in the summer of 1944, SHAEF [43] published the *Handbook for MG in Germany* to make up for the lack of policy directives coming from Washington.[44] Like the April 1944 Combined Chiefs of Staff (CCS) directive 551, it presumed that there

---

Shepard Stone, ICD officer, 8 Nov. 1984. See also local detachment reports sent to the Land level MG in the National Archives Records Administration (hereafter cited as NARA), RG 260, OMGUS files.

40. Richard Harris Smith, p. 14 ff.

41. See Rebecca Boehling, "Grassroots Democracy and Military Government: Local German Politics in the United States Zone of Occupation, 1945–49," *Zeitschrift für Kulturaustausch*, 1987/2, p. 270ff.

42. Hammond, p. 314.

43. The U.S. forces in Europe were part of a dual command structure with the British called SHAEF. Commanded by General Dwight D. Eisenhower, who also commanded the European Theater of Operations, U.S. Army (ETOUSA), SHAEF was staffed jointly with British and U.S. personnel.

44. Walter L. Dorn, "The Debate over American Occupation Policy in Germany 1944–45," *Political Science Quarterly*, 72 (1957), p. 490. Lacking guidance from Washington, SHAEF, in late 1943, established in England a strictly military

would be a normalization of social, political and economic conditions in Central Europe.[45] Despite numerous pleas for more instructions from Washington on policy directives, the strictly military SHAEF agency assigned to write the *Handbook* was left on its own to provide the necessary political guidance to unit commanders and MG detachments.[46] It developed a political guide for denazification and demilitarization and an expeditious withdrawal of troops.[47] After Morgenthau complained to Roosevelt about the leniency of the policies represented in the *Handbook*, it received only provisional authorization. For administrative convenience, each copy had to include an addendum prohibiting actions that might facilitate Germany's economic rehabilitation or the employment of active Nazis or ardent sympathizers.[48] Roosevelt also advised Secretary of War Stimson that a harsher policy than that expressed in the SHAEF *Handbook* would be necessary.[49] The president then appointed a committee consisting of secretaries of state, war, and treasury as well as the Lend-Lease administrator, Harry Hopkins, to draft short-term and long-range policies to be pursued in Germany.[50]

Before this committee reached any consensus, Roosevelt met in Quebec with British representatives to coordinate postwar policy. On 15 September 1944, FDR, after requesting Morgenthau to join him there, initialed, along with Churchill, the Morgenthau Plan, thus seemingly approving it. Although negative press reaction prior to the elections and repeated pleas from Secretary Stimson caused FDR to distance himself from the plan, Morgenthau's plan remained the only policy that the president had supported publicly.[51] In the meantime the Joint Chiefs of Staff (JCS) were given the task of drafting a directive for troops in Germany, and on 22 September they recommended what came to be known as JCS

German Country Unit, which wrote this handbook to guide MG personnel in their tasks after hostilities ended.

45. Latour and Vogelsang, p. 13.
46. Dorn, "Debate," p. 490.
47. Davis, p. 62. See also Dorn, *The Unfinished Purge*, p. 137.
48. Joseph R. Starr, *U.S. Military Government in Germany: Operations during the Rhineland Campaign*, MG Training Packet No. 56 (Karlsruhe: Historical Division, European Command, 1950), p. 38.
49. Hammond, p. 355.
50. Dorn, "Debate," p. 491.
51. Ernest F. Penrose, *Economic Planning for the Peace* (Princeton, 1953), p. 254. Penrose was an economic advisor to the U.S. representative in the EAC, Winant. See also Axel Gietz, *Die neue Alte Welt: Roosevelt, Churchill und die europäische Nachkriegsordnung* (München: Wilhelm Fink Verlag, 1986), p. 249 ff.

1067.[52] This was intended as a short-term occupation plan that was to fill the urgent need of providing some guidelines before U.S. troops reached German soil, an event only weeks away.[53] No long-term policy was to be deliberated thereafter because of Roosevelt's hesitancy to make "'detailed plans for a country which,'" as he said,"' we do not yet occupy.'"[54] The details of JCS 1067 are often not recognizable in the administration of the occupation. As the historian, John Gimbel, points out, the official policy and the views of those who administered it seemed to have had little in common.[55]

Although it was formal policy until July 1947, the impact of JCS 1067 should not be exaggerated. First, until 14 July 1945 the British-U.S. Combined Command of SHAEF (Supreme Command Allied Expeditionary Forces or SCAEF) had jurisdiction over both the U.S. and British MG and had regarded document CCS 551 and the revised SHAEF *Handbook* as de facto policy directives.[56] Second, the JCS 1067 directive was not made public until 17 October 1945, although it did serve as a guideline for the Potsdam agreement and U.S. policy in the period immediately following hostilities.[57] However, United States Forces, European Theater (USFET)[58] waited until 7 July 1945 to translate JCS 1067 into a directive with administrative rules concerned with denazification, demilitarization, disarmament, restrictions on political activity and the need for military control at all levels of government.[59] Third, the directive went through eight versions between September 1944 and April 1945 with the State, War, and Treasury Departments continuing their infighting while FDR wavered until his death.[60] For

52. Peterson, p. 39.
53. Dorn, "Debate," p. 491.
54. FDR to Hull on 20 Oct. 1944, as cited in Philip E. Mosely, "The Occupation of Germany: New Light on How the Zones Were Drawn," *Foreign Affairs*, 28 (July 1950), p. 596. Mosely was one of Hull's staff specialists.
55. John Gimbel, *The American Occupation of Germany: Politics and the Military, 1945–1949* (Stanford, 1968), p. 1f.
56. Paul W. Gulgowski, *The American Military Government of United States Occupied Zones (sic) of Post World War II Germany* (Frankfurt a.M, 1983), p. 34f. See also Starr, *U.S. Military Government*, p. 39f.
57. "Directive of the U.S. Joint Chiefs of Staff to the Commander-in-Chief of the U.S. Forces of Occupation Regarding the Military Government of Germany (JCS 1067), April 1945," Beate Ruhm von Oppen, ed., *Documents on Germany under Occupation 1945–54* (London, 1955), p. 13.
58. USFET was the postwar successor organization to ETOUSA, which was dissolved at the beginning of July 1945, after accomplishing the major tasks of military redeployment.
59. Ibid., p. 2.
60. Peterson, p. 42.

twelve days in March, a State Department draft directive even super-seded JCS 1067 and stressed the State Department concerns of securing tripartite collaboration in occupation policies. This short-lived directive advocated, among other things, MG cooperation with the leaders and personnel of freely organized labor unions and professional associations, and anti-Nazi political groupings and parties.[61] The War and Treasury Departments opposed the State Department document so strongly that FDR revoked his approval. FDR's last political direction was his signature on the "Summary of U.S. Initial Post-Defeat Policy Relating to Germany," which provided for the decentralization of governmental power and the economy, industrial disarmament, and demilitarization and a minimum standard of living to prevent unrest during the occupation.[62] The issues of how, when, in what form, and to whom German self-government was to be restored were left open.

After succeeding to the presidency on 12 April, Harry S. Truman signed JCS 1067/8. This eighth and final version of JCS 1067, a vague and ambiguous compromise, allowed each of the departments to read into it what it wanted. The deputy military governor for the U.S. Zone, General Lucius D. Clay, was able to take advantage of this leeway in formulating his directives for the implementation of MG policy,[63] as did his subordinates, whether consciously or unconsciously, on the various levels of MG. Truman made numerous personnel changes within the Cabinet. In the State Department the new secretary, James Byrnes, was assisted by Archibald MacLeish, while War Secretary Stimson was replaced by Robert Patterson. Morgenthau resigned as treasury secretary after Truman refused to let him participate in the Potsdam Conference;[64] thus ended his direct influence on the occupation.

The Potsdam Agreement defined the purpose of the occupation to be "to bring about complete disarmament and demilitarization of Germany"[65] and to "convince the German people that they have suffered a total military defeat and that they cannot escape respon-

---

61. Dorn, *Unfinished Purge*, p. 143 f.

62. Latour and Vogelsang, p. 21f.

63. Peterson, p. 42. The Office of the Deputy Military Governor was established on 18 April 1945 in order to represent the commanding general (in this case Eisenhower, who was officially the military governor of the U.S. Zone) on the Coordinating Committee of the Allied Control Council.

64. Louis J. Mensonides, "United States Foreign Policy: Germany, 1945–1959," Diss. Univ. of Kentucky 1964 (Ann Arbor, 1969), p. 31.

65. U.S. Dept. of State, *Participation of the U.S. Government in International Conferences, 1 July 1945 – 30 June 1946* (Washington, 1946?), p. 144.

sibility for what they have brought upon themselves." The occupation period was intended to "prepare for the eventual reconstruction of German political life on a democratic basis and for eventual peaceful cooperation in international life by Germany."[66] Details about the extent of economic reconstruction were left vague partly because of the complications of treating Germany as an economic unit under quadripartite control.[67] This vagueness left the way open for the continuing struggle between the State Department, with its plans for speedy economic recovery; the deindustrialization advocates, the War Department, which wanted limited liability and a speedy withdrawal from Germany; and those who saw democratization, decartellization, and demilitarization as part of an experiment in socioeconomic structural transformation. This struggle moved from Washington to London to Frankfurt to Berlin. The first American troops crossed over the German border and occupied Aachen in October 1944. Once the occupation began, the conflict over Germany's future was no longer an exclusively American issue, or even an Allied one, but rather one in which Germans were directly involved and one about which many Germans had their own definite ideas.

Training of U.S. MG Personnel

In the United States, men trained to be MG officers were prepared, for the most part, in very general ways to prepare them to serve anywhere in the European Theater of Operations or in Asia, with the assumption that MG was needed to further the conduct of the war once an area within a country was taken. Military planners did not anticipate that MG would last much beyond the end of hostilities in the country. In the summer of 1942 the Provost Marshall General's Office (PMGO) created a School for MG in Charlottesville on the campus of the University of Virginia, for prospective MG officers detailed from existing army units and for officers commissioned directly from civilian life.[68] The Charlottesville school was supposed

---

66. "Protocol of the Proceedings of the Berlin Conference of 2 August 1945," *House of Commons, Accounts and Papers*, XXIV, 1946–47 (London, 1947), p. 4.
67. See Martin, p. 158ff. Cf. John H. Backer, *Priming the German Economy. American Occupational Policies 1945–48* (Durham, 1971) and Nicholas Balabkins, *Germany under Direct Controls. Economic Aspects of Industrial Disarmament 1945–48* (New Brunswick, 1964).
68. Zink, *American*, p. 6.

to train the top MG officers[69] to lead what the PMGO considered "the ideal type of MG," namely, "one which integrates the local laws, institutions, customs, psychology and economics of the occupied area and a superimposed military control with a minimum of change in the former and a maximum of control by the latter."[70] This may have been appropriate for liberated territories, but unconditional surrender implied, and JCS 1067 would later state, that "Germany will not be occupied for purposes of liberation but as a defeated enemy nation." Also, more than "a minimum of change" would be required for "an eventual reconstruction of German political life on a democratic basis."[71]

The Charlottesville School for MG opened two years before JCS 1067 became American policy. The lack of directives for postwar Germany at the time most future MG officers were being trained at Charlottesville limited the practicability of what could actually be taught there. The courses for the occupation of Germany were based on the 1918 Rhineland experience where German officials had been "extensively utilized." It was over a month after the first classes began before the commandant of the school, General Cornelius W. Wickersham, began to reconsider the advisability of teaching prospective personnel for Germany to utilize local German officials in order to keep institutions functioning in the occupied area.[72] Wickersham concluded that "it would doubtless be unwise to continue Nazi officials in office or in key positions." His solution was to have "a trained personnel sufficient for the key administrative positions," with an adequate number of subordinates and specialists.[73] The exclusion of Nazis from local institutions stemmed from concern about military security rather than German political developments. Wickersham did not consider whether there might be other Germans who could fill these posts; his primary concern was with the recruitment of a sufficient number of Americans for MG in order

69. Gulgowski, p. 66. See also Boyd L. Dastrup, *Crusade in Nuremberg: Military Occupation, 1945–49* (Westport, Ct., 1985), p. 8.

70. Memo, Jesse I. Miller, PMGO, for PMG, 10 Jan. 42, PMGO files, 352.01, SMG, Est, as reproduced in Harry L. Coles and Albert G. Weinberg, *Civil Affairs: Soldiers Become Governors* (Washington, 1964), p. 10. Miller was a civilian consultant to the War Department at the time, who became the associate director and later director of the MG Division that was set up in the PMGO in July 1942.

71. JCS 1067 Text, as reproduced in James K. Pollock, et al., eds., *Germany under Occupation* (Ann Arbor, 1949), p. 78.

72. Memo, Wickersham, Comdt, SMG, for PMG, 17 Jun 42, PMGO files, 321.19, MG, as reproduced in Coles/Weinberg, p. 12.

73. Ibid., p. 13.

to keep local German institutions functioning. His approach, functional and practical, was oriented toward a short-term military occupation which would keep things running smoothly without much involvement with the native population. For example, language courses were an afterthought: they were only included in the curriculum after the third session.[74]

Throughout the fall and winter of 1942, various cabinet members and the president attacked the School for MG in Charlottesville because of the anti-New Deal political views of the faculty and student body, the questionable quality of students and challenges to the Army's claim to govern occupied territory.[75] Harold Deutsch, who lectured occasionally at Charlottesville, commented that the school "was an assemblage of people who did not seem particularly impressive from the standpoint of being highly selected as greatly sophisticated about affairs, German, Italian, or anything else."[76] The regular faculty was recruited primarily from officers of military training facilities, while civilian academics worked under special teaching contracts and as visiting lecturers.[77] Apparently the faculty at Charlottesville would have liked to teach more applied politics, but the provost marshall general restricted this because of departmental rivalry over MG planning and the training of personnel. The State Department's suspicions surrounding the Army's role in the civil affairs area of MG led the Charlottesville staff to take a narrowly defined legalistic and administrative approach to systems of government. This approach produced more technical competence among its graduates than a grasp of political systems and the significance of political developments.[78] The War Department, which oversaw the PMGO's office and thus the school, feared that if individual officers made personal political decisions, MG would become politicized, and differing conceptions of democracy would create an explosive situation which could destroy military discipline and its hierarchical organization.[79]

State Department advisors suggested including various civilian agencies in the training,[80] but the provost marshall general feared they

74. Bungenstab, "Ausbildung," p. 202.
75. Memo, Gullion for C of S through CG, SOS, 27 Nov 42, G-1 files, Personnel, SMG, Misc Info, in Coles/Weinberg, p. 24.
76. Harold Deutsch, Speaker in discussion at conference on Americans as Proconsuls, in Wolfe, p. 428.
77. Bungenstab, "Ausbildung," p. 202.
78. Gulgowski, p. 82f.
79. Bungenstab, "Ausbildung," p. 200.
80. See memos in Coles/Weinberg, p. 25ff.

would challenge the Army's prerogative.[81] The Army expanded its jurisdiction over MG personnel even further when CAD was created on 1 March 1943 under the War Department and the JCS. Its primary function was to provide information and advice to the secretary of war about the civil matters in those areas occupied as a result of military operations.[82] Civil Affairs (also known as G-5) officers were either commissioned from civilian life or were secured from other military units. Training programs provided general military indoctrination and specialized instruction in MG machinery and responsibilities.[83] CAD set up one-month-long training programs at Fort Custer in Michigan and up to two-month-long programs on various university campuses across the country called Civil Affairs Training Schools (CATS).[84]

CAD's Civil Affairs and MG handbooks, which were used at Fort Custer and CATS, gave little attention to the functions of MG after hostilities had ended. The historian, Paul Gulgowski, asserts that this omission helps explain why many of the detachment officers never fully realized the significance of activating trade unions, cultural and industrial interest groups, and political parties, launching reeducation programs; promoting German governmental reconstruction, or other long-range goals.[85] At Fort Custer and at the CATS training consisted of general military courses and courses on the principles of MG and on the geographical area to which officer students were to be assigned.[86] The CATS apparently put more emphasis on language study than Charlottesville.[87] It was assumed that high-ranking officers, such as detachment commanders, would not be dealing directly with the native populations, while the technical experts and subordinate officers trained at the CATS might be doing so and would be less likely to find interpreters with technical competency. As it turned out, only 5 percent of all U.S. MG personnel in Germany knew enough German to function without an interpreter.[88]

---

81. Memo, Gullion for CG, SOS, 23 Jun 42, PMGO files, 321.19, MG, as reproduced in Coles/Weinberg, p. 15.
82. Davis, p. 30f.
83. Zink, *American*, p. 2f.
84. Ibid, p. 7.
85. Gulgowski, p. 82f. Gulgowski contends that partial blame also can be attributed to the inferior quality of the MG officers trained at Charlottesville. Wickersham himself complained that only about 15 percent of the officer-students would have made suitable civil affairs officers. See Gulgowski, p. 66. Cf. Earl F. Ziemke, "Improvising in Postwar Germany," in Wolfe, p. 53f.
86. Swarm, p.399.
87. Zink, *American*, p. 9.
88. Gatzke, p. 163.

As Allied victories mounted and the need for military governors to be close to their assigned locations in Europe increased, direct commissioning from civilian life ended in the fall of 1943 with the last CATS programs for the German occupation shutting down in the United States by early 1944.[89] At the end of 1943, an administrative headquarters for civil affairs/MG in the field was set up in Shrivenham. There civil affairs officers were given assignments to MG detachments. By the summer of 1944, with Allied troops having crossed the Channel into France, these detachments were given specific training for the actual locality where they were to be responsible in the occupation. Their final stop prior to shipment to the continent was Manchester, where their training was often abruptly halted by deployment.[90] Training continued after September 1944 in some MG centers in France and Belgium where detachments were held in reserve until ready for deployment in Germany.[91]

It was only in this European phase that MG officers were prepared specifically for German occupation tasks. Sophisticated OSS Research and Analysis Branch studies on the various levels of German administration were used as teaching aids as were the British Political Intelligence Division handbooks for Germany. But the majority of MG officers did not arrive in Europe until the spring of 1944. This European (SHAEF) phase was not as well utilized as it might have been because of the limited time that most MG officers spent in Shrivenham and because of the indefinite timing for mobilization.[92]

Unfortunately many officers trained for a certain country were sent elsewhere, and many officers trained in England and France for specific detachments, including some of those trained to head detachments in Germany, never were assigned to those detachments. There were some two-hundred-odd MG detachments prepared in advance for service in particular localities that were to come under U.S. military jurisdiction. Because the occupation zones were not formally drawn until the February 1945 Yalta Conference and then were revised to include the French at the Potsdam Conference, these detachment assignments were subject to alteration. Even after the zones were finalized and hostilities had ended, it took months before more than half of the MG officers arrived at their

89. Zink, *American*, p. 7.
90. Ziemke, *U.S. Army*, p. 62.
91. Starr, *U.S. Military Government*, p. 19.
92. Walter L. Dorn, *Inspektionsreise in der US-Zone*, (Stuttgart, 1973), p. 24ff.

intended destinations. By then the situation for which they had been prepared had been transformed considerably.[93]

MG training did not usually include information about developments during the last months of the war, such as the extent of anti-Nazi resistance.[94] Most resistance, with the exception of the July 20th plot, was hushed up within Nazi Germany and rarely reached the outside world. The Association of Free Germans accused the U.S. press of suppressing news of anti-Nazi activity in an effort "to hold the entire nation responsible for the evil deeds of the Nazis." [95] This was probably caused less by any media policy than by the lack of access to such information or the means to confirm reports. This lack of specific information about recent anti-Nazi activity, in conjunction with the emotional impact of the spring 1945 disclosure of concentration camp conditions, encouraged a blanket dismissal of all Germans as Nazis, and would result in MG personnel discouraging cooperation with anti-Nazis – even former concentration-camp inmates – in occupation tasks.

The Army had problems arranging for replacements and getting long-term commitments from MG officers. Some MG officers had "vegetated" for a year or longer after attending MG and civil affairs training schools while waiting for an assignment and were completely disillusioned by the time their duties began.[96] Most of the Charlottesville graduates had accrued enough points to be discharged from active military service soon after the termination of the war. Many of them had served in North Africa, Italy, France, Belgium, and Holland before they had an opportunity to join up with a detachment in Germany. Then, generally within three months, the law permitted them to go home. Thus many of the MG officers who were best prepared to draft and implement plans for the occupation and reconstruction of Germany were almost on their way home, in spirit, if not in body, by the time they reached their ultimate goal. Those who remained had to cope with the absence of clear and

93. Joseph R. Starr, *Denazification, Occupation and Control of Germany, March-July 1945* (Salisbury, N.C., 1977) p. 6.
94. The matter of German resistance is complicated further by opportunistic claims made by some Germans after the war about having resisted passively. Here, I am referring to active resistance against the Nazis and not to any form of *innere Emigration*. One could have hardly expected outsiders to recognize these more subtle forms of alleged opposition when they are still controversial in Germany and former Nazi-occupied countries today.
95. Gerhart H. Seger and Siegfried K. Marck, *Germany, To Be or Not To Be?* (New York, 1943), p. 147.
96. Backer, p. 10.

concise guidelines about what they were expected to do in a long-term occupation, and had to deal with inadequate replacements, peers, and subordinates alike.[97]

Despite the various programs for training MG personnel, after V-E Day the U.S. MG found itself relying on any available officers, whether or not they were trained in MG or prepared for a certain location.[98] The high rate of personnel turnover, the lack of specific orientation toward an area to be occupied, the inadequate political preparation of the MG personnel, and unclear instructions on what kind of political reforms were necessary to reconstruct "German political life on a democratic basis"[99] combined to make for a very inauspicious beginning for the occupation. During this "Zero Hour," when neither central nor state governments existed, many reform-oriented Germans hoped to help create a democratic Germany but did not receive the assistance from Allied occupiers that they needed. To provide this help, MG officers needed a clear political mandate from Washington, an acute understanding of the German infrastructure, and the political shrewdness to recognize and encourage those German forces capable of implementing democratic change. In far too many cases these prerequisites were lacking.

The actual U.S. MG occupiers given the task of restoring law and order and preparing "for an eventual reconstruction of German political life on a democratic basis"[100] included various graduates of the MG school at Charlottesville, of Fort Custer and the CATS, as well as men with no MG training at all. According to Harold Zink, who was involved with the occupation from its planning stage with SHAEF and then with OMGUS and HICOG, there were "those commissioned directly from civil life, supposedly at least on the basis of professional qualifications, and trained during a period of several months for MG duties, ... those transferred from other Army units but possessing theoretically at least special professional qualifications," tactical officers with minimal MG training in Europe, and various administrative officers without any MG training at all. Those

---

97. Gulgowski, p. 257f. See also Davis, p. 118 and 135 f. Between V-E Day and 31 Dec. 1945, more than two and a half million troops left Germany and Europe; by 30 June 1946, 99.2 percent of the total theater strength of 8 May 1945 had been redeployed. The resources needed for an occupation army might have been found within the V-E Day Army, but redeployment left the Army in Germany with young replacements fresh from the United States, and as Davis said, "officered by a few career professionals and late arrivals." Davis, p. 136.

98. Zink, *American*, p. 37.

99. From JCS 1067 , as cited in Pollock, et al, *Germany under Occupation*, p. 78f.

100. Ibid.

commissioned from civilian life made up less than half of the MG officers in Germany. Most of these civilians received commissions as captains and majors in the specialist reserve. Of the volunteers, veterans and holders of political office had an edge in being selected. Few who were recruited had experience in drafting plans or doing governmental research, yet these skills were crucial to the preliminary phase of MG.[101] Besides politicians and veterans, those most frequently recruited were bankers, lawyers, public safety and health officials, engineers, and journalists.[102] Their professional experience, in combination with their MG training, should have qualified them to be at least adequate MG administrators or technocrats. But as the German historian, Lutz Niethammer, has noted, the trained recruitees frequently were given jobs that did not take account of either their newly acquired skills or their civilian field of expertise.[103]

The officers who came to MG from other military units were either scheduled or recommended for transfer at the time, and many were transferred to MG against their wishes. Of the latter, some found ways to avoid MG training, although this did not keep them from having to serve as MG officers. Unlike many of the civilian recruitees, they did have military experience.[104] But this military experience did not make up for the fact that a number of them, when they received MG posts, did little work, handled the tasks assigned to them miserably, and ultimately gave MG a lot of negative publicity in the United States and Germany because of either dishonesty, alcohol abuse, or sexual exploits.[105]

Of the MG personnel with special training, most could be classified as technical experts. The political scientist, Robert Engler, who served with MG in Germany in its early phase, contended that the fact that the Army recruited various types of technicians but few "first-class

101. Zink, *American*, p. 33f.
102. Gulgowski, p. 107. See also Robert Engler, "The Individual Soldier and the Occupation," *Annals of the American Academy of Political and Social Sciences*, 267 (1950), p. 80. Engler served with MG in 1945 and thereafter returned to Syracuse University, where he was assistant professor of citizenship and public affairs. At Charlottesville the largest group of participants in the European-oriented sessions were Americans with administrative experience, followed by lawyers and judges, and then those with skills in finance and economics. See Bungenstab, "Ausbildung," p. 201ff. See also Coles/Weinberg, p. 13.
103. Lutz Niethammer, "Die amerikanische Besatzungsmacht zwischen Verwaltungstradition und politischen Parteien in Bayern 1945," *Vierteljahrshefte für Zeitgeschichte*, 1967, H.2, p. 160.
104. Zink, *American*, p. 35.
105. Zink, *United States*, p. 85. Cf. Davis, p. 136ff.

students of public affairs and general civilian administrators revealed our failure to appreciate the fundamental issues underlying the problem."[106] These men were capable in their respective fields of expertise,[107] and most made useful contributions toward solving the problems of security, sanitation, and the restoration of public utilities, but they were inadequate in areas like denazification, political revival, and reeducation. As Engler put it: "It was far more simple for them to replace a broken water main, since both ruler and ruled could appreciate the service of a good one, than it was to select a suitable burgomaster, on the definition of which they might differ."[108]

A small subgroup of the men specially trained for MG in Germany were emigrants from Germany and Austria who, together with first- and second-generation German-Americans and a few academic types, well versed in German studies, were to function as experts for language, culture, and politics. Most members of this latter group were used in political intelligence or in the MG divisions of public safety or information control services. Few of them were career officers and thus never reached the higher ranks, which remained the prerogative of regular Army personnel who were usually much less qualified for MG duties.[109]

There were also "tactical officers assigned to MG duties in the ETO (European Theater of Operations) because of shortages of officers" trained in the United States. These tactical officers were assigned to MG at a late date and therefore received only "a few weeks of basic MG instruction in Europe." They were assigned to detachments as they were needed. Otherwise there were "officers of various sorts together with administrative personnel assigned to MG higher headquarters in Germany as the need arose."[110] It was felt that these men would need no MG background or training, although this omission proved to be a significant liability in terms of meeting the basic organizational needs of the MG bureaucracy.[111]

106. Engler, p. 80. See also Coles/Weinberg, p. 157f, who blame the lack of sophistication of civil affairs officers on "America's entire current and historical unrealism about the Army's employment in civil affairs." They go on to talk about the Army's "fallacious ... idea that there is a distinct boundary between the military and the political." They blame the pressure of administrative responsibilities for the technicians' preoccupation with means rather than ends or the so-called political neutralism.

107. Boyd Dastrup, in his 1985 book on the occupation of Nuremberg, actually uses the term "managerial elite" to refer to these recruitees. See Dastrup, p. 9.

108. Engler, p. 80.

109. Niethammer, "Die amerikanische Besatzungsmacht," p. 160.

110. Zink, *American*, p. 33.

111. Zink, *United States*, p. 35f.

There were about twice as many enlisted men as there were officers in the U.S. MG. These enlisted men were distributed among the G-5 or civil affairs divisions in SHAEF and USFET, the European Civil Affairs Division, and the various detachments. An Army Specialized Training Program (ASTP) was set up on university campuses to enlist student volunteers to fill military needs, among them, personnel for MG. But large numbers of the ASTP men were not assigned to areas within their specialty. By the time staffs of enlisted men were assembled for the various MG-related outfits (U.S. Group, Control Council for Germany and the G-5 divisions of SHAEF and USFET), very few ASTP men could be found. Thus the enlisted personnel were more or less untrained for MG duties. Some happened to have professional and language skills that would have been quite useful, but many officers preferred not to have such enlisted men on their staffs precisely because these officers found their abilities threatening.[112]

The MG detachments that were assigned to major cities, like the three under examination in this study, were usually led by career military officers. Many had received brief civil affairs training, but others had served consistently as combat commanders throughout the war.[113] One such former combat officer described his occupation responsibilities as follows:

> I had no experience that would qualify me for the job, ... After about six months as Number Two in the Landsberg Detachment, I was given the Wuerzberg assignment. ... The only duties I can recall were counting potatoes before harvesting for an economic report, acting as judge in minor MG offenses, writing a weekly summary for Munich [seat of Land-detachment with jurisdiction over all regional detachments within the Land], and visiting some innocuous regional MG field office in Augsburg, intermittently. Once in a while, someone would report a Nazi, and there would be some excitement with the Landpolizei. ... The whole operation seemed a holding action, to maintain a semblance of order. The Munich MG seemed to be indecisive, and I had no decisions to make – by order, or on my own. To keep things quiet was the aim.[114]

A survey of MG detachment reports from all over the U.S. Zone of occupation,[115] and interviews with former detachment commanding

112. Zink, *American*, p. 37ff.
113. Ibid., p. 164f.
114. Operations Research Office, Johns Hopkins University, *A Survey of the Experience and Opinions of U.S. Military Government Officers in World War II* (Chevy Chase, Md., 1956), p. 301. As quoted in Gulgowski, p. 254.
115. Ibid.

officers and with Germans who worked with MG, produced some descriptions similar to this one. There were also quite a few truly dedicated, detachment officers as well. The lack of a personal sense of duty, as expressed in this quote, was probably quite atypical, whereas the lack of understanding of the complexities of one's responsibilities, and the attitude that the aim of the occupation was "to keep things quiet" seems to have been fairly prevalent.

Military and technical staff junior officers served under the detachment commander and his assistant. If these men were not career military, they were commissioned civilians who had often worked in business, law, or public service jobs.[116] They tended to be pragmatic problem solvers, whose primary concern in Germany was to get things running again, which was the same sort of practical approach many were accustomed to taking in the business world. Their knowledge of German and European political life was limited. They often confused the lack of a political party affiliation with political neutralism and were sorely lacking in clear and comprehensive political guidance, particularly in the early phase of the occupation.[117] All of this, combined with a lack of familiarity with the German situation, increased the officers' reliance upon Germans while their ability to differentiate among Germans remained weak. It was only natural that such MG officers would prefer to have seemingly apolitical, cooperative, and experienced German administrators working under them. Such Germans would seem to be more likely to follow orders and yet be able to take administrative initiatives. On the other hand, the officers assumed that as long as such Germans were not active Nazis and were not explicitly political, they would avoid taking political initiatives. Feeling insecure and ill-prepared for their responsibilities in civil affairs, they "did not," as Paul Gulgowski tells us, "dare to rock the boat, neither in the German nor into [sic] the American direction."[118]

---

116. Niethammer, "Die amerikanische Besatzungsmacht," p. 164f.
117. Coles/Weinberg, p. 157f.
118. Gulgowski, p. 256.

Stuttgart
"rubble train"
with the city hall
in the background,
1945.

*Courtesy of the
Stadtarchiv
Stuttgart.*

Military parade of U.S. troops in Stuttgart on U.S. Independence Day, Königsbau,
4 July 1947.   *Courtesy of Stadtarchiv Stuttgart.*

MGO Lt. Col. Jackson swears Dr. Arnulf Klett in as Oberbürgermeister of Stuttgart, 8 October 1945.

U.S. troops entering Munich, Justizpalast, 30 April 1945.

German P.O.W.s
being led by U.S.
troops through
the Karlstor,
Munich, 1945.
*Courtesy of the
Stadtarchiv Munich.*

Disabled German war veteran in front of the U.S. military Officer's Club parking lot
in Munich, Neuhauser Str., 1946.   *Courtesy of Stadtarchiv Munich.*

Audience at the first postwar concert of the Munich Philharmonic playing Beethoven's Ninth Symphony in the Auditorium of Munich University, 1945.

Courtesy of Stadtarchiv Munich.

Daily rations for a "normal consumer" in a Munich display window in the Neuhauser Str., 1947.

Chapter II

STRUCTURE, JURISDICTION, AND POLICIES OF THE OFFICE OF MG-U.S. ZONE (OMGUS)

Introduction

MG detachments were assigned to the various German administrative levels of government: towns or sometimes groups of villages, cities, Landkreise, and Länder. During the first six months of occupation, all real control and responsibility rested with the lowest level of MG,[1] namely that of the detachment assigned to a German municipality or county. Counties and municipalities comprised the first German administrative units that were allowed to govern themselves in the four zones of occupied Germany. The Potsdam Agreement of August 2, 1945 stipulated: "The administration of affairs in Germany should be directed toward the decentralization of the political structure and the development of local responsibility. To this end, local self-government shall be restored throughout Germany on democratic principles through elective councils as rapidly as is consistent with military security and the purpose of the occupation."[2]

The first local elections in the U.S. Zone were held in the first half of 1946 starting with the smallest rural communities in January and ending with the major cities in May. However, the restoration of local self-government was not complete with the return of the democratic

1. W. Friedmann, *The Allied Military Government of Germany* (London, 1947), p. 58.
2. U.S. Department of State, *Germany, 1947–1949: The Story in Documents*, Publication 3556 (Washington, 1950), p. 49.

voting process. German officials still had to report to the local MG detachment, now renamed the Liaison and Security Office, but with more of a reporting - than a decision-making function. Originally, German municipal department heads reported to junior-level technical officers in the MG detachment. Later these German officials began reporting to their mayor, who in turn reported to the MG detachment commander. Although this system increased the degree of local German self-government, it also enhanced the autonomy and power of the mayor and thus potentially stymied the development of mayoral accountability. Unchecked, the mayor could filter out any information he did not want relayed to the local MG, and also could, and in numerous cases did, manipulate information to what he perceived to be to the municipality's, or his own, advantage.[3]

The local detachment commander had the same autocratic potential as the lord mayor, or *Oberbürgermeister*, in his reporting procedure to the Land-level MG, although he was subject to occasional checks. Whereas the Oberbürgermeister of major cities were in charge of *kreisfreie Städte* (cities outside of county borders), and thus were not under the authority of county commissioners (*Landräte*), some political and cultural affairs occurring in a detachment's locale did fall under the jurisdiction of other occupation authorities. There were intelligence officers from various agencies such as the Counter Intelligence Corps (CIC) and the Office of the Political Advisor (POLAD), along with information control personnel under the Psychological Warfare Division and its postwar successor organization, the Information Control Division, who operated within the same geographic region as a local detachment. These men reported their observations directly to their own superiors within their agencies, who in turn reported either to General Robert A. McClure, who headed the Psychological Warfare Division and, until 1946, the Information Control Division under USFET, or to Robert Murphy, the political advisor under the State Department, or to the deputy and later military governor, General Lucius D. Clay, the head of OMGUS.[4] Although neither intelligence nor information control personnel had direct power over the detachment, they occasionally could increase

3. For details of this reporting process, see Rebecca Boehling, "Die politischen Lageberichte des Frankfurter Oberbürgermeisters Blaum an die amerikanische Militärregierung," in *Archiv für Frankfurts Geschichte und Kunst*, 59 (1985), p. 494ff.

4. Harold Hurwitz, *Die Stunde Null der deutschen Presse: Die amerikanische Pressepolitik in Deutschland 1945–1949* (Köln, 1972), p. 46. See also Brewster S. Chamberlin, *Kultur auf Trümmern: Berliner Berichte der amerikanischen Information Control Section, Juli-Dezember 1945* (Stuttgart, 1979), p.12. OMGUS grew out of the USGCC.

the detachment commander's accountability, because they reported up to higher channels, which could – and sometimes did as in the case of Frankfurt – put pressure on OMGUS, which in turn pressured the detachment command.[5]

Americans with German background and/or knowledge of German language, culture and politics usually had lower ranks, because most had been recruited from civilian life. They were more likely to be found in intelligence and information control services than in the actual detachments. Although their paths did sometimes cross with those of the local detachment officers, they had no control over the detachment or over the German municipal administration, just as the detachment could exercise no direct control over them.[6] Because of the power structure within MG, those often most qualified to develop and interpret policies were least likely to be in a position to do so.

Structure and Jurisdiction of U.S. MG

The first military governor of the U.S. Zone of occupation, General Dwight D. Eisenhower, was the military head of the theater of operations, and, until its dissolution in early July 1945, the commander of SHAEF and USFET. His deputy military governor was General Lucius D. Clay. Eisenhower delegated almost all responsibility for MG to his deputy under the condition that Clay keep him thoroughly informed. Because Clay had been in general agreement with Eisenhower on policy, he was worried that he might lose some of his autonomy when Eisenhower left USFET in the late fall of 1945 and was replaced by General Joseph McNarney. McNarney, however, was not particularly interested in German affairs. He did exercise his command prerogatives, but for all practical purposes, Clay continued to head MG and formally became the actual military governor in March 1947.[7]

Initially President Roosevelt had foreseen John J. McCloy for the post of deputy military governor. McCloy, the assistant secretary of war, who put the JCS directive 1067 in its final form and who would become the first high commissioner to Germany in 1949 after the founding of the Federal Republic of Germany,[8] told the president

---

5. This Frankfurt case will be elaborated upon in the next chapter.
6. Cf. Norbert Frei, *Amerikanische Lizenzpolitik und deutsche Pressetradition* (München, 1986), p. 23f.
7. John Backer, *Winds of History: The German Years of Lucius DuBignon Clay* (New York, 1983), p. 104.
8. Jean Edward Smith, *Lucius D. Clay: An American Life* (New York, 1990), p. 202.

that an engineer like Clay would be the most appropriate person to deal with the disastrous conditions of postwar Germany. Clay was a civil engineer, who had served twenty-two years as a company-grade officer, alternately building dams and teaching at West Point before he became first a brigadier and then a major general in 1942. He spent most of the war in Washington using his administrative and engineering skills to solve production problems. During that time he had acquired a reputation for placing military priorities above civilian ones, for a personal independence which struck some as arbitrariness, and even for authoritarianism. Clay took a number of advisors with him to Germany, including William Draper, an investment banker turned general, as economic advisor, and two young lawyers, one who had worked under Clay in the Office of War Mobilization and the other, a mining engineer who had been Clay's executive officer while he was assigned to the Pentagon.[9] According to the historian, Edward N. Peterson, both lawyers were pragmatic and nonideological; such qualifications led to one of them being placed in charge of the task force on denazification.[10] At this high level of MG, most U.S. advisors were businessmen and technocrats without any significant expertise in political affairs or any credentials related to Germany.

General Clay's other principal aide was his political advisor, Robert Murphy. He was the only member of Clay's inner circle of native-born Americans who had studied German and had some experience in Germany, having been the American consul in Munich.[11] During the war Murphy held a subordinate diplomatic post in German-occupied Paris and later became involved in the Darlan affair in North Africa. His performance in both situations made him vulnerable to charges of anti-democratic and even "fascist" sympathies. As an outspoken Catholic, he was suspected of exhibiting favoritism toward Catholics.[12] When it came to the occupation of Germany, he tended to rely on the advice of German Catholic clergymen and to recommend that MG detachment officers do the same.[13] As the political advisor to the American representative of the Allied Control

9. Ibid., p. 5ff. See also p. 105. Cf. Smith, *L. D. Clay*, p. 212 ff.
10. Peterson, *American Occupation*, p. 81.
11. Ibid., p. 82. Interestingly enough, Morgenthau greatly distrusted Murphy, who served as Eisenhower's political advisor. See Smith, *L. D. Clay*, p. 203.
12. Harold Zink, *American Military Government in Germany* (New York, 1947), p. 214f.
13. See "Political Considerations for the Guidance of MG officers in Making Appointments in Germany," RG 84, POLAD TS/ 32/ 10, 1 of 1, NARA, State Dept. files. Parts of this are cited later in this chapter.

Council and to USFET from the fall of 1944 onward, Murphy served as the State Department's representative to MG. His Office of the Political Advisor was created in August 1944 as a division of the U.S. Group Control Council that was under State Department jurisdiction.[14] This meant that Murphy was not directly responsible to Clay or any other Army official. Both the State and the War Departments sent instructions to MG, although Clay arranged to have all instructions routed through the War Department. Clay regarded the State Department's instructions to Murphy as mere suggestions.[15]

Several of Clay's policy advisors were academics who took brief leaves from their teaching responsibilities to assist MG. The advice and opinions of these professors were usually at odds with those of the Army and civilian officials. The latter usually knew less about Germany and tended to be swayed by either war propaganda or postwar personal contacts, whereas the academics were more informed about Germans and their institutions.[16] Temporary academic advisors, like the German-speaking officers in the information control and intelligence services who were outranked by senior detachment officers, had little decision-making power. A similar power situation also existed, as will be recalled, within the OSS, where intellectuals and activists functioned as operatives and research analysts, and business executives and corporate attorneys as top-level administrators.[17] In all three cases, those persons with German language skills and/or background in German affairs and political expertise were in subordinate, advisory positions. On the other hand, those least qualified to deal with German civil affairs, beyond the administrative and technical aspects of material reconstruction, were the real holders of power, and thus instrumental in determining the lines of German political and socioeconomic development.

The civilian-military rivalry over control of the occupation continued after the war ended; the military wanted out but now the civilians (i.e. the State Department) were not ready to assume responsibility. On 26 October 1945, General Eisenhower recommended that the Army abdicate all responsibility for the non-security-related aspects of the occupation by 1 June 1946. He did not feel that the political duties involved in the occupation of Germany should be exercised by the military services except on an emergency basis. However, the State Department was absorbed with

14. Zink, *American Military Government*, p. 211ff.
15. Peterson, *American Occupation of Germany*, p. 82.
16. Ibid.
17. Richard Harris Smith, p. 14ff.

other aspects of U.S. foreign policy, specifically the spread of Communism in China and Eastern Europe, and with discouraging the appeal of Communism in Western Europe.[18] This general U.S. foreign-policy concern later strengthened the tendency in occupation policy of stressing anti-Communism over denazification and democratization, especially within the State Department's subordinate agencies, the U.S. Group Control Council and the Office of the Political Advisor.

Each year of the occupation the switch to civilian jurisdiction appeared to be imminent. It was not, however, until after the London Conference of 1948, which prepared the way for the fusion of the three western zones and the establishment of a central (West) German government, that this reorganization went beyond the planning stage. On 18 May 1949 the secretary of state formally announced an agreement to transfer nonmilitary responsibilities of the occupation from the Army to the State Department. Then on 6 June 1949 the office of HICOG replaced OMGUS.[19]

This long-delayed institutional switch to civilian jurisdiction was merely a formal change for the local and Land level of German government. By the time the Federal Republic of Germany had been founded, direct contact with the authorities of the occupation – excluding military police (MPs) – had long since become infrequent for local and many Land German officials. In the fall of 1945, when the boundaries of the Länder were re-established, the Länderrat, or Council of States, was set up in the U.S. Zone to coordinate the Länder. The three German minister presidents met under American supervision, and many local-level MG responsibilities were transferred over to the Land MG. By late 1946 much of U.S. MG supervision was exercised through the committees and subcommittes of the Länderrat.[20] The first one-and-a-half years were therefore the most crucial for MG in the municipalities and the counties; thereafter, only the large cities and counties continued to have regular detachments, now called liaison and security (L&S) units.

18. Harold Zink, The United States in Germany, 1944–1955 (Princeton, 1957), p. 43ff. Clay himself told his biographer, Jean Edward Smith, that scarcely anyone in Washington paid much attention to the occupation after the war ended and, in particular, that the State Department wasn't interested in it: "'They were interested in Germany's relations with other countries, not in Germany itself.'" Smith, L.D. Clay, p. 235. See also IfZ Munich, Walter Dorn, The Unfinished Purge, unfinished MS, p. 197.
19. Ibid.
20. Zink, American, p. 74f.

The division of responsibility and the chain of command within and among the various MG and MG-related agencies remained confused throughout the military phase of the occupation (1944/5– 1949). Besides the G-5 division of USFET and the U.S. Group Control Council for Germany, and its successor, OMGUS, there was of course POLAD under the State Department and the Information Control Division, which until the spring of 1946 reported to USFET rather than to OMGUS, and even thereafter did not adjust easily to its new master. Then there was the Army's CIC and the OSS, at least until it was dissolved in late September 1945, and its postwar clandestine successor, the Special Services Unit (SSU), which were also outside of OMGUS's jurisdiction. All of these agencies had cause to work in a particular detachment's sphere of influence and even to struggle at times over influence. This rivalry did not simplify the tasks of any of the officers or operatives of the various organizations.

Efforts, however, were made to define the jurisdiction of the various levels of MG and the tactical units of the Army. In May 1945, the headquarters of the ETO established that the chain of command should pass from the military governor through the military district commander to the MG detachments.[21] This however did little to clarify areas in which, particularly in the early stages of the occupation, the interests of the occupying tactical forces conflicted and diverged with those of the MG detachments.[22] Or as General Clay put it: "(T)he tactical commanders were not really very interested in MG."[23] Provisional detachments were organized by the occupying tactical forces until – or at least theoretically until – the MG detachment trained for that locality arrived.[24] The actions of tactical troops varied. Some commanders did not even meet their obligations of making arrangements for displaced persons or establishing security patrols, while others took charge of developments far beyond emergency measures. Unit commanders, for example, sometimes appointed acting mayors or kept the old ones in office, regardless of their political past. The *New York Herald Tribune* quoted a young lieutenant

---

21. The U.S. Zone was divided up into two military districts: the Eastern District corresponded with the borders of Bavaria, whereas the Western District was composed of Greater Hesse and Württemberg-Baden.
22. Memo from Capt. Homer G. Richey to Ambassador Murphy, 8 July 1945, RG 84, POLAD/ 458/ 81, 1 of 2, IfZ.
23. Smith interview with Clay, in Smith, *L.D. Clay*, p. 226.
24. Provost Marshall General's School, *U.S. Military Government in Germany: Operations from late-March to mid-July 1945*, Training Packet No. 57 (Frankfurt, 1950), p. 14.

commanding a tank unit, who had been busy in the town of Tüddin in the fall of 1944: "Nobody told us what to do, so I have sort of acted as military governor myself. I elected me a mayor who lives in that big house yonder, and he's doing all right."[25] Such arbitrary appointments were more likely to happen in rural areas, where a detachment had not yet arrived or would not be assigned, but they could even happen in cities as large and as important as Frankfurt, the seat of USFET headquarters until early 1946. The changeover in personnel to the regular detachment presented a situation that sometimes was not only confusing to the detachment and tactical unit personnel, but also to the Germans, who were perplexed about which Americans to turn to at any given moment.

MG Regulations and Directives

In the early stages of the occupation, directives were issued by SHAEF and USFET to the various Army groups. The Army groups supplemented these directives with instructions to the Army commanders, who in turn issued their own instructions to corps commanders, who did the same to division commanders. This procedure resulted in multiple opportunities for reformulation and misinterpretation. In August 1945 a member of the MG committee concerned with revising MG regulations stated: "By the time instructions reached a MG officer there was frequently a substantial variation between what he was told to do and what some adjoining MG officer in a different chain of command had been told to do. The situation was further complicated by the fact that MG Detachments frequently passed from one Army command to another, with the result that procedures which already had been set up [were] different from those required by the new Commander."[26] The individual officer in the field was hard pressed to determine what exactly the current instructions on a particular subject were, what had been superseded, and what to follow if there were conflicting instructions.[27] Also, because the detachments were subject

25. *New York Herald Tribune*, 2 Nov. 1944. As cited in Joseph R. Starr, *U.S. Military Government in Germany: Operations During the Rhineland Campaign*, Provost Marshall General's School Training Packet No. 56 (Karlsruhe, 1950), p. 27.

26. Col. John M. Raymond, "Military Government Regulations," in USFET, G-5, *Military Government Weekly Information Bulletin*, Military Government Conference Edition, 27–28 Aug. 1945, p. 130.

27. Ibid. Even Clay complained about not getting sufficient instructions: "'There were many times that I would have loved to have had instructions. But where

to the immediate jurisdiction of tactical commands, they did not receive regulations until they passed down through the various echelons to them.[28]

There were certain set directives involving the political, economic, and cultural life of defeated Germany, which were delineated in either the SHAEF *Handbook* or in JCS 1067. JCS 1067 included detailed policy prescriptions on denazification; reparations and restitution; industrial disarmament; property control; the dispersion of ownership and control of German industry; disbandment of cartels; formation of trade unions; land reform; political and economic decentralization; control of education; scientific research; and press, radio, and judicial reform.[29] But because most of JCS 1067 never did obtain very wide circulation at lower military levels, the much more general SHAEF *Handbook* ended up being MG's primary instruction manual. This meant that detachment officers lacked the familiarity with the details of policy needed to implement the structural changes called for in JCS 1067.[30]

As instructed by military channels, the MG detachments gave top priority to getting lines of communications and supplies to function smoothly for the troops and to providing the local population with basic necessities so as to prevent German civilians from interfering with military operations. Because of the shortage of MG personnel, these tasks required the utilization of German expertise and manpower.[31] MG personnel were placed "at all levels of German government to reestablish local administrative machinery," because USFET considered it "manifestly simpler to control Germany through German administrative machinery rather than by the undertaking of direct operating responsibilities." But first they would have to remove "Nazis and those affiliated with Nazism from places of prominence in government and industry."[32] The SHAEF *Handbook* told MG detachments: "Upon occupation of Germany, the elimination of Nazi elements will be necessary, but there will still be career

---

did I go to get them? I never knew. I don't think I ever got any instructions. "' Clay's response to his biographer, Jean Edward Smith, in Smith, *L. D. Clay*, p. 235.

28. Elmer Plischke, "Denazifying the Reich," *The Review of Politics*, 9 (April 1947), p. 166. Plischke had served as the head of the denazification desk under POLAD during the early phase of the occupation.

29. Dorn, *Unfinished*, p. 198.

30. Plischke, p. 167.

31. Ibid., p. 168.

32. IfZ Munich, RG 260, OMGWB, 12/140-3/2, 1 of 3.

servants with training, ability and a sense of duty who will prove useful to the administration of MG. Candidates for civil service had to meet certain general requirements of citizenship, education, age, health and reputation ... From an administrative viewpoint ... , the Civil Service must be credited with considerable success. By elimination of certain elements, the system may be of some practical use to the occupying forces."[33] However, it was also stated that the "German civil service, while maintaining the character of a body of trained career officials, has now lost its reputation for impartial application of the law and has become an instrument of the Nazi regime."[34] The MG reader must have been left feeling some ambivalence toward using experienced civil servants. Although told that a few individual exclusions would suffice, they were not given any guidelines on how to separate the wheat from the chaff.

An academic advisor to U.S. MG, Professor Carl J. Friedrich, emphasized in 1948 that "American policy is not 'imposing' democracy, but is imposing restraints upon those elements of the German population who would prevent democracy from being established."[35] This negative policy of restraining antidemocratic weeds through denazification was intended to make the German soil more fertile for the possible growth of democracy, but it actually played no direct role in planting the seeds of democracy, nor in watering or fertilizing the seedlings. The absence of clear guidelines and the overlapping jurisdictions of the occupation were further complicated by the psychological impact on both Germans and Americans of a collective-guilt thesis associated with the unconditional surrender and the nonfraternization policy established in September 1944 for all U.S. personnel in Germany. MG officers were impeded from seeking advice from trustworthy Germans and various politically reliable Germans who offered their services to MG were turned away because of this nonfraternization regulation.

In 1948 Merle Fainsod, the associate director of the CATS, condemned the impact that the nonfraternization directive had had on anti-Nazi Germans: "An indiscriminate policy of denying food, forbidding economic reconstruction, and outlawing any form of social contact had the effect, whatever the intent, of driving home to the Germans that, in the eyes of the Americans, Nazi and non-Nazi alike were equally abhorrent and reprehensible. Such a policy, if persisted

33. SHAEF, *Handbook for Unit Commanders (Germany)*, 15 Sept. 1944, p. 31f.
34. Ibid., p. 32.
35. Carl J. Friedrich, et al, eds., *American Experiences in Military Government in World War II* (New York, 1948), p. 14.

in, was calculated to drive antifascists to despair; it left them without hope and without any possibility or positive collaboration."[36]

The OMGUS advisor on political affairs and later Chief Historian for HICOG, Harold Zink, noted that numerous anti-Nazi Germans who came to offer their services to MG were turned away because of the nonfraternization policy. He reported that they were often treated discourteously and generally never returned to repeat their offer.[37] Zink argued that the nonfraternization policy in the U.S. Zone meant that "the American MG officers did not see fit to distinguish between Germans favorable to democratization and those thoroughly hostile to it."[38] Joseph Dunner, the intelligence section chief of USFET's Office of War Information (OWI) and later an official in the Information Control Division, admonished that the nondiscriminatory policy toward the Germans reflected either an indifference to or a lack of awareness of the strength of anti-Nazism inside Germany.[39]

The American policy of nonfraternization was eventually withdrawn: speaking was allowed as of 1 October 1945, and at the beginning of 1946, soldiers were told that they could associate with Germans as "ambassadors of democracy."[40] But, as all three of these MG officials noted, it had had quite a problematic effect upon their less-informed MG colleagues. Fainsod, Zink, and Dunner all worked either in intelligence or in civil affairs and were familiar with German history and language. But all three, in merely advisory roles, were neither high enough in military positions of power nor in possession of sufficient political influence to affect these MG policies. This was especially true early on, under the impact of the discovery of concentration camp atrocities, when the spirit of distrust of all Germans weighed on the personnel decisions that the MG detachments had to make about Germans in their area. Most MG career officers, technical experts, and enlisted men, with their deficient civil administration backgrounds, were bound to feel overwhelmed by the problems of the immediate postwar period, and intimidated by their own lack of familiarity with German language, politics, and

---

36. Merle Fainsod, "The Development of American Military Government Policy During World War II," in Carl J. Friedrich, et al, eds., *American Experiences in Military Government in World War II* (New York, 1948), p. 39.

37. Harold Zink, *The United States In Germany, 1944–1955* (Princeton, 1957), p. 135.

38. Zink, *American*, p. 241.

39. Joseph Dunner, "Information Control in the American Zone of Germany, 1945–1946," in Friedrich, *et al.*, eds., p. 290.

40. Peterson, *American Occupation*, p. 155.

culture. Recruited because of their technical and/or administrative skills, their only familiarity with Germany came – that is if they attended them – from the brief civil affairs training courses in the U.S. and Europe.

Denazification

The political scientist, John H. Herz, divided the U.S. denazification procedure into five stages. The first stage began in the fall of 1944, when the first U.S. troops occupied parts of northwestern Germany, and lasted until the spring of 1946. During the first phase, U.S. MG and tactical units handled denazification under preliminary versions of the denazification section of JCS 1067 and provisions of a SHAEF directive issued in late March 1945,[41] all variously interpreted by the different Army groups. Uniform denazification procedures for the U.S. Zone were first provided on 7 July 1945, as part of an updated JCS 1067,[42] which stipulated that:

> All members of the Nazi party who have been more than nominal participants in its activities, all active supporters of Nazism or militarism and all other persons hostile to Allied purposes will be removed and excluded from public office and from positions of importance in quasi-public and private enterprises such as (1) civic, economic and labor organizations, (2) corporations and other organizations in which the German government or subdivisions have a major financial interest, (3) industry, commerce, agriculture, and finance, (4) education, and (5) the press, publishing houses and other agencies disseminating news and propaganda. Persons are to be treated as more than nominal participants in Party activities and as active supporters of Nazism or militarism when they have (1) held office or otherwise been active at any level from local to national in the party and its subordinate organizations, or in organizations which further militaristic doctrines, (2) authorized or participated affirmatively in any Nazi crimes, racial persecutions or discriminations, (3) been avowed believers in Nazism or racial and mili-

41. John H. Herz, "The Fiasco of Denazification in Germany," *Political Science Quarterly*, Vol. 62, No 4 (1948), p. 570. See also Joseph R. Starr, *Denazification, Occupation and Control of Germany, March-July 1945* (Salisbury, N.C.: Documentary Publications, 1977), p. 36f. Starr wrote this history for HICOG in Frankfurt in 1950, although it was not published until 1977.

42. William E. Griffith, "Denazification in the United States Zone of Germany, " *Annals of the American Academy of Political and Social Sciences*, 267 (1950), p. 69. Griffith was a Special Branch officer in Bavaria during the first two years of the occupation and then chief of Special Branch in Bavaria in 1947/8. After retiring as a political scientist at MIT, he served in the 1980s as special political advisor to the U.S. ambassador to the Federal Republic of Germany, Richard Burt.

taristic creeds, or (4) voluntarily given substantial moral or material support or political assistance of any kind to the Nazi Party or Nazi officials and leaders. No such persons shall be retained in any of the categories of employment listed above because of administrative necessity, convenience or expediency.[43]

This final sentence was included to counter the tendency, which had prevailed prior to the July directive, of bypassing the denazification requirements for Germans with technical and administrative experience, whose expertise could be used to simplify U.S. Army and MG tasks.

During the second stage, the Germans were given responsibility for carrying out the new Law for Liberation from National Socialism and Militarism, which was issued on 5 March 1946. German-run tribunals (*Spruchkammer*) and appeals courts were established to try all adult Germans in the U.S. Zone who had been categorized into the five different classes of incrimination according to their suspected involvement with the Nazis. The MG then reviewed the tribunals' findings. The third stage marked the beginning of a formal relaxation of the denazification laws and consisted of a series of amnesties granted by MG in August 1946 to certain groups of incriminated persons as long as they had not been charged in the top two categories of incrimination as either Major Offenders or Offenders. These groups included youth, all Germans born after 1 January 1919, and people whose income or property fell beneath a certain level. More than 70 percent of the denazification caseload was cut by these amnesties, enabling a number of active Nazis and probable war criminals to avoid prosecution.[44]

The fourth stage was an amendment to the Law for Liberation in October 1947 that fundamentally exempted persons in the second highest class of incrimination, that of the Offenders. These Offenders were reclassified as Followers unless they had been members of the organizations declared criminal by the Nuremberg International Military Tribunal, or unless MG did not grant its approval. The amount of work involved, the difficulty in obtaining evidence, and certain forms of local pressure often precluded a thorough investigation for incriminating evidence. Numerous newly classified Followers thus became eligible for amnesty. Previously, those indicted under the lesser category of Followers, the lowest level of incrimi-

---

43. For the full text, see U.S. State Department, *Germany, 1947–1949: The Story in Documents* (Washington, 1950), p. 21–33.
44. Herz, p. 571ff.

nation, had been the first tried so that they would be able to return to work. Over time the courts' thoroughness and stringency diminished, even before the amnesties and the amendment were instituted. This meant that those Followers who were tried first generally received, relative to their incrimination, the harshest punshment.[45]

The fifth stage, a March 1948 amendment, involved the removal of the need for MG's consent for placing Offenders into the Follower category, and the introduction of the possibility of a written procedure and a system of fines rather than a trial to process Followers. At the end of the same month, an amendment was passed so that even Offenders who were members of criminal organizations could be downgraded to Followers and then amnestied or fined. With the release of those who had been interned pending trial, suspects anticipating severe punishment could easily go into hiding. Liquidation of the program was achieved for all practical purposes by the summer of 1948, with generally only appeal cases still pending. Only one-fourth of those required to register under the law were ultimately charged, and, because of amnesties and amendments, only one-quarter of those actually came to trial. Less than two-thirds of those who came to trial were sentenced, with the vast majority receiving mere fines of less than one thousand Reich Marks. Of those convicted less than nineteen thousand people were found ineligible to hold public office.[46] This ineligibility did not generally extend beyond the occupation period.

Herz concluded in his 1948 essay that the result of denazification was to bar certain persons only *temporarily* from positions of influence rather than securing their definitive or permanent elimination. He equated this with the failure "to sift out those among the ruling groups who had been most closely allied with the Nazi cause," including not only active Nazis but also those bureaucrats whose help was instrumental in the success of Nazism. Why this occurred, according to Herz, was a result of the combination of the desire of most Germans to repress the past, the difficulty of utilizing military occupation for political purposes, and the reluctance of many Americans within MG or in Washington "to deal uncompromisingly with groups and members of a class considered as related to one's own ruling group." Herz claimed that there was an even deeper reason for the deficiencies of denazification in the U.S. Zone, namely the growing bipolarization of the Cold War, whereby the

45. Ibid., p. 574.
46. Ibid., p. 574ff.

U.S. welcomed as allies not only democratic non-Communists but also fascist anti-Communists.[47]

The deficiencies in the denazification program cannot simply be ascribed to the changing priorities of the late 1940s when the Cold War heated up. Although the role of the Cold War in the outcome of the denazification program should not be dismissed, it is even more important not to ignore the various motivations behind denazification and the different channels through which denazification had to pass before its final implementation on the local level could take place. A monocausal Cold War explanation ignores the complex behavior of the individuals in MG, some of whom had political motives while others had purely selfish ones. Some took pragmatic approaches to problem solving, while others unflinchingly followed to the letter every directive, regardless of the individual circumstances. The behavior of the Germans to be denazified as well as those involved in implementing the process also affected the success of the program. Here motives also varied from the political to the personal, as did concerns, from the pragmatic ones of efficiency to the idealistic ones of democratization.

Of special importance to any study of the restoration of German self-government is why this "initial period, when, under the impact of the defeat and the revealed Nazi atrocities, conditions were still relatively propitious for a swift and radical operation, *was allowed* [emphasis mine] to pass unused." [48] In this study, the chronological emphasis on denazification is on the program's first stage under direct MG control, and on the early period of German responsibility under the Law for Liberation. Despite individual variations at the local level, molds were cast very quickly and, whether consciously or not, priorities were chosen. Individuals who were allowed to remain in their posts in the first place were much less likely to be removed for denazification purposes later on.

The historian, OSS analyst and denazification advisor to General Clay, Walter Dorn, described from his own experiences the prob-

---

47. Ibid., p. 593f. Herz was hardly alone in his analysis then or later. Twenty-seven years later, Boyd L. Dastrup described the 1945 MG crusade in the city of Nuremberg against Nazism and the way it was transformed by "pressure to establish stability and order, Nurembergers' opposition to denazification, the Americans' desire to return to the United States, and the Soviet-American rift," so that "by 1947 they (Americans) were allowing former Nazis to return to their positions in government, business, and education so reconstruction and restoration processes could be stepped up and so German support in the emerging Cold War could be won."

48. Herz, p. 593.

lems in the denazification process in a manuscript that was left unfinished at the time of his death. He noted that the approach to how National Socialism was "to be expunged effectively as an active force from the political, economic and cultural life of post-war Germany" varied according to the analysis of "what the driving forces of National Socialism actually were and how completely it had fastened its stranglehold on German life."[49] Dorn argued that what he called an outlaw theory of Nazism influenced American denazification policy most. Its supporters insisted on a "purge based on individual responsibility and the degree of complicity in the Nazi regime."[50] Dorn felt that JCS 1067 institutionalized denazification policies in a way that combined this individualized program of punishment of politicians with a Morgenthau-like plan of repression against an entire society. Both strategies avoided any revolutionary transformation of the social order in Central Europe. The plan based on the outlaw theory stressed socioeconomic continuity, i.e., reconsolidation, under the condition that the Nazi leaders be punished as international criminals and therewith be removed from the picture. This would supposedly set free the remaining non-Nazis and enable them to reconstruct a liberal order according to capitalist, parliamentary, and constitutional (*rechtsstaatlich*) principles. The other strategy foresaw the removal of the power potential of the Axis countries and a purge that went beyond the political Nazi elite. Denazification would remove a large part of the German upper class, which, in combination with political repression and the drastic destruction of the industrial plant, was supposed to reduce Germany's potential and regeneration ability.[51]

Dorn maintained that there was a certain correlation between political ideology and one's perspective on denazification. Drawing a parallel with the 1938 Munich crisis, he contended that even in the planning stages of the occupation before the war was over, "many conservatives were more apprehensive of Soviet communism than of National Socialism, while labor and socialist elements tended to be more implacable in their forthright demand for a drastic purge."[52] JCS 1067 attempted to create a compromise by promoting social democratization and harmony via a change of personnel in the top

---

49. Walter Dorn, *The Unfinished Purge*, unfinished MS, p. 12. IfZ. Like various works by other academics who participated in MG, this MS is a cross between a memoir, a political essay, and a scholarly historical reference work.
50. Ibid., p. 12f.
51. Ibid., p. 61.
52. Ibid., p.13.

leadership positions, while gradually subduing and ultimately dis-avowing the punitive aspects and the repressive consequences of denazification. This would make for both a less antagonistic occu-pation, requiring fewer MG personnel, and a more expeditious road to German economic recovery and reintegration into the capitalist system. Such an occupation would thus also satisfy many of the concerns of the War and State Departments.

There were also recommendations for more thorough structural changes within Germany. These were to prevent a revival of the Third Reich or of German authoritarian tendencies and to nurture German democratic traditions, but they came from the least influ-ential quarters. In late 1943 the R&A Branch of the OSS was given the task by the War Department's CAD of preparing manuals that would provide insights into the German social order and suggestions for changes. The result was a series of twenty-four guides on topics such as denazification, local administration, and the distribution of coal and food. The OSS series foresaw not only the removal of the Nazi elite but also the eradication of the social basis of National Socialism. The OSS's elite theory, which was based on a structural-ist analysis of society,[53] did not mesh well with the plans of MG pol-icy makers, who were primarily concerned with eliminating the ideological and personnel barriers to a parliamentary democracy along Western capitalist lines.

As Herz noted, the actual effect of denazification was an exchange of elites and only slightly altered property and socioeconomic rela-tions. One reason for this was that there never was the Stunde Null the OSS anticipated, where the German social order would have stood at the disposal of representatives of the "Other Germany." The historian and former OSS analyst, Carl Schorske, maintained in 1948 that occupation policy in the British and U.S. Zones had been:

> based on a conception of the nature of Nazism as a thing of the mind, an evil idea which would have to be rooted out through the elimination of the bearers of the idea and the re-education of the German people as a whole. This conception of Nazism involves the introduction of no change in the fundamental structure of society. Property relations are un-changed. Administration has been largely entrusted to putatively non-political, middle-class technicians. Thus the continuity of the social

53. Alfons Söllner (ed.), *Zur Archäologie der Demokratie in Deutschland: Analysen poli-tischer Emigranten in amerikanischer Geheimdienst.* Bd. I: 1943–1945, (Frankfurt, 1982), p. 146ff. Söllner maintains that this analysis was based on the work of one of the R&A emigrés, namely Franz Neumann in his *Behemoth,* which was published in 1944.

structure of Imperial, Weimar, and National Socialist Germany is maintained in the Western zones.[54]

The denazification plans of the OSS were predicated on a social-elite theory whereby Nazi incrimination and complicity were to be found not only among the highest echelons of the party hierarchy and the government elite, but also within the internal party structure. This included the leaders of the auxiliary organizations and the economic elite of the private sector. The actual U.S. practice of denazification between 1945 and 1948 stressed quantity, which meant that in the first postwar year, 1.5 million Germans had been processed via their questionnaires (*Fragebogen*). At the same time, the OSS used a qualitative measure, which kept the number of people to be investigated to a minimum. The various levels of interpretation of the schematic denazification measures, the Herculean bureaucratic task, and the retreat into amnesties that those numbers made inevitable, worked to the advantage of those with the most complicity. This was because the Followers or nominal members were sentenced first, prior to the issuing of the amnesties. All of this could have been avoided, according to the German historian, Alfons Söllner, if the criteria that the R&A Branch of the OSS had produced had been used. The denazification proceedings resulted in finding two hundred thousand Germans guilty, a number which coincided with the total number the OSS wanted to investigate in the first place.[55]

The closest the OSS structuralist approach came to realization in directive form was in a 15 August 1945 supplement to JCS 1067 and in Law No. 8, which dealt with the denazification of business enterprises. The supplemental directive added a purge of the professional classes of doctors and lawyers, under the rationale that although they had not held public office, they had held positions of wealth, prominence, and influence in their respective communities. Here, there was a hint of a social transformation, although in practice, provisions for all sorts of exceptions to dismissals and to the blocking of property were incorporated into the guidelines. The first major structural expansion of denazification measures came on 26 September 1945 with Law No. 8,[56] after General George S. Patton, who headed the eastern military district of the U.S. Zone, provoked controversy with his statement at a press conference that the difference

54. Carl E. Schorske, "The Dilemma in Germany," *Virginia Quarterly Review*, 24, no. 1 (Winter 1948), p. 30.
55. Söllner, p. 146f.
56. Dorn, *Unfinished Purge*, p. 227.

between Nazis and anti-Nazis was comparable to that between Republicans and Democrats in the United States.[57]

Law No. 8 was intended to "purify" the German economy. It limited professional/vocational participation by all active party members, regardless of their previous status, to ordinary labor. It placed the burden of proof on the accused, but most significantly, it made use of German review boards that were to be appointed at the local level by the Bürgermeister or Landrat. Neither owners of enterprises nor opportunists who had never joined the NSDAP fell under its jurisdiction.[58] As John Korman's official history of denazification points out, "less important individuals were harshly dealt with, and those with greater influence and standing were permitted to go free."[59] However, in terms of implementation, this German-run purge of business appeared, in the final analysis, to have been qualitatively more successful than the other MG-run denazification programs during the short time it was in effect.[60] German public opinion, except in business circles, was favorably inclined toward the policy, and the newly licensed trade unions, in particular, supported Law No. 8.[61] Unfortunately, with the owners still in place or only temporarily displaced by trustees, many managers and executives often only had to bide their time a short while before they were restored to their positions, whether secretly or by a change in the job classification.[62]

Directives were variously interpreted and implemented by the different levels within the military hierarchy.[63] For example, one of the armies changed the term "active Nazis" to "all Nazis," whereas another defined those who joined the party after 1936 as "not active." Yet another Army suspended denazification implementation almost altogether for reasons of expediency. Some uniformity was achieved when the Army Groups were deactivated in 1945,[64] but the mold of individual interpretation had been cast. Elmer Plischke, the early head of the denazification desk under POLAD, described in the spring of 1947 how this lack of uniformity continued down to the implementation of denazification at the detachment level:

57. Donald B. Robinson, "Why Denazification is Lagging," *American Mercury* , Vol 62 (May 1946), p. 566f.
58. Dorn, *Unfinished Purge*, p. 230f.
59. John G. Korman, *U.S. Denazification Policy in Germany 1944–1950* (Historical Division, Office of the U.S. High Commissioner for Germany, 1952), p. 43.
60. Dorn, *Unfinished Purge*, p. 231.
61. Korman, p. 38f.
62. See Gulgowski, p. 341f. See also Korman, p. 39.
63. Starr, p. 36.
64. Zink, *United States*, p. 157f.

The detachments were subject to the immediate jurisdiction of tactical commands, which delayed the process of passing denazification regulations down through its various echelons to MG officers and men in the field, and also exercised the privilege of interpreting the directives decided upon at top MG headquarters as they passed them on ... There consequently was considerable variation in the application of the denazification program among the various sections of Germany under the control of the American occupation forces.

This difficulty was augmented by the lack of direct control over denazification matters by a single, central headquarters ... and by the lack of coordination in the field by agents representing a central headquarters.[65]

The technical aspects of the implementation of denazification in the U.S. Zone were handled initially by MG detachments without any special denazification personnel.[66] Because most regular MG detachments regarded denazification as burdensome and gave it lower priority than the more mundane and translucent, but pressing, tasks of securing housing, food, water, and power supplies, responsibility for this purge was soon given to a specially created Special Branch of the Public Safety Branch of the MG's Internal Affairs Division. Germans who held or applied for any middle- or high-level position had to first fill out detailed questionnaires about their career experience and political involvement. These Fragebogen were sorted out and categorized by Special Branch officers according to the level of political incrimination. Then, if necessary, the individuals were investigated further and the appropriate action taken, whether dismissing the person from a post or blocking his or her property.[67]

Altogether some thirteen million Fragebogen, including those from expellees from the East, were completed and returned by the Germans living in the U.S. Zone. The investigation of the validity of the data and the decisions regarding action to be taken in each individual case required a considerable number of Special Branch officers and other MG personnel. Although the number of Fragebogen increased and the need for personnel to process them expanded, more and more capable military personnel were returning to the United States after their tour of duty had ended; their replacements were fewer in number and less qualified, which further diminished the efficacy of the program.[68]

The immense number of Germans who needed to be vetted for Nazi incrimination and the decreasing number of qualified MG

---

65. Plischke, p. 166.
66. Ibid., p. 159.
67. Lutz Niethammer (ed.), Editor's commentary, in Walter Dorn, *Inspektionsreise in der US-Zone* (Stuttgart, 1973), p. 88f.
68. Zink, *United States*, p. 158f.

investigators led to various concessions or compromises in the denazification program. Even in the first year and a half of the occupation period, high-level occupation officials recognized the necessity of distinguishing between active and nominal Nazis in order to reduce the task at hand. They suggested to detachments, although usually to no avail, that they rely more on the judgment of German anti-Nazis than on American personnel, most of whom were unfamiliar with the apparatus of the German system and the history of the Third Reich.[69] The size and difficulty of the MG's task ultimately led to the transfer of the denazification proceedings to German tribunals under MG supervision with the March 1946 Law for Liberation. But prior to this jurisdictional change, "a concession of justice to utility" was made in the form of the retention of certain German officials liable for dismissal but considered indispensable to the economy and to the administration of government.[70]

Local troop or detachment commanders often tried to bypass denazification dismissals because they feared dismissals would hinder their efforts to make their areas functional again for the use of military personnel and the native German population.[71] The head of the POLAD denazification desk sympathized with the detachment officer's dilemma of being torn between achieving administrative efficiency and following denazification directives:

> Many incumbent German government officials, as well as many of the industrial, utilities, and business managers, technicians, and workers were essential for the effective performance of the MG officer's responsibilities. He was torn between the twin horns of the apparently insolvable dilemma – putting the services into operation and getting things going again, on the one hand, and denazification, on the other. If he favored the former – and strong pressure to do so was often exerted upon him by his immediate superior tactical commands which needed the local German services to continue their military operations – he naturally had to slight the latter. And so it was that Nazis sometimes were retained in their former posts, occasionally for several weeks or even months after the MG detachment had taken over.[72]

69. Friedmann, p. 114. In practice, offers of German assistance were often rebuffed by detachment officers because of both the nonfraternization directives and the narrow interpretation of denazification as a U.S. operation. See Joseph F. Napoli, "Denazification from an American's Viewpoint," *Annals of the American Academy of Political and Social Sciences*, 264 (1949), p. 120. Examples of this in Stuttgart, Munich, and Frankfurt exist as well, as will become apparent in successive chapters.

70. Ibid.

71. See Dorn, *Unfinished Purge*, p. 231.

72. Plischke, p. 168.

There seems to have been much less continuous pressure to follow denazification guidelines than to keep military operations going. Only when news of specific Nazis remaining in power or being appointed to top posts reached the American public, was there an intensification of denazification. An example of this is the case in Aachen where headlines about the U.S. MG working with Nazis and discriminating against anti-Fascists caused public uproar in the United States and thus panic in Washington and within SHAEF.[73] The crackdowns were usually only temporary, with U.S. military concerns often superseding political programs like denazification.[74] As John Korman reported in the official HICOG history: "The conflicts which arose when denazification measures interfered with military commanders' desire to put things in order again as quickly as possible were many and there was considerable friction in numerous quarters as a result."[75] For example, when U.S. Army officers in charge of the German factories that supplied the Army blatantly rejected denazification in "their" factories, with the argument that '"Production comes first,"' Eisenhower responded by transferring control of these production agencies over to MG.[76] He did not realize that MG's priorities in practice were often not all that different. When MG was placed formally in charge of a company, it often kept the original factory owner or manager in the top post.

In July 1945 a survey of the progress made in denazification was conducted by USFET headquarters. Third Reich German officials had yet to be purged in numerous towns and counties that had been occupied for three to eight months. USFET reported that "it had been a widespread practice among MG detachments to retain technically qualified personnel in subordinate positions, even though they are Nazis subject to removal, until suitable replacements are found."[77] In many cases anti-Nazi Germans, even inexperienced ones, could have been trained during the time these qualified, but incriminated, personnel were retained. But such practical *and* politically responsible steps were rarely taken.

Donald B. Robinson, an officer from General Eisenhower's staff, complained bitterly in a May 1946 *American Mercury* article about

73. Lutz Niethammer, "Die amerikanische Besatzungsmacht zwischen Verwaltungstradition und politischen Parteien in Bayern 1945," *Vieteljahrshefte für Zeitgeschichte* (1967), Heft 2, p. 172ff.
74. Plischke, p. 168.
75. Korman, p. 29.
76. Robinson, p. 569.
77. Letter, Col. Stephen B. Story, USFET G-5 Division, 16 July 1945, subject: Summary of Information Furnished by Detachments on Denazification and Related Subjects, as cited in Starr, *Denazification*, p. 131.

MG's excuse of expediency for not purging Nazis from German governmental and industrial posts. He asserted that Nazi officeholders did all they could to reinforce the MG belief that only Nazis could do the work since no one else had been able to acquire experience during the previous twelve years.[78] He wrote: "To MG officers in the field, it looked better to have the town in running order than to throw out a Nazi; and it seemed safer to have a hospital functioning perfectly than to give a Hitlerite superintendant the bum's rush."[79] Robinson claimed that most American officers did not recognize the political significance of their tasks, and if they were not enjoying their stay, they were plagued with homesickness which made them concentrate more on getting home as soon as possible rather than on their assigned tasks.[80]

Administrative Appointments

If the decisions regarding whom to dismiss and retain were difficult, then those regarding whom to appoint must have been even more daunting. In some ways the appointment of Germans to administrative posts was the reverse side of the coin of denazification. New appointees were not supposed to fall under any of the categories of those to be excluded from public office.[81] Here Nazi affiliations were often used as the sole criterion, regardless of whether the membership was a mandatory one in a professional or vocational organization like the German Labor Front (DAF) or one in the SA-reserve or the SS. John Korman reported that the MG "turned to anyone who could show an unblemished record and a person who had not joined the party became more 'democratic' than one who had, no matter what the circumstances conditioning his joining might have been."[82] There seemed to be little awareness of the difference between non-Nazis and anti-Nazis, not to mention anti-Nazi democrats versus antidemocratic anti-Nazis. As the U.S. occupation historian, John Gimbel, later commented: "Americans proceeded as though the origin and evolution of democracy is a natural process that needs only to be guarded against evil agents who would block that process. They seemed to hope, in vain, that

78. Robinson, p. 565.
79. Ibid, p. 567f.
80. Ibid., p. 567.
81. Starr, p. 39.
82. Korman, p. 24.

a new democratic leadership would arise in Germany and freely and readily (instinctively?) accept the American image of democracy and thus also accept the American administrative necessities and policy changes."[83]

In the last years of the war, U.S. agencies like the OSS did try to single out potential Germans who might become this new postwar "democratic leadership." In November 1944 the OSS established elaborate criteria for the identification of non-Nazis and anti-Nazis in Germany. It pointed out that the clandestine nature of some forms of opposition sometimes prevented active resistance from being verifiable, so types of punishment such as imprisonment, job dismissals, and public criticism came to be designated as proof of resistance. Also, members of the Confessional Church (*Bekenntniskirche*) and other clergymen who had publicly voiced opposition, and any Germans who had given support and/or shelter to victims of Nazism were considered anti-Nazis. Both non-NSDAP members and Germans who refused to accept party honors or posts or government positions could be regarded as non-Nazis.[84]

The OSS also compiled so-called White, Grey and Black Lists of Germans,[85] identifying those recommended, those acceptable, and those blacklisted, according to their record of resistance or collaboration. The OSS White Lists, which included only anti-Nazis, were not particularly useful, because either those persons listed were not locatable or their most recent pasts did not correspond to their earlier records. Only a few important positions were filled according to these lists, among them the pre-1933 Oberbürgermeister of Cologne and Munich, Konrad Adenauer and Karl Scharnagl, both of whom were restored to their posts.[86] The lists rarely included lesser-known figures, such as persons known only within their municipality.[87] Various former MG officers questioned by this author could not recall ever having seen these lists.[88]

---

83. John Gimbel, *A German Community under American Occupation* (Stanford, 1961), p. 4.

84. R&A Report 2189, 15 Nov. 1944, p. 7ff. RG 59, OSS, NARA.

85. For background information on these lists, see H. L. Wuermeling, *Die Weisse Liste. Umbruch der politischen Kultur in Deutschland 1945* (Berlin, 1981).

86. Niethammer, "Die amerikanische Besatzungsmacht," p. 164f.

87. XL 22686, 6 August 1945, RG 226, OSS files, NARA.

88. Interviews held with Henry Walter, deputy detachment commander in Stuttgart and Kal Oravetz, legal advisor to G-5, USFET Headquarters from 17 to 19 Oct. 1986 in Plymouth, N.H., Ernest Langendorf, DISCC Press Control officer in Munich, on 25 Feb. 1982 in Munich; and correspondence with former detachment officers in Frankfurt, Munich, and Stuttgart.

Another source for names of potential postwar democratic leaders were anti-Nazi German exiles[89] like Dr. Helmut von Rauschenplatt in London, better known by his post-exile name of Fritz Eberhard. In 1944 Eberhard was asked to compile "lists of persons in Germany and Austria who may usefully occupy responsible positions after the defeat of the Nazis."[90] But emigrés often feared Nazi retribution against the persons they recommended as reliable anti-Nazi democrats if the lists were to be exposed prior to an Allied victory. Eberhard, who, along with other exiled German trade unionists, participated in plans to overthrow Hitler and to rebuild postwar Germany along democratic lines, did prepare political reports about conditions in Württemberg-Baden for U.S. MG intelligence, but not until he was back in his hometown of Stuttgart and the war was over.[91] In September 1944 he refused to compile such a list, because he did not want to "endanger the persons concerned."[92]

Even when names could be obtained, there was no guarantee that the people would still be alive or traceable. Of those located, some refused their cooperation prior to the formal German surrender out of fear of Nazi retribution against themselves or family members, some of whom lived in areas not yet taken by the Allies. Others felt that working with the occupying power might constitute a betrayal of national loyalties, if not in their own eyes, then in those of fellow Germans.[93] However, regardless of such reluctance, there were a number of American attempts to seek out and/or pre-select democratic Germans to replace Nazis "in places of prominence in government and industry" prior to the actual occupation.[94]

The question of returning German political refugees to Germany for intelligence purposes and/or as potential appointees arose during the latter part of the war. SHAEF had established a policy in 1944 whereby neither commitments nor negotiations were to be made with any German political elements, and this policy was interpreted by some in the State Department as precluding the return of the German exiles. However by January 1945 some officials in the

89. For more information see Ulrich Borsdorf and Lutz Niethammer (eds), *Zwischen Befreiung und Besatzung. Analysen des US-Geheimdienstes über Positionen und Strukturen deutscher Politik 1945* (Wuppertal, 1976).
90. Letter of 21 August 1944 from R.W. Southern to Dr. Rauschenplatt, ED 117, "Fritz Eberhard," Bd. 1, Bl. 31, IfZ.
91. "Fritz Eberhard," Findbuch, p. III, ED 117, IfZ.
92. Ibid., Bd. 1, Bl. 34, Letter of 18 Sept. 1944 from Rauschenplatt to a SHAEF representative.
93. Niethammer, "Die amerikanische Besatzungsmacht," p. 164.
94. See also RG 260, OMGWB, 12/140-3/2, 1 of 3, IfZ.

Manpower and Political Divisions of the U.S. Group Control Council (USGCC) felt that such refugees might be helpful in advising MG "in the very first hour," when it would be crucial to have expert information otherwise unobtainable by outsider MG officers. One of their memos to the State Department even suggested that: "(i)n some circumstances, particularly if it is found that the Nazis have killed most acceptable candidates in Germany, it might also be useful or necessary to bring back qualified refugees to fill positions in the German administration."[95]

The OSS organized a program to return exiles for political purposes. It sponsored a detachment of German political refugees, which was sent to Cologne as early as March 1945 to help in intelligence work and in the rebirth of the German labor movement. When the Political Division of the U.S. Group Control Council learned of this refugee presence, it protested to the secretary of state.[96] OSS Chief William Donovan had promised the State Department the OSS would not use refugees in Germany without its approval and would restrict their activities to intelligence gathering.[97] The matter became a political tug-of-war over jurisdiction, with the State Department and the upper echelons of the USGCC winning out over the OSS and ultimately vetoing the return of further refugees. This excluded one more potential group of anti-Nazi appointees for administrative posts.[98]

If the names of individuals who would make reliable appointees could not be verified prior to the liberation and occupation of an

95.   17 Jan. 1945 letter from Heath to the secretary of state in reference to conversation between Major David Morse, acting director of Manpower Division with Donald R. Heath of the Political Division, RG 84, POLAD TS/32/55, 1 of 1, NARA.

96.   24 March 1945 telegram from Donald Heath to the secretary of state, RG 84, POLAD TS/32/35, 1 of 1, NARA.

97.   15 June 1945 Memo from Louis A. Wiesner to Ambassador Robert Murphy, RG 84, POLAD TS/ 32/ 10, 1 of 1, NARA.

98.   It was not just within U.S. agencies that the return of German refugees was controversial. The Germans themselves, including anti-Nazis, had mixed feelings about their fellow Germans in exile. Some resented their not having had to experience the Third Reich from within and felt that if they returned, they certainly should have no special place in rebuilding postwar Germany. See "Wilhelm Hoegner Sammlung," Bd. 39, Correspondence with Hans Dill (1945–1950), ED 120, IfZ. Dill was a former SPD Reichstag and Landtag deputy and journalist, living in exile in Canada since 1939, who was trying to return to Germany (Munich) to assist in rebuilding the trade unions. The onetime Bavarian minister president, Wilhelm Hoegner, and the Bavarian trade union official, Gustav Schiefer, did not directly discourage Dill from returning, but either, in the former case, postponed responses to his pleas or, in the latter case, reminded Dill that others, who had not abandoned Bavaria in its time of need, now had a sense of solidarity and cameraderie that was crucial to rebuilding the labor movement.

area, then certain guidelines had to be provided for the arriving tactical troops and the assigned detachments of an area. The OSS criteria for the identification of anti-Nazis and non-Nazis, like much of the material that the OSS produced, rarely filtered down to the actual local level where it was needed.[99] Pressure for more concrete guidelines regarding whom to appoint grew after the first U.S. attempt at military government in Aachen in late October 1944. SHAEF discovered that almost one-third of the key administrative positions in Aachen were held by former NSDAP members and that there were no anti-Nazi appointees. Criticism of the naivete of Aachen's MG detachment was leaked to the U.S. press, which pressured the occupation authorities to take action.[100]

It was after the Aachen fiasco that the deputy assistant chief of staff of SHAEF's G-5 CAD, Brigadier General Frank J. McSherry, begged the MG's chief political advisor, Robert D. Murphy, for political directives "other than de-Nazification and the negative directive to prohibit political activity and to avoid commitments to or negotiations with any political elements." Noting "that a formal directive from SCAEF on affirmative political policy ... might commit our governments to certain political factions," he pleaded that "informal guidance ... be given to MG officers" about the formation and political utilization of trade unions, the representation of "all non-Nazi elements" in administrations, and that MG be warned against "allowing chosen officials a free hand in building up political 'machines' or 'cliques' of their own choosing" and against utilizing "the church as a source of advice on political matters" because this might "result in appointment of 'conservative' elements at the expense of other factions."[101] McSherry contrasted the situation in Germany with that in the liberated countries where USFET had "tried to stay strictly away from politics and concentrate on technical functions." He reminded Murphy that "in Germany the situation is entirely different because de-Nazification is in itself a political question."[102]

On 4 May 1945, MG Political Advisor Murphy acknowledged to McSherry the problem of the lack of "positive guidance to the MG officer who not only wants to know whom he should not appoint but whom he should appoint, both in order to obtain cooperative German

99. Personal interview with Henry Walter, deputy detachment commander in Stuttgart and Kal Oravetz, legal advisor to G-5, USFET Headquarters, 17 to 19 Oct. 1986 in Plymouth, N.H.

100. Niethammer, "Die amerikanische Besatzungsmacht ," p.172ff.

101. Letter of 31 March 1945, RG 84, POLAD TS/32/10, 1 of 1, NARA.

102. Ibid.

officials and in order to promote and encourage a regrowth of democratic forces." But he thought such guidance would have to be approached "gradually and experimentally,"[103] even though by then, MG had been set up in the entire U.S. Zone and many areas had been under occupation since the beginning of the year. In response to McSherry's concern about emphasizing to MG officers "the importance of political considerations, even at the expense of 'efficient' administration," Murphy warned against assuming that denazification would inevitably impair efficiency.[104] Yet MG officers regularly stated this assumption as an excuse for bypassing denazification directives. On the other hand, Murphy initiated no steps to place experienced personnel from the pre-1933 period, who had been purged by the Nazis, back in their posts or to train anti-Nazi Germans for these posts.

Murphy assigned several aides to put together a list of "Political Considerations for the Guidance of MG Officers in Making Appointments in Germany." The negative considerations dealt with not appointing active members of the Nazi Party or ardent sympathizers, military leader, or militarists. The positive considerations were more detailed, probably because they were being spelled out for the first time. Their relevance to this study warrants quoting them verbatim:

II. Positive considerations.

    A. In making appointments, it is highly important to make every effort to select people who are not only anti-Nazi, but who are reasonably liberal and pro-democratic in their outlook.

        1. Old political and organizational labels are indicative, though not decisive. Thus, it is a presumption that former trade unionists, Social Democrats, members of the German Democratic Party, Independent Social Democrats, and many members of the Center Party are reasonable [sic] pro-democratic and anti-Nazi. Parties to the right of the former Center Party (Nationalist Party, German People's Party) may have been anti-Nazi, but they were so generally imbued with German nationalism, militarism and conservative traditionalism as to make their members unsuitable for all purposes. In many cases members of these rightist parties are only less dangerous than the Nazis themselves. Former Center Party members should be examined with care, as this party has two divergent wings, one of which was reasonably pro-democratic and the other not.

        2. Stress must be laid on considering carefully the background of each individual being considered for appointment. *No* label from 12 years ago is conclusive.

103. Letter of 4 May 1945 from Murphy to McSherry. RG 84, POLAD TS/32/10, 1 of 1, NARA.
104. Ibid.

3. An effort should be made, within the limits of the persons available, to spread appointments over various groups. In this way, we will more easily avoid the charge of favoring this or that group among the pro-democratic anti-Nazi Germans.

4. Appointments should especially avoid giving too much prominence to elements from the extreme left or extreme right of the anti-Nazi section of the population. This is important in order to avoid charges of favoring a too radical or too conservative policy and also in order to lessen the chance of appointing persons who are not genuinely pro-democratic, although in late(sic) years they may have been anti-Nazi.

5. MG officers should study and take into consideration the political and economic background of their district in order that appointments may be reasonably representative of the local population. Thus, in a predominantly Catholic locality more appointments of Catholics, former Center Party members, etc., would be made than in a Protestant industrial community where former Social Democrats and trade unionists would be more representative. No absolute rule can be laid down and the MG officer must rely on his own judgment.

B. In many cases the MG officer will find it useful to obtain the views or advice of the local Catholic or Protestant churchmen. It must be borne in mind, however, that the record of the Church was not uniformly anti-Nazi and the MG officer should endeavor to ascertain the past position and leanings of the individual churchmen whose advice he might consider using. The MG officer must, furthermore, bear in mind that even if the advice is reliabĺy anti-Nazi, it should be carefully weighed for assurance that it is also pro-democratic and not unduly reactionary from a political point of view.[105]

How many MG officers actually received these guidelines and when and how many used them is unknown. MG officers claimed that from the start they encountered difficulties in finding persons of suitable ability, background, and experience to fill posts in local government.[106] The low number of personnel changes made in the late spring and early summer of 1945 indicate that these "considerations" made little impact on MG appointments. Again timing was crucial; by then all significant appointments had been made and unless there were specific administrative problems, few detachment commanders were going to halt progress by making changes for political reasons, unless they feared sabotage or if major Nazi offenders were involved. From the perspective of many MG officers, the least political Germans were the most attractive, less likely to

---

105. Ibid.
106. Starr, *U.S. Military Government*, p. 125.

have their own agenda or be inclined to rock the boat. Few MG officers were comfortable with explicitly political anti-Nazis, who
tended to wear their politics on their sleeves. They preferred the
more pragmatic technocrats and administrators, whose politics
seemed less partisan and were often not recognized as "political" by
these Americans. As late as mid-April 1945 the tendency of MG officers to choose "only Germans of conservative background as bur-
gomasters [sic]" was still being reported.[107] Strangely enough,
POLAD and the headquarters of the USGCC turned to MG detachments for suggestions when, in the summer of 1945, they started
soliciting lists of reliable anti-Nazis from which state ministerial
posts might be filled.[108]

Conclusion

The deficiencies in implementing denazification and making sound
administrative appointments were not only due to the nonfraternization policy, the stress on military necessity and expediency, and
the overlapping jurisdictions, but also to MG personnel's political
inexperience and their often inadequate understanding of their roles
as facilitators of democratization. This was partly caused by their
limited training and personal pragmatism, and partly by the lack of
availabilty and/or clarity of the directives and guidelines that were
passed down to them. Many MG personnel were inherently ignorant
of German political structures and cultures as well as of the political nature of the socioeconomic structure of society, whether German or their own. This further limited their ability to choose
acceptable Germans or make provisions for the training of potentially capable Germans while at the same time closely overseeing
their temporary appointees, whose experience might have been crucial but whose political pasts should have disqualified them for any
long-term positions of responsibility in a democratization process.
    As the denazification specialist, William Griffith, noted in 1950:

> Most United States field MG officers, haphazardly picked and insuffi-
> ciently trained, were, in Aachen and elsewhere, excellent at restoring
> public utilities, but much less fitted for carrying out with understanding
> – still less with enthusiasm – the revolution which United States denaz-

107. Weekly Civil Affairs Report, MG Survey No. 27, week ending 12 April 1945, OSS
    files, XL 7971, RG 226, NARA.
108. RG 84, POLAD/ 729/45, 2 of 2; POLAD/732/24, 1 and 2 of 2; RG260,
    USGCC/44-45/4/5, 2 of 4, IfZ.

ification policy implicitly involved. When forced to make political decisions, these officers most naturally favored 'stable' political elements (the Catholic Church, the one organization which had survived the collapse, and the strongly conservative former civil servants) and too often failed to appoint actively anti-Nazi officials.

These officers were temperamentally interested in 'getting things done,' not in tearing down ... .[109]

The practice of U.S. denazification policy allowed too much leeway for randomness in application and too many varying interpretations according to the convenience and expediency of the moment.

109. Griffith, p. 68.

Chapter III

FROM RESISTANCE AND LIBERATION TO CONQUEST AND OCCUPATION

Introduction

*T*he municipality *(Stadtkreis)* and the Landkreis were the first administrative units to fall under MG control. Within approximately a year they were also the first to obtain self-government in all of the four Zones of occupied Germany.[1] By the time of the signing of the Potsdam Agreement, it was clear that the eight thousand personnel allocated by the War Department for the administration of the U.S. Zone would need to work with – or through – Germans,[2] who eventually would achieve – either directly or indirectly – full autonomy in local government. Given the shortage of U.S. personnel to do the jobs themselves, and their insufficient grasp of German affairs, some level of German independence and self-governance was inevitable, even from the earliest days of the occupation.

If one takes into account the Germans' expectations of the occupation, rather than just the Americans' plans, the picture becomes even more complex. The potential for conflict increases because there is no longer just the matter of disagreements among Americans, but also among Germans and between Germans and Americans. Many opponents of the Third Reich who had survived the regime viewed the arriving Allied troops as liberators. From this perspective, they naturally expected to be regarded as the "other Germany" with whom

1. U.S. Department of State, Germany, 1947–1949: *The Story in Documents*, Publication 3556 (Washington 1950), p. 49.
2. Gulgowski, p. 122.

the Allies would want to cooperate. Early 1945 American intelligence reports predicted that while Germans in general expected a harsh occupation, most individuals expected to be personally exempted from harsh treatment, either because of their anti-Nazi credentials or because their skills and experience would be essential to postwar administration and reconstruction.[3] Those with genuine anti-Nazi credentials were actually rather few, but not as few as was perceived by the outside world. This underestimation was due to the secrecy surrounding most Gestapo arrests and because the most effective opposition had had to remain clandestine. As late as January 1945 the Political Division of the USGCC was reporting that there was "no such thing as a real 'opposition'" in Germany, only the isolated incidents of the students' revolt in Munich (White Rose), the 20 July 1944 assassination attempt and "the rather steadfast but limited open opposition within the Catholic Church."[4] This impression lent credence to the theory of collective guilt and bolstered policies such as nonfraternization and reliance on the Catholic Church for advice on "reliable" Germans.

As late as May 1945, U.S. intelligence reports stemming from POLAD, expressed amazement at the number of anti-Nazi Germans who expected the Allies to assist them in rebuilding Germany. They were astonished first, that any Germans expected to be autonomous and second, that they assumed that the occupiers would help the anti-Nazi Germans reassert control and make changes, rather than the other way around. The desire expressed by several Social Democrats for an independent German foreign policy that would not be compelled to choose between collaborating with the Western powers against the Soviet Union or with the Soviet Union against the Western powers astounded one particular agent. He found it audacious of the Germans to assume that Germany would be in a position of independence again so soon and that it might not want to belong to the Western camp.[5]

If the authors of these POLAD intelligence reports had been aware of the views of some of the emigrés who were advising the Allies, such as Fritz Eberhard, they would have been less surprised about these German expectations of autonomy. While in exile in London in 1942, Eberhard gave a radio speech advocating the

3. Report No. 6, May 1945, "What do the Germans expect to happen after the War?", RG 84, POLAD TS/32/50, 1 of 1, NARA.
4. 23 Jan. 1945 memo from Donald Heath to Ambassador Murphy, RG 84, POLAD TS/ 32/ 35, 1 of 1, NARA.
5. See note 3.

necessity of revolution in Germany once the Third Reich fell as a prerequisite to a thorough destruction of the Nazi system.[6] Like the U.S. Army, Eberhard presumed that there would be a collapse and surrender of the Third Reich as a whole, rather than the piecemeal conquest and occupation which occurred between September 1944 and May 1945. Unlike the Army, however, Eberhard was convinced that Nazism had to be destroyed from below and hence by Germans in a revolution. Perhaps lamenting the fact that the Revolution of 1918 had failed, he thought that even if outside powers could break the Nazi military and political system, a purge would have to be "carried through by the German people themselves." He recognized that there might be a period without a central authority in which diverse popular movements, not always recognizable as Nazi or anti-Nazi, would struggle against the remnants of the Nazi system, each pretending "to fight for law and order and even for democracy." Eberhard warned: "In this state of unrest the A. O. [Army of Occupation] may be forced to take over certain administrative tasks; but they must beware of a tendency for them to side with those who, having control of what is left of the administrative machine, can alone safeguard 'order.' We submit that by doing so they would prevent the creation of a new Germany."[7]

Eberhard insisted that the Allied Powers should restrain themselves from restoring "law and order" beyond their own security needs, as otherwise this would stifle the revolutionary movement needed for a thorough purge. He continued: "It must be fully realized that the birth pangs of a new order inevitably involve a certain amount of unrest and disorder and that the protection of the lives of SS men and Nazi war lords does not belong to the duties of the A. O. Non-intervention will be the wisest assistance which the United Nations can give to the creation of a new Germany. Intervention against revolution on the other hand will sooner or later lead to the return of the old powers, as there will have to be some sort of a German administration in the long run."[8] Written prior to any of the tripartite or quadripartite Allied agreements on postwar Germany, Eberhard's plans ignored the fact that the techniques and goals of the zonal powers were at odds with each other, let alone with the Germans. His assumption of a political vacuum and an

6. 6 May 1942 "Memorandum on the Policy of a United Nations' Army of Occupation in Germany and its Effect on Political Developments in Germany," ED 117, "Fritz Eberhard," Bd. 1, Bl. 260, IfZ.
7. Ibid., Bl. 260f.
8. Ibid., Bl. 261f.

autonomous German new order in central Europe was both unrealistic and impractical.

Eberhard's ideas about the necessity of revolution found little resonance among most American occupation planners. His recognition of the inherently dual character of an occupation, torn between restoring order and facilitating change, resounded however in the reports and histories of the occupation by U.S. participants.[9] Military values and priorities were the rule of the day for both tactical and MG commanders who typically focused on maintaining law and order while being extremely reluctant to disrupt existing institutions. Robert Engler, an early observer of and officer in MG, noted the military commanders' "suspicion of politics and politicians, their distrust of trade unionists, their annoyance with displaced persons, their openly contemptuous attitude towards enlisted men and those of lower rank." He commented that all of this "furnished important clues as to the nature of their training and long-time isolation from the cross-currents of democratic society ... and the propriety of using this tradition-bound organization as the instrument for the essentially revolutionary task of creating conditions favorable for the 'democratization' of Germany, once the immediate post-hostilities stage had ended."[10]

During the first year and three-quarters of the occupation "this tradition-bound organization," the U.S. Army, was supposed to play this dual role. The twenty-one months from September 1944 to June 1946, when the military had direct responsibility for governing parts of and then all of the U.S. Zone and, for a time, parts of northern Germany, represent an interregnum when the occupation had the most immediate impact upon the German people.[11] During this time, as we shall see in Frankfurt, Munich, and Stuttgart, the pattern of granting priority to military and material concerns over most civic and political ones was set for both the American rule and the German response to it.[12]

MG detachments arrived in an area anywhere from hours to days after a town had surrendered, although sometimes street fighting continued even after their arrival. In the interim prior to the detach-

9. Earl F. Ziemke, "Improvising Stability and Change in Postwar Germany," in Robert Wolfe (ed.), *Americans as Proconsuls. U.S. Military Government in Germany and Japan, 1944–1952* (Carbondale, 1984), p. 53.

10. Robert Engler, "The Individual Soldier and the Occupation," *Annals of the American Academy of Political and Social Sciences*, Vol. 267 (1950), p. 78.

11. Ziemke, "Improvising Stability," p.53.

12. Engler, p. 77.

ment's arrival, the tactical troops often proceeded with some of the first tasks of restoring order that would otherwise have fallen to the MG detachment. The extent of physical damage due to aerial and artillery bombardment or due to avid Nazis following Hitler's Nero Plan varied from town to town. The first tasks confronting the arriving detachment and/or the tactical commander included "finding shelter for the homeless, organizing distribution of food, caring for the injured and sick, and reestablishing civil administration."[13] Some areas were faced with the somewhat less immediate, but more complicated, additional chores of repatriating some of the millions of displaced persons (DPs), demobilizing the *Wehrmacht*, facilitating the return of Allied prisoners of war, evacuating Nazi concentration camps, reopening the roads and bridges, repairing the means of transportation and communication, and making provisions to receive some of the millions of ethnic German expellees from East Central Europe.[14] Most of these activities required German assistance in terms of manpower, information, and organization; a skeletal German government had to be established.[15]

In the early months of the occupation before hostilities had ceased throughout the country, many of those few Bürgermeister who were still at their posts were permitted to temporarily stay in their positions.[16] General Eisenhower's Proclamation No. 1 had provided that: "All officials are charged with the duty of remaining at their posts until further orders."[17] This assumed that municipal administration would still be intact when the area was taken by U.S. troops. Of the areas occupied in 1944 it was the rare exception for officials, especially high-level ones like mayors and department heads, to have remained at their posts, as most escaped into hiding, fearing punishment for their allegiance to the Nazi regime. The chief early concern of MG detachments was therefore not the removal of active Nazis or avid sympathizers but rather the formation of municipal administration with new personnel. MG officers reported difficulty in finding suitable appointees because so many men had been drafted into the army (*Wehrmacht*) or the civil militia (*Volkssturm*), and because all actively anti-Nazi and many non-Nazi Germans had been deprived

---

13. Joseph R. Starr, *U.S. Military Government in Germany: Operations during the Rhineland Campaign*, The Provost Marshall General's School's Military Government Department Training Packet No. 56 (Karlsruhe, 1950), p. 25f.

14. Walter Dorn, *The Unfinished Purge*, p. 211, IfZ.

15. Harold Zink, *The United States in Germany 1944–1955* (Princeton, 1957), p. 170f.

16. Gulgowski, p. 134.

17. As cited in Starr, *U.S. Military Government*, p. 71.

of the opportunity to obtain experience in public office for the last ten or eleven years. Hence the likely candidates for appointment as mayors and department heads were either advanced in age or lacking in experience.[18] Other potential appointees were still incarcerated as political prisoners or as Allied prisoners of war. Although many returned within days or weeks of the arrival of occupation troops, it was rare for these people to be appointed. Despite their political qualifications, these new arrivals would have disrupted the reconstruction process in forcing adjustments by MG and the rest of the German administration. As alluded to earlier, neither group was comfortable with visibly active anti-Nazis, either out of a sense of guilt or due to resentment on the part of many Germans or of discomfort with their politicization on the part of Americans. Moreover, many potential officeholders among the concentration camp survivors were not in sound health, physically or mentally, upon their return.

In the earliest stage of the occupation, MG officers typically sought advice from Catholic priests about whom to appoint. The result was a tendency toward conservative appointments and a not insignificant number of priests, with or without administrative experience, serving as mayors. It was not until November 1944, after the Bishop of Aachen expressly forbade the direct participation of the Catholic clergy in the MG, that the priests retired from public office and the explicit bond between the Catholic Church and MG was severed.[19] Nevertheless, clergymen continued to serve as MG's primary advisors, especially in recommending appointees.[20]Caution about indiscriminate clerical influence was not prescribed until May 1945, when POLAD's "Political Considerations for the Guidance of MG Officers in Making Appointments in Germany" came out. For the first eight months of the occupation, no set procedures had been laid out in directives for MG officers regarding the selection of new personnel for the local administration.[21]

Since the tasks of keeping military supply and communication lines open and restoring order in each assigned German community seemed more routine than political, and since the MG detachments lacked political guidelines except for those related to denazification, few officers regarded the appointment of Germans as political

18.   Ibid., p. 72f.
19.   Ibid., p. 74. The rationale behind this prohibition was probably the desire to have the clergy concentrate on religious and spiritual matters, rather than political or public administration ones.
20.   Joseph R. Starr, *Denazification*, p.34.
21.   See Chapter 2 for further details.

acts.[22] On the other hand, the active anti-Nazis, who were explicitly political, rarely seemed to fit the bureaucratic and subordinate model of the "cooperative Germans" that MG was seeking. Businessmen, old-time civil servants, and even priests, who were not perceived as political, appeared more cooperative and better suited as appointees to many MG detachments.

This naivete about politics and the political implications of apparent apoliticism was not universal in MG, but was very common among the career military and among those with technical backgrounds. The CAD deputy assistant chief of staff, Brigadier General McSherry, seemed to be one of the few in the MG upper echelons to recognize the danger of unenlightened appointments of Germans. In March 1945 he warned the POLAD chief that the appointment of Germans to administrative posts did have a political character: "It is believed that some guidance on this vital and far-reaching problem is better than no guidance at all, since in the latter case, the appointments will unconsciously reflect the political ideologies of the respective Detachment Commanders."[23]

How many of these detachment commanders were aware of their own political ideologies is unclear. But whether aware of them or not, most were inherently conservative and oriented more toward the status quo than towards democratic reforms. The HICOG history of U.S. denazification policy recorded the military's growing resentment after the Aachen scandal had created pressure for more careful screening of Germans: "Army officials found it difficult to see why a man, who did his job efficiently and was sincerely interested in reconstruction, should be removed for 'political reasons.' After all no man who liked to see his country in order and business moving along smoothly could be as dangerous as some MG claimed. A stratum of indispensable experts arose who were appreciated by the average army officer for their desire to get things running again."[24]

The strong role played by the U.S. Army's tactical commanders in the early stages of the occupation only accentuated the tendency of the occupation to emphasize the military values of subordination and authoritarianism as well as to give priority to those whose main attribute appeared to be efficiency in accomplishing technical and material tasks. Yet most of the Americans did not recognize the

22. Harold Hurwitz, *Die Stunde Null der deutschen Presse: Die amerikanische Pressepolitik in Deutschland 1945-1949* (Cologne, 1972), p. 55.
23. 22 March 1945, RG 84, POLAD/ 731/3, 3 of 3, IfZ .
24. John G. Korman, *U.S. Denazification Policy in Germany 1944-1950* (Office of the U.S. High Commissioner for Germany, 1952), p. 21f.

political implications of such decisions. In the early days of the occupation, some MG detachments who felt obliged to follow denazification procedures found themselves in direct conflict with the tactical commander in the area. The Third Army in particular was infamous for the interference of its tactical commanders in the MG process.[25]

One of the consequences of this jurisdictional rivalry was the removal of mayors soon after their initial appointments. The fact that forty-one appointed mayors were dismissed in April and the first part of May of 1945 alone indicates the mistakes made in those early appointments, especially those made by tactical commanders. Joseph Starr, an official historian of the occupation, reported that in the spring and early summer of 1945 "the most striking development in the appointment of local officials was the reliance in a few communities upon anti-Nazi groups, or upon advice rendered by pre-Hitler leaders of political parties and trade unions."[26] The fact that these groups and individuals volunteered their services to MG rather than the MG having sought them out[27] is indicative of how seldom MG drew on the knowledge and ability of anti-Nazis and how little it did to actively encourage these *political* forces.

In the context of denazification, demilitarization, and democratization, how was German local self-government to be restored without ensuring that the Germans themselves advocated and implemented these policies? The late John Gimbel maintained that over time the Americans "hoped to achieve civil service reform, educational reform, and democratization first by influencing their appointed and elected German counterparts and the agencies created by Germans freely elected at the local and state level."[28] Thus the emphasis was on finding Germans who could be convinced to implement reforms, rather than on the Americans directly implementing the reforms themselves. Since the democratic process was not restored until 1946, all local German leaders were appointed rather than elected. The majority of the appointed mayors were career civil servants, who had remained in the civil service during the Third Reich.[29] Such bureaucrats, accustomed to doing their jobs and following their orders regardless of the political complexion of

25. See Dorn, *Unfinished Purge*, p. 236 f.
26. Starr, *Denazification*, p. 34f.
27. Ibid., p. 35.
28. John Gimbel, *A German Community under American Occupation* (Stanford, 1961), p. 3.
29. Starr, *Denazification*, p. 34.

the ruling system, did not fit the profile for fulfilling the democratization goals of the occupation.

The conditions in Frankfurt, Stuttgart, and Munich at the end of the war and in the early days of the occupation created an atmosphere of chaos and uncertainty which persisted for weeks and sometimes months. This endemic confusion produced a universal longing for order, routine, and normalcy. But by granting top priority to restoring and maintaining order – both on the part of MG in making its appointments and on the part of German appointees – the opportune moment of the Stunde Null for the realization of major reforms and far-reaching structural change at the local level appears to have been lost.

Frankfurt am Main[30]

Of the 550,000 inhabitants who had lived in Frankfurt am Main before the war began, only 269,000 remained when the city was occupied by the Americans. In aerial bombings alone, 4,822 people lost their lives, half of whom were women and children. More than 12,000 soldiers from Frankfurt died in the war.[31] The first soldiers returned home in May.[32] Between August 1945 and August 1946, 1,000 people returned to Frankfurt each week, including both soldiers and those who had evacuated the city during the air raids.[33]

There were officially 1,426 Frankfurt residents who had actively resisted the Nazi regime.[34] Of the 31,000 Jews in Frankfurt prior to the Third Reich, only 140 survived the war in Frankfurt, albeit either in hiding or as "partial" or "mixed" Jews.[35] In the early summer, buses were sent to the Dachau, Theresienstadt, and Buchenwald camps to bring approximately 360 Frankfurt natives home. By September 1945, 1,044 former concentration camp inmates had returned to Frankfurt.[36]

---

30. To prevent repetition, Frankfurt, as the first city to be examined, will be given a more detailed description of its chaos and material damage at the end of the war, since its situation was not dissimilar from the other two cities.

31. *Frankfurter Rundschau*, 19 March 1974.

32. Richard Kirn and Madlen Lorei, *Frankfurt und die drei wilden Jahre* (Frankfurt a. M., 1962), p. 4.

33. OMGH 8/2-1/2, 3 of 4, RG 260, IfZ.

34. Barbara Mausbach-Bromberger, *Arbeiterwiderstand in Frankfurt a. M.* (Frankfurt a. M., 1976), p. 193.

35. Günter Mick, Den Frieden gewinnen: *Das Beispiel Frankfurt 1945 bis 1951* (Frankfurt a. M., 1985), p. 34ff.

36. *Frankfurter Allgemeine Zeitung*, 26 March 1955.

Compared to the prewar period, the number of regular welfare cases had tripled; over ten percent of the population required public assistance after the war. In addition, the expellees from Central and Eastern Europe had many special needs. From the middle of May until the end of August 1945, 92,772 German expellees arrived in Frankfurt, all of whom needed room and board, at least temporarily.[37] Whereas in December 1944 the normal consumer had been rationed 1,900 calories daily, by the end of May the daily calorie ration was down to 857. By August 1945, however, it was up to 1,240 daily, although 3,400 calories were calculated as necessary for a person performing manual labor.[38]

In comparison to other European cities, Frankfurt, in terms of its downtown area and its economy, experienced some of the worst destruction. Twelve and one-half million cubic meters of rubble was strewn about the city.[39] Of the 44,559 residential buildings in use before the war, 26 percent were completely destroyed, 27 percent were seriously damaged, 32 percent were lightly damaged and only about 15 percent were completely intact.[40] In terms of residences, slightly over 50 percent were inhabitable, but of these only half were undamaged. More than eight percent of the residences were requisitioned by the occupation troops, affecting 33,355 Frankfurt residents. Almost three-quarters of the industrial and commercial enterprises were destroyed.[41] All the churches in the inner city suffered serious damage; only five Catholic churches in the suburbs and seven Protestant churches on the edges of the city remained intact.[42] Neither trains nor streetcars were running; it took two months after the city was occupied before even two streetcar lines were back in service. Most electric lines and water and gas mains were so damaged that they would take months to repair.[43] Such was the material situation in Frankfurt when the Thousand-Year Reich came to an end there.

After waiting several days to cross the Main River because of blown-up bridges, the combat troops of the U.S. Third Army's Fifth Division occupied Frankfurt am Main on 28 March 1945, the Thursday before Easter.[44] Anticipating the arrival of the Americans, the

37. Magistratsakten (Mag) 1060/1, Stadtarchiv Frankfurt a. M. (StA Ffm.).
38. Ibid.
39. *Frankfurter Allgemeine Zeitung*, 27 March 1967.
40. OMGH 8/189-3/17, 3 of 7, RG 260, IfZ.
41. Mag 1060/1, StA Ffm.
42. Kirn and Lorei, p. 42.
43. Mag 1060/1, StA Ffm.
44. *Frankfurter Allgemeine Zeitung*, 26 March 1955.

Gauleiter had ordered the men of Frankfurt to leave the city four days earlier, although most did not, preferring to seek shelter in the cellars and air-raid bunkers until the end. The property of those who had left was looted in the interim while shopkeepers tried to sell out their stocks. As in most towns, when the Americans arrived, city life was at a standstill. After twenty air raids, the business district was a wilderness of rubble. In the railroad yards, Germans and so-called DPs, those now-liberated forced laborers and Allied prisoners of war, raided stranded Wehrmacht supply trains; seventy Soviet DPs died as a result of drinking methyl alcohol taken in one such raid. One of the few intact high-rise office buildings, the I.G. Farben building, was selected to house SHAEF and USFET headquarters. Indeed this decision prevented Frankfurt from being reassigned to the French Zone, because this building was considered one of the few in all of western Germany which was large enough to serve as headquarters.[45]

One of the few other large buildings still intact in central Frankfurt was that of the large metalworks company, the Metallgesellschaft on Reuterweg, which the tactical commander, Lt. Colonel William H. Blakefield, and his Fifth Division troops occupied. Finding the provisional director, Hermann W. Lumme, in the building, Blakefield ordered Lumme to bring him Frankfurt's Oberbürgermeister, whom Blakefield intended to leave in office for the time being. But the Nazi Oberbürgermeister (OB), Dr. Krebs, had already absconded, after instructing the remaining city employees that he could be reached in the suburb of Bad Homburg. Lumme telephoned OB Krebs and tried to convince him to return to Frankfurt. Krebs, who was reluctant to disobey the orders he had received from the German general in command, refused. An annoyed Blakefield ordered Lumme to become Bürgermeister.[46] Lumme also refused, explaining that he was a resident of Homburg and not Frankfurt. Blakefield, whose patience was wearing thin, ordered Lumme to find someone else to become Bürgermeister within one half hour.[47]

A few minutes later, Wilhelm Hollbach, editor of two now-defunct Frankfurt newspapers, the *Neueste Zeitung* and the *Illustri-*

---

45. Ziemke, *U.S. Army*, p. 226ff.
46. In Frankfurt, in contrast to other cities of its size, the Americans first appointed a Bürgermeister rather than an Oberbürgermeister, although this was the same post with a less prestigious title. Shortly before he was dismissed, Hollbach received the status of Oberbürgermeister.
47. W. Lumme, "Will America be Lost? Military Government-Ecke Reuterweg," in *MG-Information*, Zeitschrift für die Mitarbeiter im Bereich der Metallgesellschaft AG, Frankfurt a. M. (1981), H.1, p. 70.

ertes Blatt, appeared in order to ask the Americans if he could start a new newspaper.[48] Lumme got to Hollbach first, and asked the journalist if he would be willing to become the Bürgermeister. When Hollbach agreed, he was introduced to Blakefield, who summarily appointed him acting Bürgermeister of Frankfurt.[49]

Hollbach's first action as Bürgermeister was to send for his colleague, an English-speaking journalist, to act as interpreter and private secretary.[50] This man was Dr. Hans Bütow, who had been the foreign political editor of the *Illustriertes Blatt* and the *Frankfurter Zeitung* until its 1943 shutdown; afterwards, until the last days of the war, he worked for the local Nazi Party organ, the *Rhein-Mainisches Volksblatt*.[51] Bütow's mother was originally from England, and thus he spoke an Oxford English that apparently impressed Blakefield, whose approval he received.[52]

On the following day, 29 March, the MG detachment for Frankfurt arrived. Its MG commander, or *Stadtkommandant* as the Germans called him, was Lt. Colonel Howard D. Criswell. The tactical commander, Blakefield, then moved on with the rest of his division and the Third Army.[53] Like Blakefield, Criswell was a career officer, who was described by Frankfurt residents as "fanatically stringent"[54] and reservedly businesslike.[55] Hollbach himself was struck – and annoyed – by the fact that Criswell always screamed his orders to him. One day Hollbach had had enough and yelled back at Criswell, who was initially shocked but soon burst out laughing. After this incident, Hollbach reported that their dealings were rational and polite.[56] Neither Criswell nor Blakefield spoke German, which kept Bütow busy interpreting.

Although Criswell accepted Blakefield's mayoral appointee, he was hesitant to accord this new administrative head a carte blanche without investigating Hollbach further. The journalist had to fill out a Fragebogen about his past, which was then examined by a CIC lieutenant. The CIC officer endorsed Hollbach with the comment: "Says he can produce witnesses that he was always anti-Nazi. Has had six years of

---

48. No newspaper or printed matter could be published without the permission of MG. The ICD actually selected licensees to found the new German newspapers.
49. Lumme, p. 70.
50. Nachlass Hollbach (2), StA Ffm.
51. OMGH, 8/188-1/22, 2 of 9, RG 260, IfZ.
52. Nachlass Hollbach (2), StA Ffm.
53. Lumme, p. 70f.
54. 12 May 1945 diary entry, S5/193/IIN, StA Ffm .
55. *Frankfurter Rundschau*, 26 March 1970.
56. *Frankfurter Allgemeine Zeitung*, 8 May 1970. Cf. Mick, p. 25.

experience in municipal government."[57] Criswell then checked German opinion of Hollbach by forming "a non-Nazi citizens' group composed of (a) local dean of Catholic priests, the leading Protestant minister and other non-Nazi leaders of the community, and requested this group to advise him with reference to appointment of officials."[58] The "other non-Nazi leaders of the community" included: one of the founders of the German People's Party (DVP), who was also the director of I. G. Farben; the general manager of the local Chamber of Commerce and Industry (*Industrie-und Handelskammer*),[59] who had been a member of the Stahlhelm and the German National People's Party (DNVP) prior to 1933, and thereafter, although not a Nazi Party member, a member of various Nazi organizations as well as a chief of war economics (*Wehrwirtschaftsführer*) and armaments inspector (*Rüstungsinspektor*) during the war;[60] Hollbach's interpreter, Dr. Bütow; and Director Lumme from the Metallgesellschaft.[61] This allegedly representative Council, as it came to be called by the MG and the Germans, was given two applications to consider for the post of Bürgermeister. It unanimously recommended Hollbach. Col. Criswell concurred, and Hollbach received his official MG appointment on 30 March 1945.[62]

This politically right-of-center Council was soon expanded to include: a Communist, Peter Fischer, who was the self-appointed KPD representative and who had organized an extremely active anti-Fascist committee in the outlying district of Höchst; a Jew, the author, August Adelsberger,[63] who had survived the Third Reich in hiding in Frankfurt;[64] another Protestant clergyman; and a second representative of the Metallgesellschaft.[65] As local MG commander, Criswell called meetings of the Council two to three times a week. They discussed topics such as the political qualifications of the heads of industry and commerce and how to expedite the reopening of banks.[66]

57. OMGUS, 5/268-1/18, 1 of 1, RG 260, IfZ. Hollbach's municipal experience was as a city councilor for the German Democratic Party in Cologne in the latter phase of the Weimar Republic.
58. Ibid.
59. Kirn and Lorei, p. 21.
60. OMGH, 17/16-3/11, 1 of 2, RG 260, IfZ.
61. Kirn and Lorei, p. 21.
62. OMGUS, 5/268-1/18, 1 of 1, RG 260, IfZ. The identity of the other applicant is unfortunately not ascertainable from the records.
63. Kirn and Lorei, p. 21.
64. Cedric Belfrage, *Seeds of Destruction* (New York, 1954), p. 110. Belfrage was Press Control Officer for DISCC in Frankfurt in 1945. Of the 31,000 Jews who had inhabited pre-1933 Frankfurt, MG officers found 140. Ziemke, p. 227.
65. Kirn and Lorei, p. 21.
66. Lumme, p. 71.

This earliest form of quasi self-government in postwar Frankfurt, albeit purely advisory, was not in the least representative of the city's politics and traditions. Its overwhelmingly conservative and business/management composition contradicted its twentieth-century class and political structure. Both before and after the Third Reich, Frankfurt am Main was considered a Social Democratic stronghold and many, either affectionately or antagonistically, have referred to it by its nickname, "Rote Frankfurt." It is plausible that the Council's nonrepresentative nature, which included one token Communist and not a single Social Democrat, was the cause of its dissolution only five weeks later. A novel structure in the U.S. Zone primarily because it was formed at the very beginning of the occupation, it was constituted by MG and met at the Americans' beck and call. Moreover there was no systematic attempt to appoint members who were politically or socioeconomically representative of the non-Nazi municipal population. At any rate, after it was dissolved in early May by Criswell's successor, four months elapsed before a successor organization, the *Bürgerrat*, was called into being.[67] This twenty-eight-member Bürgerrat was both politically and socioeconomically more representative of Frankfurt's population than the Council had been.

In the meantime, in early April, Hollbach appointed a staff of personal advisors, most of whom had been either editors or staff writers for the *Frankfurter Zeitung*, the *Illustriertes Blatt* or the *Neueste Zeitung*. Hollbach had edited the latter two since 1934. All three were owned by the same publishing company, the *Societäts-Verlag*. Whether this staff served to offset the role of the Council is unclear, but in contrast to the members of the Council, Hollbach's advisors were handpicked and responsible to him rather than directly to MG. His staff consisted of the journalists, Dr. Hans Bütow, Karl-Heinz Knappstein, Maxim Fackler, Eberhard Beckmann, Werner Jaspert, Richard Kirn, and Gertrude Becker; and the non-journalists, Professor Dr. Ernst Beutler, H. K. G. Korell, Alfred Teves, Bernhard Grzimek, and Dr. Franz Schüler.[68]

The past records of these "personal advisors" and their subsequent fates attest to their diversity as well as their political similarities with the Council members. Unlike Hollbach, who was a decade older, they were almost all in their late 30's or very early 40's, and were about to embark on totally new careers. Only Beutler was

---

67. *Frankfurter Allgemeine Zeitung*, 26 March 1955.
68. "Amtsleiterbesprechungen," StA Ffm.

already a well-known figure in Frankfurt, and clearly qualified to become Hollbach's cultural advisor. Grzimek was a veterinarian by profession, who had written several articles on animal psychology for the *Illustriertes Blatt*,[69] and hence knew its chief editor, Hollbach. He was soon named director of the Frankfurt Zoo, although after a run-in with the local MG detachment in 1948 for falsifying his Fragebogen, he was temporarily dismissed.[70] Korell was named police advisor. He had been a member of the NSDAP at least as early as 1943, and when this came out in June 1945, he was dismissed by MG. Dr. Schüler, whom an intelligence report called "a criminally charged personality," was dismissed after two months.[71] Bütow became the official liaison between MG and the city administration in April, but was dismissed in June 1945[72] because of the political essays he had written during the war, which were filled with anti-Allied propaganda.[73] Knappstein served as welfare office advisor under Hollbach. Once political parties were allowed to form in August of 1945, he helped found the Christian Democratic Union (CDU) in Hesse. In the fall of 1945 he was appointed the Hessian deputy minister for reconstruction and much later, the West German ambassador to the United States. Fackler was the advisor for press and radio and subsequently became the political editor of the *Süddeutsche Zeitung* in Munich.[74]

The only clear-cut *anti*-Nazi among Hollbach's advisees was Eberhard Beckmann, who had been persecuted because of his SPD allegiance and his refusal to divorce his Jewish wife. The Nazis had prohibited him from continuing his career in journalism during the entire Third Reich. He was added to Hollbach's staff later in the spring and charged with helping former inmates of concentration camps resume a normal life.[75] After the first year of the occupation, Beckmann occasionally provided the Office of MG-Hesse (OMGH) with intelligence reports on the political situation in the area around Frankfurt.[76] In June 1946 the Americans appointed him head of Radio Frankfurt, which later became the Hessischer Rundfunk.

69. OMGH, 17/16-3/11, 1 of 2, RG 260, IfZ.
70. Ibid., 8/194-1/6, 3 of 3.
71. Ibid., 17/16-3/11, 1 of 2.
72. Oral information from the personnel records of Dr. Hans Bütow, provided me by an archivist because of limited access due to German personal data confidentiality restrictions, StA Ffm.
73. OMGH, 17/16-3/ 11, 1 of 2, RG 260, IfZ. See also Belfrage, p. 138.
74. Kirn and Lorei, p. 22.
75. S2/656, StA Ffm.
76. OMGH, 8/194-2/6, 6 of 6, RG 260, StA Ffm.

Thus, like his adamantly anti-Nazi American colleagues in the Information Control Division (ICD) and in the intelligence agencies, his anti-Nazi credentials did allow him to play a role in the occupation, but primarily as an advisor or analyst rather than as someone with direct decision-making powers.

Jaspert, who in the last phase of the war had written anti-Allied articles for the *Illustriertes Blatt* but was not dismissed by MG or ICD,[77] eventually became one of Beckmann's assistants at the radio station, Hessischer Rundfunk. Becker was also able to retain her post in City Press Relations despite ICD allegations that she had worked for the Gestapo clipping U.S. newspapers.[78] Kirn was head of the city's information service, and subsequently became the local editor for the second newspaper to be licensed in postwar Frankfurt, the *Neue Presse*.[79] Teves apparently served as economics advisor to Hollbach. He later returned to helping his father, who during the war had been the German consul to Bulgaria, with the large family-owned refrigeration company.[80] Thus, almost all of these advisors were able to use their positions under Hollbach as a stepping stone to more prestigious careers.

Most of Hollbach's personal staff worked with him for only a month or two, until professional administrators could be found.[81] When Hollbach himself was dismissed in July 1945, his successor retained only Becker and Fackler, both in press positions. Beckmann stands out as the only left-of-center advisor among the dozen-odd aides. The conservative bent of Hollbach's advisors only lowered the reform-minded ICD's opinion of him and most of his staff. The ICD was more involved with politics in Frankfurt than in other cities, having investigated those municipal administrators with journalism ties, and having found that several of them, including Hollbach, were trying to refound the *Frankfurter Zeitung*. A report to the 6,871st District Information Services Control Command (DISCC), the office for Hesse and Württemberg-Baden (and which was SHAEF's intelligence and media control organization associated with ICD), by a German SPD-oriented investigator, criticized Hollbach's staff vehemently. He wrote that the "mayor's staff" was composed of "bourgeois elements who still worked for Societäts-Verlag during the Nazi regime and acted in their own interest during that time. They were

77. Ibid., 8/194-3/4, 4 of 5.
78. Belfrage, p. 146.
79. OMGH, 8/188-1/22, 1 of 9, RG 260, IfZ.
80. S2/129, StA Ffm.
81. Kirn and Lorei, p. 22.

partly Pgs [*Parteigenossen*]. They are politically guilty despite the fact that privately they may have had a different opinion." The report then continued with more specific denunciations of Bütow, Grzimek, and Korell,[82] all three of whom were eventually dismissed, even if only temporarily in the case of Grzimek.

In summing up the peculiarities of military conquest and the initial occupation of Frankfurt, one is struck by the apparent absence of activist anti-Nazis. In the initial stages of occupation that subsequently took place in Stuttgart and Munich, they would play much more active, if unofficial, roles. This is not to say that anti-Nazis or active resistance did not exist in Frankfurt. Indeed Barbara Mausbach-Bromberger's book on working-class resistance in Frankfurt am Main from 1933 to 1945, as well as Emil Carlebach's and Lutz Niethammer's works on the anti-Fascist committees (*Antifa-Ausschüsse*) in 1945 prove otherwise.[83] In fact, Peter Fischer of the anti-Fascist committee in Höchst was included in the short-lived Council, but that was at the request of Criswell. This overall lack of activists could partly have been due to Frankfurt's early occupation in the spring of 1945, before many imprisoned anti-Nazis had returned from concentration camps and before many others, forced during the Third Reich to keep a low profile and move to rural areas where they were less known, had returned. In addition, numerous Frankfurt residents had left because their homes had been bombed, or to avoid the dangers of the heavy bombardments. Moreover, the guidelines from POLAD about whom to appoint were not yet available, so that the detachment commanders had the excuses both of ignorance and insufficent pressure to appoint and/or train anti-Nazis for such posts.

Nevertheless, availability was only a minor factor. With the exceptions of the clergymen, the Jewish author, and the Communist on the Council and Beckmann on Hollbach's staff, no other even potentially active anti-Nazis or political persecutees were appointed to these two dozen odd positions. Only two left-of-center appointments were made, Peter Fischer and Eberhard Beckmann. Proportionately more politically incriminated persons were appointed to these posts than proven anti-Nazis. The working class and even lower middle class were drastically underrepresented as well, a fact

---

82. OMGH, 17/16-3/11, 1 of 2, RG 260, IfZ.
83. See Barbara Mausbach-Bromberger, *Arbeiterwiderstand in Frankfurt am Main* (Frankfurt, 1976) and Emil Carlebach, "Frankfurts Antifaschisten 1945" in Ulrich Schneider (ed.), *Als der Krieg zu Ende war: Hessen 1945* (Frankfurt a. M., 1980). Cf. Lutz Niethammer, et al., *Arbeiterinitiative 1945* (Wuppertal, 1976), p. 415ff.

that ties in statistically with the lack of anti-Nazis. Industrialists and businessmen were overrepresented on the Council, as were journalists on Hollbach's personal administrative staff.

Frankfurt is the only one of the three cities where the most crucial appointment, that of mayor, was made directly by the combat commander, Lt. Col. Blakefield, rather than by a detachment commander. Blakefield was a career army man, with little background on civilian affairs, especially in Frankfurt, and seemingly scant awareness of the importance of this first appointment of a German to head the municipal administration. All the stories of Hollbach's appointment make it seem extremely haphazard. After Frankfurt, Blakefield moved on to continue fighting the war, leaving the civil-administration task he had begun to Lt. Col. Criswell, the MG commander who arrived the next day.[84]

Criswell was also a career soldier, who spoke no German and seemed to arrive with little background information on the local political situation or on whom to turn to for advice. He did put some time and effort into checking on Hollbach, but the core Council he formed to approve the Hollbach appointment included several dubious figures. Hollbach's endorsement by the CIC, which was based on his stated ability to produce witnesses verifying his anti-Nazi stance, was problematic because the CIC did not interview the witnesses or anyone else.

No one was brought in to clarify the political implications of retaining occupants of high journalistic posts during the Nazi regime. When DISCC and Press Control experts were later given the opportunity to investigate and explain, they were very critical of Hollbach, Bütow, and the entire Societäts-Verlag crew.[85] This made the MG commander and his detachment officers defensive and created even more of a rift between the reform-seeking, German-speaking, sociopolitical experts in the information services sector and the more politically naive career military men and technical experts in the Frankfurt detachment, who lacked adequate knowledge of German politics, society, and language to make sophisticated personnel decisions. This conflict-laden situation was worsened when Hollbach and his colleagues attempted to refound the *Frankfurter Zeitung* during the first year of the occupation. They found themselves frustrated by the Americans (DISCC), who granted a license to three Social Democrats, three Communists and a leftist

84. Lumme, p. 70f.
85. See 5/268-1/18, 1 of 1, RG 260, IfZ.

Catholic to form a totally new newspaper, the *Frankfurter Rundschau*. Thus the enhanced role of journalists in postwar Frankfurt politics continued even after the journalist Bürgermeister was dismissed by MG in July 1945. This situation will be elaborated upon further in the next chapter, after the first phases of the occupation in Stuttgart and Munich are examined.

Stuttgart

Stuttgart had somewhat more than 10 percent fewer residents than Frankfurt before the air raids there began, but it ended up with a similar-sized population by the time the war ended. Stuttgart had suffered less physical damage and fewer human casualties than Frankfurt. Fifty-three air raids killed some 2,750 persons in Stuttgart. Over 55 percent of the buildings were either destroyed or damaged, and 52,000 of the 150,000 individual residences were completely destroyed.[86] Approximately 4.9 million cubic meters of rubble covered Stuttgart, about a third of what covered the even worse-off Frankfurt.[87]

The population of Stuttgart decreased from 458,429 in 1939 (and 498,063 in 1942 after an incorporation of a few outlying regions), to 266,067 at the end of the war.[88] There had been 4,600 victims of aerial bombardment, of which 770 had been foreign forced laborers and Allied POWs.[89] At the front 13,510 soldiers from Stuttgart had died.[90] By the end of 1945 the population had reached 367,193, while one year later it was up to 419,000.[91] Some of this growth was due to expellees and returning evacuees as well as DPs, whose numbers totaled 13,000 by mid-1946.[92] The city office in charge of those individuals returning from concentration camps estimated in December 1945 that 2,600 Stuttgart residents had been incarcerated by the Nazis for either political, racial, or religious reasons, whereas the Welfare Office had calculated in late May 1945 that about 600 camp inmates could be expected to return to Stuttgart.[93] Of the

---

86. Edward N. Peterson, *The Many Faces of Defeat: The German People's Experience in 1945* (New York, 1990), p. 46.
87. Hermann Vietzen, *Chronik der Stadt Stuttgart 1945–1948* (Stuttgart, 1972), p. 361.
88. Ibid., p. 231 f.
89. Roland Müller, *Stuttgart zur Zeit des Nationalsozialismus* (Stuttgart, 1988), p. 537.
90. Vietzen, p. 234.
91. Ibid., p. 231f.
92. Ibid., p. 241.
93. Hauptaktei 0054, Stadtarchiv Stuttgart (StA St.). There is no breakdown of these persecuted individuals indicating how many were Jews. There were thirty-two

4,490 Jewish residents of Stuttgart in 1933, over a quarter were killed by the Nazis. At least 400 Stuttgart residents were murdered in the Nazi "euthanasia" program. Close to 150 men and women were executed for their political opposition to the Nazis, while many more died as a result of Nazi torture and incarceration.[94]

Compared to over 10 percent in Frankfurt, slightly over 4 percent of the city's population required public assistance in Stuttgart the first year after the war.[95] The food situation in Stuttgart was somewhat comparable to that of Frankfurt. At the beginning of 1945 the calorie ration for the normal consumer was 1,687, whereas it had gone down to 852 in May, but then returned to the higher level of the beginning of the year again by the close of 1945.[96] The material problems confronted by the occupation authorities upon arriving in Stuttgart were comparable to those found in Frankfurt.

Between late March and late April 1945 both American and French troops occupied the southwestern states of Baden and Württemberg. It had been agreed that the Americans would control all the towns and counties north of the Autobahn Karlsruhe-Stuttgart-Ulm as well as the cities and counties through which this important arterial road passed.[97] Despite this agreement, French troops took over Stuttgart five hours before U.S. troops of the One Hundredth Division arrived from the east during the early hours of 21 April 1945.[98] Because the French had not been included in the Yalta Conference of February 1945, they had not been involved in drawing the zonal lines of occupation or in making policy decisions. This caused a certain amount of insecurity on their part vis-à-vis the United States, Great Britain, and the Soviet Union. Württemberg's capital, Stuttgart, and Baden's capital, Karlsruhe, were taken by the French on orders from General Charles de Gaulle as important military and political hostages in order to increase their political influence in determining the future of Germany. The French quickly set up Ger-

---

Jewish municipal employees who were dismissed by the Nazis during the Third Reich. However, there had been and was still a much smaller Jewish population in Stuttgart than in Frankfurt, which had the largest Jewish community after Berlin. See Personalamt-Akten 02-0175, StA St.

94. Müller, p. 537.
95. Vietzen, p. 472.
96. Ibid., p. 252 ff.
97. Paul Sauer, *25 Jahre Baden-Württemberg, Rückblick auf die Entstehung des Bundeslandes*. Ausstellungskatalog des Landtags in Zusammenarbeit mit dem Hauptstaatsarchiv Stuttgart (Stuttgart, 1977), p. 9.
98. Friedrich Blumenstock, *Der Einmarsch der Amerikaner und Franzosen im nördlichen Württemberg im April 1945* (Stuttgart, 1957), p. 218.

man Land administrations in Karlsruhe for Baden and in Stuttgart for Württemberg in order to demonstrate and cement their claims to the two states. The Americans responded with both diplomacy and coercion. Their control of the Autobahn meant that if necessary they could cut off French supplies and transportation. This threat eventually convinced the French to withdraw from both cities. On 8 July 1945, U.S. troops and MG detachments superseded the French occupation authorities in Karlsruhe and Stuttgart. Soon thereafter, Stuttgart became the seat of U.S. MG in North Württemberg-Baden, or OMG-WB, as it came to be called.[99]

Although this study examines the role of U.S. MG in the return of self-government to the Germans, what happened in Stuttgart during the first two and a half months after the end of hostilities, before it came under American occupation cannot be ignored. The German municipal administration set up by the French is significant both in terms of continuity and change for the U.S. MG personnel policies. Unlike Frankfurt and Munich, where incoming American MG authorities had to decide on retaining Nazis in office, in Stuttgart the Americans also had to decide what to do with the appointees of their French allies. Not only was there the need to coordinate Allied policies in order not to discredit the French or the American occupation in German eyes or internationally, there was also the problem of retaining the officials the French had appointed and/or retained for the sake of continuity and expediency. These Germans were already accustomed to dealing with an occupation authority and had had two and a half months to become familiar with the postwar situation. The alternative to retaining these officials would have been to implement immediately the more stringent U.S. denazification policy, which would have resulted in a sharp personnel turnover. The decision, probably not consciously made, was somewhat of a compromise. Compared to Frankfurt or Munich, more politically incriminated administrators, at least in the U.S. MG scheme of Nazi incrimination, were retained longer in Stuttgart, but similar percentages of personnel were eventually purged.

The U.S. MG had a liaison mission in Stuttgart during the French phase of occupation as well as intelligence agents. This helped MG to keep abreast of the developments in city government, French MG, and the exceptionally active Stuttgart anti-Fascist committees. The Americans also knew about the role played by the so-called Save Stuttgart (*Rettet Stuttgart*) movement, which arose in early April 1945,

99. Sauer, 25 Jahre, p. 9.

when the Allied entry into Stuttgart was imminent. This group was formed around the future police president and the future OB of Stuttgart, in order to resist the Nazi scorched earth policy (Nero Plan) and prevent any Nazi defense of the city or Werwolf activities. It managed to get the tacit support of the Nazi OB, Dr. Karl Strölin, who for years had come into conflict with the Gauleiter Murr,[100] through the intercession of the Protestant diocesan liaison to the OB's office[101] and through a member of the well-known liberal Stuttgart family Haußmann,[102] both of whom were members of the Save Stuttgart movement. Although this group was not able to prevent the destruction of most of the city's bridges, it did save the gas, water and power plants[103] as well as the military district(*Wehrkreis*) headquarters in the Olgastrasse, which later became MG headquarters.[104]

OB Strölin had smuggled a message through the Allies' front lines announcing his preparedness to surrender the city and suggesting that an attack from the south would prevent bloodshed on both sides. The message reached the French, but Nazi headquarters in Berlin also found out about Strölin's "betrayal," and ordered his arrest via radio.[105] This order was sabotaged and did not get through until 19 April 1945, by which time all other Nazi officeholders were in the midst of fleeing the city. OB Strölin remained, and assisted the Save Stuttgart movement by preventing the Nazi-ordered destruction before the French troops moved in on 21 April.[106] On the morning of 22 April, the leading members of the emergency municipal administration, which Strölin had organized, were ordered to meet with the French commander.[107] The acting administrative chief, the city's legal counselor, Dr. Waidelich, was ordered to bring OB Strölin to the French commander so that the city could be officially surrendered. At noon OB Strölin announced the surrender on the radio, after which he was ordered to continue as OB of Stuttgart.[108]

100. Karl Strölin, *Stuttgart im Endstadium des Krieges* (Stuttgart, 1950), p. 28f. Strölin maintained that he had connections with the Leipzig OB, Dr. Karl Goerdeler, and the conspiracy of 20 July 1944 after becoming disillusioned with the *Praxis* of Nazism. See p. 32ff. This disillusionment may well have coincided with the point when a Nazi victory no longer seemed possible.

101. OSS, FIS 5, OSS, RG 226, NARA.

102. Personal interview with Dr. Wolfgang Haußmann, Stuttgart, 30 November 1982.

103. OSS, FIS 5, OSS, RG 226, NARA.

104. Hermann Vietzen, *Chronik der Stadt Stuttgart 1945–1948* (Stuttgart, 1972), p. 22ff.

105. Ibid, p. 19f.

106. Ibid., p. 22ff.

107. For information on the recruitment of French MG personnel, see F. Roy Willis, *The French in Germany, 1945–1949* (Stanford, 1962), p. 67ff.

108. Vietzen, p. 26ff. Cf. Strölin, p. 61ff.

That night the Save Stuttgart group met again, this time with the forty-year-old lawyer, Dr. Arnulf Klett, taking the lead.[109] Klett, who had won his anti-Nazi credentials by defending Communists and concentration camp inmates in court,[110] was the son of a Protestant minister, and had recently been working in the War Destruction Department of Stuttgart.[111] His main concern, which probably coincided with that of the diocesan liaison, Dr. Kruse, was with getting Bishop D. Theophil Wurm from Grossheppach, on the other side of the Neckar River, to Stuttgart, now that the bridges had been blown up. Klett's neighbors, Franz Lau and Heinz Eschwege, both left the meeting frustrated that Wurm's return should be given such a high priority.[112] Lau was a notary, who had been incarcerated in a concentration camp as an anti-Nazi political prisoner.[113] He became acquainted with Klett through Heinz Eschwege, who had an apartment in the same house as Lau. Klett had defended Eschwege when he was tried for anti-Nazi conspiratorial activity in 1944.[114] Klett, Eschwege, and Lau, once they realized their common views and their residential proximity, secretly met to listen to Allied radio reports during the last year of the war. Whereas Klett's anti-Nazism may have stemmed from his clerical upbringing,[115] Lau and Eschwege were intellectually sympathetic to the Left, although they had had no political party affiliations prior to 1933. Lau visited the French commander the following morning, 23 April, to offer his cooperation, but because he spoke no French, the commander brushed him aside. Lau then met with OB Strölin, who gave him the task of finding quarters for the French occupation troops. To assist him with his housing task, Lau decided to seek out his neighbor Eschwege, who did speak French.[116]

109. Heinz Eschwege, *Vom Niedergang und Aufstieg der Stadt Stuttgart.* Unpublished MS. (1962), Kc 248, p. 13f, StA St.

110. Lutz Niethammer, "Aktivität und Grenzen der Antifa-Ausschüsse 1945: Das Beispiel Stuttgart," *Vierteljahrshefte für Zeitgeschichte* (1975), H. 3, p. 305.

111. Strölin, p. 54.

112. Eschwege, p. 13f.

113. R&A Report 3197.2, p. 33, RG 59, OSS, NARA.

114. Eschwege, "Chronologie" in *Vom Niedergang.* Also personal interview with Heinz Eschwege, Stuttgart, 30 November 1983.

115. A 1947 investigation of Klett by the American vice consul in Stuttgart pointed out that Klett claimed to be a strict adherent to the Evangelical (Lutheran) faith, but that "people who are familiar with his past, however, say that he has been generally indifferent to religion." Klett led many to believe that he had also had no party affiliation, but in the Fragebogen he submitted to the French he admitted having belonged to the right-wing Württembergische Bürgerpartei prior to 1933. IfZ, RG 84, POLAD/ 779/ 12, 1 of 5.

116. Ibid., p. 13f.

Meanwhile, shortly before noon, a French MG officer informed OB Strölin that he could no longer remain in office, because a French headquarters order had arrived that prohibited former OBs from retaining their posts. But as a sign of appreciation for his cooperation in staying at his post despite personal danger, Strölin was allowed to recommend a successor. He was given a 2 P.M. deadline. Strölin's most obvious choices, members of the emergency administration, were excluded because of their previous membership in the NSDAP, as was his pre-1933 predecessor, OB Dr. Karl Lautenschlager, who was rejected because he was now quite old and his whereabouts were unknown.[117]

Shortly after OB Strölin received news of his impending dismissal, Lau and Eschwege arrived to report on housing for the French. Strölin asked Lau if he would accept the post of OB,[118] having both administrative experience and political persecutee status. Lau initially hesitated, but then agreed. He immediately worked up an expose with plans to dismiss all Nazi officials and civil servants. Strölin and his legal councilor, Dr. Eduard Könekamp, tried to convince Lau to keep the experienced civil servants, but Lau remained steadfast;[119] this is apparently what caused Strölin to have second thoughts about Lau. In any event, as Lau and Eschwege were leaving Strölin's villa, Dr. Klett arrived and was surprised to learn that Lau was to be the new OB. When Lau, Eschwege, and two French soldiers returned to Strölin's at 1:45 P.M. for Lau to officially assume the duties of OB, they were kept waiting outside Strölin's office. Then several French soldiers came out of the OB's office, along with Dr. Könekamp who reported that Dr. Arnulf Klett had just been named the new OB of Stuttgart. Klett then appeared, thanked Lau and Eschwege, and asked them to return the next day as members of the new city administration. Eschwege described the switch as a safeguard to prevent a "palace revolution," because Lau's plans for "changing the guard" had represented a specter of revolution to Strölin and Könekamp.[120]

Klett, in the meantime, had been able to contact Bishop Wurm. Wurm had encouraged Klett to try to play a major role in the new municipal administration. Lacking any party affiliation,[121] Klett felt he

117. Vietzen, p. 31. See also Strölin, p. 64f.
118. Eschwege, "Chronologie."
119. Eschwege, p. 28f.
120. Ibid., "Chronologie."
121. Klett apparently did not mention his previous membership in the anti-Semitic Württembergische Bürgerpartei or the pan-Germanic Altdeutscher Verband to his fellow "Rettet Stuttgart" members. See Eschwege interview. When he did

would need some group's backing. The Protestant Church was a good and solid pillar of support, especially since the French occupation authorities were generally thought to be conservative and Stuttgart's population was predominantly Protestant. Lau then understood why Klett was so anxious to get Wurm back to Stuttgart. Strölin, ostensibly, also thought it would be to his advantage to have someone with Church backing as his successor.[122] In his memoir-like description of the end of the war in Stuttgart, Strölin himself never mentions considering Lau as his successor. Rather he claims he decided on Klett after considering other unnamed candidates, for several reasons: Klett had been a trustworthy colleague in the last few difficult weeks, he had belonged to the city administration, he was not politically incriminated, he had even been briefly interned by the Nazis, and *in addition* he was known as a good lawyer.[123] Of course, except for being a good lawyer, Lau possessed all of these traits and was more of an active anti-Nazi than Klett, but he was also less solidly upper middle-class and more politically leftist in his views.

As his deputy (2. Bürgermeister), Klett appointed Dr. Könekamp, who had served as one of Dr. Strölin's professional city councilors since 1935. He had been a member of the NSDAP, but had served in the municipal administration prior to the Nazis' rise to power.[124] Known as Strölin's right-hand man, this role apparently had more to do with his experience than his activist Nazi politics.[125] The French MG approved both Klett's and Könekamp's appointments, the former more for political reasons, the latter to provide administrative experience and continuity. On 24 April the old and the new OBs met with the new administration that Klett had put together. It included five members from Strölin's staff: Dr. Könekamp and Dr. Ernst Waidelich, who had headed the emergency administration, and three other lower-level officials, who now became the heads of departments in which they had formally worked.[126] All had been

---

include this information on his Fragebogen for French MG, he tried to use the latter membership to prove his long-term anti-Nazi stance. The Verband had indeed been dissolved by the Nazis, but it belonged in a comparable league with the Stahlhelm, which was also dissolved. See Detachment E1A2 Public Safety Section, Special Branch Investigation subsection Report, 1 Sept. 1945, p. 2, RG 84, POLAD/ 779/ 12, 1 of 5, RG 84, IfZ.

122. Personal interview with Heinz Eschwege, Stuttgart, 30 November 1983. See also Niethammer, "Aktivität," p. 305.

123. Strölin, p. 64f.

124. R&A Report 3197.2, p. 32, OSS, RG 59, NARA.

125. Müller, p. 537.

126. Vietzen, p. 31f.

NSDAP members, and all were eventually dismissed by the Americans, but not until three to eight weeks after the change to U.S. MG on 8 July 1945.[127] Seven appointees had been members of the Save Stuttgart movement. They included the former police superintendant, Karl Weber, who had been dismissed in 1933 because he was a Social Democrat and who now became police president; the physician, Dr. Eugen Winter,[128] as head of the health and welfare department; the diocesan liaison, Dr. Helmut Kruse, who now became the city administration's liaison to the French MG authorities; the architect, Eugen Mertz, who was appointed head of the reconstruction department; the former president of the finance court, Dr. Alfons Wetter, who became head of the finance department;[129] the "almost OB," Franz Lau, who provisionally headed the housing office; and the radio expert, Heinz Eschwege, who became the city liaison for theater and radio.[130]

In October 1945, U.S. MG dismissed two from this latter group because of Nazi incrimination, namely Kruse and Wetter.[131] Although this latter group had resisted Hitler's Nero Plan at the end of the war, Weber, Eschwege, and Lau were the only three with records of long-term anti-Nazi activism, and they were also the only three who could be categorized as politically left-of-center. Neither Lau nor Eschwege were made department heads; they held more ephemeral, less powerful posts, indicating that Klett probably had appointed them to smooth over what had happened at Strölin's villa. Eschwege eventually became the provisional head of the State Theater and later worked for Radio Stuttgart until February 1946.[132] Lau remained the provisional head of the housing office until the summer, when Dr. Könekamp's replacement, Dr. Wolfgang Hauß-mann, took over both the housing and personnel offices.[133] Thereafter Lau returned to his job as a notary public until his sudden death in January 1948.[134] Thus Weber, as the only former Social Democrat among the original appointees, was the sole left-of-cen-

127. Ibid., p. 66f.
128. U.S. MG later removed Winter from office because of his alleged involvement in an embezzlement scheme. Klett had refused to take any action against him. Detachment E1A2 Public Safety Section, Special Branch Investigation subsection Report, 1 Sept. 1945, p. 4, 84, POLAD/ 779/12, 1 of 5, RG 84, IfZ.
129. Ibid., p. 33.
130. Eschwege, p. 35.
131. Vietzen, p. 67.
132. Eschwege, "Chronologie."
133. Vietzen, p. 66f.
134. Eschwege, Anhang.

ter full-time department head. The city administration's conservative political complexion combined with the fact that six of the ten department heads had academic titles, provided a stark contrast to industrial Stuttgart's large working-class population and its major political parties, the SPD and KPD, which had been the two strongest parties in the last pre-Hitler city council.[135]

Meanwhile because of Strölin's fears for his personal safety, the French MG gave him a license to carry a weapon,[136] a privilege most German police did not have. Later in the day on 24 April, Dr. Strölin was asked to attend a meeting about the city's food and energy supplies, where U.S. Army officers were also in attendance. Shortly thereafter, an American CIC officer arrested Dr. Strölin and took him to a prison in Kitzingen, the first station of his three-year imprisonment. Strölin had been a convinced Nazi when he became OB in 1933, and only quite a bit later did he begin to have his doubts about National Socialism. His actions during the last days of the war shortened his prison term to three years.[137] Indicative of the Americans' more stringent denazification policy, Strölin was arrested and imprisoned by the Americans, despite the fact that Stuttgart was under French occupation; the French showed no signs of ever intending to arrest him.

Stuttgart remained under French occupation until 8 July 1945. Municipal self-government was more limited in Stuttgart under the French than it was in Frankfurt or Munich under U.S. control. This was partly due to the jurisdictional conflict between the French and the Americans, as well as the interrelated establishment of the borders of the newly formed Land, Württemberg-Baden, with its Land-level government. In May 1945, Dr. Könekamp, in his capacity as the 2. Bürgermeister, was assigned the task of organizing an advisory city council. The initiative came from a group of Social Democrats, who had approached Klett about forming a council to involve the population of Stuttgart more in its local government and about training qualified anti-Nazi personnel to fill the leading municipal

135. The SPD was the strongest party in the last Weimar Republic city council, which was elected 6. Dec. 1931. It held 28 percent of the seats while the KPD was second with 17 percent. Even at the peak of the Nazis' national electoral success, the July 1932 Reichstag elections, in Stuttgart the SPD received 27.7 percent, the NSDAP 27.2 percent and, as the third strongest party, the KPD with 16.5 percent (Müller, p. 13). In the 1946 and 1948 elections, the SPD remained the strongest party each time with 35 percent, although the KPD fell to fourth place with 13 percent in 1946 and 12 percent in 1948.
136. Vietzen, p. 32.
137. Ibid.

posts, which they assumed would soon be vacated by the former Nazi Party members.[138] This advisory city council did not materialize until October and the posts were not vacated for months, nor was any training program ever set up. But the responsibility for the postponement of the council, at least until late summer, lies with French MG rather than with OB Klett. Plans for both an advisory city council and an advisory state council for Württemberg, which OB Klett had advocated, were halted by the French city commander, Colonel Mercadier, on 5 June 1945, apparently because such councils represented too much of a step toward German self-government for the French.[139] Even the discussion of such advisory councils was prohibited by Mercadier.[140]

At the grassroots level, quite a bit of spontaneous self-government did take place in Stuttgart. The anti-Fascist committees (*Antifa-Ausschüsse* or *Antifas*) in Stuttgart formed one of the largest anti-Fascist action movements in all of occupied postwar Germany. Offshoots of these anti-Fascist committees played a significant role in Stuttgart on into 1948.[141] Stuttgart's uniqueness as a city caught between two occupation Zones and two occupiers both restricted it in some ways and gave it more leeway in others. The French permitted the Antifa committees to continue to exist, albeit as work committees (*Arbeitsausschüsse*), rather than as the more explicitly political fighting committees against National Socialism (*Kampfkomitees gegen den Nationalsozialismus*), long after the political activity of such Antifa committees had been prohibited elsewhere in the U.S. Zone. Because of this, the U.S. MG in Stuttgart felt pressed to make an exception to MG policy and allow them to continue, although now as organizations within the structure of the city administration and directly under its control.[142]

The historian, Lutz Niethammer, in his 1975 study of the Antifa committees in Stuttgart, explains the movement's size and activism by pointing to Stuttgart's kettle-like shape and its decentralized structure with numerous quasi-autonomous, socially and somewhat politically homogeneous districts, which had their own Bürgermeis-

---

138. November 1945, p. 255, Gemeindebeiratssitzungsprotokolle, StA St.
139. Vietzen, p. 50. This is Vietzen's appraisal of the situation. French municipalities traditionally had much less autonomy than American ones, so these limits on local German self-government may have had just as much to do with French traditions of centralized authority as with the French distrust of Germans.
140. Ibid.
141. Niethammer, "Aktivität," p. 303.
142. Report by Brewster Morris to U.S. Sec. of State, 25 Oct. 1945, p. 7, POLAD/729/37, 3 of 4, RG 84, IfZ.

ter. Niethammer also notes the atypical cohesion of its workers' movement in the late Weimar Republic the minimal role played by the Christian trade unions, the rather militant SPD, and the pliant KPD, which after 1928 stressed trade union solidarity. This cohesion was also based on the existence of a broad network of pre-1933 workers' associations and housing complexes which further facilitated relatively autonomous workers' districts. Niethammer explained the higher level of workers' political consciousness by the proportionately high percentage of skilled laborers in Stuttgart, whose solidarity was even more accentuated under the Nazis.[143]

Both the former SPD and KPD members of the city council and the district Bürgermeister, as well as other party functionaries and shop stewards, formed the core of these *Kampfkomitees*; thus the municipal decentralization and the united working class movement of Stuttgart that was established during the Weimar Republic helped set the stage for this cooperation.[144] The postwar Antifa activism was foreshadowed during the first weeks after the Nazis came to power when Stuttgart KPD and SPD members initiated several spectacular protest actions.[145] The bombing raids toward the end of the war tended to separate the city's districts even more. When Klett took over leadership and formed his administration, many of the outlying areas of Stuttgart had their own self-administration led by these Antifa committees. They had taken on the tasks of securing food, protecting the population from plundering and violence, and

143. Niethammer, "Aktivität ... ," p. 306f. One of the unique aspects of the Antifa movements almost everywhere in immediate postwar Germany was the absence of partisan conflicts. The SPD and KPD predominated among those members who had had a previous party affiliation, but numerous members came from the old Catholic Center Party, the liberal parties, and some regional splinter parties. Even the SPD and KPD members seemed to drop their animosity toward each other in the midst of the Nazi defeat, the fear of last-minute die-hard Nazi or Werwolf actions, and the arrival of occupation troops, whom they viewed as liberators. Even once the Antifas were banned, numerous SPD-KDP joint action committees (Aktionsgemeinschaften) survived for months, usually until pressure came from above in the SPD hierarchy for its members to withdraw.

144. For more information on the Kampfkomitees and Arbeitsausschüsse, see Hauptaktei 0434-1 and 0051-1, StA St. The working class in Stuttgart had suffered considerably less unemployment during the 1920s than in most other major cities. This had to do with its highly skilled composition in mostly export-oriented industries and the fact that of the fifty-two German cities with populations over 100,000, Stuttgart had the richest population. The cohesion within neighborhoods also had to do with the concentration of workers in a few large firms, such as Bosch. See Müller, p. 7ff.

145. Müller, p. 147.

compiling lists of leading National Socialists in their districts.[146] The committees arose in Stuttgart, as in Frankfurt, Bremen, and various other cities, quite spontaneously and independently of each other.[147] Representatives of the Antifa committees approached OB Klett as early as 2 May 1945 to offer him their cooperation. On 4 and 5 May, committee representatives offered their services to the city's Department of Food and Economics.[148]

The Antifa committees were aware of the danger of being considered rivals of OB Klett's municipal bureaucracy. They went out of their way to try to convince the city administration that they were not challenging its authority. For example, on 5 May, after turning over Werwolf members to Police President Karl Weber, the committee involved wrote Weber to ask him not to consider their action a threat to his authority.[149] Indeed there was an inherent rivalry in the situation, because the majority of the Antifa committee members had either belonged to or felt sympathy with the left-wing parties in Stuttgart, whereas the majority of the city's administrative officials were decidedly right-of-center. But this political dualism did not mean that the Antifa committees planned to subvert the city administration or create a counter-administration.[150]

The leaders of the Antifa committees were often Communist, because Communists had most frequently taken the initiative, and because the KPD had the most intact underground organization of any of the former Weimar parties. Also proportionately, the Communists tended to be younger and hence more physically able to play the active roles required to lead these Antifa committees.[151] Thus, although this Communist leadership was a logical result of historical developments, conservative observers tended to exaggerate it while ignoring the fact that the majority of the members were not Commu-

---

146. Vietzen, p. 114.
147. See Carlebach, "Frankfurts Antifaschisten," p. 12ff and Niethammer et al., *Arbeiterinitiative.*
148. Vietzen, p. 114f. See also Hauptaktei 0051-1, StA St.
149. Hauptaktei 0051-1, StA St.
150. Vietzen, p. 115. Vietzen states that French MG banned the Kampfkomitees just in time before this "revolutionary group" could overthrow the order that had just been instituted (p. 116).
151. An evaluation of the political parties represented in the advisory and elected city councils of the three cities under examination here shows that the KPD was by far the youngest party. With the exception of Munich, where the FDP was not represented until 1948, the FDP was consistently the party with the oldest members as city councilors. Not surprisingly, the KPD had the largest percentage of working class members, and the SPD had the second largest. The FDP had the highest percentage of business owners and professionals.

nists, but rather from the SPD, Center Party, or the DVP, or without any previous party affiliations. The active Communist participation in the leadership of the Antifa committees made them vulnerable to "red scare" propaganda, especially from the much more conservative city government. As early as 3 May 1945 OB Klett expressed his concern to his assistant Könekamp about Communist influence in the Antifa committees.[152] Klett had informants secretly infiltrate the Antifa committees to check the members' political sympathies. An informant in the district Gaisburg committee reported that 80 percent of that committee seemed to be former KPD members, because they addressed each other as "Genosse."[153] The informant was so uninformed about working class parties that he did not know that the SPD and leftist splinter party members also used this form of address. Whether Klett picked up on this miscalculation is unclear.

While OB Klett spied on them and had his police president, Weber, keep tabs on them, U.S. MG also kept close watch over the Stuttgart Antifa committees. According to a U.S. MG study, the church hierarchy in Württemberg was among the most determined opponents of the Antifa committees. It reported that "both Vicar General Kottman and Commissioner Kruse … warned against the dangers of the anti-fascist leagues, declaring that they are 'camouflaged' bodies for the propagation of Communism, and that many Nazis are joining them."[154] Kruse, as city liaison to the French MG, tried to convince both Klett and the French of this specter of a combined Communist-Nazi front. Of course this was before Kruse himself was removed by the U.S. MG for his ties to the Nazi Party. This report of Nazi involvement was farcical propaganda, for there is no evidence of open or secret Nazi participation within the Antifas. Indeed, many observers considered the committees overzealous in their discrimination against all Nazis, whether nominal or activist.

Police President Weber initially seemed to appreciate the Antifas' help in rounding up Nazis. But in late May OB Klett put pressure on Weber to exert more control over the Antifas, complaining that the police seemed to be taking orders from the Antifa committees rather than the other way around. Klett also warned that these "elements" were trying to overthrow Weber.[155] This tactic of dividing and con-

152. Hauptaktei 0051-1, StA St.
153. Ibid.
154. FIS 5, OSS, RG 226, NARA.
155. Hauptaktei 0051-1, StA St. There is no evidence that this was true. Since Weber was the only leftist appointee and active anti-Nazi among the department heads, it is doubtful that the Antifas would have striven for his replacement. On

quering was apparently successful, because Weber ordered the Antifa committees to disband on 25 May.[156] French MG's prohibition of all political activity from the beginning of the occupation was useful to Weber in disbanding the committees, which had never been officially recognized anyway. As late as 9 May Weber had asked them to work with him as much as circumstances would allow.[157] That Weber was actually trying to retain the Antifas is quite possible. At the same time that he disbanded them, he allowed the individual members to regroup into small circles in order to continue to cooperate with him and aid in city tasks.[158] The committees did regroup, and more members of the former SPD, DVP, and Center Party joined them, although the former Kampfkomitees remained the core. A central office of these newly renamed Arbeitsausschüsse was formed under the former KPD Landtag member, Romuald Hilsenbeck, who had survived years of internment in Nazi concentration camps.[159] This central office and most of the various district committees continued to function – apparently quite democratically both in terms of structure and decision making – until 1948, under both French and American occupation, but not without attempts by Klett and others to discredit them in the eyes of the Germans and MG.[160] With the exception of the KPD, even the political parties, once they were licensed, felt threatened by the *Arbeitsausschüsse* and discouraged their members from remaining active.[161]

OB Klett seemed to understand that those forces which had been persecuted and/or suppressed by the Nazi regime would want to play an active role in the reconstruction of public life. Klett claimed that he welcomed such cooperation because of the shortage of recruits and funding to fill the posts vacated by the removal of "pro-

---

the other hand, Weber was between a rock and a hard place; he was both Klett's representative in charge of instilling order and asserting civil authority, and a previously active Social Democrat with fellow Genossen among the Antifas.

156. Hauptaktei 0434-1, StA St.

157. Ibid.

158. Hauptaktei 0051-1, StA St.

159. Hauptaktei 0434-1, StA St.

160. Ibid. The newly appointed state administration (Landesverwaltung) for Württemberg wrote OB Klett on 18 July 1945 about its discontent with the committees and councils pushing for the removal of Nazis from the administration and trying to fill civil servant posts themselves. The Landesverwaltung was annoyed that these individuals were not minding their own business, and it expressed the fear that such movements would threaten the preservation of administrative efficiency and the productivity of professional *tenured* civil servants.

161. Vietzen, p. 145.

fessionals" in the denazification proceedings. But he also stressed that his primary concern was the problem of maintaining an efficient and professionally capable and experienced civil service.[162] In late 1945 the city began paying daily stipends to these "work committee" volunteers in return for their fulfillment of certain assigned tasks. From OB Klett's perspective, this solution served two purposes. Because the individual members worked within their committees' structures, he did not have to integrate them into his administration. He was also able indirectly to control their influence and activities, eventually bringing about their depoliticization and coopting their original Antifa goals. Now rather than implementing denazification, social burden sharing, and social redistribution by developing a system of housing allotments and rubble removal based on political incrimination versus persecution, the remaining Antifas were sent off to do mundane tasks that would leave the social structure intact, like material clean up and the gathering of wood and coal supplies.

The excuse that efficiency would be lost if experienced and professional, but politically tainted, civil servants were replaced by untrained or inexperienced anti-Fascists is, on the surface, legitimate. But the U.S. guidelines had specified that, if necessary, efficiency would have to be sacrificed for the sake of denazification. Most MG officers, driven by a sort of managerial spirit, gave efficiency priority over denazification. This rationale of expediency was also used by many German administrative officials to prevent the changes that the influx of energetic anti-Fascists would have brought with it. The idea of such individuals entering "elite" municipal positions that could become available during the denazification process posed a threat to the established ruling groups, who either had belonged to the administrative elite before, as in the case of Dr. Könekamp, or who represented the economic and professional elite, such as Dr. Klett. Once the Antifa committees were co-opted by the city bureaucracy, they retained minimal decision-making power and few channels through which they could exert influence to implement change. A number of Antifa committee members did play a role in city government as advisory city councilors. But since Stuttgart's advisory city council met only nine times during its eight-month existence and was not formed until October 1945, advisory councilors could not play a significant role. Some Antifas were elected to the 1946 city council through their political parties, but only if they belonged to one of the parties licensed by MG. Many Antifas had

162. Ibid.

either never belonged to a party because of their young age prior to 1933, or because of disillusionment with traditional party politics. Despite lists of potential administrators provided by anti-Fascists, and pleas for training programs, none of these committed anti-Fascists were allowed to fill instrumental municipal posts from which they might have implemented reforms.

Neither the French nor the American MG officers were directly responsible for this personnel policy in Stuttgart. However, they were implicated because they made, or in the case of U.S. MG, confirmed, the top-level appointments of OB and 2. Bürgermeister and then gave these appointees a carte blanche to make the other administrative appointments. Once these first two MG appointments were made, positive personnel decisions were turned over to those German top-level appointees. This policy was not formally prescribed by Washington or by Frankfurt's SHAEF headquarters, but instead grew out of MG practice, a practice that had long-term negative repercussions. But before those repercussions are discussed, Munich's conquest and occupation will be examined.

Munich

Munich was (and is) a considerably larger city than either Frankfurt or Stuttgart. Relative to its size, it suffered considerably less destruction than Frankfurt and proportionately somewhat less than Stuttgart. However, a large number of DPs in Munich and its immediate surroundings, including the concentration camp inmates liberated from Dachau, complicated the material and logistical problems of postwar Munich. The population of Munich decreased from 824,000 in 1939 to 479,000 at the end of the war. But by mid-1946, the number was back up to 730,000, and by January 1947 it had reached 762,000. A total of seventy-four air raids between June 1940 and April 1945 killed 6,632 and wounded 15,800 Munich residents. This bombardment left 300,000 citizens homeless and destroyed 81,500 residences.[163] The Jewish community in Munich had been smaller than Frankfurt's but larger than Stuttgart's. Only about 250 of Munich's Jews survived concentration camps and returned to Munich in the first year following the war. Members of the Jewish community (*Kultusgemeinde*) in Munich had numbered

163. Michael Schattenhofer (ed.), *Chronik der Stadt München 1945–1948* (Munich, 1980), p. 43.

12,000 prior to 1933 and 7,000 prior to the forced deportations, whereas there were only 300 members in the fall of 1945.[164]

The daily calorie ration at the end of the war was, as in Frankfurt and Stuttgart, under 900, although it only reached about 1,200 by mid-1946. The historic old inner city was 90 percent bombed out and half of all structures (*Bausubstanz*) were destroyed. Ten million cubic meters of rubble covered the city.[165]

Munich was the last of the three cities in this study to come under Allied control, and it is perhaps not surprising that an anti-Nazi resistance organization tried to prevent the implementation of the Nero Plan and to turn over the city to the approaching American forces. During the night of 27/28 April 1945, the Freiheits-Aktion-Bayern (FAB), a resistance group of various civilian and military circles in Wehrkreis District VII, forcibly took over the Munich-area radio stations. The group called upon soldiers and civilians in the immediate listening area to end the fighting and break the last stronghold of National Socialism.[166] The revolt had been planned for over a year: all Nazi elements in the FAB core group, the Wehrmacht Interpreter Company VII, had been sent to the front by the company's leaders so that the remainder could begin training for the planned struggle to prevent Hitler's Nero Plan from being implemented in the Munich area. One week prior to the revolt, a U.S. and a French prisoner of war were secretly sent through the combat lines to inform their armies about the planned FAB revolt and to encourage an immediate halt to air bombardments.[167] Through these and various other FAB initiatives, the danger of a devastating air bombardment of Munich was averted.[168] Other FAB plans, such as convincing the federally-appointed governor (*Reichstatthalter*), Ritter von Epp, to negotiate a surrender with the Allies, failed.[169]

164. Ibid., pp. 64 , 105, and 210.

165. Ibid., pp. 43 and 166.

166. Ibid., p. 41. See also *Erinnerungsschrift zur Feier des 25. Jahrestages der FAB am 27. und 28. April 1945* (Munich, 1970), p. 6 and Extract from OSS FIS No. 1, 27 June 1945 in AG, 1945–46/1/4, 5 of 5, RG 260, IfZ.

167. *Süddeutsche Zeitung*, 26 April 1946.

168. *Erinnerungsschrift der FAB*, p. 10.

169. Schattenhofer, p. 42. This connection with Ritter von Epp was variously misinterpreted in retrospect by U.S. intelligence. An OSS Field Intelligence Study seemed to consider von Epp the real leader of the FAB until it actually staged its revolt on the 28th, when he "took a passive attitude." (AG, 1945–1946/1/4, 5 of 5, RG 260, IfZ). Von Epp's cooperation was needed by and initially offered to the FAB, but to see him as the ringleader or to associate all its members with his opportunism and elitism would be unfair. A comparison of the FAB elements with

During the twelve hours in which the FAB assumed governmental powers, it declared an open season on Nazi functionaries. Teaming up for the revolt with the socialist resistance group, "07," and a monarchist group, the FAB broadcasted that its aims were to eliminate the Nazi rule of terror and militarism; make peace with the Allies; struggle against anarchy; restore orderly economic conditions; reestablish rule by law, a just social order and fundamental human rights; and revive human dignity.[170] This vague statement was intended to unite all anti-Nazi opposition in support of the revolt. A number of sympathetic revolts did break out in the suburbs of Munich, but by 5 P.M. on 28 April the Munich Gauleiter announced that the FAB had been totally suppressed. Many of its members were captured and executed, as were many citizens who had followed its call.[171] The family of the FAB leader, the thirty-year-old Captain Rupprecht Gerngross, was taken hostage on the morning of 29 April, but their lives were spared by the news of the arrival of U.S. troops. Gauleiter Giesler fled the city after appealing to all public employees to stay at their posts.[172] Although the FAB had not been able to retain power, Munich was turned over to the hands of U.S. troops almost totally without Nazi resistance.[173]

The FAB's last-minute act of resistance was of significant symbolic value, especially because of its location and its simultaneous timing with the liberation of the Dachau concentration camp, some sixteen kilometers north of Munich. The discovery of the Nazi horror and terror against religious, racial, and political prisoners, made the idea of internal German anti-fascism seem unfathomable. The renowned journalist, Joel Sayre, writing from Munich in the 13 May 1945 *New Yorker* magazine, noted that he was "reporting the fairly incredible fact that somewhere in Germany I saw living Germans who had risked their lives fighting the Nazis."[174] The FAB broadcasts were picked up in London and Zurich and by General Patton's U.S. Third Army advancing along the Autobahn from Nuremberg toward Munich.[175]

---

those of the 20 July conspiracy would be somewhat appropriate. Both foresaw a new post-Nazi government of high-level civil servants and prominent professional and military men, rather than a truly representative, democratic one.

170. *News Digest*, 30 April 1945.
171. *Münchner Merkur*, 27 April 1955.
172. Ibid., 29 April 1949.
173. *Bayerische Landeszeitung:Nachrichtenblatt der Allierten 12. Heeresgruppe für die deutsche Zivilbevölkerung*, 1 June 1945.
174. *New Yorker*, 13 May 1945.
175. *Sunday Times*, 29 April 1945.

The 12th Army Group newspaper for the Bavarian population stated as late as 1 June 1945 that "Munich is the only city in Germany in which a larger united action against the Nazi regime took place."[176]

Although this uniqueness is an exaggeration, many Americans were obviously surprised and impressed by the FAB action, or at least the American journalists were. One would therefore assume that the FAB might have formed the core of Munich's postwar municipal administration. But in actuality, only one FAB member played a role of any significance in the new city administration.[177] The FAB was given an office by the Americans, and its members were asked to serve as advisors and informants to the CIC in Munich.[178] But this special status did not last long. Only weeks after the FAB decided it did not want to work directly for the CIC, the FAB office was ordered closed by unnamed American authorities and any further activities were prohibited.[179]

The FAB leaders, Dr. Gerngross and Dr. Ottheinrich Leiling, both felt that the U.S. MG did not sufficiently appreciate the FAB, because, according to the U.S. policy of unconditional surrender and nonfraternization, "there were not supposed to be any good Germans." The FAB revolt thus created unwelcome inconsistencies.[180] More realistically, the FAB, like the Antifa committees in Stuttgart, was considered sufficiently political and autonomous to pose a challenge to MG's appointed municipal administration; therefore the prohibition of political activity in the U.S. Zone was applied to it as well.[181] This is plausible because Leiling and Gerngross, who were both Protestant, complained to MG about the overwhelming presence of former members of the BVP, the Bavarian counterpart to the Catholic Center Party, and thus of the Catholic Church in the upper ranks of the new city administration.[182] The appointed OB, Dr. Scharnagl, was aware of these complaints, but, as one of those trying to refound the

176. *Bayerische Landeszeitung*, 1 June 1945.
177. Personal interview with Dr. Rupprecht Gerngross, Munich, 28 February 1982.
178. Ibid. This was corroborated in a personal interview with another FAB member, Dr. Ottheinrich Leiling, Munich, March 1982.
179. Ibid. Leiling and Gerngross, like most Germans I interviewed, referred to various U.S. authorities simply as "die Amerikaner," without differentiating between those with the Army, CIC or MG, let alone the various MG divisions. Whenever, upon my questioning, Germans were able to identify the the institutional affiliation I have included this information.
180. Ibid. Quote from Gerngross. Dr. Leiling agreed with this statement in his own separate interview.
181. See POLAD/ 730/31, 1 of 1, RG 84, IfZ for a mention of this prohibition being based on current political directives.
182. Secret Memorandum from Captain Homer G. Richey to Ambassador Murphy, 6. June 1945, POLAD/729/37, 1 of 4. RG 84, IfZ.

BVP (which became the CSU), had little sympathy.[183] Indeed it was in his personal and his party's political interest to suppress the FAB. To speculate further, one other possible factor in this prohibition could have been the OSS's appraisal of the FAB as a right-wing organization, strongly connected with the former federally appointed governor (*Reichstatthalter*), Ritter von Epp.[184] At any rate, even though FAB leaders were used as sources for American intelligence information in the area,[185] they otherwise played no significant role after the first days of the occupation.

The actual conquest or liberation was itself somewhat anticlimactic after the FAB action two days earlier. At 4:05 P.M. on 30 April 1945 the Munich City Hall was officially surrendered to a major of the U.S. Seventh Army.[186] At 6:30 A.M. the following morning, the Munich MG detachment under Colonel Walter H. Kurtz[187] and his assistant, Major Eugene Keller, Jr., arrived at City Hall and took command. The detachment for Munich had been formed in England in May 1944, where it had studied information about the city and its surrounding area and had developed a tentative plan of operations. The OSS provided Black, Grey and White lists of prominent Munich citizens.[188] Several of the twenty-four detachment officers had served in the MG Corps of the U.S. Army. Their task had been to deal with problems involving the civilian population either in enemy or liberated territory so that the armed forces could concentrate on actual combat problems. This personnel, according to Keller, had been "chosen from civilian volunteers with experience in the problems of civil government and administration, as far as practicability permitted."[189]

183. POLAD/730/31, 1 of 1, RG 84, IfZ.
184. AG, 1945–1946/1/4, 5 of 5, RG 260, IfZ.
185. POLAD/ 730/ 31, 1 of 1, RG 84, IfZ.
186. Schattenhofer, p. 42.
187. The name of Lt. Col. Walter Kurtz does not appear in most renditions of MG command in Munich. Rather his assistant, Major Eugene Keller Jr., who is referred to as Lt. Col., is named as the detachment commander in official histories, such as Earl Ziemke's *The U.S. Army in the Occupation of Germany* (p.253). But OMGUS files, specifically RG 260, OMGBY, 10/78-7/4, and Schattenhofer's *Stadtchronik* document Kurtz's four-month leadership stint in Munich, which was cut short by his unusual death caused by a falling rock from the top of the city-hall building. See Schattenhofer, pp. 67, 83, 86.
188. Bürgermeister und Rat (BuR) 2524b, Bl. 172, Stadtarchiv München (StA Mü). In this 1959 "Chronicle of Personal Reflections," the then retired Keller wrote that "we knew Munich better than we did our own home towns."
189. Ibid, Bl. 171. This description resembles the personnel trained at Charlottesville, but apparently neither Kurtz nor Keller had been trained there.

In terms of the recruitment and training of the Munich detachment, Keller's "Personal Reflections" contrasts with the historian,
Lutz Niethammer's more critical account.[190] Munich seemed to have
been assigned detachment personnel who were better trained for
their civilian administration assignments than most cities in the U.S.
Zone; also that personnel seemed to have possessed more background information on Munich and Munich personalities. Therefore,
the detachment could put its actual training into practice. Besides
having apparently better trained personnel, with explicit knowledge
about Munich, this exceptional preparedness was probably also
affected by the fact that Munich was occupied later than most areas
in the U.S. Zone. There was a little more time to learn about contemporary Munich from Germans inside of Germany, rather than
just from emigrés, who had not lived in Munich for as long as twelve
years. There was also more time to learn from the mistakes other
detachments had made during the early stages of the occupation.
Other factors included Munich's uniqueness as the largest city in the
U.S. Zone and its infamy as the "Hauptstadt der Bewegung," where
more die-hard Nazi resistance could be expected. The U.S. MG
would have had to counter this with the most detailed, precise MG
preparation and the most qualified personnel possible.[191]

The deputy city commander, Major Eugene Keller Jr., was of Alsa-
tian descent, spoke German,[192] and was an engineer in civilian life.
He and his detachment had been informed about the activities of the
FAB. They also knew about the sixty-four-year-old former OB of
Munich, Karl Scharnagl,[193] about whose whereabouts they inquired
as soon as they arrived in Munich on 1 May 1945. No one knew
where he was, although he had been seen in Munich recently.
Among the group of Germans who greeted the Munich detachment
upon their arrival at city hall was the pre-1933 OB of Würzburg, Dr.
Franz Xaver Stadelmayer, who, after claiming to be familiar with the
layout of the City Hall, led Major Keller to the OB's chambers. Once
there, Keller appointed the fifty-four-year-old Stadelmayer acting
OB of Munich. Stadelmayer was told that he would be expected to

190. See Niethammer, "Die amerikanische Besatzungsmacht," p. 159 ff.
191. In Stuttgart the time factor did not play much of a role, because it was not occupied by the Americans until July. But there, the U.S. MG commander had had no
civil affairs training, and the other personnel had been previously assigned to
other detachments, where they should have acquired MG experience, but not
information on Stuttgart personalities.
192. Personal interview with the former press officer in Munich, Ernest Langendorf,
Munich, 2 March 1982.
193. It will be recalled that his name was on one of the OSS White Lists.

assist MG in re-creating some semblance of civilian administration.[194] Before he became OB of Würzburg, Stadelmayer had
directed a publishing company. He had been a member of the BVP
until its dissolution in 1933. After apparently resisting pressure for
several years, he had applied for Nazi Party membership in 1942,
although he only became a member in July 1944. Stadelmayer
openly admitted his membership to Keller,[195] who explained to him
that he would be acting as provisional OB only until Karl Scharnagl
could be found.[196]

Keller was most appreciative of Stadelmayer's administrative
experience and his knowledge of Munich and its people, both while
he served as acting OB and thereafter, when he became Scharnagl's
deputy, or 2. Bürgermeister.[197] As city employees in Munich were
called back to duty, they were each required to fill out a question-
naire or Fragebogen. This was also the case for Germans hoping to
occupy or to retain influential positions in the professions and
industry, as well as with MG. These Fragebogen were then screened
by a team headed by the Special Branch denazification officer, the
Jewish-German emigré, Captain Kurt Baer. Baer, according to MG
reports, worked according to the SHAEF directive, which made it
clear "that the first concern was not the efficient operation of local
government, but the denazification of Germany."[198]

Initially both MG and the city administration were housed in City
Hall. On 3 May the pre-1933 OB of Regensburg, Dr. Otto Hipp, was
called upon to assist Stadelmayer as 2. Bürgermeister.[199] Hipp was
sixty years old, a native "Münchner," and former chairperson of the
Bavarian assembly of cities (*Städtetag*). Like Stadelmayer and Scharnagl, Hipp was a former BVP member, and all three knew each
other well as fellow OBs and party colleagues. Hipp retained this
post as 2. Bürgermeister for less than six weeks, after which he

194. BuR 2524b, Bl. 172, StA Mü.
195. BuR 2525b, StA Mü.
196. Hauptausschusssitzung vom 18. Juli 1946, p. 642, Ratssitzungsprotokolle (RP)
719/3, StA Mü.
197. Ibid., BuR 2524b, Bl. 173.
198. Fg 14, p. 3, IfZ.
199. In Munich the deputy to the OB is called the 1. Bürgermeister, and his assistant
the 2. Bürgermeister, whereas in Stuttgart and Frankfurt a. M. there is only one
assistant to the OB, and he is called the 2. Bürgermeister. For the sake of sim-
plicity and uniformity, the deputy to the Oberbürgermeister in all three cities
has been referred to as the 2. Bürgermeister. In the case of Munich, where it
briefly had two assistant Bürgermeister, the terms 2. and 3. Bürgermeister have
been used.

accepted the more prestigious post of Bavarian minister for culture and education.[200]

On 4 May, Major Keller received news of Scharnagl's whereabouts.[201] A master baker by trade, Scharnagl had feared last-minute persecution by the Nazis and went into hiding during the final days of the war.[202] He was brought to City Hall and asked to take over the duties of OB. When Scharnagl hesitated, MG reassured him that it would assist him and that he would not be worked "to the point of collapse." Scharnagl then accepted and was officially inaugurated the next morning. Both Dr. Hipp and Dr. Stadelmayer were retained as co-deputy Bürgermeister.[203]

Major Keller found Scharnagl to be well qualified for the job, from the standpoint of both civil administration and familiarity with democratic principles. Keller was also generally pleased with Scharnagl's selection of municipal department heads. The deputy commander, however, did remark that some MG directives were "quite naturally … often contrary to German thinking and customs." Thus, to bridge these differences better and "to better supervise Civil Government and render assistance where possible, MG was organized into (16) departments similar to those in civil administration."[204]

The initial Munich detachment commander, Col. Walter H. Kurtz, seemed to play a more behind-the-scenes role during the four months he served in Munich prior to his accidental death on 27 September 1945.[205] He did however take the initiative in contacting Cardinal Michael Faulhaber within forty-eight hours of the detachment's arrival in order to obtain personnel recommendations for the city administration.[206] Col. Kurtz, Major Keller, and the Upper Bavarian district MG commander, Col. Keegan, were all Roman Catholics, and all turned to Cardinal Faulhaber for advice. Kurtz, in fact, was reported to be fanatically Catholic.[207] Major Keller, who

200. BuR 2528, StA Mü.

201. BuR 2524b, Bl. 173, StA Mü.

202. Hans Wacker, "Kurze Lebensbeschreibung von Dr. h.c. Karl Scharnagl," Part of the preliminary section to the then unfinished Ph.D. thesis on Scharnagl, University of Munich. I have not been able to ascertain if this section was included in the completed dissertation.

203. BuR 2524b, Bl. 173f, StA Mü.

204. Ibid., Bl. 174, StA Mü.

205. OMGBY, 10/78-7/4, 3 of 9, RG 260, IfZ. See also Schattenhofer, p. 83.

206. Personal interview with Dr. Erwin Hamm, former professional Munich department head under Scharnagl, Munich, 1 July 1983.

207. Fg 14, IfZ. Charles E. Keegan, who was Irish-Catholic and a former New York city councilor, was removed from his post in the summer of 1945 for too much

became the Munich MG commander after Kurtz died, was quite taken with Faulhaber, to whom he reportedly often referred as "a prince of the Church."[208] Even Keller's successor, Col. James H. Kelly, who headed Munich's detachment from October 1946 until July 1949, was a Catholic of Irish descent.[209] Faulhaber certainly approved of the appointment of so many BVP members, especially the OB Karl Scharnagl. Scharnagl's brother was a bishop under Faulhaber's jurisdiction, and Karl, himself, had been very active since his youth in various Catholic lay organizations.[210] Karl typically described MG officers according to whether they were "good Catholics," anti-Catholic, or "anti-Church," as he put it, which was often his translation for non-Catholics.[211]

The churches seemed to play a considerable role in the person-nel policies and selections not only in Stuttgart with Bishop Wurm and the Church – City administrative liaison, Dr. Kruse, but perhaps even more in Munich. In Frankfurt the clergy of both Christian reli-gions had been strongly represented with one Catholic priest and two Protestant ministers in the short-lived, ten-member, MG-appointed Council. But thereafter, religious influence seemed to have waned considerably in predominantly Protestant Frankfurt. In Munich, at least in the first year, Cardinal Faulhaber not only influ-enced the appointment to posts, but he also determined, to a certain extent, who could and could not exert influence on MG and ulti-mately on the city government.

Dr. Gerngross, the leader of the FAB, accused Faulhaber of dimin-ishing the MG's confidence in the FAB because of his dislike for Gern-gross, who was both Protestant and married to a non-Bavarian.[212] Both Gerngross and Leiling, another Protestant, had been asked to meet with Faulhaber after the revolt. The Cardinal praised the FAB for saving both German and American lives, but warned them about the dangers of becoming revolutionaries or traitors, apparently in refer-

leniency in denazification. OB Scharnagl was convinced that this "hervorragen-der Katholik" (outstanding Catholic) was brought down by the anti-Catholic men in MG, "freemasons, Jews, etc.," who, according to Scharnagl in June 1946, had gotten the upper hand in MG. Scharnagl stated this at the Dienstag-Club meeting on 4 June 1946. As cited in: Klaus-Dietmar Henke and Hans Woller (eds.), *Lehrjahre der CSU: Eine Nachkriegspartei im Spiegel vertraulicher Berichte an die amerikanische Militärregierung* (Stuttgart, 1984), p. 57.

208. Personal interview with Dr. Ottheinrich Leiling, Munich, March 1982.
209. BuR 1655, StA Mü.
210. Wacker, see note 202.
211. Henke and Woller, p. 57.
212. Personal interview with Gerngross, Munich, 28 Feb. 1982.

ence to their working too closely with the MG. He suggested a return to orderliness, because, as he emphasized: "Wir wollen doch ordentliche deutsche Männer bleiben."[213] Apparently even for the hierarchy of the German Catholic Church, the idea of too much cooperation with the former enemy bordered on disloyalty for the "ordentlichen Deutschen." Faulhaber's only other conceivable motive for the warning could have been to minimize the FAB's influence on the MG, which he wanted to retain for the Catholic, former BVP members. Regardless of his motive, a problem now arose for many Germans willing to work with the MG, many of whom were rejected or discouraged because, as in the case of the Antifa committees, their antifascism was considered too politicized. Others were rejected because they were considered opportunists, as in the case of MG's view of the FAB leaders.[214] Still others were discouraged by fellow Germans, particularly more conservative ones, who used nationalist arguments to portray cooperation with the MG as unpatriotic.[215]

Conclusion

The initial occupation period in Frankfurt, Stuttgart, and Munich was characterized both by a disproportionately large representation of conservative middle- and upper-class special-interest groups in upper-level municipal posts, and by strong clerical influence, either upon the appointees filling the posts or upon MG in its selection process. In none of the three cities during this initial occupation period, when MG rule was most direct and MG influence strongest, were active anti-Nazis appointed to key posts, nor did they play any major role in recommending individuals to MG. Not only were they not encouraged to do so, but they were frequently discouraged when they did try to do so. The only exception to this was the appointment of fairly active anti-Nazi former Social Democrats to the post of police president in all three cities.[216] Perhaps this was because the German police represented one of the most nazified institutions in all of Hitlerian Germany.

Active anti-Nazis, especially those who had been persecuted by the Nazis, were relied upon to aid in the denazification process,

213. Personal interview with Leiling, Munich, March 1982.
214. OMGBY, 10/90-1/20, 1 of 3, RG 260, IfZ.
215. Niethammer, "Die amerikanische Besatzungsmacht," p. 164.
216. Those filling the post of police president in Munich and Frankfurt will be identified in detail in the next chapter.

either by compiling lists of Nazis or by seeking out incriminating evidence, which gave them the reputation of denunciators. After March 1946, when denazification was turned over to German tribunals, active anti-Nazis formed the core of the tribunal personnel, a role that further alienated them from the rest of German society, Nazi and non-Nazi alike. This almost exclusively negative role of accusation and judgment that was accorded many anti-Nazis[217] by MG kept them in an isolated ghetto with little opportunity to implement the political or socioeconomic reforms that they might have been able to initiate had they been appointed to key municipal posts, such as that of OB or Bürgermeister. As it was, they remained almost as powerless as they had been under the Nazis, except in the areas of journalism and culture, where different occupation elements were in control.

217. The term "anti-Nazis" is used here to describe a rather heterogeneous group of individuals who had opposed the Nazis and now sought to play active political roles in postwar Germany. This was out of a sense of either duty, because of their failure to have stopped the Nazis, or determination to use the opportunity of the collapse of the Third Reich to create a more socially just and equitable, democratic, civil society with social, economic, and political changes that would prevent the rise of fascism and even authoritarianism again. Many such anti-Nazis, probably even most, had only vague ideas about what those changes should be or how to achieve them, but few even had a chance to try their hand at it. The Antifas constituted only one such semiorganized group of anti-Nazis.

Chapter IV

The Stunde Null

American Occupiers, German Appointees, and Predemocratic Municipal Administration

Introduction

As early as late March 1945, when Frankfurt, the first of the three cities, was occupied, SHAEF had become aware of MG officers' tendency to give priority to "efficient administration without regard to some of the political implications of Military Government in Germany."[1] The July 1944 *Civil Affairs Guide* presumed that new anti-Nazi authorities would have assumed power on their own before MG took over and therefore instructed the MG detachments to lend assistance to these anti-Nazis, even if they appeared to be "inexperienced, inexpert and crude." Criticisms were expected to "come from those among the former personnel who [would] emphasize their own non-political attitude and their expert qualification as against the partisan and lay qualities of the new rulers." It warned "that those representing themselves as neutral experts will have been the collaborators of the Nazis, while the new men, as anti-Nazis, could not acquire expert training under Nazism." MG officers were instructed to "use active anti-Nazis" in the first phase of occupation even if they were "technically less qualified than persons politically unreliable."[2] But instead, the troop commanders or the MG commanders fell back on the old municipal structures and, at

1. POLAD TS/32/10. 1 of 1., RG 84, NARA.
2. R & A 1655.1., RG 59, OSS, NARA.

times, the former personnel to fill any administrative void they found.[3] In these three cities, most medium- and low-level civil servants remained at their posts, giving the impression of a relatively intact structure that could simply be repaired by filling in the upper echelons. In terms of expediting the return of efficient administration and a smooth transition to the occupation, these German bureaucrats and the U.S. commanders both had a stake in retaining and maintaining these structures.

Like Fritz Eberhard,[4] the OSS authors of the *Guide* presciently anticipated that allegedly neutral German experts would attempt to discredit the untrained anti-Nazis. MG detachments were generally more receptive to the arguments of the German experts, who emphasized their own skills and credentials as essential to the fulfillment of MG's goals. The policy advisor to the ICD, William Harlan Hale, critically observed in December 1945 that wanting to get "things in Germany to hum" was as natural for the heads of the technical divisions of MG like Transport and Economics as it was for those of the CAD. He noted that most officers were "recruited directly from American business life. They are specialists at making things go." The detachment officers who had been through Civil Affairs training were more likely to be veterans of city administration, but "these, too, were chosen not on the basis of their knowledge of Nazi Germany or of the ways to cure it, but because they were experts at keeping civic machinery going."[5] Hale also placed blame on those who had trained the detachment officers, claiming that they "seemed to see their job less as one of uprooting Germany's Old Order than of quickly restoring some sort of civil order out of chaos."[6] The erosion of American policies like denazification and democratization, according to Hale, was "taking place in the interests of efficiency or of 'administrative necessity.'"[7] Hale identified "conscious attempts to modify" U.S. policy. He complained that there had "been distinct reluctance in several circles inside MG to carry out the policies of disarming German industry, of delivering reparations to our Allies, and of encouraging anti-Nazi political and social forces inside Germany."[8]

---

3. See Friedmann, p. 102.
4. See Chapter 3.
5. William Harlan Hale, "Our Failure in Germany," *Harper's Magazine*, vol. 181, no. 1147 (December 1945), p. 517.
6. Hale, p. 517.
7. Ibid, p. 518.
8. Ibid., p. 519.

German civil servants, industrialists, and managers, all groups that had been singled out in denazification directives, but because of their key individual roles in the economy and administration, were unlikely to be pursued, also exploited the argument in favor of utilizing experienced personnel for reasons of efficiency.[9] This was especially true after Secretary of State James Byrnes gave his September 1946 reconstruction speech in Stuttgart, confirming the now official U.S. goal of an expeditious German economic recovery. By then the United States had measurably distanced itself from its denazification goals. In the midst of the developing Cold War, organizations like the OSS and ICD were either dissolved, as in the case of the former, or purged of the personnel which had continued, throughout 1946, to stress denazification, structural reforms, and democratization, as in the case of the latter.[10] These fervent anti-Nazi and reformist, if not at times revolutionary, elements were rendered powerless by their association with leftist ideas in the midst of growing anti-Communism in the United States and among MG authorities. With the removal of pressure from ardent social planners to transform and reconstruct the political and socio-economic basis of German life, it was much easier for MG to supervise and facilitate material reconstruction and to concentrate on reintegrating Germany into the West.[11]

By the time the expeditious economic reconstruction of Germany along capitalist lines became official U.S. policy, many MG detach-

9. See Hermann Graml, "Die Alliierten in Deutschland," in *Westdeutschlands Weg zur Bundesrepublik 1945–1949*. Beiträge von Mitarbeitern des Instituts für Zeitgeschichte (Munich, 1976), p. 41f.

10. Personal interview with James Aronson, chief of press, DISCC, Western District, New York, 27 Dec. 1985. Aronson stated that as early as December 1945, pressure was put on both leftist German newspaper licensees and leftist DISCC and ICD personnel to tone down their anti-Nazism, while at the same time, less and less tolerance was displayed toward Communists and socialist views. This led many in ICD and DISCC, who felt powerless and disillusioned, to return to the States. Their replacements were described by Aronson, as "a new breed, who had not been through the war and were not concerned with the struggle against fascism." A case in particular involved the emigré, Joseph Dunner, a press control officer with DISCC, who was dismissed and sent back to the United States in January 1946 for showing too much preference towards Social Democrats and presumably Communists. When it was learned that he had belonged to a Communist-affiliated youth group during the Weimar Republic in Frankfurt, his return to the States, which had been under consideration, was expedited. See 5/263-3/2, 1 of 2, RG 260, ISD. IfZ.

11. Cf. the recollections of those pursuing reforms, such as Cedric Belfrage in his *Seeds of Destruction* (New York, 1954) and James Stewart Martin in his *All Honorable Men* (Boston, 1950).

ments had already helped clear the way for the German support of such policies by appointing sympathetic Germans to influential posts. On the municipal level, this may not always have been conscious. The ostensibly neutral experts and right-center Weimar Republic politicians, who made up the majority of the appointees, were selected as the more cooperative and pragmatic Germans over former SPD and KPD members, whose role was largely confined to cooperation with denazification.[12] The latter were likely to have a different economic system in mind, with centralized government planning, extensive social programs and a strong role for labor. By most American political standards, the Social Democrats and Communists, with their seemingly dogmatic leanings, were less attractive than their right-center counterparts, who were more pragmatic about obtaining their goals and more willing, even if superficially, to appease MG.

A new guideline exemplifying MG's preference for German – supposedly apolitical – expertise over leftist politicization appeared in a November 1945 Field Intelligence Study on "Political Representation and Party Issues in the Gross-Hessen Government." The study was produced by the Special Services Unit (SSU), an overall less left-wing successsor organization to the recently dissolved OSS. The SSU assumed that experts, on the one hand, and members of "Left parties," on the other, were incongruous and incompatible. In discussing the newly formed Hessian ministry, which was politically balanced with four Social Democrats and one Communist on the Left and two Christian Democrats and three nonparty men on the Right, the study noted that the "Christian Democrats are apparently generally regarded as belonging to the bourgeois or 'expert' category."[13] The explicit assumption was that "bourgeois" was synonymous with "expert" and that the SPD and KPD members were not experts. This view prevailed despite the fact that among the SPD cabinet members there was a lawyer, a former city councilor and labor union official and a farmer, who certainly possessed some expertise in their respective ministry fields of justice, reconstruction, denazification, and agriculture.[14] Whereas the "bourgeois" equals "expert" assumption went unquestioned, the "expert" equals conservative theory was dismissed as a leftist perspective. The authors remarked that "from the standpoint of the Left, … a ministry of experts, although it might call itself non-political, would be by its very nature conservative." Indeed the unaffiliated minister presi-

---

12. OSS R & A 1655.1, OSS, RG 59, NARA.
13. OSS/SSU, Field Intelligence Study (FIS) 42, 26 Nov. 1945, p. 3, RG 226, NARA.
14. Ibid.

dent, a noted conservative jurist, was so concerned "that the Left representatives in the cabinet would be able to outvote the bourgeois members" that he had insisted on sole executive responsibility, and denied his ministers any real power. The other two unaffiliated Land officials, a tax expert and a career judge, were also members of the propertied groups in German society and known for their conservatism.[15] But since such typically middle-class, business and professional types did not belong to any political party, these SSU authors, who frequently did not consider themselves as having any explicit political orientation either, saw no reason to categorize them as conservative.

During the first year of the occupation, these initial OB and Bürgermeister appointments were crucial in determining MG's relationship with the various political factions. The MG detachment tended, either consciously or not, to adopt its appointees' biases and political positions. This also occurred on the state level, for example in the case of the SSU and Hessian Minister President Geiler and his cabinet.

During the Weimar Republic, municipal administration and OBs, in particular, had become more politicized.[16] This was due to tighter municipal budgets in the midst of postwar economic difficulties,[17] but also to the new universal adult suffrage that increased party competition and allowed the previously underrepresented but better organized mass parties such as the Center Party and the SPD to play a larger role in city administration. The broadly based SPD officials tended even then to be more party politicians (*Parteipolitiker*) than the Center OBs, who were more often experts first and politicians second (*Fachpolitiker*), or than DDP (German Democratic Party), DVP, or DNVP OBs, who represented relatively small party factions in city councils.[18] MG, which made a distinction between experts and partisans, preferred less explicitly political administrators for local government.

Hale, the ICD policy advisor, singled out the OBs of Cologne, Munich, and Frankfurt as examples of MG-appointed right-of-center German officials, who did not have the impulse to make denazification and democratic reforms work. On the other hand, he cited

15. Ibid, p. 1f.
16. Wolfgang Hofmann, "Oberbürgermeister als politische Elite im Wilhelminischen Reich und in der Weimarer Republik," in Klaus Schwabe (ed.), *Oberbürgermeister. Deutsche Führungsschichten in der Neuzeit*, Bd. 13 (Boppard am Rhein, 1979), p. 32.
17. These were due to Matthias Erzberger's financial reforms.
18. Hofmann, p. 33ff.

Siebeke, the Bürgermeister of Marburg, as an example of MG's lack of support for appointees who did try to make those policies work. Hale described him as "a very tame Social Democrat, whose influence our local MG detachment nevertheless felt it necessary to curb by surrounding him with an aggressive group of reactionary German Nationalist officials headed by the county councillor." Hale complained that such choices were not dictated in Washington, but rather represented local MG decisions "not to upset the civic applecart." He then noted: "'Safe' as such preferences on the part of MG officers may be, their cost is high in terms of the growing disillusionment and discouragement of those anti-Nazi forces in Germany which had awaited our coming and had dedicated themselves to building a new democratic and peaceable Germany." Furthermore, after talking to anti-Nazi concentration camp survivors at the time of their liberation and then seeking them out several months later at their homes, Hale lamented, "that these forces, although never strong, were stronger when we came than they are now."[19] Thus the full potential for change in this Stunde Null was never realized, due, to a large extent, to who was and who was not appointed.

Examples of direct MG intervention to prevent political parties from playing their legitimate legal role in the democratic process can be found in the first municipal elections in two of the three cities of this study, Frankfurt and Stuttgart. In Stuttgart, a Württemberg-Baden MG officer actually threatened the local SPD and CDU leadership with MG intervention unless they retained the unaffiliated Dr. Klett in office by voting for him in the May 1946 elections.[20] In Frankfurt the newly elected city council with its SPD majority elected an SPD OB and a majority of SPD department heads. MG expressed its disapproval of this left-wing majority by dismissing the elected SPD 2. Bürgermeister on the grounds of political incrimination during the Third Reich. The detachment also threatened to find grounds to dismiss additional SPD elected officials unless more CDU members were included among the department heads. Under this coercion, SPD members were compelled to vote for CDU members in a new election.[21] The MG detachment in

19. Hale, p. 521.
20. The MG officer deeply disliked party politics and was particularly fond of Klett because of his lack of affiliation. He argued: "Er (Klett) hatte keine politische Maschinerie hinter sich, aber er hatte etwas aufzuweisen." Charles Lincoln, *Auf Befehl der Militärregierung*. Trans. by Hans and Elsbeth Herlin (Munich, 1965), p. 140ff.
21. Mag 1058, Beschluss vom 6. Sept. 1946, and Mag 1050/1, Bd. 2, StA Ffm. Also personal interview with Emil Carlebach, who was present at the SPD meeting

Frankfurt was thus able to counteract the electoral defeat of the considerably more conservative, but officially nonaligned, appointed OB, Dr. Kurt Blaum, by reducing the political influence of the SPD in the Frankfurt city government.

Besides the posts of OB and Bürgermeister, the other administrative appointments which had to be made in each municipality were those of the department heads. These were made in the months following the war by the OB himself, although they were subject to MG approval. While the local MG detachment concentrated on dismissing politically incriminated German personnel, the German OBs filled the posts left vacant by denazification. Therefore, ultimately the OB had more power in personnel decisions than even MG, whose power was, after its OB appointment, de facto restricted to dismissal. The entire character of municipal government in the first year of the occupation, prior to the return of the democratic process in municipal affairs, was thus shaped by MG's selection of the OB and then the OB's own personal and personnel decisions. The political scientist, Gerhard Loewenberg, notes that a large number of MG's earliest appointees developed prominent political careers because they were "favored by an early start at a formative moment. In this way military government strongly influenced the composition of the new political class."[22] Because of the significance of these appointments in that first year, this chapter will focus on the Americans in the detachments and in the affiliated MG organizations, the activities of the OBs during this time when they were directly responsible to MG and, particularly, their appointments of department heads.

As noted previously, there were three groups of Americans involved in the U.S. occupation on the local level. The most powerful MG group, in terms of local German administration, consisted of high-ranking, usually career, military officers who usually headed the detachments (MGOs) and their deputy MG officers (DMGOs). The second group included military and technical staff officers, usually captains or lieutenants, who often had worked in business or in the civil service in civilian life. They usually served as MG counterparts to German municipal department heads. Members of both of

---

following the dismissal of the 2. Bürgermeister, Frankfurt, 30 May 1983, and personal interview with the former city councilor, Rudi Menzer, who was also present at that meeting, Frankfurt, 6 June 1983. See also Nr. 975, Abt. 502, Hessische Hauptstaatsarchiv. This incident will be described in detail in Chapter 6.

22. Gerhard Loewenberg, "The Remaking of the German Party System," in *European Politics: A Reader*, Mattei Dogan and Richard Rose, eds. (Boston, 1971), p. 267.

these groups tended to have a limited knowledge of Germany, which increased their reliance upon Germans and decreased their ability to differentiate among Germans. Their natural preference was for cooperative, experienced German administrators, who would both follow orders and take administrative, but not political, initiatives. The third group of U.S. occupation personnel was made up of German emigrés, who had joined the U.S. Army to liberate their homeland from the bonds of National Socialism, and of Americans, who had either personal ties to Germany, or who had had some academic training in German history, language, or politics. These "experts" on Germany usually held low ranks or temporary military ranks which commanded less authority than the regular military.[23] They were often very reform oriented in their designs for postwar Germany and frequently somewhat leftist in their politics. They often worked as intelligence agents and information control officers, where they were rarely directly involved with the local MG detachment.[24] Although the only appointments that this group made were in the media field, it was concerned at times[25] with overseeing the behavior and investigating the past of the MG detachment's German appointees, especially if they had ties to the media.

One can also classify potential German appointees, who were usually either ardently anti-Nazi, with a history of active opposition and persecution, or merely passively non-Nazi, into three sociological groups. First, there were the older pre-1933 political, administrative, or managerial elites, who could be restored to their old positions, thus providing continuity with the Weimar Republic. These elites actually consisted of two groups, those who were non-Nazi and often right-of-center or centrist, and those who were explicitly

23. Personal interview with James Aronson, former press chief, DISCC, W. Military District, New York, 27 December 1985.
24. Cedric Belfrage, personal letter to me, 22 Nov. 1984. Belfrage, a DISCC Press Control officer, was involved in newspaper licensing in Aachen, Frankfurt, and Wiesbaden. He noted that he "never knew much about the inner workings of MG, only that they generally fostered Nazis while our [DISCC] outfit was carrying out the denazification order from Eisenhower."
25. Hale, p. 522. In June 1945, for example, ICD officials complained to Robert Murphy about MG's failure to denazify and demilitarize in the field. Murphy instructed them to keep him informed, which resulted in weekly intelligence reports being researched by ICD and distributed to all higher staff sections and the War Department. Hale lamented the lack of action taken by Murphy and his State Department superiors. It should be noted that some actions did result, for example, when OB Hollbach was thoroughly investigated and dismissed from his Frankfurt post the following month, July 1945.

anti-Nazi, and often left-of-center or leftist. Then there were the generally younger members of the spontaneous antifascist activist groups. These Antifas hoped to take advantage of the breakdown of the Nazi system in order to reconstruct Germany along what they considered more democratic, and in some cases, socialist, lines.

Members of these antifascist action committees were not likely to appeal to pragmatic U.S. MG detachment officers, because their emergence represented autonomous German political activism and spontaneity at a time when political activity was prohibited in the U.S. Zone. Many of these antifascist activists were too young to have had a clear-cut political profile prior to 1933 or, for other reasons, had difficulty proving their anti-Nazi credentials. If they did have political affiliations prior to 1933, they were most often, although not exclusively, with one of the parties of the Left, which also made them suspect and too politicized in the eyes of many MG officers. Few had had administrative experience, and if they had had some prior to 1933, given their politics, it would have further decreased their chances of being considered as appointees. From the perspective of U.S. MG, their initial disqualification seems to have been foremost due to their overt political activism.[26]

Most U.S. MG detachments preferred to restore those Weimar elites who had no Nazi incrimination, because they would provide the dual qualifications of not having been Nazis while possessing administrative experience. Such elites would have been at least fifty years old. Of those local-level Weimar political elites, who were and had been actively *anti*-Nazi and who might still have had the energy and resolve to reenter municipal government, most were aligned to one of the parties of the Left, which often made them appear too political and dogmatic to appeal to the characteristically pragmatic MGOs and their deputies. On the other hand, the *non*-Nazi business and bureaucratic elites of the Weimar Republic were less likely to wear their politics on their sleeves. If they had belonged to a pre-1933 political party, it had probably been a middle-of-the-road or right-center party characterized by pragmatism and, unlike the SPD and KPD, had disappeared after 1933. The political nonalignment and administrative or managerial experience of the pre-1933 business and bureaucratic elites made them the optimal *non*-Nazi German appointees to municipal posts in the eyes of most MG detachment commanders.

26. As Hale relayed from a fall 1945 MG headquarters report, "There are numerous reports of petitions and requests from anti-Nazi organizations, whose impertinence seemingly grows in geometric progression with each new member." Hale, p. 521f.

Thus, in summary, there were six distinguishable groups of Germans, who were not Nazis, and of American occupiers, who eventually aligned themselves into two bi-national factions according to their degree of politicization, pragmatism, and idealism. The first faction was made up of the pragmatic U.S. MG detachment officers and their technical staff, and the non-Nazi, seemingly apolitical, experienced middle-class German administrators and businessmen, from among whom the MGOs and DMGOs selected their OB and Bürgermeister appointees, and from whom in turn the OBs chose their department heads and other top-level local officials. What made this faction cohesive was the common practical goal of getting German society and the economy, as well as municipal services, functioning again as soon as possible. The second group included the reformist, politicized emigrés and U.S. experts on Germany from information control and intelligence services and the two anti-Nazi German groups they supported. These comprised the older Weimar Republic political elite of the SPD and KPD and the often younger antifascist activists, whose political inclinations were usually leftist and whose social background was typically working class. The shared goals of the members of this faction were sweeping denazification and the establishment of a new democratic order that had at least a social welfare state, if not a socialist-oriented economy, in order to redistribute economic, social, and political power within German society. Thus, even prior to the stark polarization of the Cold War in late 1946, the lines in U.S.-occupied Germany were not drawn according to nationality or between occupied and occupier. The evidence presented in this chapter should provoke a reassessment of much of the literature of the 1970s which saw "the Americans" as advocates of a "restoration" in opposition to numerous untainted Germans as the promoters of a "new order", a categorization which drastically oversimplifies the complex reality of postwar Germany under the U.S. occupation.

Frankfurt am Main

MGO Criswell had been replaced in early May by Col. Robert K. Phelps and his deputy MGO, Major Francis E. Sheehan. Including Blakefield, the tactical commander, Frankfurt had had three different U.S. colonels in command within little more than a month. Phelps remained in Frankfurt for over a year, through the summer of 1946, while Sheehan remained until March 1946, when he was transferred to Wiesbaden, the seat of MG for the Land of Hesse (OMGH). The duties of the MGO in Frankfurt were more difficult than in other cities of the U.S. Zone, because, as Phelps put it, at the seat of USFET headquarters, one had "to try to please all the brass in and around his district." In regard to this brass, Phelps noted in August 1945 that he and his top officers felt "quite out of sympathy with prevailing policy."[27] This comment came after MGO Phelps had been forced to dismiss the appointed Bürgermeister Hollbach in July, despite his apparent desire to allow Hollbach to continue in office. Phelps and Sheehan were both apparently career army officers.[28] Neither spoke any German, nor did they seem to have had much previous contact with German affairs. It does not appear likely that either attended any civil affairs training courses to prepare them for the German occupation. Sheehan, who had played a more active role in civil administration than Phelps, had the reputation among Germans of cultivating only affluent and influential Germans. One other officer, the civil affairs expert, Captain LaFleur, was reported by Germans to have been familiar with German politics and society, and to have been both objective and politically well informed.[29] But his rank of captain diminished his potential impact upon policy decisions.

Frankfurt's acting Bürgermeister, Wilhelm Hollbach, remained in his post only until 4 July 1945. His dismissal marked a victory for the ardently anti-Nazi and often leftist DISCC and intelligence agents in MG. Because Hollbach was both a journalist interested in founding or refounding a newspaper, in this case, the *Frankfurter Zeitung*, and the head of Frankfurt's municipal administration, he fell into both the local MG's and ICD's sphere of influence. His short-lived term of office provides a revealing microcosm of the struggle between the reformist specialists in the ICD and/or DISCC, who were seeking a fundamental transformation of German society and promoted the encouragement of active anti-Nazis, and the more pragmatic, allegedly apolitical MG detachment officers. The latter recognized the necessity of some denazification, as long as it did not interfere with restoring an orderly administration and as long as the replacements (appointees) cooperated with MG and seemed to be "respectable," and thus, in their minds, traditionally bourgeois, pragmatic Germans, with experience as civic leaders.

27. ED 122, Bd. 1, p. 35, IfZ.
28. Ibid. This inference is based on MG correspondence about promotions for the two.
29. Personal interview with Emil Carlebach, Frankfurt a. M., 30 May 1983.

Wilhelm Hollbach was fifty-one years old in 1945, a decade older than Stuttgart's OB Klett and a decade younger than Munich's OB Scharnagl. He was born and grew up in Aachen, served in World War I and thereafter had worked for various newspapers in Weimar, Mannheim, Cologne, and eventually Frankfurt. In Mannheim he became involved in the Democratic Youth Movement of the DDP and the politically left-of-center ex-servicemen's association, the *Reichsbanner Schwarz-Rot-Gold* .[30] In Cologne he was a member of the DDP's local steering committee and an elected member of the city council while Konrad Adenauer was OB.[31] In 1931 the Frankfurt Publishing Company, which was owned by the Societäts-Verlag and which published the *Frankfurter Zeitung* , offered Hollbach the opportunity to modernize and run the *Neueste Zeitung* and the *Illustriertes Blatt*. [32] Hollbach took this position and soon also became news editor of the *Frankfurter Zeitung* until all three newspapers were shut down during the final phase of the war.[33] From late May 1945 on Hollbach was secretly investigated by the Information Control section, DISCC, and in June by Frankfurt's own MG detachment.

DISCC's investigation was prompted by the fact that a "well-defined clique around Bürgermeister Hollbach," all of whom had formerly worked for the *Frankfurter Zeitung* (FZ), was applying to DISCC to refound the FZ. The fact that IG Farben had bought out the original Jewish owners of the FZ's publishing company (Societäts-Verlag), and in 1938 had sold the company to one of the secret companies founded by the NSDAP publishing house, the Eher Verlag, did little to endear former FZ employees to U.S. Information Control personnel. On 28 May 1945, DISCC sardonically reported that the "FZ liberals" had been "cleverly used by Goebbels to soften down anti-Nazi feeling abroad, where the FZ had prestige." DISCC was of the opinion that the political difference between the FZ and other newspapers during the war years was quite small. Hitler's order to stop publication of the FZ was understood by DISCC as having been based on the same rationale used in closing down hundreds of other papers, namely, to save newsprint and personnel. DISCC also was of the opinion that by September 1943, the FZ's "usefulness abroad had ceased, most of the world being by then solidly lined up against Germany."[34]

30. Personal papers of his daughter, Dr. Elgin Hollbach, Frankfurt a. M.
31. Nachlass Hollbach. StA Ffm.
32. Richard Daub, *Journalismus zwischen Zwang und Freiheit* (Frankfurt a. M., 1981), p. 29f.
33. Nachlass Hollbach, StA Ffm.
34. OMGH, 17/16-1/11, 1 of 2, RG 260, IfZ.

The authors of the DISCC report were, therefore, solidly opposed to any revival of the FZ. They had little use for its former staff, and, in particular, Hollbach, whom they suspected of having been a Nazi Party member,[35] although then, as now, there was no evidence corroborating their suspicions. They were appalled that Hollbach had neglected to mention on his Fragebogen his management of the *Illustriertes Blatt*, which they considered a "scurrilous propaganda sheet with great influence and circulation." Even if it were true, as Hollbach maintained, that he had not written a line after 1933 and had not been a NSDAP member, they felt he was "too compromised with the Nazis to be acceptable." The report then commented on the "curious" fact that Hollbach had been appointed and vetted as Bürgermeister by an MG detachment that had never even heard of the *Illustriertes Blatt* until it saw copies bearing Hollbach's name as responsible editor in mid-May.[36] By mid-June the chief of SHAEF's Psychological Warfare Division (PWD),[37] Robert A. McClure, was most concerned that Hollbach still held "a strong position in the newspaper game in the Frankfurt vicinity and that most of his gang of Nazi collaborators are still hanging around expecting to republish the local newspaper." McClure feared that Hollbach's "presence in Military Government with his complete unreliability from our point of view, will react unfavorably on our whole Military Government structure, particularly since he occupies a key position at the seat of U.S. Military Government."[38]

Four officers of the Frankfurt MG detachment compiled an extensive report on Hollbach for MGO Col. Phelps, who apparently had begun to feel pressure from DISCC and PWD headquarters. The report explained Hollbach's omission in his Fragebogen of his editorial and supervisory work on the *Illustriertes Blatt* and the *Neueste Zeitung* by stating that his connection there had been "incidental to his main employment with the [*Frankfurter*] *Zeitung* ."[39] In actuality, the reverse seems to have been the case. Hollbach probably thought it would have been to his advantage to play up his FZ duties, assum-

35. Ibid. Neither the OMGUS files nor the Berlin Document Center files indicate that Hollbach ever belonged to the NSDAP or any of its affiliated organizations.
36. Ibid.
37. When SHAEF was dissolved, most of the PWD personnel went over to ICD under USFET and later OMGUS.
38. OMGUS, 5/268-1/18, 1 of 1, RG 260, IfZ. Frankfurt was the seat of U.S. MG until January 1946, when OMGUS was set up in Berlin as a sovereign authority. Until then, MG had been placed under the authority of USFET, whose headquarters was in Frankfurt.
39. Ibid.

ing that the *FZ* 's liberal reputation would not be placed in question. Since employees of all three newspapers were paid by the Societäts-Verlag,[40] this was easy enough to do. The MG detachment report decided that there was "no basis for believing that Hollbach was a member of the Nazi Party or a strong Nazi sympathizer." Without recommending either his dismissal or his continuation in office, the report did criticize Hollbach for not being "an experienced administrator" and for having "surrounded himself with former members of the Nazi Party," albeit more as "a matter of expediency, in endeavoring to obtain experienced civil service officials, than a leaning toward former Party members." It concluded that by including such men in his municipal staff, Hollbach's position had "been somewhat compromised and an unfavorable impression ha(d) been created on some agencies coming in contact with his office."[41] This reference was obviously to DISCC and PWD. Cedric Belfrage, a Press Control officer in Frankfurt, who had previously been involved with newspaper licensing in Aachen and Wiesbaden, stated that MG "generally fostered Nazis while our [DISCC] outfit was carrying out the denazification order from Eisenhower."[42] It is probable that neither the local MG detachment nor Hollbach intentionally fostered Nazis, but MG sometimes indirectly fostered Nazis by allowing MG appointees like Hollbach to retain or appoint Nazi Party members and Nazi sympathizers as well as tainted opportunists.

As early as April 1945 Hollbach sought ways to bypass MG denazification directives through such machinations as hiring former party members for midlevel posts at the earliest possible moment, without recording the dates of employment to disguise the fact that they were new employees. It was in fact much easier for former employees to be rehired on the basis of experience and civil service seniority rights than for NSDAP members to get a job for the first time with the city. Hollbach started this illicit practice after the first month of the occupation when MG began issuing its dismissal orders.[43]

Both Hollbach and his successor, OB Kurt Blaum, retained three of the six municipal department heads, who had held their posts at the end of the war. None of the three had been NSDAP members. The chief administrative director,[44] Willi Emrich, who had been a party member, stayed at his post until 16 June 1945, when he

40. Nachlass Hollbach, StA Ffm.
41. OMGUS, 5/268-1/18, 1 of 1, RG 260, IfZ.
42. Personal letter from Cedric Belfrage, 22 November 1984.
43. Mag 1058/1, StA Ffm.
44. This position was not classified as a department head.

was dismissed by MG. This occurred despite a series of appeals from Hollbach and others that he be retained since he had never been a Nazi and had helped the pre-1933 Jewish OB, Dr. Landmann, receive his pension and emigrate to Holland.[45] The pre-1933 SPD 2. Bürgermeister, the sixty-nine year-old physician, Dr. Karl Schlosser, resumed his former position under Hollbach until June, when he retired due to his age.[46] Schlosser was replaced by the former OB of neighboring Hanau, Kurt Blaum, whom Hollbach had recommended to MG.[47]

Several high-level administrators and assistant department heads from the Third Reich were retained and made acting heads of the departments in which they had held subordinate posts. Only in one case had the newly appointed department head been a member of the NSDAP. A local MG investigation showed that while this party member, Rudolf Prestel, had served as assistant public welfare department head during the Third Reich, he had been "a convinced enemy of nazism." However, because "he was a Party member," the local MG detachment insisted upon his dismissal in June 1945.[48] When Prestel's case came up before the German denazification tribunal in late summer 1946, he was exonerated. Evidence proved that he had used his party membership to keep several welfare institutions running, to save the lives of many children, and to protect politically and racially persecuted officials from the Nazis.[49] In the 1946 Magistrat elections, Prestel was elected head of the department of public welfare and youth by the newly elected city council.[50] Prestel, who had been a party member in name only and had actively risked his life to protect various persecuted individuals, had been dismissed by MG in 1945. At the same time, others who had not joined the NSDAP, but who, for example, as technical experts, had compromised themselves more with the Nazi regime, remained city employees and usually received promotions because of their experience. Some high-level officials dismissed by MG were allowed to remain in the same department in a subordinate position,[51] where they created problems of authority and morale. Their new superiors, only recently their subordinates, frequently felt inferior to their more

45. OMGH, 17/16-3/11, 1 of 2, RG 260, IfZ.
46. Abt. 503, Nr. 3821, Hessisches Hauptstaatsarchiv.
47. "Amtsleiterbesprechungen 1945," Sitzungsprotokoll vom 4 Juli 1945, StA Ffm.
48. OMGH, 17/16-3/11, 1 of 2, RG 260, IfZ.
49. Abt. 501, Nr. 241, Hessisches Hauptstaatsarchiv.
50. *Mitteilungen der Stadtverwaltung Frankfurt*, Nr. 29, 22 July 1961, StA Ffm.
51. OMGH, 17/16-3/11, 1 of 2, RG 260, IfZ.

experienced former bosses, who continued to exert indirect influence over key government offices.

Hollbach's top-level city administration did include one avid anti-Nazi, who because of his anti-Nazi stance and his SPD politics had lost his job of fourteen years as criminal investigator in 1933. The now fifty-seven-year-old Ferdinand Mührdel had been responsible for the arrests of close to forty-five thousand National Socialists during the Weimar Republic, an accomplishment which earned him the nickname of "Nazifresser [Nazi-devourer] Mührdel"in the Nazi press.[52] He had been imprisoned by the Nazis for ten months when they first came to power and then prohibited from holding any job in Frankfurt for five years.[53] From 1940 to 1945 he had worked as an office manager in the Societäts-Verlag,[54] where he apparently met Hollbach. He was appointed police president of Frankfurt by MG on 29 March, and was finally formally recognized by Hollbach two months later.[55] As Frankfurt's chief of police, Mührdel supported the idea of purging Nazis and militarists from the police, but Mührdel based his criteria not just on mere party membership, which MG wanted him to do, but rather on whether someone had profited professionally or materially by cooperating with the Nazi regime. Despite his experience with the Frankfurt police and his unquestionably anti-Nazi credentials, he was dismissed by the Frankfurt MG detachment on 14 August 1945. The detachment told MG headquarters that the reason for Mührdel's dismissal was his deficiency as an organizer,[56] but it told Mührdel that it was due to his insufficient cooperation with MG. This discrepancy indicates hesitation on the part of the detachment to consult with its superiors on varying interpretations of denazification and about its own authority in these procedures; perhaps the detachment was fearful of being reprimanded for its behavior.[57] Mührdel's colleagues felt that his upright republicanism had led him into conflict with MG, which wanted orders to be followed without question or controversy. Mührdel suffered a physical and mental breakdown in 1950 as a

---

52. *Frankfurter Presse*, 6 July 1945.
53. Ibid., 7 June 1945.
54. S1/98, Nr. 54, StA Ffm.
55. S2/5228, StA Ffm. Why Hollbach delayed this confirmation is uncertain. Perhaps he had a different – politically less leftist – candidate in mind.
56. OMGUS, 5/8-1/5, 8 of 12, RG 260, IfZ.
57. It will be remembered that it was at this time that MGO Phelps complained about feeling in disagreement with prevailing MG policy. See ED 122, Bd. 1, p. 35, IfZ.

result of the frequent Gestapo interrogations he had endured during the Third Reich,[58] not to mention the impact of his dismissal by MG. He eventually returned to police work and, after his recovery in the 1950s, became chief of the Hessian State Criminal Police.[59]

Another Social Democrat named Weyand, who was appointed as acting police president to replace Mührdel, held that post for less than a week. He was perhaps even more actively anti-Nazi than Mührdel, having held posts until 1933 in the republican defense organizations, the Reichsbanner and the Iron Front, and then spending fifteen months in concentration camps and almost a year in hiding from the Gestapo.[60] Why he was not retained any longer is impossible to determine from the records.

Weyand's successor as of 1 September 1945 was the trained jurist, Dr. Rudolf Siegert, an older, experienced bureaucrat of sixty-three, who leaned toward the new CDU.[61] Siegert had headed the police division of Hesse's Ministry of the Interior from 1923 to 1933, and had been neighboring Aschaffenburg's police president from April 1945 until MG brought him to Frankfurt in late August.[62] Dr. Siegert remained in office for only a year. The official reason given for his resignation was that he had been suspected of being an official in the Reich Ministry of the Interior and an SS-*Standartenführer*. This seems to have been a cover for the fact that MG, which had given him its complete support, had urged him to resign when the SPD stepped up its pressure to have him dropped because of his personnel policies. As early as October 1945 an OSS report indicated that this Dr. Rudolf Siegert was not to be confused with another Dr. Siegert who had played these SS and interior ministry roles.[63] The use of this excuse (confusing Dr. Rudolf Siegert for this other Dr. Siegert) one year later as the official MG reason for his resignation/dismissal is suspicious. In February 1946, U.S. intelligence agents reported that Siegert had brought several men from Aschaffenburg with him, who were not allowed to work with him officially because of their Nazi pasts, but to whom he had given specially commissioned tasks and whom he paid as special advisors. The report commented that antifascists under Siegert's jurisdiction "who looked too deep into the cards of high-ranking officials" had been

58. OMGUS, 5/8-1/5, 8 of 12, RG 260, IfZ.
59. S2/5228, StA Ffm.
60. OSS, R & A 3197.3, RG 59, NARA.
61. OMGH, 8/ 194-3/4, 3 of 5, RG 260, IfZ.
62. S2/5228, StA Ffm.
63. OSS, R & A 3197.3, RG 59, NARA.

replaced by more "reliable" men.[64] The MG detachment, however, took no action. After the May 1946 elections in which the SPD received the majority, an SPD representative let MG know that the SPD could not support Dr. Siegert as police president, because under his supervision "the police force was employing militaristic and reactionary elements." The SPD state chairman, Willi Knothe, had complained publicly about Siegert's policies, and thereafter Siegert's Public Safety counterpart in the MG detachment "had maintained a hostile attitude towards the SPD," according to the Social Democrats. Hence the SPD felt that to approach the Public Safety officer about Siegert would have been to no avail.[65] Siegert resigned on 13 September 1946. While some sources suggest it was voluntary,[66] the resignation, however overdue, was apparently based on an MG decision, but not one based on denazification.

Siegert's successor was Willi Klapproth, a Social Democrat who remained police president until his retirement in 1954. The fifty-two-year-old Klapproth, who was younger than his three postwar predecessors, had also been persecuted by the Nazis, having lost his position as a police commissioner and civil servant in 1933 and then having endured twenty-four Gestapo interrogations.[67] He apparently went out of his way to remain on the good side of MG and especially with the new MGO, Major Gerald C. Sola.[68] His long tenure of office, under the same MGO until 1949, attests to the success of this tactic.

In the meantime, German anti-Nazi discontent with the Hollbach administration was growing. By June 1945 the American occupation authorities were receiving negative reports on German public opinion in Frankfurt, especially from the traditional supporters of the leftist and centrist political groups. Frustration due to MG not utilizing the available anti-Nazi personnel for the posts still being held

64. OMGUS, 5/8-1/ 7, 4 of 7, RG 260, IfZ.
65. OMGH, 8/194-2/9, 3 of 6, RG 260, IfZ.
66. S2/ 4272, StA Ffm.
67. Protokoll der Stadtverordnetenversammlungssitzung vom 17. Oktober 1946, StA Ffm.
68. Personal interview with Rudi Menzer, Frankfurt a. M., 6 June 1983. Sola, a high school graduate, who as a civilian was vice president of Standard Oil of Brazil, had received MG training in Charlottesville for approximately one year in 1943. He had a "very limited" knowledge of German, but was apparently generally well liked in Frankfurt, where, as a sign of this, he received the city's Goethe award in 1949. This biographical information comes from a letter from his son, Gerald C. Sola, Jr., and his response to a survey I conducted of former detachment officers in Frankfurt, Munich, and Stuttgart, 20 July 1986.

by Nazis and not having set up training programs for anti-Nazis so that they could fill such posts was growing. The outlawing of the antifascist organizations in Frankfurt in the late spring was interpreted by many as a boost for the Nazis, whereas followers of the leftist and center parties were losing confidence in MG. This disillusionment with MG was compounded by empty promises made to the Left by Hollbach. The soon-to-be Hessian SPD party chairman, Willi Knothe, reported that Bürgermeister Hollbach had told him and other left-wing leaders "that they carry a lot of weight in the town." But when they tried to use that weight by actually suggesting qualified anti-Nazis for specific posts, politically incriminated individuals were appointed.[69]

On 20 June 1945, USFET G-5 Deputy Chief McSherry informed PWD Chief McClure that he had suggested to Colonel Phelps "that he seek a new burgomeister [sic]." McSherry noted that Hollbach had an "understudy," namely the 2. Bürgermeister, Dr. Kurt Blaum, so that "in due course," Hollbach would be dismissed. This action was not because of any certainty that Hollbach was a Nazi or even a Nazi sympathizer, "but in order to be absolutely certain that we [MG] do not have a questionable acting burgomeister [sic] in Frankfurt."[70] Ironically enough, perhaps to cushion the fall, Hollbach was granted the more prestigious title of OB on 26 June by MG, even though it knew that he would be forced to resign in the immediate future.[71]

Major Sheehan, Frankfurt's deputy MGO, informed Hollbach on 4 July 1945 that he would have to give up his post as acting OB because of an order from a higher authority within MG. Both MGO Phelps and Sheehan assured Hollbach that the Allied MG had always been satisfied with him and that no accusation of Nazi sympathies was being made. Otherwise, no information about Hollbach's dismissal was provided to him or to any other German authorities.[72] Phelps and Sheehan suggested to Hollbach that he return to his field of journalism, but not in the city of Frankfurt.[73] Apparently unbeknownst to them, the ICD had already limited Hollbach to at most subordinate positions in journalism and later blacklisted him from journalistic work altogether in the entire U.S. Zone.[74]

69. OMGH, 8/ 194-3/3, 4 of 4, RG 260, IfZ.
70. OMGUS, 5/ 268-1/18, 1 of 1, RG 260, IfZ.
71. Mag 1090/ 103, Bd. 1, StA Ffm.
72. "Amtsleiterbesprechungen 1945," 4 July 1945, Sitzungsprotokoll, StA Ffm.
73. Nachlass Blaum. Cf. Nachlass Hollbach, StA Ffm.
74. Abt. 501, Nr. 946, Hessisches Hauptstaatsarchiv. For ICD list see OMGUS, 5/265-1/19, 1 of 5, RG 260, IfZ.

MG also advised him not to seek any other position within the city administration, and his successor, OB Blaum, was instructed by MG that Hollbach could not be employed by the city.

In evaluating Hollbach's political guilt, it seems clear that he was neither an avid anti-Nazi nor a Nazi. He had not joined the NSDAP, an accomplishment in itself considering his various high-level journalistic posts. He had also, at some personal risk, helped various racially persecuted individuals during the Nazi regime. His personnel policies as head of the city of Frankfurt were, nevertheless, quite problematic. He had not only retained or hired some politically incriminated individuals, but had also not practiced a positive policy of encouraging anti-Nazis through either hiring or training. Yet his case ended in personal tragedy. Hollbach never got over his unexplained dismissal. Plagued by what he considered a dishonorable discharge, Hollbach continued to press the various levels of MG for explanations, which he never received. He did eventually do some minor publishing in the French Zone of occupation, but within a year of his dismissal as OB, he began having alcohol and drug problems, which afflicted him until he died in a dismal state of poverty and depression in 1962.[75] His dismissal may have marked a victory for the adamantly anti-Nazi reformers in DISCC and PWD, but because the reasons for his dismissal were never clarified to him or to the German public, and because his replacement was even less of a democrat or of a proven anti-Nazi, the victory was at best a bittersweet one.

Hollbach's "understudy," the sixty-one year-old Dr. Kurt Blaum, was an experienced administrator, who had served as administrative director in his birthplace of Strassburg, as a government councilor (*Regierungsrat*) in the State Interior Ministry of Württemberg and, from 1922 until 1933, as the elected OB of Hanau, twenty kilometers southeast of Frankfurt am Main. Like Hollbach, he had been a member of the DDP. During the Third Reich, Blaum avoided membership in the NSDAP, but acquired no anti-Nazi credentials and had very close, and from the perspective of denazification and democratization, very problematic, ties to the armaments industry. From 1934 until 1942, Blaum wrote and published texts on civil administration. As a captain in the reserve, he worked with the armaments commando in Frankfurt during the war. He also worked as a director of the motor manufacturing combine, Klöckner, Humboldt, Deutz in

75. Personal interview with Dr. Elgin Hollbach, Frankfurt a. M., 27 July 1983. See also Nachlass Hollbach, StA Ffm. Because of his dismissal, he received no pension from the city.

Oberursel, outside Frankfurt from 1942 to 1944.[76] During this period the factory was producing armaments, and Blaum ostensibly served as the chief of war economics (*Wehrwirtschaftsführer*) there.[77] On 1 April 1945, Blaum was appointed OB of Hanau by MG, a position he retained until June, when he became Hollbach's 2. Bürgermeister.

Even after Hollbach was dismissed, DISCC did not drop its surveillance of Frankfurt's city administration. Its investigation of Blaum's leadership of the municipal administration and of whether he had corrected Hollbach's practices revealed a more orderly and clearly defined organization than that of his predecessor. "A feeling of reverence and respect" was noted, along with, however, a more limited awareness, on the part of the OB's office, of "conditions in the city" now that OB Blaum had all but eliminated Hollbach's practice of using personal advisors to keep the OB informed. A city-hall atmosphere of "*Beamtenhochtum*" resulted from Blaum's creation of "a kind of smooth autonomous administrative island," which established a barrier against intruders and isolated the OB and his staff from the public. Because Blaum did not want an assistant or 2. Bürgermeister, many on his staff and the public, in particular, were convinced that he wanted to be the unequivocal "Number One."[78] Finally, apparently under pressure, OB Blaum recalled the almost seventy-year-old Dr. Schlosser to the position of 2. Bürgermeister in November 1945. This was, as he put it, "in agreement with MG" and "by way of reparation" since Schlosser had held the post from 1932 to 1933 when the Nazis had forced him to step down.[79] OB Blaum probably did not "agree" with MG about needing an assistant, but if he had to have one, it was certainly no accident that he selected the retiring Dr. Schlosser, whom the SPD considered to be only a nominal Social Democrat even before 1933.[80] Blaum could thus have a token Social Democrat as his deputy and set a reparation (*Wiedergutmachung*) example.

The Social Democrat and political persecutee, Eberhard Beckmann, who was the only personal advisor retained by OB Blaum,

---

76. Nachlass Hollbach, StA Ffm.
77. OMGH, 17/16-3/11, 1 of 2, RG 260, IfZ. Blaum avoided mentioning his involvement with armaments production in his Fragebogen for MG. He was never called to task on it, despite the fact that this role was exposed and criticized in the freshly licensed *Frankfurter Rundschau*.
78. Ibid.
79. Mag 1050/7, Bd. 2, StA Ffm.
80. Ibid. Oral information from Schlosser's personnel records provided to author, StA Ffm.

clandestinely reported to DISCC on Blaum's personnel and administrative practices. He noted that Blaum had tried to get around
MG's denazification guidelines and had also avoided giving special
consideration to those persecuted by the Nazis for religious and
political reasons. Blaum appeared to have convinced the detachment of the danger of weakening the traditional structure and the
authority of the municipal administration, were he to denazify too
radically or to install new democratic employees without sufficient
administrative experience. Beckmann noted with trepidation that
Blaum encouraged the German tendency to follow orders and avoid
change within his staff rather than encouraging the democratic
initiative and innovation that the postwar situation required. He
suggested that the addition of new staff members might aid in
implementing the denazification policies more, acknowledging that
this was far from certain, since "Blaum, as a clever man, under-
stands quite well how to circumvent any measures that might disturb his system. The possessor of a well-built and well-oiled
machine," Beckmann continued, "can always prove that the addition
of new elements will impair its smooth functioning."[81]

DISCC continued to keep an eye on Blaum's administrative
methods. It reported in November 1945 that Blaum's style of
leadership verged on the *"Führerprinzip."*[82] The only newspaper that
was licensed in Frankfurt at that point, the *Frankfurter Rundschau*,
openly criticized Blaum in an article for his wartime work in the
armaments industry and for his administrative policies as OB. This
prompted a counterattack on the article's author by Blaum's supporters, including former *FZ* journalists and one of Hollbach's
appointees. The author was a left-wing former Catholic and former
Center Party member, who was one of the seven licensees of the
Frankfurter Rundschau, which, to the dismay of Hollbach and several
former *FZ* employees, had been licensed as a brand-new newspaper. This new founding made the refounding of the *FZ* even less
likely. Blaum's supporters tried to discredit the article's author –
and the newspaper as well – by publicly accusing this licensee of
making an ambiguous speech in 1933 which could have implied
support for the Nazis.[83]

Once this conflict surrounding Blaum became public, the Frankfurt KPD, which had been licensed after the ban on political acivity
was dropped in late August, began strongly to advocate Blaum's

81. OMGH, 8/194-3/3, 4 of 4, RG 260, IfZ.
82. Ibid., 1 of 4.
83. Ibid.

dismissal. Frankfurt's MG detachment, which was quite aware of the situation, "exerted pressure on all parties to keep the entire affair quiet." After its perceived defeat in the Hollbach dismissal, the MG detachment did not want to lose its second OB appointee. Unlike the case with Hollbach, this time the OB did not fall under the direct jurisdiction of DISCC. In its November 1945 report, DISCC recognized its powerlessness and admitted its frustration:

> While it is conceded that the removal of Blaum and his bureaucratic machine would be a most desirable event, we are faced with two unhappy situations.
>
> 1. The Rundschau does not have sufficient power to produce the desired result ... .
> 2. The local MG detachment, whether it bases its decision on lack of replacement, ignorance of the situation, or just to stick to its appointee, is fostering the development of a local political machine which is marked by inefficiency, lack of proper cooperation with our policies and ideals and is a living symbol of the archaic bureaucracy which has for many years characterized German municipal government. Certainly no new progressive spirit is being shown by the present German municipal government of the city of Frankfurt.[84]

In late January 1946, the Frankfurt MG detachment polled general public opinion concerning OB Blaum. It had improved somewhat since the autumn, but criticism was still strong, especially in regard to his wartime activities, his treatment of persecutees, and his undemocratic rule. While on the one hand it was said that: "from a communistic point of view Dr. Blaum is too indulgent with the known Nazis," another opinion was that: "all former Nazis, however apparently look upon him as the ideal man for the position of Bürgermeister."[85] From this particular MG detachment's perspective, uncompromising anti-Nazism had come to be equated with Communism. The vivid images of the horrors of the concentration camps had already faded by early 1946 as the clouds of the Cold War began rolling in.

Kurt Blaum remained in office until after the first democratic elections were held in 1946. Frankfurt public opinion was reflected in the SPD victory in both the city council and OB results. With the support of the local MG detachment and the Frankfurt CDU, Blaum announced his candidacy in the July 1946 OB election by the first

---

84. Ibid. It is interesting here that DISCC also used the argument of inefficiency in its critique of the "political machine." In this case, however, it was targeting authoritarian bureaucracy as inefficient.
85. OMGUS, 5/8-1/7, 4 of 7, RG 260, IfZ.

elected postwar city council, despite the SPD's absolute majority in the new council. The CDU endorsed Blaum with the argument that no one could deny his excellent administrative credentials. But the SPD city council faction, denying this "fact," retorted that Blaum was "an authoritarian man who had not created any democratic foundations upon which to base his administration."[86] Almost 80 percent of all the Bürgermeister and OBs appointed by the Americans in Hesse were able to retain their posts in the 1946 elections. Of the 20 percent that did not remain in office, almost half did not run for office. Blaum was one of the approximately 10 percent who ran and lost.[87] After this electoral defeat, Blaum continued as a civil servant, but in state rather than municipal government. He became president of the Polytechnical Society and the Hessian Red Cross. In 1952 he received the Federal Republic of Germany's greatest service award, the *Grosses Bundesverdienstkreuz*, and in 1954 the city of Frankfurt awarded him its *Ehrenplakette*. Unlike his dishonored predecessor, Blaum died tranquilly on 26 November 1970.[88]

Stuttgart

The official transition from French to U.S. occupation authority took place at noon on 8 July 1945. The Stuttgart MG detachment had been formed from two detachments, so that the MGO had been able to select the very best personnel from both. The officers who were chosen were generally able to perform duties for which their civilian background or subsequent MG training or experience had prepared them. Most of the twenty-eight officers had had one to two years of civil affairs training, and were quite young, in their twenties or thirties.[89]

The MGO, Lt. Col. Charles L. Jackson, was a career officer in the infantry. He was only thirty-two years old when he took command of Stuttgart,[90] and had had only two weeks of MG training in France in the spring of 1945. A West Point graduate, he had seen quite a bit of action during the war, and had worked his way up to batallion commander. He did have three brief temporary MG assignments prior to becoming MGO of Stuttgart, including two subordinate posts in Hesse and a two-week stint as MGO in Weimar immediately before that

86. Protokoll der Stadtverordnetenversammlung vom 25. Juli 1946, StA Ffm.
87. OMGH, 8/190-2/ 9, 1 of 6, RG 260, IfZ.
88. Oral information provided to the author from Blaum's personnel file, StA Ffm.
89. OMGUS, 5/10-1/12, 10 of 10, RG 260, Hauptstaatsarchiv Stuttgart.
90. Ibid.

area was incorporated into the Soviet occupation Zone.[91] Jackson was characterized by his Land-level MG superiors as "young, aggressive, energetic and interested in the work of Military Government." His superiors felt that the combination of his personal characteristics and the presence of his deputy MGO, the fifty-one-year-old Major Edwin A. Norton, who had had considerable MG experience, compensated for his relative lack of MG experience. Norton had been in the Army for three years, two of which he had spent in civil affairs training, while the last year he had spent with one of the two detachments dissolved to form the Stuttgart detachment. In civilian life, he was executive vice president of an ice and coal company. His MG superiors considered him well-suited for the job because of his executive ability and his dedication to the work.[92]

But Norton only remained in Stuttgart until the fall of 1945 when he was reassigned to a unit in the United States. At that point the thirty-five-year-old Trade and Industry officer, Major Rolland H. Stimson, was promoted to Stuttgart DMGO until his transfer to Pforzheim in July 1946. Stimson had been in the Army since 1941, although he had been commissioned as a second lieutenant ten years earlier after serving four years in South Dakota State University's R.O.T.C. Prior to the war he had been an instructor of chemistry at a junior college. His undergraduate major in chemistry and his M.A. in education would hardly seem to have destined him to be a trade and industry specialist, although this is what happened. He received two weeks of MG training in Wiesbaden and a month-long preparation for his assignment with the Stuttgart detachment. For three months from the late fall of 1945 until early 1946, Stimson served as acting MGO while Jackson was on an R&R leave in the United States.[93] By late August 1945 the Germans began complaining about the problems caused by the discontinuity of the short tenure of MG officers;[94] this was certain to have an even stronger impact upon Stuttgart, which had recently had to make a difficult adjustment from French to U.S. MG.

Jackson recognized the French MG's appointment of Dr. Arnulf Klett as acting OB, but delayed for three months before formally administering Klett's oath of office in order to establish his political

91. Response to my survey of MG officers and letter from Col. (Ret.) Charles L. Jackson, 6 August 1986.
92. OMGUS, 5/10-1/12, 10 of 10, RG 260, Hauptstaatsarchiv Stuttgart.
93. Response to author's survey of MG officers and letter from Rolland H. Stimson, 22 September 1986.
94. Fritz Eberhard's Berichte an die OSS, ED 117, Bd. 89, p. 5, IfZ.

reliability.[95] In the interim, SPD supporters[96] tried unsuccessfully to have OB Klett replaced by the last Weimar Republic OB and a Social Democrat, Dr. Karl Lautenschlager, whom they claimed should have been reinstated.[97]

The first order of business between Klett and MGO Jackson was a purge of former Nazi Party members from the city administration. During the next two and a half months, over twenty-five hundred former party members were dismissed from the city administration.[98] MGO Jackson emphasized to OB Klett that all Nazis and those with Nazi tendencies would have to be removed. He remarked that he realized that this would cause difficulties, because frequently the most important officials had had Nazi connections. The city commander told the OB to consider carefully where he would turn for personnel to replace those being dismissed.[99] Klett had to have all new appointments for department heads and other high posts approved by MGO Jackson. For middle range positions within the various departments, the counterpart MG officer was to be consulted. The MG detachment did not require prior consultation for German appointments to lower level positions.[100]

A meeting between the MGO and the OB on 2 August is indicative of their shared emphasis on technical expertise over political qualifications in their personnel decisions. Jackson urged that Klett seek out the best-qualified people for his administration. Klett responded that that was precisely his practice: in filling posts, his first priority was technical qualification, and only secondly did he consider political leanings. Jackson replied that at the present, political criteria were of no relevance; as long as the applicants were not Nazis, their technical or professional suitability would be the decisive factor, and he promised to back Klett in this 100 percent. Jackson then mentioned that political appointments could not be made, since "politics" did not exist. He added that he wished to be informed of any transgression of the MG ban on political activity.[101] Jackson interpreted "politics" as the state of being political within the confines of political parties, which were not permitted to form in

95. OMGWB, 12/222-1/8, 1 of 3, RG 260, IfZ.
96. Political parties in the U.S. Zone were permitted to begin organizing and to submit applications for licensing to MG as of late August 1945, when the ban on political activity was removed.
97. Hermann Vietzen, *Chronik der Stadt Stuttgart 1945–1948* (Stuttgart, 1972), p. 68.
98. Ibid., p. 66.
99. Hauptaktei 0314-8, Sitzungsprotokoll vom 23. Juli 1945, StA St.
100. Personalamt 02-010, StA St.
101. Ibid.

the U.S. Zone until late August 1945. Jackson's narrow interpretation of "political" led him to also deny that the denazification program was a political matter.[102]

Jackson's naivete enabled Klett to hire anyone who was not formally a Nazi, to disregard the promotion of anti-Nazis, and to avoid seeking out individuals representative of the city's varied political directions and social strata for the city administration. Jackson's lack of knowledge of German and his minimal training in civil administration, along with his narrow view of politics increased OB Klett's autonomy. Klett, like OB Blaum in Frankfurt, remained unaffiliated with any political party, although both wavered between the CDU and the DVP, which later became the FDP. Because Klett used his nonpartisan status to convince MG of his objectivity and neutrality,[103] he seemed, to the local MG, less likely to be biased toward or against any party.

Jackson's older, more experienced deputy MGO, Norton, was less easily manipulated by OB Klett, but because he was only a deputy and in Stuttgart for merely a few months, his influence on major detachment policy decisions was limited. Occasionally if Jackson was detained from attending one of his regular weekly meetings with OB Klett, Major Norton would take his place. On one such occasion in mid-August, Klett complained to Norton about the SPD's

---

102. Hauptaktei 0052-1, StA St. In the 20 November 1945 Hauptausschusssitzung, MGO Jackson stated: "Es wird erneut betont, dass in dieser Denazifizierung keinerlei Politik enthalten sein darf." (As translated in the German protocol). In a 20 September 1986 letter to the author, Charles Jackson contended that he had used the words "political" and "politics" in reference to "politicians in their partisan activities." His attempt to clarify what he considered political and his views on denazification further confirmed my impression that his narrow definition underestimated the difference between non-Nazis and anti-Nazis and the importance of having the latter over the former as well as the political implications of choosing technical expertise while disregarding the political leanings of appointees. Jackson was irritated at the suggestion that MG "should influence the selection of German administrative personnel by insisting that an appropriate percentage or number of Germans [based on party affiliations] be selected for, appointed to or hired for municipal positions." Jackson went on to state: "It is hard to visualize how being an active anti-nazi would in itself qualify anyone with being necessarily entitled to or being even qualified for any position in the new German government per se. One would have to prove himself worthy of such a position. Think of how many people were active anti-Vietnam in the 60's and 70's as compared to the few who have gone on to succeed in business or politics. Not many have come to my notice."

103. Since Klett was only twenty-eight when the Nazis came to power, it is not all that unusual that as a new lawyer he had not yet joined a party.

political intrigues against him.[104] According to the German protocol of the meeting, Norton made light of Klett's concern by commenting that it would be better if the Germans would work rather than talk politics, advice aimed at Klett as well as at the SPD.[105]

Fritz Eberhard, in a 25 August 1945 report for the OSS on Stuttgart, noted the growing frustration of the anti-Nazis, provoked by MG's and the city administration's behavior toward them. Anti-Nazi civil servants, most of whom were lower-level, sensed a strong distrust from MG officers, who did not even seem willing to talk to them. Eberhard reported that while some still hoped to convince the Americans that there was "another Germany," most had been over-come by resignation.[106] Many were also horrified by the extent of MG's bureaucracy and the intrigues that had developed between the different U.S. authorities, as well as by the obstacles placed in the way of Germans trying to establish communication with MG.[107] Such Germans had to have written permission from OB Klett or one of his representatives in order to contact MG,[108] which naturally meant that either self-censorship or Klett's censorship occurred if anything critical of Klett's administration was to be relayed. Anti-Nazis expressed dissatisfaction with MG's schematic denazification policies, but they, according to Eberhard, also blamed the German authorities for not making the necessary removals at the beginning of the occupation.[109] Denazification had been complicated in Stuttgart by the fact that the French MG had been much less stringent and schematic in their practices than U.S. MG policy required.

Klett's top-level administration was purged quite gradually, but thoroughly, from 30 July to 1 December 1945.[110] The first administrator to go, and the one whose continued presence had distressed Stuttgart anti-Nazis most, was Klett's 2. Bürgermeister, Dr. Eduard Könekamp, who had headed the departments of economics, police, education, culture, and housing under OB Strölin during the Third Reich,[111] and had been a member of the NSDAP since 1933.[112] Under

---

104. Hauptaktei 0314-3, StA St. The reference is not clear, but this probably referred to the SPD's attempts to have Klett replaced by the former OB, Dr. Karl Lautenschlager.

105. Ibid.

106. 25 August 1945 OSS report, ED 117, Bd. 89. IfZ.

107. 1 December 1945 OSS report, ED 117, Bd. 89, IfZ.

108. 11 December 1945 translated memo from Jackson to OB Klett, Verbindung mit der Stadtverwaltung, Hauptaktei 0314-0, StA St.

109. 31 October 1945 OSS report, ED 117, Bd. 89, IfZ.

110. Vietzen, p. 66f.

111. 25 August 1945 OSS report, ED 117, Bd. 89, IfZ.

112. Hauptaktei 0314-10, StA St.

OB Klett, Könekamp had not only been 2. Bürgermeister, but also had headed the personnel office, which meant he exercised a great deal of influence over hiring and firing city employees. He had also been in charge of organizing the advisory city council (*Gemeindebeirat*), greatly influencing appointments to it and how much power it had.

Dr. Könekamp was replaced by a member of the Save Stuttgart movement, the forty-two-year-old attorney, Dr. Wolfgang Hauß-mann. Like the detachment leadership in Stuttgart at the time, the heads of the municipal administration were exceptionally young. Haußmann, whose Swabian family's liberal party ties stretched back to the Revolution of 1848, had played a backseat role in the early postwar months because of a gunshot wound he received while returning from trying to print leaflets against Hitler's Nero Plan in the finals days of the war.[113] Haußmann was soon to be one of the postwar founders, along with Theodor Heuss and Reinhold Maier, of the Deutsche Volkspartei, which later became the FDP. During the Weimar Republic, Haußmann had been the Württemberg state chairman of the DDP's youth group, the *Demokratische Jugend*. He later served on the DDP's executive committee for two years before being forced out of politics by the Nazis. Haußmann would head the DVP (FDP) faction in the Stuttgart city council from 1946 until 1953, when he became the state Minister of Justice. In 1955 he was selected to hold the post of national vice-chairperson of the FDP, and three years later he founded the Central Office for the Investigation of National Socialist Crimes in Ludwigsburg.[114] After the first elections were held in 1946, Haussman did not continue as 2. Bürgermeister despite his immense popularity as displayed by the fact that he received the highest number of votes of all city councilors. He turned down the suggestion that he run for OB, in spite of the support granted him by the SPD faction. With a newborn daughter and recurring health problems from his gunshot wound, he decided to throw his support to Klett. Klett, however, had apparently become wary of Haußmann's popularity and decided to prevent Haußmann from continuing as his deputy.[115]

Dismissed soon after Könekamp, were two other department heads and one of Klett's personal advisors, because of their membership in the NSDAP from 1933 on.[116] A month later, two more department heads were dismissed because of joining the NSDAP in

113. Personal interview with Dr. Wolfgang Haußmann, Stuttgart, 30 November 1982.
114. *Stuttgarter Zeitung*, 3 July 1963.
115. Personal interview with Dr. Wolfgang Haußmann, Stuttgart, 30 November 1982.
116. Vietzen, p. 66.

1937.[117] The U.S. MG considered it less incriminating to have joined in 1937 than in 1933, because the 1937 Nazi Civil Service Law had placed added pressure on civil servants to join the party. Five of the six dismissed by October had served under OB Strölin either as department heads or their assistants. From October to December, three former members of the Save Stuttgart movement were dismissed. They were: Bishop Wurm's liaison, Dr. Kruse, who had also served as Klett's liaison to MG, because he had applied for party membership in 1937; the finance department head, Dr. Alfons Wetter, who had apparently belonged to the NSDAP at some point; and the head of the reconstructuion department, the architect, Eugen Mertz, who had served under OB Strölin, but had never joined the Party.[118] Mertz was the only one of the key post holders dismissed by U.S. MG, who had neither been a member nor an applicant for membership in the NSDAP. Given his experience, it is not clear why he was dismissed. Of all three postwar cities examined here, at least initially, Stuttgart, under U.S. occupation, retained the largest number of top officials who had served during the Third Reich and who had been Nazi Party members. This was the case until the U.S. MG detachment slowly ordered their dismissal, in their order of incrimination, according to MG's schematic classification and dates of membership in the NSDAP.

Most of the replacements for these department heads were high-level civil servants, who were simply promoted to heads of the departments in which they had been working. However, a few cases of reinstating persons dismissed by the Nazis for political reasons did occur. One such case was the rehiring of the former department head, Josef Hirn, who had been dismissed in 1933 because of his SPD membership. The forty-seven year-old Hirn was then elected 2. Bürgermeister in 1946.[119] Another reinstatement and a major promotion occurred in the case of Karl Weber, who had headed the Save Stuttgart movement. Weber had been a detective with the Stuttgart police up until 1933 when he was dismissed because of his SPD membership. Weber was appointed police president by Klett and remained in that post until 1948, having been elected to it in the 1946 elections.[120]

A considerable amount of controversy surrounded Klett and his administration. Fritz Eberhard had stated in a late August 1945

---

117. Hauptaktei 03141-10, StA St.
118. Vietzen, p. 67.
119. Ibid.
120. Ibid., p. 547.

report for the OSS that Klett was not sufficiently anti-Nazi and that he exercised his official duties in too authoritarian a manner.[121] The adamant anti-Nazis, who were most strongly represented among the parties of the Left, never came to the support of Klett or his close advisors. This was especially apparent in debates in the advisory city council, especially from members of the Antifa-Arbeitsausschüsse, and in the 1946 and 1948 OB elections, when a growing polarization of the Right, which supported Klett, and the Left, which did not, manifested itself. Because the Left played such a minimal role in Klett's 1945/46 administration, the advisory city council, which had representatives from all the parties, was the only municipal structure in which it had any voice. This voice was minimized by the fact that the council had only an advisory status; it was the last such council to be formed in the three cities, and was the only one that was dependent on the OB to convene. Klett convened it only nine times, considerably less often than the councils in Munich or Frankfurt convened.

Klett was scrutinized by the Investigative Subsection of the Stuttgart detachment's Special Branch in late summer 1945, because of the combination of new information acquired through receipt of his Fragebogen from the French, his proposal of several '"outright Nazis"' for the Württemberg Land administration, and pressure from the Württemberg Interior Ministry to discipline Klett because of the Nazi and criminal elements among his appointees. The Americans learned, apparently for the first time, that Klett had indeed had political affiliations prior to 1933, namely as a member of the anti-Semitic Württemberg Middle-Class Party (Württembergische Bürgerpartei) and the pan-German-oriented Altdeutscher Verband. The investigation revealed that Klett had knowingly appointed people with criminal pasts (embezzlement, extortion, etc.) and that he had refused to take action against a high-level police official he had appointed, despite considerable evidence that the man had been an SS trustee at the Dachau concentration camp with a long record of brutality. Klett had entrusted this man with all police arrests and investigations. When a fellow lawyer, who had been sentenced to death for political reasons by the Nazis, confronted Klett with elaborate evidence of the police officer's role in Dachau, Klett responded that the man "is my strongest support in the police; he has suffered for years, too. I shall not govern without him. He, [the man's name was provided here], will make order." Klett completely ignored growing public protests

---

121. 29 August 1945 OSS report, ED 117, Bd. 89. IfZ.

over this police official, who, however, was eventually arrested by the French and given over to the American CIC, who turned him over to be tried for war crimes.[122]

The investigative report concluded that the Klett regime was causing MG to be "fast losing the necessary respect and trust it needs to aid the organization of democratic elements in Stuttgart; [and] several ugly rumors regarding 'protection' given Dr. Klett by certain French and American officers have reached this office." The report went on to warn that "when a German official claims that no replacements are available a large number of discretionary cases are allowed to continue in office; in short, Military Government cannot de-nazify [sic] without the active aid of the Germans themselves. The approach of a Special Branch is negative, with the aim of prevention. It is the German who plays the positive role of suggesting candidates." Special Branch then recommended that Klett "be summarily removed from office" and "that a vigorous anti-Nazi be appointed in his place to begin a thorough cleansing process," which would "be declared the prime aim of the new appointee for several weeks with administrative efficiency recognized as only a secondary goal during that period."[123]

This report with its dismissal recommendation was not heeded, nor does any paper trail indicate that there was even any follow-up at the time. But, interestingly enough, the report resurfaces as an enclosure to a 24 February 1947 "Confidential Biographic Data" report, prepared by the American vice-consul in Stuttgart, apparently for POLAD. Alluding to the information about Klett in the enclosure and to its own somewhat glossed-over version of this information, this 1947 report, very much unlike that of the Special Branch some seventeen months earlier, concluded that despite some "unsavory appointments" it was "generally conceded by most elements of the local population and MG officials that the Oberbürgermeister and his recruits … have done a superior job of governing the city."[124]

In the interim between the original 1945 investigation and its use as an enclosure in February 1947, a Württemberg MG officer had stepped in and coerced the freshly elected Stuttgart city council into electing Klett as lord mayor in mid-1946. This could have been one of those officers about whom there were "ugly rumors regarding 'protection' given Dr. Klett." Certainly by 1947, and even by mid-

122. POLAD/779/12, 1 of 5, p. 1ff, RG 84, IfZ.
123. Ibid., p. 6.
124. 24 Feb. 1947 "Confidential Biographic Data" report by the American vice-consul, Seymour M. Finger, p. 2, POLAD/779/12, 1 of 5, RG 84, IfZ.

1946, the emphasis on denazification had changed. Agencies like the Special Branch no longer played the same role in Military Government, which had turned over denazification to the Germans in the spring of 1946. Most striking about this case is how negligible an impact this quite involved Special Branch investigation had on MG as a whole, even in September 1945 when it was sent to Lt. Col. Perry. It also exhibits vividly how individuals like Klett, who were probably not appropriate appointees in 1945, could retain support from enough corners within MG to stay in office, despite displays of very problematic personnel choices, disregard for MG rules, and lack of German political support.

The Württemberg-Baden MG officer, Charles Lincoln, who was the former U.S. MG liaison to the French MG in Stuttgart, connived to keep OB Klett in office in 1946. After the city council elections in May, the OB was to be elected by the city council itself. Lincoln threatened the local SPD and CDU council leadership, which planned to vote the unaffiliated Dr. Klett out of office, partly because both parties were interested in choosing a more representative figure for OB in terms of party politics. Lincoln told them that MG would intervene if Klett were not confirmed by them in his OB office. Under this pressure, both parties backed down and agreed to have their municipal government representatives elect Klett. Lincoln, who was lying and had no authority to make such a threat, was quite proud of his accomplishment and felt he had saved the day for the continued proper functioning of the city. In his memoir-like book Lincoln bragged about "his little intrigue" as having served the citizens of Stuttgart. His rationale for this intrigue was his dislike of party politics and his feeling that Klett had proven himself to be a capable OB.[125] This move on the part of an MG representative surely did not symbolize a very positive lesson in democracy for an MG that was supposed to be fostering democratization. However, Klett's administrative successes, his outgoing personality, and the lack of widespread public knowledge about some of his appointees' pasts apparently sufficed for him to be able to acquire genuine mass support by the time of the 1948 municipal elections, elections in which no MG representative intervened.

Munich

After Karl Scharnagl had been reinstated as Munich's OB on 4 May 1945, he began searching for men to head the city's fifteen depart-

125. Lincoln, p. 140ff.

ments. MG's Special Branch officers prepared action sheets for all the city personnel after examining their Fragebogen. It was calculated that of two hundred thirty-three city employees in positions of authority and responsibility immediately prior to the occupation, forty-one had reported for duty after the Americans had arrived. Of these forty-one, fifteen were dismissed, seven were cleared, and nineteen were allowed to work temporarily until their Fragebogen were processed further.[126] Of the original fifteen acting department heads, nine were removed by MG during the third week of May.[127] Three of these nine had been pre-1933 department heads under OB Scharnagl, whom he had recalled. All three had joined the NSDAP. But despite the fact that OB Scharnagl was convinced that they were not Nazis, Special Branch officer, Captain Baer, had them removed.[128] In Munich, unlike Stuttgart and Frankfurt, Special Branch seemed to be, at least according to the Germans, taking charge of the actual dismissals rather than the MGO. Munich was occupied a little later than the other two cities; thus Special Branch as an institution designed to implement denazification, was slightly more settled and active within U.S. MG. It is also possible that there were more precise tasks for the various MG officers and branches in Munich and that there was an MGO who was more willing to relegate authority. It is also likely that Captain Baer was an especially active Special Branch officer; he was described by the welfare department head, Erwin Hamm, as the "all-powerful man in Munich."[129]

OB Scharnagl had been able to find a number of experienced administrators to head the city departments, although several of them who were either nominal Nazis or in some way had collaborated with the Nazis were eventually dismissed by MG. This group included the first postwar police president,[130] Hans Ritter von Seisser, the sev-

126. OMGBY, 10/78-1/4, 1 of 9, RG 260, IfZ.
127. OMGBY, 13/142-1/7, 1 of 11, RG 260, IfZ.
128. Personal interview with Dr. Ludwig Schmid, former Munich city councilor, both in advisory and elected city council, Munich, August 1982.
129. Personal interview with Erwin Hamm, Munich, 1 July 1983.
130. It is not clear that von Seisser was actually the first police president. Documents in the Stadtarchiv München indicate that von Seisser took on this position on 7 May 1945. But a man by the name of Frenkel preceding von Seisser appears on a list of police presidents without any further information. Otherwise, interestingly enough, the name Frenkel has been purged from the Munich municipal records. See Verzeichnis vom Direktorium A. A weekly MG report from the Munich detachment for 27 July to 3 August 1945 notes that von Seisser was installed on 1 August 1945. See OMGBY 13/142-1/7, 4 of 11, RG 260, IfZ. The professional city councilor Erwin Hamm claimed he recalled Frenkel, and that

enty-one-year-old former commander of the Bavarian State Police, who had been involved in the 1923 Beer Hall Putsch, and gotten a bit too close to the NSDAP during the latter years of the Weimar Republic.[131] He served as police president until his mid-August dismissal by MG. Dr. Josef Ochs, who had worked in the Wiesbaden municipal administration prior to and during the Third Reich, headed Munich's municipal enterprises until late November 1945. A member of the Center Party until 1933, Ochs had waited to join the NSDAP until 1940, but was expelled three years later because of help he had offered to Jews. Scharnagl's first appointed fiscal department head was Dr. Emanuel Backhaus, a lawyer and notary public, who had worked in economic and communal affairs in Bremen. Backhaus had not joined the NSDAP, but had served as Wehrmacht economics officer in Nazi-occupied Norway from 1940 to 1942 and was dismissed in late April 1946, shortly before the municipal elections. The sixty-three-year-old former SPD judge in Munich, Dr. Peter Michael Reitmaier, served from July to August 1945 as the head of the district police. He was dismissed because he had applied for membership in the NSDAP in 1938, although he had never been accepted. Dr. Alfred Kroth, a trained lawyer, was the only former KPD member to be appointed department head in any of the three cities during the first postwar year. The thirty-three-year-old Kroth was dismissed by MG on 24 September 1945, shortly before he was to join the new Minister President Wilhelm Hoegner's cabinet, because he had entered the Nazi Party via the Hitler Youth, albeit as a Communist spy. This espionage mission was completely confirmed to MG through various interrogations. Despite OB Scharnagl's special appeal to the MG authorities on Kroth's behalf, he was nevertheless dismissed.[132]

Scharnagl had better luck with his appointees, Dr. Josef Zink; Dr. Erwin Hamm as the city legal advisor; the former Bürgermeister, Paul Berrenberg; Dr. Anton Fingerle as superintendent of schools; and the Social Democrat, Dr. Karl Sebastian Preis, who had headed Munich's

---

the reason his appointment as police president was so carefully hidden was that it was discovered after a few weeks that Frenkel was a homosexual who had been appointed by a homosexual officer in MG, and that this was the reason for his dismissal. Hamm claimed that Frenkel served four to five weeks, and that von Seisser did not actually become police president until early June, at which point his appointment was predated. Personal interview with Dr. Erwin Hamm, Munich, 1 July 1983.

131. Michael Schattenhofer (ed.), *Chronik der Stadt München 1945–1948* (Munich, 1980), p. 47 and p. 50.

132. BuR 2528, StA Mü.

housing department from 1919 until 1933. The heads of the three technical departments and of the construction department had all worked under the Nazi OB Fiehler, but had not joined the NSDAP, and were thus all retained with the approval of MG.[133] Scharnagl apparently personally knew all the men listed above except for Dr. Hamm and Dr. Fingerle. Dr. Hamm's sister had been OB Scharnagl's personal secretary until the OB's 1933 dismissal. When Scharnagl asked his secretary, who had been re-hired, if she knew of a clean lawyer ("*sauberen Juristen*"), she suggested her brother.[134] The thirty-three-year-old Dr. Fingerle was a Gymnasium teacher, who had been drafted as an interpreter into Captain Gerngross's company and then became a member of the FAB. But this FAB association probably had nothing to do with his appointment. Instead it was conceivably his friendship with the pre-1933 head of the city's public libraries, Professor Dr. Hans Ludwig Held, that led to his appointment, or the fact that he had taught the sons of Scharnagl's 2. Bürgermeister, Dr. Franz Stadelmayer.[135]

Replacements for the dismissals included three Social Democrats: Franz Xaver Pitzer, as police president; Karl Erhard, who had been the pre-1933 city shop steward; and the city councilor from 1925 to 1933, Thomas Wimmer, who was initially appointed 3. Bürgermeister and then 2. when Dr. Franz Stadelmayer resigned on 10 November 1945.[136] Two former BVP members, the Weimar Republic city councilor, Max Gerstl and Dr. Karl Lacherbauer, who served as 3. Bürgermeister when Wimmer became 2. Bürgermeister, were also appointed as replacements.[137]

During this postwar year of pre-democratic municipal government, 30 percent of Munich's department heads were representatives of the SPD and KPD (although only one was from the KPD), far more

133. Ibid.
134. Personal interview with Dr. Erwin Hamm, Munich, 1 July 1983. Hamm was one of the early members of the CSU and continued to play a leading role in Munich's government until his retirement in the late 1970s. He married the FDP city councilor, Hildegard Brücher, who is much better known as Hildegard Hamm-Brücher, the FDP candidate for Bundespräsident(in) in 1994.
135. Johannes Timmermann, "Anton Fingerle zum Gedächtnis," in *Münchner Anzeiger*, 26 March 1982, p. 26.
136. Dr. Stadelmayer resigned after pressure was placed upon him by MG, despite the fact that MG had instructed OB Scharnagl to keep him as 2. Bürgermeister a few months before. Scharnagl had actually appointed him to the post for twelve years. On 1 December he was forced to give up his seat in the advisory city council. See BuR 2525b and RP 719/3, Hauptausschusssitzungsprotokoll vom 18. Juli 1946, p. 642, StA Mü. See also Weekly Munich Detachment Report, 7-14 November 1945, OMGBY, 13/142-1/7, 9 of 11, RG 260, IfZ.
137. Ratskartei. StA Mü.

than in either Stuttgart or Frankfurt am Main. Erhard, Wimmer, Gerstl, and Scharnagl had all been imprisoned together in the Dachau concentration camp after the July 1944 assassination attempt on Hitler, when almost all pre-1933 centrist and leftist officials, from the municipal level on up, were arrested and imprisoned for periods of from several weeks to several months. This shared experience brought them closer together and convinced them that after the Nazis' overthrow they should all emphasize their common concerns rather than their partisan differences as they had during the Weimar Republic.[138] Of the thirty-six appointed members of the Munich advisory city council, which met from August 1945 until May 1946, ten had been in the Dachau concentration camp as political prisoners.[139]

The combination of this shared persecution and the comradeship that developed out of the experience, as well as the multiparty representation within the OB's professional staff created the basis for extremely genial cooperation between the various political parties and individuals and an atmosphere of mutual respect. One apparent consequence of this was the establishment of training programs for inexperienced anti-Nazi personnel, such as the special police training schools. This atmosphere sets Munich apart from Frankfurt and Stuttgart, not just during the first year of the occupation, but well into 1948. This changed somewhat after the 1948 elections, when seven different political groups were represented in the city council, causing the political poles to widen and the percentage of those sharing the common experience of persecution during the Third Reich to decline. The fact that OB Scharnagl represented continuity with Munich's administrative and political past as its pre-1933 elected OB, unlike Hollbach, Blaum, or Klett, and that he was of the lower middle-class rather than solidly middle-class probably also positively affected the rapport among the municipal administrators and with the city in general.

In Munich, the only one of the three cities where the pre-1933 OB was restored to his old post, there was not only less reliance upon the old bureaucracy of the Third Reich, but also more reinstatements of concentration camp victims and political persecutees.[140]

---

138. Hubert Sturm, "Thomas Wimmer," Hauptseminararbeit bei Professor Friedrich Prinz, University of Munich, 1980, p. 4. See also BuR 2533a, StA Mü.
139. BuR 1537, StA Mü.
140. OMGBY, 13/142-1/7, 3 of 11, RG 260, IfZ. As early as 20 July 1945, the MG detachment noted that of 231 reinstated office employees, eight-six were concentration-camp victims. Besides those, eight politically persecuted victims had been reinstated into the higher civil service brackets.

One reason for this could have been OB Scharnagl's familiarity with running Munich, which would have made him less dependent on experienced civil servants than others, such as the young lawyer, Dr. Klett or the journalist, Hollbach, who had had practically no experience in municipal administration, or even than OB Blaum, who had administrative experience, but not in Frankfurt. Another reason might have been that Munich appeared to have a more intact Weimar Republic political elite that had been and still was anti-Nazi.

It would be wrong to assume that OB Scharnagl always displayed objectivity and showed no partisan or religious preferences. In late July, representatives of the former DDP in Munich suggested names of individuals to be considered for the advisory city council.[141] OB Scharnagl had requested names from all the other Weimar democratic parties already in the early summer.[142] But Scharnagl did not even consider the DDP's list, because his list had long since been completed, and because, as he wrote the DDP members, party politics were not to play a role in this council. He even stated in his response to the DDP delegation that he would not raise a finger to revive his old party, the Bavarian People's Party (BVP), [143] and yet he did become a charter member of the Christian Social Union (CSU), the BVP's successor. Scharnagl apparently went to extraordinary lengths to avoid including the Protestant Liberals, who eventually joined up with the old DVP to form the FDP, or Liberal Democratic Party (LDP), as it was first called in Munich. In late November 1945, when Dr. Stadelmayer resigned as 2. Bürgermeister, the Munich LDP tried to get the well-known Bavarian liberal, Thomas Dehler, appointed to the post. Munich's MG detachment had apparently encouraged Dehler's candidacy, but the advisory city council, which was allotted more responsibility and power than its counterparts in Frankfurt and Stuttgart by their respective OBs, did not accept Dehler. Of course the council had no LDP representatives.[144] The fact that the LDP was the last major party to form and be licensed in Munich for the 1946 elections was certainly partly because OB Scharnagl excluded it and its predecessors from the advisory city council. The fact that it had less than two percent of the popular vote in those elections can also be traced back, at least in part, to OB Scharnagl's exclusive party politics.

141. BuR 1636, StA Mü.
142. BuR 1537, StA Mü.
143. Ibid., BuR 1636.
144. Berthold Mauch, *Die bayerische FDP, 1945–1949* (Munich, 1981), p. 22.

Conclusion

Overall, Munich had a more progressive, representative, and cooperative municipal administration in 1945/1946 than either Frankfurt or Stuttgart. Curiously enough, the PWD and its successor, the ICD, did not play a role in Munich or officially in any part of Bavaria until October 1945, when General George Patton, who had served as the military governor for Bavaria, was removed from his post. Patton had refused the assistance of the "Sykewarriors," as he called them, in the area under his jurisdiction, because he felt he had enough information and intelligence resources.[145] Any early progressive trends must be attributed to the German municipal government itself and/or the detachment in Munich under MGO Keller. In Stuttgart and especially in Frankfurt, the presence of PWD and DISCC was quite noticeable, and indeed it constituted a democratic, reform-oriented anti-Nazi presence. But their influence seemed to wane after the autumn of 1945, after the Hollbach affair. OB Blaum remained in office in Frankfurt despite DISCC's efforts to dislodge him, and OB Klett continued to have the full support of MGO Jackson, even without that of the Stuttgarters or of acute intelligence agents like Fritz Eberhard.

The MGO detachments won out against the would-be reformers in DISCC and PWD and the activist anti-Nazi German groups because, among other reasons, they were more likely to give in to their or their predecessors' appointees, instead of constantly harping on denazification and personnel changes, which DISCC, PWD, and various intelligence organizations had been pressing them to do. More interested in a smoothly running administration, the detachments were more inclined to accept their German appointees' arguments about the value of experienced civil servants and the need to avoid politics. Their acceptance of German arguments of expertise and efficiency over political qualifications meshed well with the developing trend in general U.S. occupation policy of granting top priority to German economic reconstruction and a swift return to what was perceived as normalcy.

By mid-1946, the tone and analytical direction of U.S. intelligence reports had also changed, becoming more and more aligned with those of MG detachment reports. There were still some progressive

145. Lutz Niethammer, "Die amerikanische Besatzungsmacht zwischen Verwaltungstradition und politischen Parteien in Bayern 1945," *Vierteljahrshefte für Zeitgeschichte* (1967), H. 2, p. 196.

elements left in Information Control, but the OSS had been dissolved, and people like Eberhard Beckmann, Fritz Eberhard, and Cedric Belfrage no longer worked for OSS or DISCC. The rumblings of the Cold War helped purge leftist reformers from posts of influence within MG intelligence agencies. This further decreased the potential for structural reforms within Germany, so that grassroots reforms from the municipal level on up became almost an impossibility.

Kurt Schumacher campaigning for the SPD on the Königsplatz in Munich, 24 Nov. 1946.   *Courtesy of the Stadtarchiv Munich.*

Gardening on a rubble-strewn lot in downtown Frankfurt, Neue Kräme, summer 1946.

"Bus" transportation between the main and eastern train stations in Frankfurt,
Braubachstr., summer 1946.
Courtesy of the Institut für Stadtgeschichte, Frankfurt a.M.

Make-shift living
quarters in
bombed-out
building,
Frankfurt,
summer 1946.

Chapter V

GERMAN GRASSROOTS DEMOCRACY AND U.S. MG

Early Manifestations of Local Self-Government

Introduction

A 1944 U.S. *Civil Affairs Guide* for postwar Germany stipulated that the local level was to be "the starting point for political reform in Germany," because "city government had been the one point where there existed a strong tradition of self-government in Germany."[1] There were limits, however, to how much self-government the American occupying authorities actually welcomed and supported. The revival of local German self-government did not initially mean an introduction of popular democracy "except insofar as the persons who were appointed to office were (supposed to be) democratic."[2] According to the U.S. occupation authorities, the prerequisite for a revival of "democratic political life even on the lowest level" was the democratization of local government and the formation of democratic political parties.[3] Nevertheless, German democratic political revival was postponed until 27 August 1945, when political activity

---

1. *Civil Affairs Guide*, 22 July 1944, p. 2, R&A 1655.15, RG 59, NARA.
2. Gillen, *State and Local Government in West Germany, 1945–53*, Edited by the Historical Division of the Office of the U.S. High Commissioner for Germany, n.p., 1953, p. 5.
3. Ibid.

and the formation of political parties were permitted on the local level in the U.S. Zone of occupation. Prior to that time, when a ban on all political activity was in effect, U.S. MG's primary objective had been to revive public order and municipal administration. "Political activity was not the need of the moment," according to POLAD, but rather "the need was for a period of practical emergency organization and for political stock taking."[4]

Public order, a smoothly running bureaucracy, and an expedient material reconstruction took priority for most MG detachments over any goals of democratization, whether in the form of government accountability to the citizenry or genuine civic participation in government. This was true even after the ban on political activity had been lifted and basic material needs had been addressed. The ban had suppressed the potential for German grassroots democratic initiatives, such as the formation of new political parties or a rethinking of party politics to stress party discipline less and inner party democracy more. At this time, such initiatives would have had the strongest impact and could have provided the impetus for structural change. Some such initiatives were attempted, but for the most part they were discouraged or stifled by either the local MG or its German appointees. If grassroots reform initiatives were inhibited at the municipal level, where democracy and self-government were to be restored first, then there was even less chance for far reaching democratization on the Land, zonal, or later, national level. Once all the cogs of the bureaucratic wheel had been well greased and were functioning smoothly, this propitious moment for initiating the process of reconstructing local democracy in Germany was gone.[5]

Such local democratic initiatives might have influenced the higher echelons of administration and government as higher levels of German government were restored; they could have presented a model and a tradition at a time when no other form of German self-government existed. The discouragement of initiatives, such as attempts to nurture political persecutees by providing them with administrative and vocational training, surely had a negative impact on those striving to implement democratic change. As an OSS report on the Antifas in the Frankfurt area reported only a few weeks after they were banned: "Actual Antifa activity is declining, or at least changing its emphasis. Although members still present complaints to MG … and are still cooperating with CIC in running down Nazis, their

---

4. Perry Laukauf, Dispatch enclosure to the Sec. of State, 21 Nov. 1946, POLAD/ 746/ 9, 2 of 3, RG 84, IfZ.
5. Cf. Söllner, p. 193.

initial impetus is spent. MG states that they have 'caused little trouble in the past two weeks.'"[6]

The appraisal by POLAD of the May 1945 situation did not take into account that months had passed since most areas had been occupied. The December 1944 SHAEF directives that prohibited "political activity of any kind except as expressly permitted by the Supreme Commander" were not officially applied in the U.S. Zone until May 1945.[7] This meant that German political initiatives could have emerged legally, and in fact they did, in the interregnum between the liberation/occupation of an area and the official end of the war in Europe when the SHAEF ban was implemented. There were some Germans who initiated grassroots reforms from the earliest days of the occupation and others who tried to introduce new political options by forming new parties and/or challenging traditional party structures and hierarchical discipline. The Antifa committees, for example, took action by implementing denazification and restitution through the redistribution of housing on the basis of need and according to who had suffered political discrimination and/or persecution. They also assigned Germans the task of rubble removal on the basis of their Nazi political incrimination. These were policies which were almost identical to those some local MGs implemented in their own areas of command in the early postwar weeks. Yet because the American occupation authorities regarded this Antifa activity as "political," these grassroots democratic action committees were prohibited throughout the U.S. Zone in the spring and summer of 1945, except temporarily in Stuttgart.[8] An anti-Communism that fed on the fact that the Antifas were often led by Communists was, however, often more directly behind the enforcement of the prohibition. This becomes clear in the POLAD description of the Antifa committees as "pseudo-political organizations" that were "often Communist inspired and Communist-used."[9]

6. 18 June 1945 report, p. 4 , OSS, XL-11911, RG 226, NARA .
7. Perry Laukhuff, Dispatch enclosure to the Secretary of State, 21 Nov. 1946, POLAD/ 746/ 9, 2 of 3, RG 84, IfZ. Even then, members of the old Weimar parties were unofficially permitted to begin organizing and meeting to refound or to consolidate forces, as in the case of what came to be called the CDU or CSU in several towns and cities, such as Marburg, Kulmbach, Nuremberg, Würzburg, and Munich. See Schott, p. 46f, notes 267 and 276.
8. See Chapter 3. These Antifa activities involved material concerns, but they were not separated from the larger political framework of the collapse of the fascist regime and the promise of a new democratic social order.
9. Perry Laukhuff, dispatch enclosure to the secretary of state, 21 Nov. 1946 POLAD/ 746/ 9, 2 of 3, RG 84, IfZ. See also Ch. 3.

Another example of German grassroots reform initiatives occurred when certain Germans who were not included in the municipal administration placed pressure on the appointed OBs to form advisory city councils. These "outsiders" were seeking some level of reform-oriented input into municipal decision making in those crucial first months of the occupation. The U.S. MG gave permission to its appointed OBs to form citizens' councils with exclusively advisory functions. Such advisory councils were formed a few months after the OBs' appointments to their posts. This occurred, however, before the 27 August 1945 lifting of the ban on political activity and authorization for the formation of political parties on the local level.[10] Since these were advisory committees, not formally composed of political factions (since, technically speaking, no political parties existed yet), MG did not consider these a violation of the ban on political activity. Technically the members fell under the category of administrators rather than politicians as far as MG was concerned. These councils were not formed at the OBs' or MG's initiative,[11] but rather at that of Germans, who, at least until that point, had been excluded from positions of municipal influence. On the other hand, these advisory councils were eventually supported by MG and the OBs as a way of competing with, or co-opting, the activist, and, from their perspective, overly autonomous, role of the Antifa committees.

The acting OB usually recruited advisory councilors from the major pre-1933 political parties other than the NSDAP or DNVP, which had been represented in the last elected Weimar Republic city councils. In fact, they generally asked former leading members from those parties to suggest party lists, from which the OBs then chose advisory council members.[12] Thus, ironically, the apolitical appointees of the apolitical Americans relied on the officially nonexistent political parties to form the supposedly apolitical advisory

10. Gillen, p. 6.
11. One possible exception to this occurred in mid-August, two weeks before the ban on political activity was lifted in the U.S. Zone, when the MG-appointed Regierungspräsident (president of the Regierungsbezirk [RB]) of Mainfranken in conjunction with MG for the RB, instructed all mayors and Landräte to form advisory councils of party representatives from the non-Nazi 1933 parties according to their strength at that time, and of representatives of business, cultural life, and the church. In this case, it is unclear whether the Regierungspräsident or the Mainfranken MG took the initiative or whether pressure came from below, from Germans. See Schott, p. 37.
12. This was the case in all three cities under examination here. See BuR 1537, StA Mü; Hauptaktei 0621, StA St; and Mag 1060/1, Bd. 1, StA Ffm. It was also apparently the case in Würzburg. See Schott, p. 37f.

councils. This not only had implications for the refounding of the political parties, but also for the potential success of any grassroots groundswell, which was virtually squelched by this pattern of restoration of parties from above, even on the local level. Germans who were too young to have had political party affiliations prior to 1933 or who had simply not found their political niche prior to the Third Reich were excluded from this top-down party development as well. This does not mean that there were no democratic initiatives from within the major parties that were eventually licensed, but rather that there were limits as to how much influence new members could have within the party and that there was less likelihood for change within the parties, when Weimar elites reestablished them.

A final example of democratic anti-Nazi initiatives and the problems encountered in the attempt to implement changes can be seen in the structure of some of the initial boards of licensees for the first newspapers and also in the original content of those newspapers. The ICD and its subordinate agency, DISCC, sought out unincriminated proven anti-Nazis as licensees for the first postwar German newspapers. This would facilitate free expression and open up access to national and international news, as well as provide a forum for discussion of the directions that this new postwar Germany might take. Rather than turning to the prominent journalists of the Weimar period, many of whom were either in exile or had incriminated themselves politically with their continued work during the Third Reich under the aegis of the *Reichskulturkammer*, ICD and DISCC, with their often leftist stance, generally selected younger, less experienced, but active anti-Nazis as licensees in the first months after the war. These early newspaper licensees were frequently from the Left with allegiances to either the KPD, SPD, or left wings of the Center or Democratic Parties.[13] The first German newspaper selected to be licensed in the U.S. Zone of occupation was the *Frankfurter Rundschau,* and the selection of its licensees was based mainly on their anti-Nazi credentials. An attempt was also made to include individuals of diverse political backgrounds – at least from the political middle to the left – so that the new newspapers would provide a forum for multiparty cooperation.[14]

13. Cf. Frei, p. 19f. Frei notes a significant degree of personnel continuity on the middle and low level of the editorial hierarchy, as opposed to the actual licensees, to whom I am referring here. Of the initial new licensees in these three cities, most had been politically active during the Weimar Republic, but mostly as quite young men, too young to have climbed the ladder of any party hierarchy very far.

14. DISCC report by Cedric Belfrage, 28 May 1945, OMGH 17/16-3/11, 1 of 2.

Whether intentionally or not, this attempt to include different political allegiances also gave an advantage to the old traditional parties of the Weimar Republic, which sometimes, after the parties' formal reestablishment following the end of the ban on political activity, exerted party control and even censorship on their licensee members. This party discipline and censorship was exercised especially when certain members cooperated too closely with the licensees of other political affiliations. This inclusive policy also brought ICD or DISCC into conflict with more conservative and allegedly apolitical agencies within MG, ultimately resulting in a political purge of licensees and ICD and DISCC personnel, because of leftist and/or too ardent anti-Nazi sentiments.

By September 1946, when Secretary of State James Byrnes in Stuttgart announced the U.S. policy of expediting material reconstruction and the implicit goal of rebuilding Germany along capitalist lines, anti-Communism and, to a certain degree, antisocialism had taken priority over anti-Nazism in MG policy toward the Germans. Since the most ardent anti-Nazis were often leftists, they – Germans and Americans alike – were no longer in step with MG policy. Thereafter, more and more traditional German journalists returned to leading positions in the press, and more conservative ICD officials replaced the more leftist ones, thus creating more personnel continuity in journalism with the Third Reich and the Weimar Republic, and curtailing a grassroots democratic experiment in the press.

This chapter will explore these various manifestations of grassroots reform-oriented input into local-level government during the first year of the occupation prior to the first municipal elections and the formal restoration of democratic municipal self-government. Not only will the German Antifa committees, the advisory city councils, and the political parties be examined, but also the limits imposed upon these various groups by U.S. MG as well as by the newly appointed German city administrations. This will reveal the limits imposed upon grassroots initiatives during the first phase of the occupation, the very time when they would have had the most impact because old structures were not yet back in place and there was still a window of opportunity for change. Whereas the primary German actors appointed by MG in postwar Frankfurt, Munich, and Stuttgart were addressed in the preceeding chapters, this chapter will focus more on those individuals who attempted to institute reforms from below as self-government was restored gradually to their cities. It will consider the difference the support by MG or its

German appointees of such attempts might have made for the political development in those cities, for the overall development of the U.S. Zone, and ultimately, for the Federal Republic of Germany.

Antifa Committees

In the final days of the war and in the period immediately following the cessation of hostilities, spontaneous anti-Fascist activist groups sprang up in most major cities of Germany.[15] There was no communication or organized connection between these so-called Antifa committees. In fact, often in the midst of the postwar destruction and the disruption of normal lines of communication, neighborhood or district committees were unaware of the existence of a committee only a few kilometers away.[16] The historian Leonard Krieger has described this Antifa phenomenon as:

> ostensibly formed on the united-front principle that would not so much unite as transcend all former political divisions in the fight against the survivals [sic] of Nazism, but they were actually run by communists, a communist-social democratic coalition, or socialists open to cooperation with communists. They were ostensibly non-political, devoted to the urgent practical issues of the purge and reconstruction as necessary public preconditions of politics, but actually they interpreted both of these putatively technical aims institutionally to include far-reaching measures of socialization and democratization. They were ostensibly informal associations, but they actually operated as municipal governments where they could seize control and as a kind of pressuring citizens' council where they could not. The antifa movement did not survive long under the occupation. All the occupying powers – Soviet Russia included – preferred more regular and traditional forms of political, and non-political, organization, and the antifas quickly ran into the sands of history, whence nary a trace of them is to be found. Unlike the rest of Europe, moreover, where the resistance organizations suffered an analogous literal fate in favor of a more orthodox dispensation, in Germany they have not even survived as a political symbol. And yet their meaning for immediate postwar Germany remains a tantalizing question. Omitting the issue of communist inspiration or participation for our diagnostic purpose as an instance of the genetic fallacy, we must avow the antifas to have been novel, reconstructive, and democratic in their pro-

15.   Lutz Niethammer, et al, *Arbeiterinitiative 1945: Antifaschistische Ausschüsse und Reorganisation der Arbeiterbewegung in Deutschland* (Wuppertal, 1976), p. 12. See also Starr, *Denazification*, p. 127.
16.   "Action Groups in Post-Collapse Germany," May 1945 OSS report, p. 1, Enclosure to 29 May 1945 Political Advisor Report to the U.S. Sec. of State, POLAD TS/ 32/28, 1 of 1, RG 84, IfZ.

grams, and both activist and politically committed (despite their protestations) in reality; we must avow them too to have gotten the jump, when they appeared, on the elite groups and to have been disbanded finally by occupying rather than German powers. But we must also avow them to have been small in membership (aside from the reportedly impressive cases of Leipzig and Bremen) and, for their influence, more dependent upon an anticipated collaboration with the occupying authorities than upon any clear evidence of support from a German population whose own organizations were in temporary eclipse. The antifas clearly could no more have become long-range democratic institutions than such supraparty councils or soviets ever have been able to, but whether they could have triggered new departures in German politics must remain an open question.[17]

Krieger's descriptive analysis provides a basis upon which to examine the composition, purpose, goals, and significance of the Antifa committees and similar organizations in Munich, Frankfurt, and Stuttgart. First, if we examine the question of a united front, it is true that the Antifas in Munich, Frankfurt, and Stuttgart were able to transcend political divisions, at least until the officially sanctioned revival of the political parties. Even then, there existed SPD – KPD working committees or fronts to continue this transcendence of traditional political party divisions and animosities. Indeed Antifa committees were often run by Communists, because the lines of continuity among Communists that were maintained during the period of illegality during the Third Reich allowed for quick reemergence and organization. To a lesser extent, this was also true of Social Democrats and members of socialist splinter groups like the Socialist Labor Party (SAP), who were also well represented among the Antifa leadership.[18] Often there was a coalition group consisting of a Social Democrat, a Communist, and a Center or Democratic Party member that led an Antifa group, like the one in Höchst on the outskirts of Frankfurt.[19] In Stuttgart the core group was made up of former KPD members and an equally large portion of members without any previous political affiliation.[20] Antifas strove to achieve political parity and a united front of all anti-Fascists regardless of previous political, religious, and union affiliations in order to denaz-

17. Leonard Krieger, "The Potential for Democratization in Occupied Germany: A Problem in Historical Projection," *Public Policy*, Vol. XVII, 1968, p. 49f.
18. Action Groups in Post-Collapse Germany," May 1945 OSS report, p. 2, Enclosure to 29 May 1945 Political Advisor Report to the U.S. Sec. of State, POLAD TS/ 32/28, 1 of 1, RG 84, IfZ.
19. "Erinnerungen aus 1945," S1/30, Peter Fischer Nachlass, StA Ffm.
20. Lutz Niethammer, "Kampfkomitees und Arbeitsausschüsse in Stuttgart, "in Niethammer, et al, *Arbeiterinitiative 1945* (Wuppertal, 1976), p. 582.

ify, democratize, and create a lasting peace along with German reconstruction.[21] Because this goal of recruitment was rarely met, the groups were vulnerable to charges of being "Communist inspired and Communist-used."[22]

When the Antifas stressed the practical aspects of their activities for the reconstruction of everyday life, it may well have been a way of circumventing the ban on political activities. Their denazification work included: compiling lists of former Nazis and attesting to their level of complicity or responsibility for work details, arrests, or dismissals from employment;[23] tracking down Nazis who were trying to cover up their identities; allocating furniture and residences to Germans based on their level of resistance to or complicity with the regime;[24] searching through lists of potential voters to determine who was to be temporarily excluded based on their Nazi past;[25] training members in democratic administration for prospective civil service positions;[26] proposing Antifa personnel to serve on municipal committees; and putting pressure on the appointed local governments to create advisory councils so as to allow democratic input into municipal decision making.[27] They also helped organize the more prosaic activities of woodchopping and delivery, rubble removal, and housing appropriations.

All these Antifa activities had political implications. Denazification was a very political process with the political goal of purging Nazis from political and socio-economic life and restricting their activities according to their level of complicity until – if ever – they

21. Ibid. See also "Resolution zur Lage und die Aufgaben der antifaschistischen Arbeiter, Bauern, Bürger," S1/30, Peter Fischer Nachlass, StA Ffm and Starr, p. 127. This excluded Nazi or right-wing party affiliations such as the DNVP.

22. Perry Laukhuff, Dispatch enclosure to the Secretary of State, 21 Nov. 1946, POLAD/ 746/ 9, 2 of 3, RG 84, IfZ. See also Ch. 3.

23. Zentralstelle der Arbeitsausschüsse Gross-Stuttgart an die württembergische Regierung, 12 January 1946; Kampfkomitee Ortsgruppe Botnang an OB Klett, 2 May 1945, Hauptaktei 0052-2, StA St. For Frankfurt, see S1/30, Peter Fischer Nachlass, StA Ffm, and "Anti-Fascist Organizations and Tendencies in the Frankfurt Area," 18 June 1945, OSS report, XL 11911. RG 226, NARA. For Munich, see OB Scharnagl an den Münchner Antifaschistischen Wirtschaftsausschuss, BuR 1647, StA Mü.

24. Chef der Stuttgarter Polizei an OB Klett, 21 June 1945, Hauptaktei 0051-1. StA St.

25. OB Scharnagl Bekanntmachung, 30 July 1945, BuR 1778, StA Mü.

26. OB an Zentralstelle der Arbeitsausschüsse-Stuttgart, 20 Okt. 1945, Hauptaktei 0434-1, StA St.

27. OB Klett an Dr. Könekamp, Finanzgerichtspräsident Wetter und Ministerialrat Klein, 16 July 1945, Hauptaktei 0434-1, StA St.

became reeducated and rehabilitated. The Antifa training aimed to create a new elite to fill the void left by denazification. The training also was political and represented the positive side of the purge policy toward Germans, which elsewhere was so sorely lacking. Unfortunately, this training was not encouraged by MG, and when it was initiated by the Antifas themselves, it never received the full support of the German municipal administration and was eventually stopped, ostensibly because the revival of *Volkshochschulen* made it redundant.[28] Even the more mundane tasks of collecting wood, removing rubble, and appropriating and assigning housing had very political overtones, particularly in the early phase of the occupation, because the Antifas called on *Parteigenossen* (Pgs) to help with these tasks and to give up or share their housing with those persecuted by the Nazi regime. This was a kind of restitution or *Lastenausgleich* of a political nature long before the economic equalization of burdens of the early Adenauer era emerged. Thus their intentions in these actions were clearly political and indeed should be seen within the framework of "far-reaching measures of socialization and democratization." The Antifas' political commitment was to an anti-Fascist, democratic, and for some, a socialized Germany, and their activism reflected their genuine desire to accomplish these goals.[29]

In terms of the formality of their structure, in all three cities Antifas were created both spontaneously and informally. In none of the three cities did they actually operate as municipal governments, although they did occasionally function as district administrations in outlying areas such as Höchst, on the outskirts of Frankfurt, Alte Haide in Munich, Gaisburg, Zuffenhausen, or Unter- and Obertürkheim in Stuttgart.[30] There are no signs that the Antifas in Munich, Frankfurt, or Stuttgart were interested in taking over the entire city administration or functioning as soviets or *Räte* per the 1917 Russian or 1918 German models. They wanted rather to have a major impact upon city developments through their neighborhood and district grassroots organizations. They did exert pressure on

---

28. See " Aufruf der Zentrale der Arbeitsauschüsse-Gross-Stuttgart an alle Mitarbeiter," 18 Sept. 1945, Hauptaktei 0434-1, StA St.

29. This call for socialization was a red herring for many Americans, although German political sentiment in the immediate postwar period reflected serious consideration of some level of socialization from the CDU to the KPD.

30. See Niethammer, "Kampfkomitees," p. 504ff. and 14 June 1947 Brief an die Aussenstelle München-Stadt des Bayerischen Landesamtes für Vermögensverwaltung. MSo (Sonderministerium) 6-421, Bayerisches Hauptstaatsarchiv.

the city governments to implement denazification[31] and to establish either advisory city councils, district councils, or Antifa advisory committees to help each municipal department. The mayors of the major cities in Württemberg actually saw the formation of advisory city councils as serving the purpose of replacing the Antifa committees and, for this explicit reason, encouraged their formation.[32] In Stuttgart the Antifas suggested to OB Klett that he appoint not only a thirty-two-member advisory council, but also a larger group of Antifa representatives who would participate in the various departments of the municipal administration. The Antifas also asked to send a rotating member to attend the city council meetings so that each area of expertise and "each direction in a democratic respect" would have their perspective represented.[33] This Antifa representation was never granted, and the advisory city council, whose formation had originated from an Antifa proposal for more democratic input into the municipal administration, was actually used to pull the rug out from underneath the democratic initiatives and the reform potential of the Antifas. They were then hired as temporary municipal workers and, as such, coopted into the broader, more traditional top-down structure of the municipal government. In most places Antifas were denied all access to municipal administration. After their dissolution, their function as a democratic influence on municipal decision making was replaced with allegedly representative advisory councils in which the Antifas were rarely granted representation and to which the pre-1933 non-Nazi political parties sent the majority of representatives, comprised of men and a handful of women recommended by the old party elites.

In Munich there are no records of such Antifas in the city or Bavarian state archives prior to the Antifa-Wirtschaftsausschüsse in December 1945[34] and the Aktionsausschüsse of 1946.[35] However,

---

31. In the first municipal elections of 1946, Nazi Party members were excluded from active and passive rights of citizenship.
32. Protokolle der Sitzung der Landesverwaltung des Innern mit den Oberbürgermeistern der grösseren Württembergischen Städten, 31 July 1945, Hauptaktei 0434-1, StA St.
33. Gemeindebeiratssitzungsprotokolle, 12 Oct. 1945, p. 195. StA St. From what we know of Antifa groups, they seem to have functioned quite democratically, with their leadership and decisions based on elections. See Hauptaktei 0434-1, StA St.
34. OB Scharnagl an den Antifaschistischen Wirtschaftsausschuss, 15 Dec. 1945, BuR, 1647, StA Mü.
35. Aktionsausschuss München-Süd an den Oberbürgermeister, 3 April 1947. BuR 1647, StA Mü. This action committee mentions in this letter that it began its activities (specifically, rubble removal) on 3 August 1946.

the social historian Lutz Niethammer notes that there was a prohibition of Antifas in Munich as of 16 May 1945,[36] indicating that indeed they must have existed there at that early date. Munich represents an interesting case because, while other major cities were experiencing the phenomenon of predominantly leftist Antifa committees, the more conservative, even monarchist-tinged FAB dominated the scene there, and played some of the same early roles as the Antifas in other cities, at least in their means, as anti-Nazi grassroots organizations, although with differing goals.[37]

A May 1945 OSS report divided "action groups in post-collapse Germany" into the left-wing local Antifas and the "conservative forces which had more or less unwillingly allied themselves with Nazism, and which were therefore allowed to maintain contacts and an interchange of ideas" and thus were now able "to exercise some sort of organized influence on the course of events." Although "these rightist groupings range[d] all the way from the military clique around Doenitz which managed to make itself the accepted surrender government to local Chambers of Commerce," the FAB was considered, by the author of this OSS report, to be "the most spectacular example of conservative anti-Nazi initiative."[38] The activities, goals, and treatment of the FAB by the local MG have been described in Chapter 3 and thus will not be repeated here. What should be emphasized however is that, whereas the Antifas represented an impetus for a major break, not just with the Nazi past, but with the Weimar and Wilhelminian past as well, the FAB and other conservative forces focused on "the preservation of some sort of continuity in German social and economic life and the avoidance of violent changes."[39] Such forces included the Business Owners' Organization in Stuttgart, the Vorläufige Württembergische Wirtschaftsrat, which stood in direct opposition to the Antifas and was eventually dis-

---

36. Lutz Niethammer, *Entnazifizierung in Bayern* (Frankfurt, 1972), p. 135. See also Lutz Niethammer and Ulrich Schröder, "Die regionalen Befreiungsbewegungen in Südbayern und Österreich," in Niethammer, et al, *Arbeiterinitiative 1945*, p. 637. Unless Niethammer is referring to Antifa groups in the greater metropolitan Munich area, which did exist, it is not clear from his sources exactly who these "Munich" Antifas were and whence they originated.
37. Cf. Chapter 3.
38. "Action Groups in Post-Collapse Germany," May 1945 OSS report, p. 3ff, Enclosure to 29 May 1945 Political Advisor Report to the U.S. Sec. of State, POLAD TS/ 32/28, 1 of 1, RG 84, IfZ.
39. "Action Groups in Post-Collapse Germany," May 1945 OSS report, p. 4, Enclosure to 29 May 1945 Political Advisor Report to the U.S. Sec. of State, POLAD TS/ 32/28, 1 of 1, RG 84, IfZ.

solved by U.S. MG because it rivalled the Chamber of Commerce.[40] While the new, autonomous organizations, whether more on the Right or on the Left, were ultimately banned by U.S. MG, the more traditional structures received both the approval and encouragement of the local MG and the German municipal administration. These included the Chambers of Commerce and Industry and professional organizations of industrialists and business people with less overtly political goals, which "were quickly revived to look out for the interests of the business community."[41]

The same May 1945 OSS report did not acknowledge the political implications of encouraging such traditional conservative forces interested in restoring the status quo ante while discouraging the forces of change, i.e., the prohibition of the Antifas. "With the Nazis gone, these elements (leaders of the business community) occupy the most important positions in German society; they want to remain in these positions and to use their influence to bring Germany back to something like normal as quickly as possible."[42] Naively, the report concluded that whatever the political complexions of the activists, be they conservatives or leftists, their activities and programs were:

> not political in the traditional sense of the term. Defeat, destruction and total occupation have relegated normal political issues to the status of academic questions in Germany; denazification and the day-to-day problems of maintaining a bare existence have taken their place as the foci of public life. It is with these basic issues that the active forces among the German population are attempting to deal. The Left puts the emphasis on rooting out all traces of Nazism as the prerequisite to a new start; the Right concentrates on attempting to conserve whatever is potentially valuable from the shambles left by the Hitler regime. Such opposition as exists between the two tendencies is not a reflection of a normal political struggle for power. Rather it grows out of differing approaches to the problem of reconstituting the very bases of organized existence.[43]

40. Bericht der 4. Sitzung des Hauptausschusses des Vorläufigen Württembergischen Wirtschaftsrates, 23 May 1945, p. 5, "Vorläufige Württembergische Wirtschaftsrat,"(VWW), Wirtschaftsarchiv Baden-Württemberg. For VWW denunciations of the Antifas, see Otto Debatin, *Der Vorläufige Württembergische Wirtschaftsrat des Jahres 1945: Eine Chronik* (Stuttgart, 1955), especially p. 12. Cf. Hauptaktei 700/14, StA St.
41. "Action Groups in Post-Collapse Germany," May 1945 OSS report, p. 4, Enclosure to 29 May 1945 Political Advisor Report to the U.S. Sec. of State, POLAD TS/ 32/28, 1 of 1, RG 84, IfZ. Although the term *Industrie- und Handelskammer* or "Chamber of Industry and Trade" was new, these structures, with some leadership purges, were the same as the old Wirtschaftskammer, and even earlier, the Handelskammer.
42. Ibid.
43. Ibid.

What the author of this report missed went beyond the differing approaches to the essentially different concepts of a political and social order, what he called "organized existence." If, on the one hand, the conservatives wanted to restore a Wilhelminian Germany, or even a quasi Third Reich without war or Hitler and Nazi terror, the leftists, on the other hand, wanted a real break with the past, which even the Weimar Republic had not represented, in order to democratize and socialize "the very bases of organized existence." This was not "a normal political struggle for power," because this was not a normal time in terms of traditional party politics; if not a Stunde Null, it was at least an interregnum. The primary enemy of both groups, the Nazis, had been defeated. This did not, however, mean that they now shared common goals. The rivalry between continuity and change, as reflected in their support or lack of support of a thorough denazification via the reallocation of housing and goods or in the training of new elites, had considerable significance for Germany's future social, economic, and political structure.

To be sure, the Germans were not acting autonomously or in a void, but rather within the context of an unconditional surrender and quadripartite military occupation. Whichever group or tendency the occupying power(s) supported gained the advantage, if not the exclusive opportunity, to implement its program. Once the democratic process was restored, this could theoretically be altered by popular ballot.[44] The democratic process was restored on the municipal level three years before the founding of the Federal Republic and nine years before the occupation formally ended in the Western Zones. The occupying authorities, in this case those of the United States, were able to continue exercising their influence on and their support of those Germans whose postwar vision corresponded most closely with theirs and thus influence elections. This influence was most direct from 1945 until 1949, but it continued in less overt ways until at least 1955.[45] Belonging to an organization like the appointed

44. Even though one of the reasons for licensing the parties on the local level first was to provide for grassroots developments, on the local level the top-down organization allowed little say to the rank-and-file or new members, who had almost no opportunity to receive enough party support themselves to run for election. Voters could only choose among those candidates whom the parties placed on their election lists, and in 1946, voters could only choose among those parties licensed by MG.

45. The American military presence continued or replaced one of the other Allies beyond the occupation in various cities and towns in the 1950s with NATO bases. The U.S. military's contributions to the local economy as well as the impact upon the local culture were part of this influence. See the recent

municipal administration, which was formed by MG, or the advisory city council, usually gave the MG-appointed administrators and MG-approved councilors an advantage in the 1946 and later elections.

The Marshall Plan and the Western Allies' currency reform gave clear signals to West Germans as to whose side one should be on to achieve the most rapid material reconstruction and a return to normalcy. Most people support approaches that provide material gains, without considering their possible short-term nature or any long-term negative implications of such material improvement. Understandably, in light of widespread shortages, most Germans, including former Nazi Party members, were more concerned with their material situations, in terms of having a warm, safe place to live, enough food to eat, and steady employment, than with sacrificing expediency in these material aims in order to guarantee or facilitate a long-term structural democratization.[46] Those who had risked their lives in the committed acts of anti-Nazi resistance during the war or who exhibited civil courage and personal self-sacrifice in the early post-war period,[47] and who had less to lose materially and more to gain in terms of fulfilling their twin ideals of denazification and democratization, were clearly in a minority. The continuation in power of most appointed officials and their lower-level bureaucrats together with the high priority given by MG to restoring order and reviving the economy meant the victory of continuity over change.[48] The potential for democratic structural change represented by some of the Antifas' activities scarcely survived after their formal prohibition in the early summer of 1945, and virtually expired after the reinstitution of democratic elections in the spring of 1946. If they had been tolerated longer and actually worked together with by MG and MG's

---

dissertation by Maria Höhn, "GIs, Veronikas, and Lucky Strikes: German reactions to the American Military Presence in the Rhineland-Palatinate during the 1950s," Ph.D. dissertation, University of Pennsylvania, 1995, and the essays in Reiner Pommerin, ed., *The American Impact on Postwar Germany* (Providence and Oxford, 1995).

46. Cf. Kocka, "1945," p. 145 ff.

47. Antifas, who volunteered their work and received no special ration allotments, and MG-appointed officials risked attacks from die-hard Nazis and the threat of Werwolves in the initial post-hostilities phase. Even the appointed, and later the elected, city councilors sacrificed income and time to sit in unheated, sometimes unsafe, rooms to try to help run their cities.

48. Kocka, p. 153 ff. Kocka, with whom this author wholeheartedly agrees, argues that bureaucratic continuity in the German postwar period was just as important as the capitalist economic continuity in terms of limiting change in twentieth-century (West) German history.

appointed German officials, they may well have had an opportunity to cull active public support for their denazification and personnel training plans and their model of civic activism.[49]

As Krieger stated, the Antifas, like all other German groups seeking influence in the immediate postwar period, were "more dependent upon an anticipated collaboration with the occupying authorities than upon any clear evidence of support from a German population whose own organizations were in temporary eclipse."[50] In fact, they were dependent upon both the occupying authority and the occupiers' German administrative appointees.

In Frankfurt, MGO Criswell, as early as 27 April 1945, banned the Antifa committees[51] after they had organized the removal of rubble and garbage (having "recruited" former Nazis who had not fallen into the mandatory arrest categories for this task), distributed intact residences to the bombed-out homeless to the fairest extent possible, and tried to uncover possible construction and repair materials.[52] In mid-April Social Democratic Police President, Ferdinand Mührdel, informed the OB that the U.S. MG welcomed the Antifas' initiatives as long as they supported and did not compete with the police. But according to Mührdel, the police wanted the Antifas disbanded and only tolerated them because of the expressed wish of the MG.[53] Although it was MGO Criswell who imposed the ban shortly thereafter, he clearly did so with the agreement, if not at the initiative, of acting OB Hollbach and apparently with the approval of his police president.

The Frankfurt Antifas themselves were probably unaware of the role of the appointed German administrators in their dissolution. Of course, MG could and would have overridden its appointees, had it wanted to do so. The Frankfurt Antifas expressed their disappointment over not being recognized "as legitimate representatives of German anti-fascism," and over the ban against "contact with MG," which was apparently imposed upon them. According to a mid-June 1945 OSS report on anti-Fascist organizations and tendencies in the Frankfurt area, the Antifas felt "that not even traditional American

49. This nonpartisan, or actually multipartisan, grassroots model was much more democratically based than traditionally centralized political parties, with rigid hierarchies and party discipline.
50. L. Krieger, p. 50.
51. S5/158, Chronik Hey, p. 20, StA Ffm. See also Emil Carlebach, "Frankfurts Antifaschisten 1945," in *Als der Krieg zu Ende War: Hessen 1945,* ed. Ulrich Schneider et al. (Frankfurt, 1980), p. 18.
52. Carlebach, "Frankfurts Antifaschisten," p. 12.
53. "Amtsleiterbesprechungen 1945," 12 April 1945, p. 2, StA Ffm.

suspicion of radicals and inexperience in the role of military governors [could] explain away the consistent rejection of aid from anti-fascists and the retention in office of known Nazis and Nazi sympathizers. They claim that this frustrated disappointment is shared by the population at large, and that covert Nazi anti-American propaganda is gradually finding fertile soil among people who a few weeks ago 'wept with joy at the sight of the first American tank."[54]

Responding ten days afterwards to this report, the POLAD chief warned the secretary of state about growing anti-American and anti-MG sentiment. But instead of reversing the ban on the Antifas, Murphy's office recommended "some informal use of local non-political groups" or "individual members of such groups as are democratic and represent more than extremist minorities ... as a modification for the first time of the absolute ban on political activity."[55] Ultimately this resulted in the authorization of advisory city councils rather than a recognition or even toleration of the Antifas. The Antifas, however, did not entirely disappear in Frankfurt. As late as 24 September 1946, the chief of political activities of the Hessian Land-MG approvingly noted their continued activity and questioned why the Frankfurt detachment had judged them "detrimental to good government." In the meantime, these Antifa committees included members of several legalized parties; the report commented that "such citizen groups are a normal adjunct of good government in the United States. There is no reason why a different criterion is to be applied to the City of Frankfurt." One such organization in which the Antifas had a major presence and which therefore the local detachment wanted to ban was the local workers' welfare organization, theArbeiterwohlfahrt. In defense of it, this Land-MG report pointed out that "by its very nature it includes members of the wage earning groups and it is only logical that it be dominated by workers' political parties such as the SPD and the KPD."[56] Although there is no sign that the local detachment reversed its policies toward antifascist groups, regardless of what form they might have taken after their dissolution, it is important to note that not all segments of or factions within MG were uniformly against the Antifas.

Robert Murphy wrote the secretary of state on 20 July 1945 that "since the inception of MG in our zone, one of the difficult problems

54. OSS, XL-11911, 18 June 1945, p. 4f, RG 226, NARA.
55. Robert Murphy Airgram to Sec. of State, 28 June 1945, p. 2f, POLAD/730/1, 1 of 1, RG 84, IfZ.
56. OMGH, 8/193-2/3, 2 of 4, RG 260, IfZ. This particular Political Activities chief's views on the Antifas hardly exemplifies MG comments about them.

with which local detachments have dealt has been the activities of antifascist movements."[57] Yet at the same time that Murphy was complaining about the Antifas, his POLAD office forwarded on to Washington a USGCC Joint Intelligence Committee report which recommended that such movements "be authorized and used by MG, subject to the surveillance of MG at all times."[58] Even after the ban on political activity, anti-Fascist groups in Stuttgart and Munich were "used" by the local city administrations to perform primarily manual tasks in Stuttgart and denazification tasks in Munich.

While Stuttgart was still under French occupation, OB Klett decided to use the French MG's ban on political activity to disband the Antifa committees. This was clearly due to the initiative of Klett himself, who pressured Police President Weber into ordering the committees to disband on 25 May 1945.[59] Yet at the same time that Weber ordered their dissolution, he encouraged the individual members, apparently with Klett's permission, to regroup into small circles which would continue to cooperate in performing city tasks.[60] In reality, this regrouping constituted a total transformation of the Antifas in Stuttgart. They became paid "volunteers", and as such came under the direct jurisdiction of the municipal administration, which assigned them their tasks and paid those who were working regularly. This transformation served two purposes for OB Klett: Because the Antifas still retained their committee structure, he was now immune to their pressure to integrate them into his formal administration. At the same time, indirectly he was able to control their influence and activities, eventually bringing about their depoliticization and the subversion of their antifascist goals of structural social reform. This was accomplished by restricting their activities to manual tasks, which fell under the jurisdiction of the municipal administration, and by removing them from the public limelight and thus from positions of potential power locally.

In Munich even the Aktionsausschüsse, a less politicized form of the Antifas, were transformed and brought under the direct control

57. POLAD/ 730/1, 1 of 1, RG 84, IfZ.
58. Ibid. There may have been political differences of opinion between Murphy's POLAD office and USGCC in the early phase of the occupation, but Murphy's position on the Antifas seemed to win out. Murphy, in his memoirs, described the USGCC as "a haphazard organization ..., which had been laboring for months under the impression that it was going to govern the American Zone." He mentioned how it had prepared a guide for MG that " not only tolerated but encouraged friendly relations between American soldiers and German civilians." See Robert Murphy, *Diplomat Among Warriors* (New York, 1964), p. 249 f.
59. Hauptaktei 0434-1, StA St.
60. Hauptaktei 0051-1, StA St.

of the city government. In September 1947, when they still existed in over twenty districts, the elected city council voted to abolish them altogether and to try to incorporate them as much as possible within the district committees (Bezirksausschüsse) that were being formed.[61] Yet in early 1946, when a district committee had already been formed primarily from former Antifa members, district police, using the argument of the population's unease over the existence and activities of a grassroots district committee, appealed to OB Scharnagl to suppress this group. Scharnagl responded that such committees could not be permitted to exist both because the MG had not yet vetted the members of such committees and because committees, in particular district committees, were not allowed to form themselves, but rather should be formed through nomination by the three political parties (BVP/CSU, SPD, KPD), the Churches and the district police.[62] This provides a clear-cut example of the OB's rejection of grassroots democracy and his preference for structures formed by the traditional party leadership from the top down.[63] Ironically, the excuse of an "uneasy" popular opinion was used to squelch one of the remnants of the Antifas' grassroots activities. Like Klett's use of French MG's ban on political activity to dissolve the Stuttgart Kampfkomitees, Scharnagl took advantage of U.S. MG regulations to implement his own policy of restricting the Antifas in Munich. In other words, the banning of the Antifas was not just, as Krieger maintains, an MG policy, but rather one in which the MG-appointed administrations had an equal, if not greater, interest.

In Stuttgart the Arbeitsausschüsse, which were paid by the city and had formerly been the Kampfkomitees, also received little gratitude or support from the city administration. The Stuttgart Arbeitsausschüsse focused their activities on acquiring and distributing wood for heating purposes, constructing and repairing residential areas, setting up rent committees to negotiate between landlords/ladies and renters, registering POWs and, as they themselves described it, encouraging and cultivating democratic principles. Throughout their existence, they

---

61. Stadtrat-Vollversammlungsbeschluss, 30 Sept. 1947, BuR 1647, StA Mü.
62. BuR 1647, StA Mü. This "representative" model corresponds closely to the political guidelines used for the top-down formation of advisory municipal councils in 1945.
63. As will be shown in the next section, most parties which were formed first were formed from the top down. This limited the extent to which most political parties embodied or practiced grassroots democracy. In this early period, any new party, if it could get licensed in the first place, was excluded from the advisory city council and had few channnels through which it could exert influence.

were confronted with critiques that they had outlasted their purpose and with attempts by municipal officials and political parties to get rid of them altogether.[64] When the Central Committee of the Arbeitsausschüsse invited representatives from the KPD, SPD, and DVP to try to organize cooperation in late 1945, the SPD and DVP rejected any cooperation and implicitly accused the Arbeitsausschüsse of trying to influence and lead the parties. Relaying their sense of feeling threatened by this supraparty grassroots structure, they let the Central Committee know they considered the Arbeitsausschüsse a temporary structure that would have to disappear once democratic organs, like an elected city council, were created.[65] The OB and various department heads, as well as some city councilors, both advisory and appointed, felt threatened by the continued existence of the committees. Partly to appease this feeling and partly to clarify their status, the leaders of the central committees sought out OB Klett to set up jurisdictions and to reassure him that they did not intend to take over the city government.[66] This, however, merely postponed their eventual demise, which took place on 29 February 1948, when the city terminated all payments to the Stuttgart Arbeitsausschüsse.

Klett and Scharnagl, both politically on the Right, distrusted the Antifas, and ultimately had them dissolved because of their predominantly leftist composition. In Stuttgart, Police Chief Weber reported to OB Klett in late September 1945 that he had no general objection to the activities of the Antifas, but that because the majority of their members consisted of Communists, their activities were distrusted or totally rejected by segments of the population.[67] Certainly, many in the German population were adamantly anti-Communist and distrusted any group or activity which involved Communists. The Roman Catholic hierarchy of Württemberg was "among the most determined opponents of the Kampfkomitee(s)," according to a July 1945 U.S. Field Intelligence Study, because, according to the vicar general and his liaison to MG in Stuttgart, the Antifas were "camouflaged' bodies for the propagation of Commu-

---

64. "Zwecke und Ziele der Aktionsausschüsse," Vermerk der Zentrale der Aktionsausschüsse, 25 Sept. 1946, Hauptaktei 0434-1, StA St.

65. Vietzen, p. 145. The non-Communist parties felt threatened by other supraparty structures, such as the VVN, not only because of the KPD participation, but because such structures were not under the parties' tutelage and could provide an unsupervised forum for political cooperation and the potential breakdown of interparty barriers and party discipline.

66. See Rechtsrat Dr. Ruisinger an OB Klett, 9 Nov. 1945, Hauptaktei 0434-1, StA St.

67. Hauptaktei 0434-1. StA St. It is not at all clear that at that point the majority of the members were Communists.

nism" and many Nazis were joining them.[68] There is no evidence of this latter "fact," which was probably used to manipulate public opinion and MG against the Antifas.

Karl Brehm, an Antifa activist and municipal employee in Stuttgart, who had set about organizing stewards' councils until unions could be introduced into the municipal Technical Works, was denounced by a former Nazi Party member to MG for allegedly trying to start up a Communist Party there. Brehm denied any such activity, but promised to go through the appropriate channels before continuing any union organization. He also stated he would report any other Nazi sabotage efforts to the police.[69] Brehm was apparently not punished by French MG or by the Stuttgart police, but there is more than a note of irony to the fact that a former Nazi denounced a former Communist for political activity this early on in the occupation and that Brehm, rather than the Nazi, was interrogated by the Stuttgart police on orders of MG.

The MG was more than passively involved in overseeing and placing restrictions on the Antifas. The Americans were particularly concerned that the KPD might be using the Antifas to maintain pressure for joint action by the Left.[70] In Frankfurt and Munich, united fronts of SPD and KPD members were formed inthe summer of 1945 after the Antifas were banned. This seems to have been more a result of the banning than of premeditated intentions. It certainly had nothing in common with the move toward the founding of a Socialist Unity Party (SED) in the East, despite the Americans' and some SPD leaders' fears to the contrary.[71] In Frankfurt, however, a joint SPD – KPD committee was formed in late May to sponsor united front activities[72] "in contrast to the Antifa conception which aimed at a homogeneous anti-fascist front and not at a joint party

68. OSS, FIS 5, 2 July 1945, p. 4f, RG 226, NARA.
69. Karl Brehm had been a member of the KPD until 1933 and a leader of the Internationale Arbeiterhilfe. This was apparently cause enough for his incrimination, at least according to the Pg denouncer. See Vermerk des Chefs der Polizei, 4 May 1945, Hauptaktei 0051-1, StA St.
70. OSS, FIS 43, 1 Dec. 1945, p. 15, RG 226, NARA.
71. Daniel E. Rogers argues that U.S. MG feared that disaffected SPD leaders in the U.S. Zone might "ram their local group into fusion with a local KPD branch," and therefore "permitted mergers only at the state level." It also tried to strictly limit the activities of united action committees. See Dan E. Rogers, "Transforming the German Party System: The United States and the Origins of Political Moderation, 1945–1949," Journal of Modern History, vol. 65, no. 3 (Sept. 1993), p. 530.
72. OSS, XL-11911, 18 June 1945, p. 6, RG 226, NARA.

project." In Munich, a united action committee met for the first time on 11 June 1945, signed a united action agreement on 8 August, and continued to meet until January 1946, when pressure was put on the SPD members by their local, more conservative party leadership to withdraw from such unified action.[73] A similar committee did not exist in Stuttgart, apparently because this Antifa organization with its representation of the KPD, SPD, Center Party, and DDP was allowed to continue there until 1948. Thus, ironically, the ban that was enforced in Munich and Frankfurt to prevent joint action by the Left resulted in these bipartisan action fronts of the Left that MG had been so concerned about avoiding in the first place.

The Antifas were thus either coopted into organizations paid and ultimately controlled by the city administrations, as in the case of Stuttgart, or replaced by advisory city councils with some token Antifa representation, as in the case of Frankfurt. The refounding of the political parties also eventually spelled the demise of the united front that the Antifa movement represented. Although SPD – KPD united action committees, which were often organized by rank-and-file members, grew directly out of the shared Antifa experience, including that of discrimination by the city administrations and the ultimate MG ban, the revived parties, with their old leadership, particularly in the case of the SPD, saw to it that the old party boundaries and rivalries were restored. The reemergence of the political parties certainly made inroads into the membership and popularity of the Antifas. If the Antifas had been less marginalized in the early months of the occupation, their model of bottom-up organization, consensus building, and multiparty/supraparty cooperation might have resulted in more rethinking of the old party structures and traditions, such as rigid conformity to party discipline (following the party line) and hierarchical behavior, which provided few channels for influence from new or even rank-and-file members. With this development in mind, the formation of the advisory city councils in Frankfurt, Munich, and Stuttgart will be explored next.

73. Protokolle der Aktionsgemeinschaft SPD-KPD München, Du 005. Georg Fischer Nachlass, IfZ. See also OMGBY, 10/110-2/19, 2 of 2, RG 226, Bayerisches Hauptstaatsarchiv. This conservative leadership tended to see any cooperation between the SPD and the KPD as a subterfuge for the coerced formation of a united party under Communist auspices, to some extent even before pressure for the united SED was growing in the Soviet Zone. See Horst Schmollinger and Dietrich Staritz, "Zur Entwicklung der Arbeiterparteien in den Westzonen," in *Das Parteiensystem der Bundesrepublik*, ed. Dietrich Staritz (Opladen, 1980, 2nd ed.), p. 110ff.

Advisory City Councils

All municipalities were permitted to have exclusively advisory citizens' councils. These councils were appointed by the Bürgermeister or, in the case of larger cities, by the OBs, because the OB was ultimately responsible to MG for all decisions made and/or actions taken by any municipal organization or administrative official. Whereas members of the Antifas and of the traditional parties of the Left took the initiative in suggesting such councils to the OBs in Stuttgart and Frankfurt,[74] OB Scharnagl himself took the initiative in Munich.[75] Despite the fact that the Left often took the lead in suggesting these councils, they were also used by the OBs and MG to reduce the influence of the Left, who many MG officers and their German appointees felt had the organizational advantage over the groups of the Center and the non-Nazi Right.[76] Yet it was not just the desire to even things out between the sides of the Right and the Left that led to this move on the part of MG and the OBs, but rather it was to help out those political groups with whom they felt the most sympathy.

A 24 September 1945 OSS report remarked that since the beginning of the occupation in April, in Frankfurt the Social Democrat, Willi Knothe, with the support of various Communists, had made numerous attempts:

> to create an advisory body of representative community leaders to assist MG and the German administration. Several such bodies, called Beiräte, were created and disbanded between May and August. They remained advisory, and apparently did not provide the link between administration and people which their proponents hoped of them. In August, Knothe, with representatives of the Communists and Christian Democrats, presented a petition for the establishment of a Bürgerrat (City Council) to assist the Mayor in the city administration. He presented a list of representatives of various political and community groups to be included. The principle was adopted by MG and mayor Kurt Blaum. But the list of

74. Sitzung der Inneren Abteilung, 28 Nov. 1945 , Gemeindebeiratsprotokolle, StA St and Bürgerratssitzungsprotokolle, 6 Sept. 1945, StA Ffm.

75. BuR 1537, StA Mü.

76. Political Advisor Murphy to Sec. of State, 28 June 1945, POLAD/ 730/1, 1 of 1, RG 84, IfZ. Because the KPD had maintained a clandestine organization of sorts during the Third Reich, it was often the first party to apply for licensing when political parties were allowed to form. Without understanding the reason that the KPD was often the first party to be licensed on the local level, some higher level offices within U.S. MG even charged their local MG detachments with leftist sympathies. See Rogers, p. 529. Rogers himself fails to note the legitimate reasons why the KPD was licensed before the other parties.

names submitted by Knothe and his group was accepted only in part. The Mayor wished to make it clear that the active political groups outside the government had no right to name a council which was to be an organ of his administration. To that end, he dropped certain names and added a group of individuals upon whose support he could rely. The Social Democrats, Communists and Christian Democrats felt that this action partly negated the purpose of the Council. The mayor also determined that the City Council should not meet regularly, but only on his own initiative.[77]

This OSS portrayal of events, although largely correct, fails to mention the conflict in Frankfurt between MG and OB Blaum over how the Bürgerrat was to be formed. On 3 August 1945, OB Blaum sent MGO Sheehan a list of twenty-five persons who had never belonged to the NSDAP; he had chosen them on the basis first, of their membership in "the professional classes," then on what he called the "ideological point of view," which actually meant religion, and, lastly, according to the political composition between 1929 and 1933 of the city council's non-Nazi and "non-militaristic" members, with the latter presumably a reference to the DNVP. At that time, the political representation had consisted of 36 percent so-called middle-groups, 15 percent Center Party, 34 percent SPD, and 15 percent KPD; now Blaum proposed 45 percent middle-group members, 14 percent Center Party, 23 percent SPD and 18 percent KPD, as well as one clergyman each for the Protestant, Catholic, and Jewish religions. He tried to justify the disproportionate representation of the "middle-group" by claiming that this reflected the political complexion of the present population, which was showing "less activity in the public, especially at the American and German offices than their number would suggest."[78] Blaum, himself a Protestant, leaned in the direction of the LDP, which later became the FDP.

The MG did not accede to Blaum's desire to create "a mirror image of the various professional classes of the population" in the Bürgerrat, but instead insisted on the exclusive criterion of political parties, which were licensed soon thereafter. MG specifically requested that there be 28 members with seven representatives from each of the four parties: CDU, KPD, LDP (FDP) and SPD. Among these 28 were four women. Blaum then fought hard to have this principle of party parity changed to representation based on the elections of 1929 and 1933. Citing the political affiliations of recently elected

77. FIS 23, 24 Sept. 1945, p. 29f, OMGUS (CAD), 15/109-2/7, 1 of 6, RG 260, IfZ.
78. Mag. 1060/1, Bd. 1, StA Fffm.

works council members and the low percentage of active KPD members among them, Blaum tried to get the number of Communist representatives, in particular, reduced.[79] At MG's insistence, the notion of parity for Frankfurt's four major political parties was retained for the composition of the advisory Bürgerrat. This nevertheless worked to the disadvantage of the SPD, since it had received 34 percent of the seats in the last free elections. This SPD underrepresentation and the inaccuracy of Blaum's estimate of postwar political alignments were exposed in the May 1946 municipal elections when the SPD won an absolute majority of seats.[80]

In Munich and Stuttgart the OBs eventually based the proportion of seats allotted to the various political parties and interest groups upon their representation in the last free Weimar Republic city councils, although efforts were also made to allow for city district and vocational representation.[81] In Stuttgart, OB Klett first called together a committee to make preparations for an advisory city council on 31 August 1945. This eleven-member committee, chaired by Klett, included three members of the Arbeitsausschüsse, a trade union representative, two religious leaders and two municipal department heads, as well as two business representatives and a high-ranking police official.[82] No women were included, despite the fact that two women, the cochairpersons of the former Association of Women's Clubs of Württemberg, had volunteered their services and submitted a list of seven other potential women to be included, and that the chairperson of the Women's Section of the Württemberg Evangelical Church had also submitted a list of potential female members.[83] Klett asked the all-male group to help develop guidelines for the advisory council and to suggest appropriate councilors from their various interest groups. He originally planned to choose thirty-two members from among those suggested. These thirty-two then would have to turn in Fragebögen and be approved

79. OB Blaum an die Militärregierung, 5 Dec. 1945, Mag. 1060/1, Bd. 1, StA Fffm.
80. The 1946 municipal elections in Hesse had a 15 percent minimum clause which resulted in the exclusion of the KPD and the FDP in Frankfurt until 1948. In 1946, in the Frankfurt city council elections, the SPD received 39.3 percent of the vote, the CDU 33.6 percent, with the KPD (11.6 percent) and the LDP (11.3 percent) falling beneath the minimum and thus losing their votes to the top two parties.
81. See BuR 1537, StA Mü and Hauptaktei 0621, StA St.
82. Rechenschaftsbericht 1945, Hauptaktei 0621, StA St.
83. Vietzen, p. 151. The local MGO in Würzburg requested that the advisory council there include two women after the mayor had put together an all-male fifteen-member council. Women representatives were then added from the SPD and CSU. Schott, p. 38.

by MG.[84] The U.S. MG in Stuttgart requested that professional and vocational categories constitute the basis for representation in the city council, because political parties were not yet permitted.[85] Thus in Stuttgart, MG did not want the political parties to play a role in the representational structure of the city council, but used the vocational structure of the city as the primary guideline. The opposite had been the case with MG in Frankfurt, where OB Blaum had been prevented from forming the Bürgerrat on the basis of "professional classes."

Between the first and second meetings of the Stuttgart preparatory committee, the Württemberg Interior Ministry, led by the Social Democrat, Fritz Ulrich, issued guidelines for the formation of advisory councils to assist the Bürgermeister or OBs in the large cities. These guidelines, which came from a ministry headed by a Social Democrat, suggested that cities of overone hundred thousand should have a thirty-six-member council, of which half should come from preexisting committees such as the Arbeitsausschüsse, and the other half from a proportional representation of the various vocational and labor-management organizations. The council was intended to serve as an arbitrator or consultant (*Gutachter*) to the OB. Citing the head of the Land-MG, who considered the function of the advisory city councils to be to take advantage of "the democratic spirit of the already existing committees," OB Klett construed these "already existing committees" to apply just as easily to his own preparatory committee as to the explicitly mentioned *Arbeitsausschüsse*. The preparatory committee, at its second meeting on 18 September 1945, apparently concurred with Klett's interpretation and decided to apply its own formula to the composition of the advisory council, whereby its own eleven members were to be joined by twenty-one representatives of the parties, which in the interim had been licensed, and by four members appointed by the OB.[86] The *Arbeitsausschüsse* were thus completely omitted from the group of preexisting committees from which the advisory council was chosen.

At its third meeting on 25 September, the preparatory committee came up with thirty-two members, while reserving the remaining four spaces for any new parties which might emerge. When, by late October, no new parties had been licensed, OB Klett made his own four appointments. Although not publicly represented as a party-oriented composition, the political breakdown was as follows: SPD

84. Gemeindebeiratsprotokolle, 1. Sitzung des vorbereitenden Ausschusses für den zu bildenden Gemeindebeirat, 31 August 1945, StA St.
85. Vietzen, p. 150.
86. Ibid., p. 152. See also Gemeindebeiratsprotokolle, 18 Sept. 1945, StA St.

28.5 percent, KPD 22 percent, DVP 11 percent, CDU 11 percent, church representatives 8.5 percent, and those without party affiliations 19 percent, although one-third of this latter group were known to ally themselves with the DVP. Among the final thirty-six were four women.[87] Although the parties of the Left had considerable representation in the advisory council, in Stuttgart they played less of a role in municipal government than in the other two cities, because Klett only convened the council nine times.

Although Munich was occupied last, its council was formed first, and its initial session was on 1 August 1945. Because Munich was the only one of the three cities where the pre-1933 OB was restored to his old post, it had experienced leadership and apparently did not feel the need to rely as much on the bureaucracy of the Third Reich. OB Scharnagl was also more aware of who was available, experienced and not incriminated than his OB colleagues, the journalist Hollbach, the Hanauer Blaum in Frankfurt, or the young lawyer Klett in Stuttgart. This had repercussions for the municipal civil service, but probably even more so for the advisory city council.

Already in August 1944, when the former BVP Munich OB and the Social Democratic city councilor, Thomas Wimmer, were imprisoned in Dachau together, they discussed plans for post-Nazi Germany. Wimmer and his fellow Social Democrat, the former head of the Munich trade unions, Gustav Schiefer, who had also been in Dachau with Scharnagl and Wimmer, volunteered their services to OB Scharnagl soon after his appointment.[88] Scharnagl requested names from Wimmer and other leaders of non-Nazi parties in the early summer of 1945,[89] after getting permission from MG on 26 May to form an advisory council of thirty-six members.[90] Including Wimmer and Schiefer, ten of the thirty-six had been inmates in Dachau during the Third Reich. Their incarcerations lasted from a few weeks following the 20 July assassination attempt against Hitler (when thousands of former Weimar Republic political figures were

87. Ibid., p. 151f. Klett probably felt more comfortable with party representatives chosen by party leaders, because the individuals would have been more likely to have been known quantities, accustomed to party discipline and behavior, than the more activist-inclined Antifas. This representation of the parties of the Left actually corresponded completely with the first postwar municipal elections, when the SPD and the KPD together received twenty-three of forty-eight seats.
88. Stadtratssitzungsprotokolle, 7 Jan. 1947, p. 5f, RP 720/1, StA Mü.
89. BuR 1537, StA Mü.
90. Michael Schattenhofer, ed., Chronik der Stadt München 1945–1948 (Stadtarchiv München, 1980), p. 54.

incarcerated) up to several months in a few cases.[91] According to Scharnagl's report to the MG, the composition of the advisory council took into consideration, "all layers (classes), all professions and all political and all intellectual" tendencies within Munich society.[92] Scharnagl, however, excluded former DDP members, apparently because two lists from competing contingents of the DDP were submitted later than the others,[93] long after he had completed his own list. Although Scharnagl officially justified his decision with the excuse that party politics were not to play a role in this council,[94] he obviously did not want to include this Protestant Liberal party; it represented the starkest competition for potential clientele with his own newly founded party, the CSU, which hoped to transcend the old exclusively Catholic lines of the BVP. When the Munich LDP (which formed from the old DDP and DVP and later became the FDP) suggested, with MG support, that the well-known liberal, Thomas Dehler, fill the newly vacated spot of 2. Bürgermeister in November 1945, the advisory city council, which, alone in Munich, was given the power to make this decision, turned him down.[95]

The Munich advisory council included 30.5 percent former members of the SPD, 26.5 percent former members of the BVP, 6.5 percent former KPD members, 6.5 percent Protestant Church representatives, 3 percent Jewish representatives, 3 percent house-owner representatives, 3 percent agricultural representatives, and 21 percent representatives of the economy and of the intellectual and cultural life of Munich.[96] This compares favorably with the last Weimar city council, which had had the following representation: SPD 34 percent, BVP 24 percent, KPD 6 percent, house-owner representatives 4 percent, and aside from the NSDAP and DNVP contingents and two small bourgeois splinter groups, no DDP or DVP representatives.[97] The Munich MG detachment insisted on the inclusion of two women after two male civil servants were rejected on the basis of conflict of interest, but only one woman was actually appointed.[98] Munich was the

---

91. Ibid., p. 67.
92. OB Scharnagl an die Military Government, 30 July 1945, Official Translation, p. 3, BuR 1636, StA Mü.
93. BuR 1537. StA Mü.
94. BuR 1636, StA Mü.
95. Berthold Mauch, *Die bayerische FDP, 1945–1949* (Munich, 1981), p. 22.
96. OB Scharnagl an die Military Government, 30 July 1945, Official Translation, p. 3, BuR 1636, StA Mü.
97. These statistics were calculated by the author on the basis of city council lists in the Adressbücher in the Stadtarchiv München.
98. BuR 1537. StA Mü. Cf. footnote 83 for Würzburg.

only city of the three which had not come up with any female councilors on its own initiative and with only one, it still had the smallest percentage. It had 3 percent as compared to 11 percent in Frankfurt and 9 percent in Stuttgart. This low percentage cannot be explained by the unavailability of women in 1945 or the sparsity of women involved or interested in municipal politics: Munich's 1932 council had had 8 percent women, and in its second postwar municipal elections, women won almost a quarter of the seats.

Except for these restrictions on women and liberals, Munich's advisory council displayed more democratic tendencies than those of the other two cities. This does not necessarily mean that its membership was inherently more democratic, but it certainly signifies that the council itself was allowed to function more democratically. For example, the Munich council was more active than its counterparts in Frankfurt and Stuttgart, meeting twenty-seven times prior to the May 1946 elections as compared to Frankfurt's nineteen sessions and Stuttgart's nine. Munich's council was the most like its elected Weimar predecessors in both its composition and its function; the largest percentage of its members had served as councilors during the Weimar Republic (22 percent as compared to 19 percent in Stuttgart and 18 percent in Frankfurt), and it, alone among the three cities, determined its own meeting times. A further sign of democratization was the change in occupational representation that in 1945 more closely mirrored the city than in 1932: workers, professionals, and the self-employed were better represented in the 1945 council than they had been in 1932, whereas teachers and the general middle class saw their (over-)representation decline considerably.[99] Of course, another factor influencing the behavior of the Munich council was that the 22 percent veteran municipal politicians were serving under the same OB that they had previously and they, like Scharnagl, were probably repeating previous patterns of behavior, knowing how to calculate each other's responses. It is also possible that the quality of the Munich detachment had something to do with the democratic nature of the advisory council. The political scientist Harold Zink, who served from 1945 to 1949 with the USGCC and its successor organization, the Political Division of OMGUS, described the Munich detachment as the most effective MG detachment in Bavaria in the summer of 1945.[100]

99. These statistics were calculated by the author on the basis of city council lists in the Adressbücher and similar lists in the Stadtarchiv München, Stadtarchiv Frankfurt, and Stadtarchiv Stuttgart.

100. See Zink Memo to Donald R. Heath in Foreign Relations of the United States 1945, Vol. 3: European Advisory Commission; Austria; Germany (Washington, 1968), p. 946.

If Munich's advisory council appeared to be the most democratic, then Stuttgart's was the least. Stuttgart's council was formed the latest of the three cities and met on an average of only once a month. It seemingly played the least active role in municipal affairs, not only because it met so seldom, but because, like Frankfurt's council, it could meet only when convened by the OB. In both Frankfurt and Stuttgart, there was less representation of workers in the advisory council than in 1932. In Stuttgart, where half of the advisory council was supposed to have come from the *Arbeitsausschüsse,* and thus predominantly from the working class, the percentage of workers in the city council dropped from 33 percent in 1932 to 14 percent in 1945.[101]

Stuttgart's advisory council was constrained in its democratic potential because of OB Klett's insistence that "'Politics don't belong in city hall,'"[102] but also, ironically enough, because of MGO Jackson's reprimand to the council for criticizing the OB rather than acting "democratically."[103] After the council's first meeting on 12 October 1945, when plans were made to set up committees for the council, OB Klett unilaterally changed the number and composition of the standing committees as well as postponed their meetings. Thus at the first meeting of the council's steering committee, which was not called by OB Klett until 28 November, considerable discontent was expressed. The council's second plenary session, virtually its first business meeting because the opening session had been largely ceremonial, did not take place until 30 November. By that time the press had gotten wind of the council's discontent with the delay and published an anonymous member's poem comparing the way the council was being handled with Hitler's rubber-stamp parliaments.[104]

The plenary session began with councilors' demands for an explanation from Klett for the seven-week delay. Instead of a response by OB Klett, MGO Jackson interjected and attempted to justify the delay by referring to the heavy workload of the OB and his office, which had left no time for a council meeting. Jackson's intercession, which was apparently planned, took Klett off the hook. It was made clear to the councilors that Jackson was defending Klett

101. These statistics were calculated by the author on the basis of city council lists in the *Adressbücher* and similar lists in the Stadtarchiv Stuttgart. Most of the KPD and SPD members in the advisory council were not working class.

102. Gemeindebeiratssitzungsprotokolle, 30 Nov. 1945, p. 255, StA St. The advisory councilor, Rudolf Gehring (SPD), criticized Klett for not understanding that almost every municipal activity was political and for advocating the notion that "Politik gehört nicht aufs Rathaus."

103. Gemeindebeiratssitzungsprotokolle, 30 Nov. 1945, p. 285, StA St.

104. Vietzen, p. 154.

and therefore that they could neither directly confront the OB nor further question or contradict the MGO. In practice, this behavior further diminished the possibility of democratic exchange and also prevented the councilors from becoming involved in all those tasks with which they had hoped to help Klett.[105] When MGO Jackson requested that the various department heads report on their concerns, the various councilors lamented the lack of opportunity they had been given to take a position on these concerns. One councilor pointed out that he was not being negative for the sake of being negative, but rather, that in a democracy it is "not only a right, but under certain circumstances also an obligation" to express public criticism. "This criticism should not be disparaging or destructive, but encouraging and constructive."[106] Following the councilors' applause, MGO Jackson reprimanded the group. He claimed that he had apparently come to the wrong meeting. He had thought the council would make suggestions to the OB, but instead, after listening for three hours, he had not heard any concrete suggestions. Recognizing, he said, "that you have not had the opportunity in twelve years for such a democratic exchange, your ideas of democracy have become a little rusty." Complaining that the councilors' critiques were often "naive" and "crazy," and that they did not provide any solutions, Jackson called a meeting for the following week, "at which time he wanted to see another type of meeting," where only "constructive criticism" would be expressed. The MGO then admonished them that they were "also an advisory council for the MG."[107]

Jackson's patronizing stance was strongly resented by the councilors, who let their feelings be known in the next steering committee meeting four days later and again in the 7 December plenary session. Councilor Gehring, who was also a district Bürgermeister, complained that, given the amount of restraint that Germans had to practice under military occupation, the least they could expect from MG was that it also show them some consideration. As he put it: "If we are not allowed to really openly express our opinion and say what we think is right, then the others should also not go beyond the limits that lead to real infringements." Gehring went on to express his regret that they were not given the opportunity to engage in discussion with Jackson, "in order to give (him) a picture of what we understand under democracy."[108]

105. Ibid., p. 153ff.
106. Gemeindebeiratssitzungsprotokolle, 30 Nov. 1945, p. 258, StA St.
107. Ibid., p. 285.
108. Protokolle, Innere Abteilung, 1945–1946, 4 Dec. 1945 Sitzung, p. 4, StA St.

At the plenary meeting three days later, all four parties in the council formulated a collective public statement about the criticisms they had expressed at the last plenary session which Jackson had so deprecated. Calling their own critiques positive, because they pointed out which problems needed to be solved next and how they should be "mastered" in the opinion of the council, the council then noted its surprise about Jackson's comments, which had given the public the impression that the council was not equal to its job. Pointing out that all of those who had spoken at the previous session were experienced parliamentarians, who resented being treated in public as "parliamentary children, who first needed training in municipal politics," the statement retorted that the councilors' ideas of democracy had not in any way become "'rusty'" in the last twelve years. The purpose of the last plenary session had not been to present concrete motions, but rather to do that in committees.[109] The implication was that MG, under the guise of playing the teacher of democracy, was not practicing democracy. Indeed, MG's intervention and comments did nothing to further democratization in Stuttgart's municipal politics. Instead, it provoked the council's resentment while strengthening OB Klett's tendency to ignore it, knowing he had the MGO's backing due to his overt distrust of the councilors' abilities.[110]

In the case of Frankfurt, the discontent of the left-wing parties of the advisory council regarding OB Blaum's authoritarian ways led to his eventual defeat in the 1946 OB election.[111] Although the SPD and the KPD had half of the seats in the council, the Left had marginal influence on municipal politics while Blaum was OB. Like Klett, Blaum wanted to keep politics out of City Hall and paid little attention to the council, whose composition was not at all to his liking. In late September 1945, an OSS report on Frankfurt described the political situation there as follows: "In its simplest terms, the political problem of Frankfurt boils down to the fact that the administration is in the hands of the business men and professional administrators, while the left parties on the outside are trying to secure not merely more positions for themselves in the government, but responsibility of the adminis-

---

109. Gemeindebeiratssitzungsprotokolle, 7 Dec. 1945, p. 293 f, StA St. The various council committees corresponded to the city's departments and made suggestions to the appropriate department head. Although the committee members could not hold the department head or the OB accountable, they did actively research the issues and make concrete proposals.
110. Gemeindebeiratssitzungsprotokolle, 30 Nov. 1945, StA St.
111. See Chapter 4.

tration to the political party leadership as a first step toward the establishment of a politically-based city government. Underlying this problem is the precedence accorded by occupation policy to the restoration of administration over the revival of political life."[112]

The first meeting of the Frankfurt advisory city council produced an explosion when OB Blaum complained to the council that "the tempo of denazification in the city administration had been so rapid that 'the tool of reconstruction was being knocked out of his hand." The representatives of the Left protested Blaum's statement, because, according to an OSS report, "deeply conscious of the strength derived by the right from the imperial professional bureaucracy retained under the Weimar republic, they fear[ed] that the slightest compromise on the purge issue [would] enable the bureaucracy which supported Nazism to survive under the guise of technical expertise."[113]

Because of its lack of influence via the council, the Left turned to the public, publishing an editorial against the OB and a news story on the session in the *Frankfurter Rundschau*. This was the only newspaper licensed in Frankfurt at the time, and it was controlled by seven licensees, six of whom were either Communists or Social Democrats, including Willi Knothe, Hans Etzkorn, and Emil Carlebach, who were also members of the advisory council. In the next session, one of Blaum's close friends, a manager of the large Philip Holzmann Construction Company and leader of the LDP toward which Blaum leaned, accused the Left of misrepresenting the OB. According to this OSS report, Blaum's partisans, "who seem to include all the Liberal Democratic leaders and much of the business community, feel that the left is abusing its control over the only press organ in the city."[114] Thus the political debate extended beyond the council itself; after the Left had used its influence on the press to inform and shape public opinion, Blaum's supporters on the Right felt compelled to retort.

The press in Frankfurt, at least until the elections in May 1946, played a more direct role in democratization, in terms of holding the city's leaders accountable and creating a forum for open discussion and civic involvement, than the advisory city council. If the council could exert no influence over the OB, the press could, especially since Blaum had political ambitions and wished to continue in office once elections were restored. As will be recalled, the press was also

112. OMGUS, 15/109-2/7, 1 of 6, OSS FIS 23, 24 Sept. 1945, p. 29, RG 260, IfZ.
113. Ibid., p. 30f.
114. Ibid., p.31.

under American control, but not of the MG detachment, but rather – at least at this early stage – of the much more reform-oriented DISCC and ICD.

In terms of continuity, the carryover of advisory city council members into the May 1946 elected councils varied a great deal. In Munich, where OB Scharnagl had written the heads of the former political factions in the last Weimar Republic city council in order to secure lists of their suggestions for their party representatives and had followed these lists fairly closely,[115] 54 percent of the honorary councilors elected in May 1946 had belonged to the advisory council. This fits in with the trend of continuity from the Weimar Republic and the related fact that these were trusted and experienced politicians, who had been able to practice some limited democracy during the previous year. In Stuttgart, where OB Klett had asked a preliminary committee of representatives he chose from some of the various political groupings to compile lists,[116] some 44 percent of the elected city councilors had been advisory councilors. In Frankfurt, where OB Blaum had met with representatives, or at least those he designated as representatives, of the old Frankfurt Weimar Republic parties as well as business and industrial leaders, and had acquired long lists from which he chose seven councilors per party,[117] only 8 percent of Frankfurt's 1946 city council were members of the advisory Bürgerrat. This was partly because only two of the four major parties had survived Hesse's minimum 15 percent clause,[118] and partly because some of the parties' representatives in the Bürgerrat opted for Land rather than local-level politics. It was also probably because of a public rejection of Frankfurt's municipal administration during the previous year under Hollbach and Blaum; apparently a rejection of those advisory councilors associated with their administration. The fact that OB Blaum, unlike Klett and Scharnagl, had

---

115. BuR 1537, StA Mü.

116. Hermann Vietzen, *Chronik der Stadt Stuttgart, 1945–1948* (Stuttgart, 1972), p. 150f.

117. Magistrat der Stadt Frankfurt a. M. (ed.), *Frankfurt am Main 1945–1965: Ein 20-Jahresbericht* (Frankfurt, n.d.), p. 289. See also Mag 1060/1, Bd. 1, StA Ffm.

118. The state of Hesse introduced a 15 percent clause in 1945 for all upcoming local and state elections in order to prevent a multiplicity of small parties. This was of course unnecessary as MG, at that time, had only licensed the main four. But after parties like the LDP, a forerunner of the FDP, and the KPD each won over 10 percent of the votes but less than 15 percent, and were denied seats in local elections, the clause was changed to 5 percent for the 1946 elections for the state constitutional convention. However, until 1948, when the second postwar municipal elections were held, many Hessian towns and cities, such as Frankfurt, only had two parties represented in their municipal councils, the SPD and the CDU.

not adhered closely to the parties' lists when he put together the council also played a role.

Frankfurt was the only city of the three where the OB was not returned to office by an electoral victory in 1946. Both in terms of the composition of the city council and the department heads there was relatively little continuity between the 1945/46 Frankfurt municipal government and the succeeeding administrations during the next decade under the former city director of Düsseldorf, the quite popular Social Democrat, Dr. Walter Kolb. Thus, unlike in Munich and Stuttgart, 1946, perhaps more so than 1945, represented a watershed in Frankfurt's municipal history.

Political Parties

The Allied occupation authorities felt that the formation of democratic political parties was a prerequisite for the revival of democratic political life in Germany. After the Soviets authorized the formation of "anti-Fascist parties" on 10 June 1945, the United States followed suit three months later, granting permission for party organization on a district basis on 27 August 1945, and on a zonal basis in February 1946. Both the British and French MGs authorized the formation of political parties in December 1945. Preconditions for the authorization in all four zones was that the parties be anti-Nazi and democratic. They also all discouraged, albeit by different means, the formation of new, or what they considered, splinter parties.[119]

In the U.S. Zone, local MG permission was provisional until it went through USFET's G-5 (Civil Affairs) division. To even submit application for licensing, twenty-five sponsors were required to fill out Fragebögen and to provide detailed statements of their party program to the local MG authorities. If any of the groups were found to be "militaristic, undemocratic, hostile to Allied purposes, or prejudicial to military security and the maintenance of order," their authorization could be withheld, or if already granted, withdrawn.[120]

119. Friedmann, p. 128.
120. J.F.J. Gillen, *State and Local Government in West Germany, 1945–1953*, ed. by the Historical Division of the Office of the U.S. High Commissioner for Germany (n.p., 1953), p. 5ff. Daniel E. Rogers argues in the Sept. 1993 *Journal of Modern History* that U.S. MG discriminated against Left and Right extremes equally "in a halting yet continuing attempt to bring stable, moderate democracy to postwar Germany." The discrimination against the Right took the form of withdrawing licenses or not granting Land-level licenses for parties such as the Bavarian

Regulations on political parties in the U.S. Zone were revised in April 1947, although many of the clauses simply reiterated old ones. For example, expellee and refugee parties continued to be prohibited, because it was felt that these outsiders should be absorbed into German life as quickly as possible and prevented from forming a right-wing party with irredentist demands for their lands in Eastern Europe.[121] In this April directive and in another one in July, it was stressed that MG officers should show impartiality toward all authorized parties and party personalities. The fact that it was reiterated in July indicates that impartiality had not been the case. Another change involved the cessation of the requirement that constantly updated party membership lists be submitted to MG after the Germans had protested this lack of privacy. Also MG was no longer to intervene in internal party disputes.[122]

Impartiality was often not the case on the local level, and there are numerous examples of MG intervention beyond granting or withdrawing licenses, not so much directly in interparty affairs, but certainly in intraparty ones, especially prior to these 1947 directives. The fact that intervention had occurred does not indicate that it was previously encouraged, but simply that the MG officers had assumed that they they had that leeway of personal preference and intervention in the Germans' political affairs.

Sometimes an MG detachment's intervention was manipulated by an OB or a department head who wanted the extra weight of MG backing in order to strengthen his own political preference and weaken his opponents'. Generally, local MG detachments got their information on political parties and their activities from the weekly

---

monarchists (BHKP) or the National Democratic Party in Hesse. On the Left, Rogers claims that the KPD was discriminated against only in terms of restrictions on freedom of expression and with anti-Communist propaganda, and that even this only occurred after 1947 when the head of the U.S. Zone, General Clay, began practicing a policy of containment. Rogers, p. 515 ff. Based on my research, I would agree that MG prohibited extreme right, reactionary parties, which promoted authoritarian, undemocratic ideas, but that in its preference for what it considered middle-of-the-road politics, it discriminated against the KPD much earlier than 1947 and in various cases, which I have shown, such as the 1946 municipal elections, against the SPD and even before, the Antifas and other left-oriented groups.

121. See Rogers, p. 524 f.
122. Seymour R. Bolten, "Military Government and the German Political Parties," *Annals of the American Academy of Political and Social Sciences*, 267 (1950), p. 57f. See also Alf Mintzel, "Besatzungspolitik und Entwicklung der bürgerlichen Parteien in den Westzonen (1945–1949)," in Dietrich Staritz, ed., *Das Parteiensystem der Bundesrepublik* (Opladen, 1980), p.80.

OB reports, from CIC and, after the dissolution of the OSS, from other less skilled intelligence sources. Numerous CIC reports were extremely biased against Communists and Socialists, and many intelligence reports contained blatant errors, such as designating Kurt Schumacher as the KPD chief of the British Zone,[123] or characterizing the FDP's Dr. Wolfgang Haußmann, whose family had been Liberals since the 1848 Revolution, as a Social Democrat during the Weimar Republic,[124] when actually he had been a DDP delegate in both the state and federal parliaments.

The OB's weekly reports to MG were often extremely subjective. In Frankfurt, OB Blaum composed them himself without relying directly on any departmental reports, and they were sometimes translated verbatim – although not acknowledged as such – as the local detachment's weekly report to the Land-MG.[125] The Frankfurt MG was probably the most ill-informed and most easily influenced by its appointees. This is especially ironic, since Frankfurt was initially the headquarters of U.S. MG and was expected to set an example for the rest of the zone. OB Scharnagl showed more objectivity by synthesizing reports from the police and the other department heads to come up with his reports to MG.[126] The Munich police submitted reports directly to CIC on public opinion and the activities of the political parties as well.[127] In Stuttgart the police president sent weekly reports, first to French MG and then to U.S. MG, on public opinion, along with his own analyses of the causes and effects of public opinion, while OB Klett sent activity reports of the city administration to MG and "situation reports" to CIC.[128] The local MG detachments submitted bimonthly political-activity reports to the Land-MG, which sent them on to the OMGUS zonal headquarters.[129] Since local detachments were the source of most of the information used by higher-level offices to make policy decisions, the role of city administrations and their portrayal of political activities in their cities cannot be overestimated.

---

123. 2 Dec. 1946 Special Brief of Political Affairs, p. 5, MA 1427/2 Walter J. Muller Nachlass, IfZ.

124. 1 Oct. 1945, Stuttgart Detachment's Political Activities Report, p, 7, OMGUS, 5/10-1/12, 1 Of 10, RG 260, IfZ.

125. Rebecca Boehling, "Die politischen Lageberichte des Frankfurter Oberbürgermeisters Blaum an die amerikanische Militärregierung 1945/1946," *Archiv für Frankfurts Geschichte und Kunst*, 59 (1985), p. 494ff.

126. BuR 1668, StA Mü.

127. BuR 260/10/I, StA Mü.

128. Hauptaktei 000-8/7, StA St.

129. Gillen, p. 5ff.

The formation of the advisory councils preceded the U.S. authorization for the formation of political parties on the local level. The supposedly apolitical appointees of the apolitical MGOs fell back on the officially nonexistent political parties to form the supposedly apolitical advisory councils. Thus the major Weimar Republic political parties were de facto restored, although sometimes in a somewhat conjoined state, as in the case of the transfigured Center Party, DDP, and DVP. This occurred despite the existing prohibition of political activity in the U.S. Zone. Beyond the formation of these councils, the Allied MGs often permitted informal organizational activity by the surviving leaders of the Weimar parties, allowing them a head start with long-term implications.[130] An almost immediate restoration of the old Social Democratic and Communist political parties occurred. Centrist and liberal parties took a bit longer to coalesce, because they included former splinter parties, such as the national Staatspartei, or the more regional Wirtschaftspartei, Christlicher Volksdienst, Freie Bürgerliche Mitte, and Bayerische Mittelstandspartei. Because this initial restoration and/or reconfiguration of the four political parties, KPD, SPD, CDU/CSU, and FDP, was based upon the appointed mayor's reliance upon the old local party elite for the suggestion of council members, the hierarchy of power among the individual members of the parties was also immediately restored. This happened, whether consciously or unconsciously, under the auspices of the U.S. MG.

The precipitate restoration of the pre-1933 political parties inhibited the formation of new political parties, when parties were officially permitted to form in late August 1945. Because no new parties, if they were able to emerge at all, had representation in the advisory city councils, they lacked any opportunity for formal participation in local self-goverment, however limited, until the advisory councils were replaced by the first elected city councils in May 1946. Even then, the absence of visibility during the first postwar year hurt new parties in the elections and generally doomed them to a short-lived, if not obscure, existence. Barred from entering the public arena until the mid-1946 elections, they were by then also faced with percentage clauses as high as 15 percent in order to win seats in the city councils.[131] New parties were also regarded skeptically by the MG detachments, which had received instructions to

---

130. Gerhard Loewenberg, "The Remaking of the German Party System," in *European Politics*, M. Dogan and R. Rose, eds. (Boston, 1971), p. 267f.
131. Cf. note 118.

prevent a return of the extreme multiparty system that was blamed for the downfall of the Weimar Republic.[132] If the parties were not licensed, they could not run for election. Political officers actually discouraged applications from what they termed "small splinter groups," instructing new party sponsors to seek agreement with one of the "four major parties."[133]

New parties trying to get licensed were effectively discouraged until the four major parties were firmly ensconced after the first elections. In Württemberg-Baden the Land- MGO, Colonel Dawson, recognized the four major parties "as fast as their application could be checked, and their sponsors screened." According to a MG officer at the time, "it was Colonel Dawson's policy to discourage applications from small splinter groups. He advised their sponsors either to seek agreement with one of the major parties or to be content with permission to form societies rather than political parties per se."[134] In Munich a member of POLAD, Captain Richey, filed a report concerning the lawyer, Dr. Keller, who wanted to found a Völkerrechtspartei in late September 1945. Richey discouraged Keller, telling him that most "internationally minded Germans would either associate themselves with the SPD or the KPD." Richey went on to speculate that Keller and his group of intellectuals would not "ever amount to anything." Richey described Keller as "an interesting example, however, of what seems to be occurring around here at the present time, namely the emergence of all sorts of small political groups with some hair-brained program." Keller's "hair-brained program" was to direct Germany's consciousness toward Europe rather than concentrating on Germany.[135] From the perspective of MG officers, who were accustomed to a two-party system, the "four major parties" were already more than enough. This MG stance was of course welcomed by the "four major parties."

New parties however did arise, although most were not licensed until after the 1946 elections, when the four major parties were firmly in place. One was what, in today's parlance, would be called a feminist party, namely, the Neue Partei, which only got MG ap-

132. "Political Analysis of the Weimar Republic," 10 Oct. 1945 OSS, XL 35658, RG 226, NARA.
133. "Political Activity in North Württemberg-Baden," 1 Dec. 1945, p. 12, OSS, FIS 43, RG 226, NARA.
134. Moses Moskowitz, "The Political Re-education of the Germans: The Emergence of Parties and Politics in Württemberg-Baden," *Political Science Quarterly*, 61, no. 4 (1946), p. 545.
135. IfZ-Munich, RG 84, POLAD/ 729/ 37, 3 of 4, 5 Oct. 1945.

proval after it changed its name from "Frauenpartei,"[136] but which then managed to get two representatives elected to the 1948 Stuttgart city council.[137] Others were the Arbeiterpartei, an alternative socialist party,[138] the Union der Mitte, the Freie Wählervereinigung, the Neue Sozial-Demokratische Partei Deutschlands, the Nationale-Demokratische Partei, the Schwäbischer Bund in Stuttgart, another branch of the Arbeiterpartei in Frankfurt, the Bayerische Heimats- und Königspartei, the Wirtschaftliche-Aufbau-Vereinigung, and the Bayern-Partei in Munich. Except for the monarchistic Bayerische Heimats- und Königspartei,[139] which was already licensed in Munich in January 1946 but dissolved because of its monarchistic stance before the May elections, the Wirtschaftliche-Aufbau-Vereinigung, licensed on 8 December 1945,[140] and the Schwäbischer Bund, licensed on 20 October 1945,[141] all of the other parties were licensed, or in the case of the Neue SPD, rejected for licensing because its founder had been a member of the NSDAP,[142] after the May 1946 elections.

With the exception of the Arbeiterpartei, which represented an alternative for discontented Social Democrats and Communists, almost all these other parties were on the Right of the political spectrum, with the Nationale-Demokratische Partei in Stuttgart[143] and the Bayerische Heimats- und Königspartei, the Wirtschaftliche-Aufbau-Vereinigung, and the Bayern-Partei in Munich on the far Right. Given the treatment of the Antifas in the first months of the U.S. occupation, the combined MG - OB onslaught discouraged new organized political initiatives on the Left. Also, the early disillusionment of many active anti-Nazis with the lack of active support from MG led them either to retreat from politics altogether or join forces with the stronger, old traditional parties of the Left, possibly hoping to avoid falling prey to a policy of divide and conquer.

The U.S. MG was particularly concerned about the possibility of complicating "the political stage to the Right of the Communists and Socialists" by licensing "small 'Splitter' groups," that might "weaken considerably the non-Communist and non-socialist political forces." In a 23 November 1945 memorandum on "American policy and pos-

136. Hauptaktei 0061-4, StA St.
137. Vietzen, p. 180.
138. OMGWB, 12/221-2/2, 3 of 8. RG 260, Hauptstaatsarchiv Stuttgart.
139. Peter Jakob Kock, "Die Grundlegung des bayerischen Nachkriegsföderalismus," Ph.D. dissertation, Ludwig-Maximillans-Universität-München, 1981, p. 159.
140. OMGBY, 10/90-1/20, 1 of 3, RG 260, IfZ.
141. Hauptaktei 0061-6, StA St.
142. OMGUS, 5/10-1/12, 1 of 10, RG 260, Hauptstaatsarchiv Stuttgart.
143. OMGWB, 12/221-2/4, 21 of 22. RG 260, Hauptstaatsarchiv Stuttgart.

sible prevention of too many political parties representing the Center and Right," a member of Murphy's POLAD staff lamented the clauses in the Potsdam Agreement permitting and encouraging all democratic parties, because he wanted local MG "to prevent the emergence of too many parties." Using the excuse of the negative experience of the Weimar Republic's multiparty system, the author asked Murphy if MG could "not also refuse to permit the organization of local political groups which do not seem to have any real support on a larger geographical or national basis, on the grounds that too many 'splitter' parties should be prevented."[144] Indeed, MG managed to keep out most new parties until after the 1946 elections, which effectively eliminated them from politics until at least 1948. The 1946 regulation against MG intervention was indeed warranted, but it came too late. Also, because it applied only to internal party affairs, MG could shape German political developments by preventing the emergence of grassroots, local parties, even before zonal, not to mention, national parties were permitted. Grassroots developments, officially encouraged by MG policy, were in fact actively discouraged by MG officers.

Only one new party succeeded in entering the city councils in Frankfurt, Munich, and Stuttgart in 1946, the Wirtschaftliche-Aufbau-Vereinigung (WAV) in Munich. The situation was somewhat different in 1948. The Neue Partei did get two seats in the Stuttgart city council. In Munich, the particularistic, xenophobic Bayern Partei (BP),[145] which attracted some former Bayerische Heimats- und Königspartei (BHKP) members,[146] was the second largest party, with thirteen of

144. POLAD/ 729/ 37, 4 of 4, RG 84, IfZ. Dan E. Rogers argues that "the American occupation discriminated against both Left and Right extremes in a halting yet continuing attempt to bring stable, moderate democracy to postwar Germany." Rogers, p. 515. Rogers tends to see moderation as the U.S. motive, rather than as a byproduct of a general avoidance of many or splinter parties or the de facto, but probably unintentional, practice of giving the older Weimar parties the head start. Cf. Loewenberg, p. 268.

145. In the 22 July 1948 session of the city council's Hauptausschuss, the Bayern Partei fought to rid the city of its single Chinese restaurant, with the excuse that "Wir Bayern gehen nicht nach China, um dort eine Laden aufzumachen ... Übermorgen kommen sonst 40 oder 60 Polen, die was aufmachen wollen, dann kommen die Griechen und die Jugoslawen, und so geht es weiter." The BP motion was defeated. RP 721/5, 22 July 1948, p. 1440, StA Mü. The BP was licensed on the Kreis level in Oct. 1946, but U.S. MG delayed its licensing on the Land level until March 1948 because of its Bavarian separatism, and in order to prevent it from detracting too much from the development of the CSU as an all-Christian party, firmly aligned with the CDU. See Mintzel, p. 78.

146. Kock, p. 164. The BHKP had been licensed on the Kreis level, but then was banned because of its monarchistic and antidemocratic tendencies on 9 May

fifty seats in the 1948 council. The WAV, whose chairperson's criminal record and activities eventually led to the party's demise, was also able to win three seats in the 1948 elections.[147]

Munich's 1948 city council had seven different factions, while Stuttgart had five, and Frankfurt had four. Munich's two new parties, the Bayern-Partei and the nonparty, the one-member Parteilose Katholiken, and the somewhat older WAV, which were all to the Right of the CSU, constituted a third of the city council. But even with this large percentage, the traditional parties continued to dominate the council. The largest party was the SPD, which then took over the post of OB, while Scharnagl fell to the position of 2. Bürgermeister. Indeed, POLAD's concern that the licensing of new parties on the Right might "weaken considerably the non-Communist and non-socialist political forces,"[148] in other words the CDU/CSU and the FDP, did seem to have some validity in the Munich case. Thus, although Munich had the largest number of new parties, their conservative, even at times reactionary, nature prevented them from constituting a democratizing force, not to mention a force for change. Instead, most of these particular parties wanted to turn the clock back to even before the Weimar Republic, by creating a more authoritarian and less secular and less ethnically diverse Bavarian society.

The minor role that any new progressive parties were predestined to play had major implications for the continuity of the ideology and the hierarchical structure of the revived parties of the Weimar Republic. The lack of new competition from new sources early on allowed these old parties and their transfigured successor parties to sink comfortably back into many of their old structures, ideologies, and traditional party rivalries. In Munich, for example, the CSU began very much as a revived Bavarian People's Party (BVP) in terms of its membership and its world view. Such continuity prevented any internal spring cleaning of the parties, in terms of a reassessment of ideas, methods and structures, which surely all

---

1946. Daniel Rogers is critical of MG's ban of the BHKP and the NPD in Hesse. He argues that neither party was actually undemocratic, but that the U.S. banned them in order to restrain the far Right. See Rogers, p. 516 ff. The former referred to the divine right of kings, while the latter promoted the exclusion of women from active and passive citizenship and granting votes to men according to their age. Most modern western definitions of democratic platforms would not include such divine right concepts or anti-one person-one vote franchises.

147. Schattenhofer, p. 384. The neo-Fascist Deutscher Block (DB), founded in October 1947, was an offshoot of the WAV. See Mintzel, p. 78.

148. POLAD/729/ 37, 4 of 4, RG 84, IfZ.

the parties needed after the experience of their collapse or dissolution during the Third Reich. Such a critical self-evaluation might have resulted in new alignments and a real democratization of the parties from the bottom up, rather than from the top down, as it actually took place. This restoration from the top down of the old structures and attitudes and of, to some extent, the surviving old elites inhibited internal party reform.

The continuity of party leadership also prevented the channeling of new ideas into the parties from new members, who experienced the effects of party discipline, even exclusion from the party, if they dared to question the party line as established by the party elite.[149] Such dissenters included members of the Antifa committees, which were model democratic, grassroots, reform-oriented groups, but which departed from traditional partisan politics. Other dissenters included the female city councilors in Munich, who collaborated across party lines to introduce various motions. Almost a fourth of Munich's extremely heterogeneous council were women, the highest percentage of women ever in Munich's history, although only one belonged to a new party. These women councilors introduced cross-party motions, to the dismay of their male colleagues and party leaders.[150]

Such dissenters had little decision-making power within the party hierarchy and could generally be quelled from above. For example, Kurt Schumacher himself intervened in local-level politics when he forbade any Social Democrats from serving as licensees of the *Frankfurter Rundschau*, whose licensee board had been a model of multiparty – albeit predominantly on the left – cooperation (one Center Party, three SPD, and three KPD licensees). The SPD chairperson for Hesse, Willi Knothe, an original licensee, who had since resigned, informed SPD journalists that they would be expelled from the party if they volunteered their services as licensees to MG (ICD).

149. This was especially true for members who exemplified cross-party cooperation by remaining in anti-Fascist organizations, such as the Union of Persecutees of the Nazi Regime (VVN) and the SPD-KPD Arbeitsgemeinschaften. For the specific case of Frankfurt, see Emil Carlebach, "Frankfurts Antifaschisten 1945," in Ulrich Schneider (ed.), *Als der Krieg zu Ende war: Hessen 1945* (Frankfurt, 1980), p. 12ff. A more general account can be found in Günther Plum, "Versuche gesellschaftspolitischer Neuordnung. Ihr Scheitern in Kräftefeld deutscher und allierter Politik," in *Westdeuschlands Weg zur Bundesrepublik 1945–1949* (München, 1976), p. 97f.

150. For examples, see the following protocols: RP 722/9, Personalausschusssitzung, 7 April 1949; RP 722/1, Stadtratssitzung, 29 March 1949; RP 722/2, Stadt-ratssitzung, 12 April 1949, StA Mü.

Rather than fighting the accusation that the *Frankfurter Rundschau* was really a Communist newspaper, the SPD hierarchy strengthened the accusation by withdrawing its licensees. The Americans in ICD, however, outwitted Schumacher et al. by bringing in an SPD journalist-in-exile, Karl Gerold, from Switzerland, and getting a commitment from him to serve, before he was aware of the SPD policy or subject to party discipline.[151]

Whereas SPD, KPD, and some Center Party and Democratic Party members cooperated extensively in Stuttgart in the Arbeitsausschüsse,[152] in Frankfurt and Munich SPD-KPD Arbeitsgemeinschaften were formed immediately after political parties were allowed to function openly. In Frankfurt there was even a Four-Party Committee of the SPD, KPD, CDU and LDP(FDP) that consisted of five members of each party who met to discuss all important political problems, in order to find solutions congenial to all four factions.[153] OB Blaum let it be known that he was against such committees, because he did not believe that they had any practical significance. He also pointed out that MG had not approved of such committees.[154] This Four-Party Committee, chaired by the CDU, concentrated on practical concerns like a winter emergency program, and on suggestions for the new Hessian government and for the formation of an advisory council on the Land level until Land elections were restored.[155] Supplementing the underutilized advisory council, the committee functioned until the spring of 1946 and worked hard to prevent a smear campaign in the election.[156]

It is striking that in Frankfurt this considerable amount of informal party cooperation existed alongside a great deal of conflict and lack of party cooperation in the city council. By 1948 the SPD, FDP,

151. OMGH 8/190-2/9, 5 of 6, RG 260, IfZ. Cf. Cedric Belfrage (Press Control officer for the FR), *Seeds of Destruction: The Truth about the U.S. Occupation of Germany* (New York, 1954), p. 213. See also Emil Carlebach, *Zensur ohne Schere Die Gründerjahre der "Frankfurter Rundschau" 1945/47* (Frankfurt am Main, 1985), p. 93ff.

152. Although the leadership of the local SPD and DVP distanced their parties from the Arbeitsausschüsse after the fall of 1945, they did not not officially discourage their members' participation, apparently in hopes of diluting KPD influence. See Vietzen, p. 145 and 25 Oct. 1945 report by Brewster Morris to Sec. of State, p. 7, POLAD/729/37, 3 of 4, , RG 84, IfZ.

153. *Frankfurter Rundschau*, 27 Nov. 1945.

154. Ibid., 31 Dec. 1945.

155. Wolf-Arno Kropat, *Hessen in der Stunde Null 1945/47* (Wiesbaden, 1979), p. 71. In this case, cross-party cooperation was led by the Right and not by the Communists.

156. 12 Jan. 1946 Entschliessung des Aktionsausschusses der vier Parteien, OMGH, 8/2-1/6, 2 of 5, RG 260, IfZ.

and CDU were refusing to work with the KPD members in the city council almost altogether. Apparently this open animosity stemmed from the escalating Cold War tension in the midst of the Berlin Blockade and the related recent local divisiveness between the KPD and SPD, parties that previously had worked particularly closely together in their own joint action group (*Aktions-Einheit*) in Frankfurt. In the 16 August 1948 session of the city council the head of the LDP faction announced that the three other parties had decided to exclude Communists from all affairs of the council to the extent that they could, because the KPD had eliminated itself by its uncooperativeness. When the KPD faction leader, Emil Carlebach, tried to contradict him, the LDP representative criticized the KPD for the Berlin Blockade and for trying to sabotage the Marshall Plan. He also warned that Carlebach and the KPD would not be able to prevent "the three democratic parties" from working together to raise Frankfurt out of its terrible defeat. His speech was reportedly cheered by the LDP, CDU, and SPD.[157] Even an MG informant noted, after this particular session, that "the attitude of the three parties SPD, CDU, and LDP during the quarrels (in city council meetings) clearly indicate that they are determined to exclude the KPD in [*sic*] future from any cooperation. They are opposing the KPD and unanimously vote against every motion introduced by the KPD."[158] In December 1948 the head of the CDU faction expressed his regret that democracy forced him to have to allow Communists to speak, and called upon his fellow councilors to eradicate (*ausmerzen*) the KPD.[159] Although the SPD clearly did not take issue with these criticisms, and apparently cheered them on, there are no examples of Social Democrats attacking Communists directly as did the CDU and LDP. However, without SPD support, it is doubtful that the CDU or the LDP would have taken such an uncompromising position, especially since the SPD was the strongest party in the 1948 council and because Frankfurt was ruled by an SPD OB.

The SPD was of course the most direct rival of the KPD in terms of traditional working class-support. There were Social Democrats who wanted to continue working closely with the KPD, at least on some issues, and there had been a strong anti-Schumacher wing that tried to keep the SPD out of the Cold War struggle against the

---

157. Stadtverordnetenversammlungssitzungsprotokolle 1948, 16 Aug. 1948, p. 56 ff., StA Ffm.
158. MG informant's report, 16 August 1948, OMGH, 8/45-2/30, 2 of 3, RG 260, IfZ.
159. Stadtverordnetenversammlungssitzungsprotokolle 1948, 2 Dec. 1948, p. 39f., StA Ffm.

KPD. But Schumacher had managed to become the almost undisputed leader and, as such, was able to threaten those who continued to cooperate with Communists in structures such as SPD-KPD working committees, newspaper licensee boards, and the Association of Persecutees of the Nazi Regime (Vereinigung der Verfolgten des Naziregimes or VVN).[160] At the national conference of SPD leaders on 5 October 1945, representatives of the "new" or left-wing Socialists differed from the dominant SPD line, according to an OSS report, "in their espousal of closer cooperation with the Communists." Yet even this group accepted Schumacher's leadership because, although he had held a place in the pre-1933 party hierarchy, they did not consider him one "of the 'old men' of the SPD from the Weimar period."[161]

Schumacher worked closely with younger Social Democrats with whom he had become acquainted through illegal work during the Third Reich and through shared concentration camp experiences.[162] This helped endear him to the often younger, left-wing Socialists. On the other hand, "the old line party organizers" welcomed his leadership because of "his orthodox attitude toward the importance of an independent organization of Social Democracy and his reserve toward the Communists."[163] The Stuttgart SPD fell in line behind Schumacher relatively quickly because of his ties there during the Weimar Republic, when he had been a journalist and head of the local SPD. He had even turned down a high administrative post in Württemberg in the spring of 1945 in order to focus on reconstructing the SPD.

In Frankfurt, Wilhelm Knothe, the leading SPD member in the advisory city council, who soon chaired the Hessian SPD, made several trips to Hanover in the summer and fall of 1945 to visit Schumacher. He was given the task of "swinging" the other SPD organizers in Hesse "into line behind Schumacher."[164] It was after Knothe became an ardent backer of Schumacher that he resigned from the licensee board of the *Frankfurter Rundschau* and, under Schumacher's orders, put pressure on other Social Democrats, not to accept a license with the newspaper as long as there were Communists on the board.[165] This was another factor behind the grow-

160. Plum, p. 97f.
161. OSS, FIS 37, 3 Nov. 1945, p. 8f., RG 226, NARA.
162. Ibid., p. 2.
163. Ibid., p. 8f.
164. Ibid., p. 2.
165. OMGH 8/190-2/9, 5 of 6, RG 260, IfZ. Cf. Belfrage, *Seeds of Destruction*, p. 213. See also Carlebach, *Zensur ohne Schere*, p. 93ff.

ing tension in the Frankfurt city council between the KPD, whose *Rundschau* licensees were all eventually forced to resign by MG for political reasons, and the SPD, as well as the other parties. It is interesting to note that, to a large extent, the source of this tension originated outside (above) the city and from the high levels of the party hierarchy as well as in international East-West relations.

Munich's Social Democrats were unique in Bavaria for having established an effective Arbeitsgemeinschaft with the Communists and for trying to convince the rest of their southern districts that the SPD needed to exert major efforts to broaden its labor base. They were opposed by MG-appointed SPD Minister President Wilhelm Hoegner, who was more inclined toward recruitment from the Right, and the Franconian wing of the Bavarian SPD, which was unwilling to formalize any relationship with the KPD.[166]

From 1945 until 1949, of the three cities, Munich's city council exhibited by far the best relations between the SPD and the KPD. While animosity would best describe the situation in Frankfurt at the time, Munich's SPD faction was extremely class conscious and protective of the workers on the eve of the currency reform, which the SPD, like the KPD, feared would benefit industry and commerce while hurting the workers and organized labor in particular.[167] The discussions over a strike to protest the practice of hoarding goods and the black market in November 1948, as well as numerous debates concerning a broad social *Lastenausgleich*, point out that in the Munich city council, the SPD and KPD were usually aligned against the CDU and the other parties on the Right, rather than the KPD versus the other parties.[168] Overall, there was less partisan conflict among the traditional parties in Munich, although statements and motions by members of the Bayern-Partei and the WAV often heated up discusssions in the council considerably.

Of course, the Germans were not operating in a void. Their political party preferences and prejudices were influenced, not only by their own previous political affiliations, but also by the preferences and biases of the occupying power and international events. In terms of an MG bias towards certain German political parties in the three cities under examination here, the first year of the occupation should be broken down into phases. During the first phase, which lasted from the initial occupation until the horror over the concen-

---

166. OSS/SSU, FIS 39, p. 20ff, RG 226, NARA.
167. Hauptausschusssitzungsprotokolle, 4 March 1948, RP 721/4, StA Mü.
168. Hauptausschusssitzungsprotokolle, 11 Nov. 1948, RP 721/5, StA Mü .

tration-camp discoveries faded in the late summer of 1945, persecuted Communists were sought out by MG Public Safety and Civil
Affairs personnel for advice and help in denazification as well as for
a few important posts either in labor relations, denazification, or
journalism. Especially during the strict nonfraternization period,
which corresponded with the liberation of the concentration camps,
Communism was regarded as the one label that one could positively
equate with reliable anti-Nazism. Intelligence reports from the OSS
and other groups on Communist Party activity during the early
months of the occupation abound with comments about the moderation and cooperation displayed by the Communists.[169] They also
discuss the energy, capability, and youthfulness of the KPD leaders,
who were often contrasted with the experienced, but less lively veteran leaders of the other parties, especially the SPD, who were trying to revive the old Weimar past.[170]

Many Germans were surprised that the Americans had anything
to do with the Communists, although most realized that, as a political group, the Communists had been the most strongly opposed to
the Nazis and the most persecuted by the Nazis. During this early
phase, MG officers displayed a certain amount of respect toward the
Communists, which was noticeably absent in their behavior toward
most other Germans.[171] Social Democrats, on the other hand, were
harder to gauge for most Americans. There had been active resistance among Social Democrats, and many had been persecuted by
the Nazis, but in both areas, the SPD's record was not as uncompromising as the KPD's. The MG officers often trusted clergy or active
lay members of churches more than Social Democrats, because at
first it was assumed that the churches, as institutions, had resisted
the Nazis, which was actually not generally the case. Heterogeneous

---

169. 1 Oct. 1945 Detachment F-10, Stadtkreis Stuttgart Political Activity Report, RG
260, OMGUS, 5/10-1/12, 1 of 10, Hauptstaatsarchiv Stuttgart. It is important to
remember that the OSS and ICD/DISCC contained numerous Americans with
more leftist views than OMGUS personnel generally, and that to the extent that
these groups influenced the occupation, it was in these first months.

170. FIS 23, 24 Sept. 1945, p. 13, 19f. , OMGUS, 15/109-2/7, 1 of 6, RG 260, IfZ. As
late as April 1947, the Stuttgart detachment was complaining about "the dead-
beats" of the parties, who were "the old men with old minds and (who) are
unable to clean the tarnish from their thinking." See OMGWB, 12/221-2/1, 3 Of
9, 8 April 1947, RG 260, Hauptstaatsarchiv Stuttgart.

171. OMGBY 10/90-1/20, 1 of 3. RG 260, IfZ. Also personal interviews with the former city councilors Dr. Ludwig Schmid (CSU), Oskar Neumann and Adelheid
Liessmann (KPD), and the journalist Georg Wulffius in Munich, and the KPD
councilor and journalist, Emil Carlebach, in Frankfurt.

groups, including those with monarchist leanings, such as the FAB, were regarded skeptically, especially if their anti-Nazi credentials had been earned after Nazi defeat was imminent.[172]

In the second phase, once the shock of the concentration camps had worn off and before parties were officially allowed, MG officers tended to rely on either those who were nonaligned, or representatives of the more conservative parties, who seemed less politicized and thus more pragmatic, such as Kurt Blaum, Arnulf Klett, and Karl Scharnagl. The Communists, who had been used as advisors in the early phase, were not appointed to high posts except in the area of denazification, a task which, with the qualified exception of the SPD, the other parties tended to avoid because it might make them unpopular with their fellow Germans and prospective party members.

By this second phase, there had been frequent turnovers in MG detachment personnel; when the men who were trained specifically for civil affairs reached the end of their military stint and returned home, even less prepared officers and enlisted men took their place. To these MG officers, the SPD supporters were still suspect, now not so much because they had not sufficiently resisted the Nazis, but because they had joined in various action committees with the Communists,[173] or because of their overt politicization. By the fall of 1945, the FDP (LDP) and CDU/CSU, with the latter in the forefront, had often won MG over to their side. This was partly due to their more pragmatic, seemingly less political nature. In the case of the CDU/CSU, especially in Munich, the religious, middle-class traits played a role.[174] With the FDP (LDP), especially in Stuttgart, but also in Frankfurt, the old-style economic liberalism won many MG hearts.

The final phase of the first year set the trend for the rest of the occupation. This began in early 1946 when the Communists had become completely suspect to high-level MG. Churchill's March 1946 "Iron Curtain" speech coincided with the victory of the State Department's policy of anti-Communism in Europe and Asia over any leftist tendencies in organizations like the now-defunct OSS. This was

---

172. Ibid.

173. See Carlebach, "Frankfurts Antifaschisten...," p. 21.

174. Personal interview with Georg Wulffius, who advised the Munich detachment in its licensing of political parties, 3 May 1982, Munich. The American consulate general's office in Munich on 20 August 1945 noted that "certain SPD functionaries in Munich have stated that they now feel that American Military Government has started to pursue a policy in its supervision of political activities here in that it now favors the CSU. They state that the reason for this 'partiality' is that we now wish to build up a strong Catholic bloc against Soviet Russia." POLAD/ 746/7, 1 of 8, RG 84, IfZ.

reflected internationally in the United States' active opposition to tripartism in France and its discouragement of Communist Party participation in postwar Italian parliamentary politics. In Germany, U.S. MG's spirit of collective guilt and anti-Nazism had given way to anti-Communism. The fact that MG considered the Communist Party to have the "keenest leadership and best organization"[175] only made the Communists appear more dangerous and devious to MG.

Anxiety about which way the SPD would go – more to the Center or to the Left – continued to grow. Some pro-Left American elements in intelligence agencies and the ICD were skeptical about the SPD because of the growing strength of the Schumacher wing and its willingness to abandon strict anti-Fascist policies in order to jump on the bandwagon of anti-Communism. On the other hand, the supposedly apolitical elements in MG were concerned that the "S" in the SPD stood for "Socialist" which, for many Americans, had become synonymous with communist.[176] By the spring of 1946, reports of Communist infiltration into the SPD started appearing in detachment reports. In May 1946 the Munich detachment announced in May 1946 that "the latest estimate is that 20 percent of the SPD are Communists."[177] The source of this information is not specified, nor was it confirmed by either the SPD or the KPD. It is much more likely that it was based on rumor and the spreading shadow of the perceived threat of a Soviet and/or Communist takeover in Germany.

By the spring of 1947, MG intelligence reports, which were no longer researched or written by the progressive or leftist Americans who had either resigned in disillusionment or been purged, were stressing that "Communism has gripped key offices or institutions, and the sympathy of a larger percentage of a destitute population than is generally realized. The full significance of the facts can best be appreciated when considered relative to the unknown but suspected existence of party workers incognito." This same Stuttgart detachment report then went on to suggest conducting a witch hunt within MG to weed out possible Communists: "Since Communism is

175. Weekly Political Activity Report for Frankfurt, 15 Nov. 1947, OMGUS, 5/8-1/7, 7 of 7, RG 260, IfZ.
176. The author Günter Plum maintains that there was a stronger willingness on the part of a significant wing of the SPD in all of the Western occupation Zones to unite with the KPD or at least to retain such action committees than is generally accepted. This was especially true at the time of Kurt Schumacher's 5 Oct. 1945 speech at Wennigsen, where he denounced any such union. See Plum, "Versuche gesellschaftspolitischer Neuordnung," p. 97f.
177. May 1946 Detachment E-213 (Munich) Monthly Historical Report, p. 7, OMGBY, 10/78-1/3,1 of 5, RG 260, IfZ.

a world wide movement, and has secured such influence in the United States for example, as to have resulted in a congressional investigation there, it is reasonable to infer that because Germany occupies such a critical position in world affairs today, that the shrewdest Communistic minds may have infiltrated MG. It is believed that a thorough investigation of key MG officials as well as indigenous civil officials in critical positions, would not be a too drastic measure at this time."[178]

By the summer of 1949, when the MG for Württemberg-Baden conducted a survey on local self-government in Stuttgart and the growth of democratic attitudes, it complained about the citizens' lack of political awareness and involvement, although so-called citizens' meetings or *Bürgerversammlungen*, which had been initiated in 1948, had become quite popular. The report criticized the establishment of political parties for not being "very appropriate to promote democracy." It went on to note that "party dogmatism makes cooperation and compromise, two fundamentals of the democratic process, very difficult. As the political line of the parties is usually decided by top men in higher quarters, membership has not much influence. Moreover the totalitarian ways of the KPD as well as the centralism of the SPD make no fertile soil for democracy." Lamenting the fact that twenty to thirty-five-year-olds were showing "practically no evidence of political interest and democratic attitude,"[179] the intelligence officers who authored this report obviously made no connection between how MG had allowed political parties to form and discouraged grassroots democracy in the first place, particularly among young Germans, and the current absence of active democratic political development. They also disregarded the impact of the Nazi experience and the defeat on the many returning Wehrmacht personnel and POWs as well as the necessary focus of many Germans on day-to-day survival.

178. 12 May 1947 Stadtkreis Stuttgart Intelligence Report, p. 1, OMGWB, 12/221-2/1, 1 of 9, RG 260, IfZ.

179. 1 August 1949 Stuttgart Liaison and Security Office Report, OMGWB, 12/141-2/1-29, 37 of 47, RG 260, IfZ. It is particularly interesting that the KPD, in all three cities, had by far the youngest city councilors, with most in their thirties, and presumably the youngest active members. Part of this can be explained by persecution by the Nazis and the likelihood that older KPD members would not have been as likely to have survived it. Of course this twenty- to thirty-five-year-old group was the one which had reached adulthood either just before or during the Third Reich, had belonged to the Hitler Jugend or Bund deutscher Mädel, had served in the Wehrmacht, and was likely to be the most disillusioned by politics.

Conclusion

The different forms of democratic initiatives that Germans in Frankfurt, Munich and Stuttgart took during the first postwar year were not entirely without effect, yet they did not result in major structural change or groundbreaking, lasting reforms. Compared to the Third Reich, local government was democratized in the sense that many political parties were eventually authorized and Germans were allowed to elect their own municipal officials. However, the restraints placed on grassroots political activity by both U.S. MG and its appointed German officials in 1945 and 1946 inhibited not only the development of new and refounded political parties, but also the potential for a fuller democratic transformation of German society and the economic order.

The only actual provision made by MG for German democratization was that its appointees be democratic.[180] Given the undemocratic nature of most bureaucracies, placing democrats into leading positions in nondemocratic structures, such as the appointed city administrations and the advisory councils, could not guarantee democracy. One must also take into account that most MG officials, in practice, equated democratic Germans with non-Nazi, pro-American, anti-Communist Germans, who seemed to mirror themselves. This differs considerably from Webster's definition of a democrat as "a person who believes in and practices the principle of equality of rights, opportunity, and treatment."[181] One grassroots democratic movement, that of the Antifas , was anti-Nazi rather than just non-Nazi, not anti-American, but also not pro-American capitalism and either non-Communist or sometimes even pro-Communist. The Antifas' activities, their heterogenous political composition and their plans for a thorough denazification of German society all represented models of civic involvement and non-hierarchical cooperation, however, which could have further democratized the structures of postwar German society and politics. But they needed the approval, if not the support of the occupying authorites in order to pursue their plans and continue their activities, and this they did not have.[182]

The MG ban on political activities in the spring of 1945 did suppress the Antifa movement, but it did not prevent a revival of the old

---

180. Gillen, p. 5.
181. *Webster's New World Dictionary of the American Language* (New York, 1970), 2nd College Ed., p. 375.
182. They may well have run out of steam before too long, but they would definitely have left more of a political legacy.

parties of the Weimar Republic. The OBs' reliance on the old Weimar political party leaders for the selection of the members for the advisory city councils assured a revival of the old parties and their hierarchies. This prevented a grassroots formation and democratization of the parties. Political life was revived, but not revitalized. The early restoration of the old parties, in combination with the MG practice of discouraging new parties, made it very difficult for any new parties to acquire political influence and to succeed in elections.

The advisory councils were often formed to take the wind out of the sails of the Antifas and other grassroots movements. The democratic potential that the councils represented by including more of the community in the municipal decision-making process was inhibited by the motivation behind their formation. This led to their not being particularly representative and to their having minimal power. The OBs, with the exception of Scharnagl in Munich, had not wanted these councils in the first place, but managed to use them to create a facade of democracy while continuing in their own autocratic ways.

The press, when free and open, functions both as a prerequisite and a corequisite to democratic political life. In Frankfurt, the licensee board of the *Frankfurter Rundschau* represented a model of relatively youthful, multiparty cooperation. Initially these licensees worked very closely together with their ICD and DISCC supervisors, who allowed them a great deal of journalistic freedom. The *Rundschau*'s critiques of OB Blaum and the city administration made them more accountable to the citizenry of Frankfurt and contributed to Blaum's political demise in the 1946 elections. This was especially important in Frankfurt because the advisory council found itself so powerless vis-à-vis the administration. Yet in 1946 the multiparty structure of the newspaper began to collapse, as the SPD leadership discouraged SPD-KPD cooperation and even prohibited collaboration on licensee boards. Gradually more censorship was exercised towards the remaining licensees, as ICD and DISCC personnel changes resulted in more conservative, openly anti-Communist supervisors. Thus the *Rundschau*'s democratizing function was also impeded by increasingly anti-Communist policies on the part of Americans and Germans.

The growing political emphasis on anti-Communism and an expeditious economic reconstruction led MG and many Germans to de-emphasize anti-Nazism and denazification and ultimately, whether consciously or not, to limit the degree of democratization of German society. German political groupings were dependent on MG support for any genuine success. Directly, they needed MG authorization for their continued existence, while indirectly, they needed their approval and active encouragement to gain the support of the German electorate. Most Germans, after the experience of wartime and postwar shortages and material discomfort, wanted an expeditious return to normalcy and material well-being. The Americans and the German political parties they supported seemed to represent the best hope for this. Because of their predominantly leftist advocates, long-term political reform and socio-economic structural change came to be associated with Communism.

The growing influx of expellees from Eastern Europe and refugees from the Soviet Zone of occupation added fuel to MG's anti-Communist propaganda in the U.S. Zone. To most Germans, material well-being seemed incongruous with Communism and, by extension, increasingly with any form of socialist-oriented experimentation. As Jürgen Kocka has pointed out, the experience in the Soviet Zone of occupation affected the widespread early postwar mood of German anticapitalism. This anticapitalist atmosphere was based on the perception of connections between German capitalism and the rise of Fascism, and this perception appeared politically all the way from the Left to the center Right of the CDU. In the Soviet Zone, the nationalization of the means of production did not suffice to establish real democratization, indeed it was accompanied by threats to and restrictions of personal freedoms and a lack of economic prosperity. This observation, in combination with American MG policies, the growing political strength of German business interests, and concerns for a quick economic recovery, lessened the appeal of socialization for many Germans and weakened their determination to implement serious socioeconomic change.[183] Many Germans were willing, consciously or unconsciously, to sacrifice the ideals of structural political and socioeconomic democratization in return for U.S.-style capitalism – which most Americans equated with democracy – as long as it meant an end to the very real chaos, disorder, and shortages of the postwar period.[184]

183. Kocka, "1945," p. 147 ff.
184. The voices of those who continued actively to question traditional German political party and state structures became rarer and more muted, with fewer and fewer having concrete alternatives in mind.

Chapter VI

U.S. MILITARY GOVERNMENT IN RETREAT

The Return of German Self-Government and the Results of Democratization Initiatives

Introduction

*D*irect U.S. MG control on the local level ended with the restoration of the democratic process in 1946. Elections were held first in the smallest municipalities and counties in January 1946, and then in May 1946 in the major cities[1] such as Frankfurt, Munich, and Stuttgart. After all the local elections and those for the constitutional conventions for the Länder had been held, and after Secretary of State Byrnes gave his famous September 1946 Stuttgart speech on reconstruction, the military governor, General Lucius D. Clay, issued a directive outlining the new relationships between MG and German public authorities. This directive, which was to go into effect once the Länder had adopted constitutions some two months later, stipulated that MG would achieve its objectives through observation, inspection, reporting and advising, and by only exercising its veto power in cases where economic, social, political, and governmental measures were considered to be in clear violation of MG objectives. Although this still allowed MG quite a bit of leeway, the directive did signal a new role for MG in its relations with the Germans, in particular with their political parties: rather than licensing and supervising, it was now supposed to just observe and advise.[2]

---

1. Elections were held last in the cities outside or independent of counties (*kreisfreie Städte*), which included all three of the cities in this study.
2. Bolten, p. 56. Bolten was the executive officer of the Political Activites Branch of CAD.

Moves toward German autonomy were reflected even earlier in organizational changes within MG. As of 15 November 1945, local German officials would handle all operational functions, but they would remain under the supervision and control of the local MG detachments. Each detachment's size would be reduced to include "only those officers who (were) performing duties peculiar to MG and whose duties (were) not paralleled in the German government."[3] In other words, a detachment officer would no longer serve as a counterpart to each department head and major city official, and Germans would have more autonomy and less interference in their municipal tasks.

Part of the reason behind this reorganization was the steadily decreasing number of available MG personnel due to the completion of soldiers' tours of duty and the granting of their requests to return to the States. The other factor was the difficulty MG was experiencing while actively participating in many of the German tasks, partly because of cultural and administrative differences, and sometimes because of insufficient language skills and expertise in the area to which they were assigned.[4] Enough personnel was to be retained on the local level to supervise elections, but thereafter, "surplus" personnel was to be transferred to the Land-MG. The city detachment was to be withdrawn within thirty days of the 1946 local elections, and MG L&S offices would be placed in their stead. The L&S offices would "be responsible for liaison between occupational troops and civil government; for calling for the use of occupational troops as necessary to prevent or put down disorder within the Landkreis or Stadtkreis concerned; for periodic non-specialized reports of the general operations of civil governments and trends of public opinion; and for such other duties as are necessary to carry out these basic responsibilities."[5]

The L&S offices, with usually two officers and a small administrative staff, were considerably smaller than the detachments had been.[6] They stayed in place throughout the OMGUS period, although,

---

3.   1 Oct.1945 USFET memorandum to the commanding generals in the Eastern and Western Districts of the U.S. Zone entitled "Reorganization of Military Government Control Channels in order to develop German Responsibility for Self-Government," POLAD/ 730/ 20, 2 of 4, RG 84, IfZ. This date did not represent any sort of watershed for German-MG relations in the three cities under examination here. However in other cities, such as Coburg, it apparently did. See Beyersdorf, p. 62.

4.   For an elaboration of this theme, see the analysis originally written in Frankfurt in 1950: Starr, *Denazification*.

5.   POLAD/730/ 20, 2 of 4, RG 84, IfZ.

6.   Ibid.

like the detachments, they experienced quite a bit of personnel turnover. When HICOG replaced OMGUS in 1949, the L&S offices were replaced by individual resident officers. Thus, up until the finalization of the Occupation Statute in 1955, representatives of the U.S. occupation continued to oversee Germans on the local level, both in the county seats and in major cities, as well as on the Land, zonal and national levels. But the administrative level at which MG exercised its supervision of German developments changed considerably during the 1945–1955 decade, in order to reflect the gradual extension of German autonomy from the lowest (local) to the highest (national) level.

By the time local and Land elections were completed and MG's role changed from direct control to indirect supervision, the focus of MG-German relations had moved from the local to the state and zonal, and soon thereafter bizonal level. Neither local MG nor local German officials had any real influence over policy developments, and numerous local decisions were constrained by higher authorities. The more traditional top-down hierarchy that was now firmly ensconced severely limited the possibility for bottom-up developments. Whereas the MG role of overseer was more likely to involve individual acts of local intervention in the early phase of the occupation, after 1946, MG exercised its influence more often from above on the zonal level. The task of overseeing German elections and other political, social, and economic developments provided MG with ample opportunities to get involved.

The extent of this "oversight" varied from overt intervention, as in the case of the MG legislation for civil service reform and the prevention of nationalization initiatives in Hessen, to more covert intervention, as in the case of the previously mentioned 1946 Magistrat elections in Frankfurt and the 1946 OB election in Stuttgart. MG involvement in German political life also included an anti-Communist campaign, formally initiated in 1948, which included a program of anti-Communist propaganda, the surveillance of individuals and groups, the creation of obstacles for political campaigning, and the provision of material aid to all other non-Communist parties in order to disadvantage the KPD in elections. This anti-Communist campaign was initiated despite a 1947 State Department report on the KPD's democratic behavior and intentions in the Western Zones.[7]

---

7. April 1947 report by Herbert Marcuse, POLAD/460/4, 2 of 4, RG 84, IfZ. This report will be elaborated upon later in this chapter. The KPD city councilors in Munich, Frankfurt, and Stuttgart all exhibited democratic behavior in the council and committee meetings.

The success and/or failure of MG attempts to influence German political, economic, and social developments during this "supervisory" phase of the occupation depended to a large extent on how consistent MG was in its policies, whether or not it had German allies, and whether these German allies were on the Right or the Left of the political spectrum. An alignment of MG with the German political forces of the Right usually succeeded, as can be seen in the anti-Communism campaign and the dominance of free enterprise over nationalization or socialization of industry. An alignment of MG with the German Left, or at least with some elements of it, as in the case of civil service reform, failed. This can be seen in the fact that as soon as Germans regained enough autonomy, they reversed these MG directives, whose implementation, as will be shown, they had fairly successfully postponed anyway.

In the case of denazification, a policy with much more support from the German Left than from the Right, U.S. MG wavered between an initially very stringent, but quantitatively unrealistic implementation, and sweeping amnesties which exempted numerous Germans with more political incrimination than those tried early on. This wavering allowed German elites the leeway to grant selective reprieves – which often became exemptions – to many incriminated Germans, whose expertise and/or property was deemed essential to an expeditious economic reconstruction. The inconsistency in denazification, and the fact that the less incriminated Nazis were tried first and received harsher sentences during the early, more adamantly anti-Nazi phase of the occupation, while the accused offenders in the top classifications of incrimination got much more lenient sentences or fell under various MG amnesties, had serious repercussions. This led to shortcomings in the program and a resentment on the part of both the less incriminated and those anti-Fascists and others who had been persecuted during the Third Reich.

This chapter will examine the influence of MG on the 1946 and 1948 elections in Frankfurt, Stuttgart, and Munich and on municipal decision making and general political trends after 1946 in the areas of denazification and the reinstatement of former Nazis to their positions of employment. The propagation of anti-Communism, civil service (*Berufsbeamtentum*) reform, and economic reconstruction will also be discussed. These later political developments, which all involved some aspect of real or perceived democratization, cannot be examined exclusively on the microcosmic level of the municipality. The higher levels of German administration must now be integrated into this analysis because it is there that reform, if it took place at all, was accomplished through either MG decree or German legislation. Many reform initiatives had started at the local or grassroots level. If they had not been successfully adopted there, they were unlikely to break through higher levels of administration that were formed and/or restored after the municipal administrations.

These higher levels of administration were staffed by individuals with usually even more bureaucratic and/or administrative experience than that of the initial MG-appointed municipal administrators. The appointed as well as the elected Land, zonal and bizonal German officials were more likely to have had a higher status within their area of bureaucratic expertise or within their political parties than their municipal counterparts. These elites also displayed a stronger tendency toward continuity rather than change or reform, and a greater stress on bureaucratic efficiency than was present on the municipal level. Higher-level German officials, both appointed and elected, who had not been actively involved in the Stunde Null interregnum, were more likely than local-level Germans, who at least had been caught up in the atmosphere of flux and grassroots democratic initiatives, to share MG goals of an expedient economic recovery and a postwar Germany modeled on and allied with American-style capitalism and parliamentary government. It is therefore in this larger context, that the scope of MG influence and the results of German and American reform initiatives, after the democratic process was restored, must be considered.

Elections

The first postwar elections were the first elections in Germany since 1933. The experience of the demise of the Weimar Republic, the lack of democracy during the Third Reich, the defeat in the war, the unconditional surrender, and the total occupation were all factors influencing the voter's approach to the polls. As was the case in most of Europe, Frankfurt, Munich, and Stuttgart experienced a rise in the popularity of the Left, in particular the Social Democratic Party. However, the general electoral results in 1946 did not vary drastically from the last pre-Depression elections in 1928, at least as far as the major political parties and their predecessors were concerned. In both Stuttgart and Frankfurt, the SPD received the largest number of votes in 1946. In fact, because only two parties were represented in the Frankfurt city council with its unusually high 15 percent minimum clause, the SPD received the absolute majority of council seats, much more than its 39.3 percent of the vote would have otherwise merited. In Munich, a 1920s stronghold of the Bavarian People's Party, the CSU was the largest party in 1946, although this changed in 1948, when the SPD received a plurality. In fact the SPD was the party which received the largest number of seats (and votes) in all three cities in the 1948 city council elections.

The MG influenced elections through its licensing of political parties, while displaying a clear-cut preference for keeping the number of parties down, primarily because of its fears of a repeat of the Weimar political sitiuation.[8] This ultimately worked to the advantage of the older, more traditional parties of the Weimar Republic, like the SPD and the KPD, as well as the new CDU and the FDP, whose leadership and rank and file had carried over and/or consolidated themselves to a large degree from the old Weimar parties of other names (BVP/ Center Party, DDP/ DVP/ Staatspartei). These older parties were able to (re)organize much more quickly, due to their old organizational ties and their representation in the 1945–46 advisory city councils. MG's practice of licensing political parties discouraged new parties and provided a crucial headstart for the successors of the old parties of the Weimar Republic.[9]

The 1948 elections witnessed the emergence of a number of new parties in the municipal and Land-level parliaments. By 1948, MG did less to discourage new parties than it had done in the earlier phase of the occupation, primarily because by then new parties no longer required MG licensing. In Munich, six different parties were represented in its 1948–52 city council (the four from 1946 plus two new ones), with the new Bayernpartei winning the second largest number of seats (26 percent).[10] Stuttgart, on the other hand, had one new party and Frankfurt had none, although the FDP and the KPD were now, thanks to the repeal of the high 15 percent minimum clause in Hesse, represented in the 1948 council.

Whereas MG had influenced the development of German politics primarily via its selective use of the ban on political activity, the licensing of political parties, and the discouragement of the found-

---

8. Many Germans feared the effects of too many parties as well. But they were more concerned with limiting parties via minimum election result clauses than with restricting the number of parties even allowed to run for election through licensing. They were also less concerned with too many parties on the local level as opposed to the state or national level.

9. See Chapter 5.

10. Michael Schattenhofer, ed., *Chronik der Stadt München, 1945–1948* (Stadtarchiv München, 1980), p. 384.

ing of new parties in the first year of the occupation, its influence took new forms once local and state elections were restored in 1946. Some bias against Communists became apparent as early as late spring of 1945, when some U.S. policymakers were expressing distrust of Communist concentration-camp survivors and the Free Germany movement. A visit by members of Robert Murphy's staff to the Buchenwald concentration camp in late April 1945, prior to the German surrender but after the camp had been liberated and controlled by the Americans for over two weeks, revealed, according to a report by one of the visitors, "a hot bed of Communist propaganda and political activity." To the dismay of the author of the report, the name "comrade" was being used among the former inmates and "propaganda material" signed by the "National Committee of Free Germany, Leipzig District" was present in the camp. Particularly upsetting was the fact that the U.S. MG officer in charge of the camp had decided not to "stop this political activity" since Buchenwald would soon be in the future Soviet Zone. Expressing his disapproval to the head of the USGCC's Political Group, the report's author reminded his boss that "the State Department has a secret but definite policy of in no way supporting or aiding the Free Germany Movement;" that there was an MG ban on political activity; that the reaction could be provoked "that perhaps Goebbels was right and the Americans are indeed turning Germany over to the Communists;" and finally that journalists could "place the American Government in an embarrassing position by describing its apparent toleration of Communist political activity."[11]

Official U.S. occupation policy was to be one of political neutrality, but officials like the author of this report clearly felt that "toleration of Communist political activity" should not be required by a policy of political neutrality. In 1946, POLAD reported to the secretary of state, with some dismay, that OMGUS was requiring all MG personnel "to be politically neutral and aloof." The concern expressed here was with MG personnel *not* indicating "a preference for any individual or group of individuals,"[12] and therefore a dislike for others, i.e., Communists.

MG suspicions about KPD members and alleged Communist sympathizers were based more and more on affiliation or contact with Communism rather than on specific activities against MG policies. In Berlin, POLAD put together a "top secret" list of "biograph-

11.   29 April 1945 Memorandum from Brewster Morris, POLAD/730/55, 1 of 1, RG 84, IfZ.
12.   POLAD/ 746/7, 4 of 8, RG 84, IfZ.

ical data on German Communists and others of possible importance in that field" in early May 1948. Suspects included people who were members of the KPD, but also an almost equal number of non-KPD members, who were considered suspect because of previous socialist leanings or contacts with Communists, or even because of membership in the VVN. This latter organization had a large number of KPD members in it, especially after the SPD hierarchy in the western zones tried to force fellow Social Democrats out of it in 1948 as a way of proving that Social Democrats had nothing to do with Communists.[13] One of the non-KPD suspects on this list was the well-known Stuttgart anti-Nazi lawyer and postwar state attorney general, Dr. Richard Schmid, due to his earlier membership in the SAP and his trial for high treason by the Nazis. Also included on the list was Dr. Karl Barth, for allegedly negotiating "with Communists" and for having "almost a hypnotic influence over (the) well-organized liberal section of (the) Evangelical Church," along with Georg Reuter, the general secretary of the Bavarian Federation of Trade Unions, because he had been described by a KPD functionary as "the man for us."[14]

As early as the summer of 1946, a State Department document, reviewing U.S. policy toward Germany in preparation for a meeting of the Council of Foreign Ministers, directly admitted that "the United States cannot tolerate a Communist dominated Germany."[15] One of the recipients of the report within POLAD asked for modification of this statement because "if left on the record it would indicate that we are hypocritical in our profession of political neutrality." He suggested instead: "The United States cannot tolerate a Germany dominated by a Communist party subservient to Soviet aims."[16] This

---

13. 3 Nov. 1948 Intelligence Report, OMGWB, 12/221-2/3, 3 of 16, and 8 Dec. 1948 SK Stuttgart Intelligence Report, OMGWB, 12/221-2/4, 18 of 22, RG 260, Baden-Württembergisches Hauptstaatsarchiv-Stuttgart, and 27 Oct. 1948 OMGBY Intelligence Division Memorandum to ODI, "Land-Wide Survey on Possible KPD Influence of [sic] Infiltration in Office of VVN." ODI, 7/22-2/12-13, 2 of 7, RG 260, IfZ. For the specific case of Frankfurt, see Emil Carlebach, "Frankfurts Antifascisten 1945," in Ulrich Schneider (ed.), *Als der Krieg zu Ende war: Hessen 1945* (Frankfurt, 1980), p. 12ff. A more general account can be found in Plum, p. 97f.
14. POLAD/33/97, 1 of 1, RG 84, IfZ.
15. State Department Policy Committee revised draft of July-August, 1946, p. 7, Enclosure to 7 August 1946 telegram from Dean Acheson to Political Advisor Robert Murphy, POLAD, 17/24-2/5, 1 of 2, RG 260, IfZ.
16. 4 Sept. 1946 Memorandum from Donald R. Heath to Mr. Galbrath and Mr. Mason, POLAD/746/8, 1 of 3, RG 84, IfZ.

POLAD official recognized that some might interpret political neutrality to include a "toleration of Communist political activity," although he was less concerned with the real contradiction between the stated policy and the actual practice than with the possible outward perception of hypocrisy.

On 19 August 1947, Robert Murphy reported to the State Department his desire to revoke "the authorization for the KPD to operate in the US zone." The State Department responded on 21 October 1947 with reasons why it was not yet ready to ban the KPD, including the fact that it had issued a new directive that would "provide MG with a sufficiently flexible authority to deal with the problem of the KPD as it might develop." This new directive stated: "Every authorized political party should have the right freely to state its views and to present its candidates to the electorate, and you will tolerate no curtailment of nor hindrance to the exercise of that right; if, however, you find that an authorized party is adopting or advocating undemocratic practices or ideas, you may restrict or withdraw its rights and privileges."[17]

The State Department felt that the Communist Party should not be banned in the U.S. Zone "until such time as the Communists have made unequivocally manifest to the German people their own true anti-democratic character." In the meantime, however, the State Department emphasized that "its rights and privileges should be restricted wherever and whenever, in the judgment of MG, KPD actions exceed the bounds of propriety." It was warned that "care should be taken naturally that the Communists are not made to appear as martyrs in the eyes of the German population, but whenever necessary we should rap them on the knuckles."[18] The selectiveness with which the State Department intended the MG to implement the neutrality policy is made even more clear in the concluding paragraph of the State Department's letter to Murphy:

> (W)e do not believe that there is any reason for MG to afford the same assistance to the KPD as to the other parties. To be sure, the new directive states in paragraph 8, b: 'you will likewise give support to the principle that MG and the German authorities should afford non-discriminatory treatment to duly authorized political parties.' In so far as non-discriminatory treatment under present circumstances may involve material assistance, say in the form of automobiles, gasoline, newsprint, office equipment, etc., I think that the non-Communist parties should be

17. POLAD TS/33/29, 1 of 1, RG 84, IfZ.
18. Ibid. Of course considerable anti-Communist sentiment already existed among the German population, dating back at least to the 1918 Revolution in Germany.

favored in material aid over the KPD. The principle of neutrality, however, should be carefully observed in our treatment of the genuinely democratic parties.[19]

For some offices within OMGUS, there was disappointment that only the KPD could be targeted in this program rather than all forms of socialism. The Elections and Political Parties Branch of OMGUS's CAD decided that this new October 1947 "anti-communist program" would have to be concentrated on the "left' flank," because a "frontal' attack against socialism" would be doomed to failure, since "more than half of the German electorate ha[d] expressed itself in favor of some form of socialism." Tactically it suggested instead "an expose of Communism as the gravest danger to the existence of democratic institutions, civil liberty and political freedom," because this would have "a universal appeal which cuts across party and social lines and lends itself to mass support." Feeling that Communism presented the largest threat in the spheres of economics, trade unions, and politics, the appropriate counterattacks were to be the Marshall Plan and the strengthening and encouragement of "the non-communist elements," which would be accomplished primarily through "material aid in the form of paper and the opportunity to use other information media." To counter the political influence of the KPD, MG had a more complex agenda, which elaborated upon the 21 October 1947 State Department letter to Murphy:

> In the political sphere, the democratic non-communist political parties must be relied upon to perform the major role in this program. This will involve a basic change in MG policy towards political parties. Our policy of indifference (sometimes called 'neutrality') towards the views and actions of political parties should give way to a policy of active material and moral aid to cooperating parties. Programs and procedures ... should be 'sold' to the parties as being in the mutual interest. It should be the function of political activities officers to promote these [anti-communist] programs through contact with the parties. Above all, newsprint and all the other information media should be supplied in sufficient quantities to effectively counteract the high-pressure propaganda attacks of the Communists. Other aids such as facilitation of travel, international contacts, availability of reference material should serve to increase the prestige and sense of responsibility of the parties. In a word, any aggressive attack against Communism must start with material aid.[20]

By the spring of 1948, this "aggressive attack against Communism" included a focused program of data collection by both Ger-

19. Ibid.
20. CAD, 17/256-2/7, 1 of 1, RG 260, IfZ.

mans and MG investigative agencies for deposit with the new OMGUS Coordinating Committee. This agency served as the recipient "of information regarding German personalities against whom MG may decide to proceed." Military Governor Lucius D. Clay, who, on his own initiative, had announced an American propaganda campaign against Communism in a press conference on 28 October 1947,[21] justified this data collection with MG regulations that reserved "to MG certain rights to intervene directly in German affairs when the objectives of MG are jeopardized. It is considered that the tactics of the Communist party in attempting to penetrate key positions and organizations in the U.S. Zone for the purpose of undermining the democratic German governments in Germany constitutes a potential threat to the objectives of the Occupation and to the security of the U.S. forces in Germany."[22]

A year prior to this report, the former OSS R&A agent, Herbert Marcuse, had been sent to Germany by the State Department to report on political developments in the Western Zones.[23] Marcuse drew a totally different picture of the KPD in the Western Zones than what Clay was to use to justify his policy of intervention. In fact, Marcuse claimed that "the Western CP follows loyally the democratic party line," and that "this was more than accommodation." He went on to say:

They feel that the development of political consciousness and activity is preconditioned upon the economic reconstruction of Germany. That is why they are seriously interested in this reconstruction – even if it leads to a temporary strengthening of capitalist forces ... They advocate, not socialization, but democratization of the economy, and they concentrate their efforts on the institution of the Mitbestimmungsrecht. ... They are willing to enter coalition governments and to share responsibility wherever their democratization program is really carried through. They are training new members, not as Communists, but as efficient and active workers, farmers, craftsmen, etc. who are anxious and capable of playing a responsible part in the direction – not only in the performance – of a democratically controlled economic activity.[24]

Marcuse's analysis seemingly had no impact on POLAD or on MG. In fact, the OMGUS Coordinating Committee was quite suc-

21. Wolfgang Krieger, *General Lucius D. Clay und die amerikanische Deutschlandpolitik 1945–1949* (Stuttgart, 1987), p. 302f.
22. April 1948 memo from Clay to deputy commander in chief, EUCOM, ODI, 7/22-2/12-13, 2 of 7, RG 260, IfZ.
23. 28 March 1947 letter from E. Allan Lightner, Jr. to Brewster Morris, Office of the Political Advisor, POLAD/460/4, 2 of 4, RG 84, IfZ.
24. April 1947 report by Herbert Marcuse, POLAD/460/4, 2 of 4, RG 84, IfZ.

cessful in not only reporting on what it considered "the extent of Communist influence in the U.S. Zone,"[25] but in getting Germans to take direct action against Communists who were their subordinates. In the case of the Hessian police, where supposedly the "KPD penetration" had reached "at least 2.9 percent of the police positions" by April 1948, the MG office of the chief of intelligence for Hesse was relieved to report to OMGUS that most of those Communist infiltrators, who had been with the police since 1945, were now "known to their anti-communist superiors who are seeking grounds to dismiss them."[26]

This problem of finding excuses for dismissals arose for MG as well. In November 1948, the Office of the Director of Intelligence (ODI) expressed frustration that it had no legal grounds on which to dismiss Communists in "sensitive positions as potential threats to U.S. forces." In contrast to Marcuse's view of the KPD's autonomy, the ODI felt that "there is no doubt that the continued employment of Communists in sensitive positions constitutes a potential threat at this time since they are subject, as all Communists are, to directives from Moscow." The only suggestion for removing this potential threat, short of outlawing the KPD, which the ODI felt would drive the KPD underground and ultimately strengthen it, was to keep such personnel "under careful surveillance" in the hope of discovering overt acts which would then subject such persons to trial and removal.[27]

Pressure increased within the higher echelons of MG to ban the KPD in late April 1948, only weeks before most larger municipalities were to hold elections. A lengthy report by the OMGUS Coordinating Committee recommended against it, not because of democratic principles, but rather because of fears it would aid the Communists' infiltration of other parties[28] and make the movement stronger and less detectable. Instead it suggested that the minister presidents recommend to their Landtage the "implementation of those sections of their constitutions dealing with loyalty to the governments and

---

25. 29 April 1948 report of the OMGUS Committee, ODI, 7/22-2/14, 1 of 1, RG 260, IfZ.

26. 1 April 1948 Weekly Intelligence Report for Hesse, ODI, 7/28-2/17-23, 1 of 4, RG 260, IfZ.

27. ODI, 7/20-3/10, 1 of 3, RG 260, IfZ.

28. Already in the spring of 1946, reports of Communist infiltration into the SPD were appearing in detachment reports. The Munich MG detachment announced in May 1946, without clarifying its source, that "the latest estimate is that 20 percent of the SPD are Communists." See May 1946 Detachment E-213 Monthly Historical Report, p. 7, OMGBY, 10/78-1/3, 1 of 5, RG 260, IfZ.

inform them that MG expects them to exercise the inherent right of every government to rid itself of disloyal persons."[29]

Although MG never did ban the KPD, it certainly intervened against it in its material-aid policies for campaigns, and in its close surveillance of important party members. MG's encouragement of anti-Communism among the other parties also had an effect on party cooperation within the city councils and the Land governments. In Hesse, MG congratulated itself for the fact that in April 1947 "both the SPD and the CDU expressed increased anti-Communist sentiments during the week. They fear further strong Communist infiltration in labor unions."[30] Fighting a losing battle, a KPD city councilor in Stuttgart appealed to his colleagues to stop wasting their energy on a witch-hunt against the Communist Party and, instead, to consider seriously some of his proposals to counter the negative economic effects anticipated in the immediate period following the upcoming currency reform. He also complained about the animosity and poison expressed routinely by the press against the KPD and the USSR.[31]

The MG, eventually, was able to encourage anti-Communist propaganda in the press via its ICD, which, since 1946, was staffed by more anti-Communist officers, rather than the early overtly anti-Fascist journalists like Cedric Belfrage and James Aronson.[32] In 1948, MG introduced a media-centered "propaganda drive against communism and direct MG action against the most flagrant anti-American communist activities."[33]

Only four months after the Basic Law was promulgated in May 1949, HICOG, the successor organization to OMGUS, issued Law Number 5, which gave it the right to implement measures such as

29. ODI, 7/22-2/14, 1 of 1, RG 260, IfZ.
30. 5 April 1947 OMGH ICD Weekly Summary, OMGH, 8/188-1/22, 5 of 9, RG 260, IfZ.
31. Gemeinderatssitzungsprotokolle, 6 Oct. 1948, p. 480, StA St.
32. Interview with James Aronson, New York, 27 Dec. 1985 and Letter from Cedric Belfrage, 22 Nov. 1984. Cf. Chapter 5 for the developments with the *Frankfurter Rundschau*. Harold Hurwitz maintains that there were two stages of ICD personnel removal. Without clarifying what the one prior to 1947 one was, he explains that the purge that took place beginning in the summer of 1948 included not just Communists, but also non-Communists, "fellow travelers," and even some active anti-Communists, as well as "a number of Germans who were independent leftists." See his contribution to the conference discussion in the book edited by Robert Wolfe, *Americans as Proconsuls. U.S. Military Government in Germany and Japan, 1944–1952* (Carbondale, 1984), p. 342f.
33. 29 April 1948 Report of OMGUS Committee on Extent of Communist Influence in U.S. Zone, ODI, 7/22-2/14, 1 of 1, RG 260, IfZ.

shutting down newspapers, censoring campaign posters, and even trying and sentencing German citizens in special courts for criticizing U.S. foreign policy.[34] This law was directly aimed at the KPD and so-called sympathizers, but because it goes beyond the chronological scope of the OMGUS phase, it will not be elaborated upon here. Suffice it to say that the campaign of the American occupation authorities against the German Communist Party did not end with the founding of the Federal Republic. In fact, it escalated in the 1950s and found frequent support from the German authorities,[35] eventually culminating in the Federal Republic's 1956 ban on the KPD.

Besides its influence on the political parties, MG also determined the guidelines for who could actually vote. In November 1945, OMGUS set up provisions for all 1946 local elections to be held in the U.S. Zone. These provisions took into account local government codes and Land legislation in force on 30 January 1933. Adults of German nationality who were twenty-one and over and who had resided in the voting community for a minimum period of not more than one year would generally be able to vote. Exceptions to this included those politically incriminated due to their association with the NSDAP. This included: (1) those in the mandatory arrest category; (2) those who had joined the NSDAP prior to 1 May 1937 or who had been active members having joined after this date; (3) anyone having held any office in the Party, the SA, the Hitler Youth, the Bund deutscher Mädel, or in the Nazi organizations for students, professors, women, drivers, and pilots; (4) any members of the SS; and (5) any "known Nazi sympathizers and collaborators."[36] Municipalities were required to publish lists of presumably qualified voters prior to the elections. Any qualified voter could then file a written, signed petition requesting that someone's name be stricken from the list if he or she thought the person in question fell under one of the categories requiring voting disqualification. A municipal election committee would then consider the challenge and give the person being challenged an opportunity to be heard. Local and Land MG

34. *Stuttgarter Zeitung*, 17 August 1950.
35. In some cases, the Germans even tried to outdo their American "teachers." In Frankfurt in 1950 the police president tried unsuccessfully to convince MG to shut down a so-called Communist-steered newspaper, after the High Commission for Hesse had shut down the *Sozialistische Volkszeitung* in the late summer of 1950 for propagating so-called anti-Allied material, namely advocating holding a plebiscite on the issues of remilitarization and the negotiating of a peace treaty. Mag 2110/1, StA Ffm.
36. AG, 1945-46/1/1, 5 of 5, RG 260, IfZ.

also had the authority to disapprove of candidates who were nominated by either parties or citizens' groups that met "the requirements set up for the regular political parties."[37]

In 1948 the Germans themselves gained more direct control over the elections and the Landtage were now able to set the guidelines for voting. The major change involved voter disqualifications. Generally, those Germans found guilty by the German tribunals (*Spruchkammer*) of having more than a minor (*Minderbelasteten*) incrimination during the Third Reich remained disqualified, although someone with a minor incrimination could be excluded if a voting disqualification was directly included as part of his or her sentence.[38] Due to the large number of amnesties granted by U.S. MG, and to the considerably smaller number of Germans still disqualified under these new rules, the number of qualified voters grew considerably.[39]

In addition to having an effect on who could vote and when, and on what level a party was licensed, if at all, MG also was influential with regard to who was elected. In most cases, MG appointees and their appointed city councilors and department heads ran in 1946 for the offices they had been holding provisionally. The extent to which MG appointees were confirmed through the elections in their positions as OB, Bürgermeister, department heads, and city councilors varied considerably in the three cities under examination here. In Stuttgart and Munich, the MG-appointed OB and Bürgermeister were both confirmed in their positions in the 1946 elections. In the 1948 elections, Klett remained OB in Stuttgart, but, unlike 1946, his deputy was now a Social Democrat. In Munich, the CSU OB, Karl Scharnagl, now became the deputy, whereas the former Bürgermeister, the Social Democrat, Thomas Wimmer, now took over Scharnagl's position as OB. In Frankfurt, neither the MG-appointed OB nor his deputy were elected in 1946. Initially the city council elected two Social Democrats for these positions, although the Bürgermeister was forced by MG to resign and was replaced by a CDU member. In 1946, MG in Frankfurt let it be known, through its dismissal of this Bürgermeister, that it preferred a politically mixed or

---

37. Ibid.
38. Vietzen, p. 173.
39. The numbers also increased due to the return of POWs and the expellees and others who had immigrated and/or returned since 1946. Interestingly enough however, the voter turnout in 1948 was considerably less (58 percent rather than 79 percent) in Stuttgart than it had been in 1946, whereas it only decreased marginally in Munich, which still had over 80 percent turnout in 1948. See Vietzen, p. 160 and p. 177, and Schattenhofer, p. 168 and p. 370.

coalition municipal administration, even if one party – especially if this one party happened to be the SPD – had an absolute majority in the council.[40] In 1948, Frankfurt's OB Kolb was reelected with the help of the SPD council majority, but a different Christian Democrat became his deputy. In terms of the political affiliation of the OBs and their deputies, all three cities ultimately had politically mixed leadership in 1946 and 1948.[41]

Like MG's appointees, most of the officials who had been either appointed or indirectly elected to serve as department heads in 1946 had served in municipal government prior to Hitler's acquisition of power. The 1946 popularly elected city councilors, on the other hand, had, more often than not, not served on pre-1933 city councils. Experience in office seemed to be a much more important factor for the selection of bureaucrats than in the selection of democratic representatives. Whereas approximately one-fifth of the members of the advisory councils, in all three cities, had been city councilors during the Weimar Republic, only 10 percent of those elected in Frankfurt in 1946 had had this experience, as compared to 15 percent in Stuttgart and 17 percent in Munich. These percentages would increase, however, particularly in the case of Munich, if one were to include the number of those city councilors elected in 1946, who had had experience as either district (*Bezirk*), Landtag, or Reichstag representatives. In the case of the two working-class parties, their representatives were often experienced as either party or trade union officials. The representatives of the other parties, to the right of the SPD, were often prominent business people, and not men and women without any sort of political or public profile. Rather than having acquired that profile from having held elected or appointed municipal positions during the Weimar Republic, they had come to it within the business community or within their political party or union hierarchy. This was clearly related to the way the members of the advisory councils had been chosen: the appointed

40. This reference is to the Altheim incident, which will be descibed in the next pages.
41. OB Klett in Stuttgart was not formally affiliated with any political party, although his political orientation leaned much more toward that of the CDU and FDP than the SPD. In 1947 the American vice consul in Stuttgart reported that "persons who know him intimately believe that he is still inclined toward the right." However, his opportunistic pragmatism was emphasized in the report with the following information: "Lt. Col. Irwin Harlow, Commanding Officer of the Stuttgart detachment of MG, believes that Klett will continue to refuse all invitations to join a party until after the peace treaty, when it becomes clear which party will be dominant." 24 Feb. 1947 report, p. 2, POLAD/ 779/ 12, 1 of 5, RG 84, IfZ .

OB had chosen leading political party figures and business leaders to draw up lists of members of their party or interest group.

The continuation of the members of the advisory council into the first postwar elected city council is striking, especially in contrast to the lack of personnel continuity of the former with the Weimar city councils. In Munich, 54 percent of the 1946 city councilors had been members of the advisory council. In Stuttgart, it was 44 percent, whereas in Frankfurt, it was only 8 percent. The low percentage in Frankfurt should be considered an anomaly. Frankfurt's unusually high minimum clause, 15 percent, in its 1946 election, made almost a quarter of the votes cast, namely those for the KPD and the LDP/FDP, invalid. The two parties represented in the 1946 council, the SPD and the CDU, had each had seven representatives in the twenty-eight-member advisory council, whereas now they had thirty-two and twenty-eight, respectively, in the sixty-member elected council. The elected council's size had more than doubled compared to the advisory council in Frankfurt. This contrasted with Munich, where the size was increased slightly and Stuttgart, where it was increased by one-third. Two-thirds of Stuttgart's and three-fifths of Munich's advisory councilors were elected to the city councils, whereas less than a quarter of Frankfurt's advisory councilors remained in office after the 1946 elections.[42] One other factor that might explain Frankfurt's decreased personnel continuity was that it was the only city of the three where the appointed OB was not confirmed in office in the elections, an indication that some voters might have wanted a fresh start after the controversial OB Blaum regime. These figures show that having served in the advisory council had a major impact on a council candidate's political party's decision to have him or her run for election. Tenure on an advisory council also placed a candidate in an advantageous position on the party list and had a positive effect on a candidate's popularity with the public.

The decisions made by MG's appointed officials in putting together the advisory city councils had an influence far beyond 1946. In fact, many of those advisory councilors elected in 1946 were reelected in 1948, if they chose to run again. The rate of continuity in the 1948 elections, as compared to the 1946 ones, was slightly over 40 percent in Frankfurt and Munich, and just over 50 percent in Stuttgart. In this way, through its appointees, MG influenced municipal elections throughout the entire occupation period.

---

42. I developed these statistics by comparing biographical data contained in the three city archives on the members of the 1945, 1946, and 1948 city councils.

Viewed from another perspective, it was a disadvantage for a potential candidate of the 1946 city council to have *not* been appointed in 1945. Indeed, people outside the old Weimar political party structure and/or people low on the totem pole within the party hierarchy were at a distinct disadvantage, not only in the pre-democratic period of the occupation but also once elections were restored. Whereas collaboration with the occupation authorities might have worked against appointees, it apparently did not in these major cities, nor was it successful against the acting OB's appointees. Rather, it worked to their advantage.

The U.S. MG also had some individual preferences when it came to election results. But there was no guarantee that MG's preferences would always coincide with the electoral results, particularly when the democratically elected city councils had the power to elect the OB and the professional department heads. Intervention by MG in the elections included the two previously mentioned cases of meddling in the 1946 city councils' election of leading administrators. In Stuttgart, the election of the OB by the elected city council was largely determined by the Württemberg-Baden MG officer, who threatened the local SPD and CDU council leadership with intervention if the parties did not keep the unaffiliated Dr. Klett in office.[43] In Frankfurt, MG did not intervene until after the council and the administrators had been elected.

Frankfurt MG had encouraged the city council's election of Dr. Blaum, its appointee, as OB. The CDU in Frankfurt had also supported Dr. Blaum's candidacy, but the SPD won an absolute majority of seats in the city council (*Stadtverordnetenversammlung*) and this SPD-led council elected an SPD OB, Walter Kolb, the former city director of Düsseldorf, and a majority of SPD-affiliated department heads to the Magistrat.[44] Reacting against this SPD majority, MG threw down the gauntlet when it dismissed the elected SPD 2. Bürgermeister, Dr. Karl Altheim, on the grounds of political incrimination during the Third Reich and a concomitant Fragebogen falsification. This action was taken immediately following elections, despite the fact that MG had apparently known of this incrimination for almost a year while Altheim had served as a department

43. Charles Lincoln, *Auf Befehl der Militärregierung*, Trans. by Hans and Elsbeth Herlin (Munich, 1965), p. 140ff. See Chapter 4 for a more complete description and analysis.

44. The Magistrat was the collective body of all municipal department heads in the Prussian municipal administrative system, of which Frankfurt had become a part in the 1860s.

head. The timing of the accusation was, according to witnesses, designed to force the city council to elect more CDU members as department heads in the Magistrat.[45]

In the Frankfurt MG detachment's report to the Office of the Director of Intelligence on Altheim's arrest four days after he and the rest of the administration were sworn into office in Frankfurt, details were given of Altheim's omission of the fact that he briefly had held the rank of Rottenführer in the SA, and that he had applied for membership in the NSDAP in April 1933, although he was never accepted. The report noted that witnesses attesting to Altheim's anti-Nazi stance included three leading SPD members, two of whom had worked for either MG intelligence or Special Branch. Rather than questioning the evidence, the report had a tone of distrust regarding the SPD witnesses. Three points, which apparently were not completely unrelated to the Altheim situation, were added after the information on Altheim: first, that the newly elected SPD OB, Walter Kolb, had gone to Düsseldorf three days before "without informing this office [L&S Office – Frankfurt] of his departure or the probable date of his return"; second, that two of the other elected department heads refused, apparently in protest of the Altheim dismissal, to take their posts; and third, that "with three vacancies existing in the City Administration, the CDU party apparently is already making plans to come to some agreement with the SPD."[46] The recipient of the report, in forwarding it on to the OMGUS chief of the Analysis and Reports Division of ODI, commented: "The arrest itself is unimportant and appears to be warranted but the timing is unfortunate in that it followed the ceremony inducting Altheim into office by a matter of hours, and is causing much adverse comment by Germans in Frankfurt."[47]

Reading between the lines of this MG report, one finds an apparently obtuse connection between Altheim's arrest and the CDU's "making plans to come to some agreement with the SPD." This con-

---

45. Beschluss vom 6. Sept. 1946, Mag 1058, and Mag 1050/1, Bd. 2, StA Ffm. Also personal interview with Emil Carlebach, who was present as a journalist at the SPD meeting following the dismissal of Altheim as 2. Bürgermeister, 30 May 1983. Rudi Menzer, who was also present at that meeting, confirmed Carlebach's version in a separate personal interview, Frankfurt, 6 June 1983. See also Nr. 975, Abt. 502, Hessisches Hauptstaatsarchiv.

46. Confidential letter from Major Gerald C. Sola, LSO-Frankfurt commanding officer, to Lt. Col. O'Steen, chief of intelligence, 2d MG Battalion, 5 August 1946, OMGH, 17/125-1/6, 2 of 5, RG 260, IfZ .

47. Confidential letter from Lt. Col. O'Steen to Lt. Col. F. W. Potter, 7 August 1946, OMGH, 17/125-1/6, 2 of 5, RG 260, IfZ.

nection is implicit, however, in other documents, especially in a memorandum signed by the three highest Hessian Land officials, where the ministers condemned the mixing of Land politics with municipal politics,[48] after some leading Frankfurt Social Democrats complained to the Land government about the MG intervention into municipal politics,[49] in particular, in "the formation of the Frankfurt Magistrat."[50] The senior ministry officials decided not to have the entire cabinet discuss the matter, but rather they recommended that "for reasons of the defense of democracy under the realization of legality, the Frankfurt city council factions of the SPD and the CDU should accept the suggestion of a mixed Magistrat along with the measure of uniting the position of Welfare and Health in the hands of Dr. Prestel."[51] The "realization of legality" was apparently a reference to the fact that all levels of German "self"-government were subject to the tutelage of the occupation authorities, which ultimately allowed little leeway for the "defense of democracy," except for that of an MG definition of democracy, which meant a stronger representation of the opposition, in this case – and certainly not coincidentally – the CDU, than the elections had warranted.

Dr. Prestel, who had been dismissed by MG in June 1945 from his position as head of public welfare, but then exonerated in a German denazification tribunal a short time before the elections,[52] was now elected to the Magistrat immediately following Altheim's dismissal/resignation. His election to the Magistrat could be interpreted as somewhat of a retort to MG on the part of the Germans. Of the original nine members of the Magistrat elected on 25 July 1946, eight were members of the SPD and only one, the long-time city treasurer, a member of the CDU.[53] As a result of Altheim's arrest, the treasurer would have been next in line to become the 2. Bürgermeister, but because he had also applied to join the NSDAP, although never had joined, and was fearful of suffering a fate like Altheim's, he refused

48. Mag 1050/1, Bd. 2, StA Ffm.
49. Nr. 975, Abt. 502, Hessisches Hauptstaatsarchiv.
50. Mag 1050/1, Bd. 2, StA Ffm.
51. Ibid. The exact German text reads as follows: "Aus Gründen der Verteidigung der Demokratie unter Verwirklichung der Gesetzlichkeit empfehlen die Unterzeichneten den Frankfurter Stadtverordneten-Fraktionen der SPD und CDU, den Vorschlag der Wahl eines gemischten Magistrats mit der Maßgabe anzunehmen, daß Fürsorge und Gesundheit in der Hand von Herrn Dr. Prestel vereinigt werden."
52. OMGH, 17/16-3/11, 1 of 2, RG 260, IfZ. See also Nr. 241, Abt. 501, Hessisches Hauptstaatsarchiv.
53. Stadtverordnetenversammlungsprotokoll von 25 July 1946, StA Ffm.

to accept the 2. Bürgermeister's post.[54] This city treasurer, a CDU member, however, was not charged by MG, although ultimately he resigned completely. Whether MG would have acted in the same manner against a CDU department head is unclear, but Altheim's arrest and the seemingly related other resignations resulted in the CDU suggesting four new members for the Magistrat, two of whom were CDU members while the other two, including Prestel, were unaffiliated. These CDU nominations were then "unanimously elected" by the council.[55]

After the Frankfurt SPD's unsuccessful appeal to the Hessian Land government for assistance against MG's dismissal of Altheim and against MG's use of this dismissal as a ploy to force the SPD to include more non-SPD members in the Magistrat,[56] the Hessian SPD criticized MG's intervention in its leadership meeting on 16 August 1946. ICD infiltrated the meeting and reported that a heated debate had occurred about whether to support Altheim "to the fullest of the party's ability," in order "to show some measure of defiance to MG, since MG was obviously discriminating against the SPD." Other examples of MG discrimination against SPD officials were cited, including the unexplained removals of two Frankfurt police presidents, Mührdel and Weygand, by MG[57] and MG's shielding of CDU officials in other parts of Hesse. The Hessian SPD executive committee ultimately decided that it "should not make an issue of the Altheim case, and should by no means defy a decision of MG" and therefore concluded that it would ask Dr. Altheim to resign from his position as 2. Bürgermeister and from the city council.[58]

Dr. Altheim did resign, and was sentenced to eight months' imprisonment for falsification of his MG Fragebogen, having omitted his NSDAP application and his having briefly held the rank of SA-Rottenführer.[59] But further evidence that this action against him had very little to do with his alleged political incrimination is seen in the

54. ICD Political Activity Report, 8 August 1946, OMGH, 8/194-2/9, 1 of 6, RG 260, IfZ.
55. Stadtverordnetenversammlungsprotokoll von 25 July 1946 (with updated results), StA Ffm.
56. Personal interview with Emil Carlebach, 30 May 1983. Rudi Menzer, an SPD city councilor, who was also present at that meeting, confirmed Carlebach's version in a separate personal interview, Frankfurt, 6 June 1983.
57. See Chapter 4.
58. ICD Political Activities Report, 23 August 1946, p. 8f, OMGH, 8/194-2/6, 5 of 6, RG 260, IfZ.
59. ICD Political Activities Report, 15 August 1946, OMGH, 8/194-2/6, 5 of 6, RG 260, IfZ . See also Frankfurter Neue Presse, 15 August 1946.

fact that when he later approached the commanders of the Frankfurt and the Hessian-Land MG on 3 July 1947 about working for the city as a special advisor to the OB, both MG officers insisted that they had "no objections at all" and encouraged him to do so. The heads of both the SPD and the CDU city council groups also approved of his employment with the city.[60] It is interesting to note, however, that OB Kolb, who had encouraged Altheim's resignation in 1946 during the Hessian Land – SPD debate because he wanted to avoid a run-in with MG for the sake of the city administration and the SPD, and probably for his own sake as well,[61] apparently required Altheim to check with MG and the party leaders to make sure that there would be no objection before making the appointment. OB Kolb, unwilling to go out on a limb for Altheim and even make the inquiries of MG and the parties himself, made Altheim pursue his own clearance. In 1954 and again in 1960, Altheim was elected as a department head to the Magistrat, an office he held until his death in 1961. In 1959, on the occasion of his sixtieth birthday, he was awarded the medal of honor of the city for his service to Frankfurt. In the laudations, Altheim was praised by the Bürgermeister for his *thirty-two* years of service to the city of Frankfurt and for the well-being of its citizens;[62] his year-long dismissal in 1946, of which eight months was spent in jail, was simply ignored.

In Munich, one of the department heads was prosecuted by MG for falsification of his Fragebogen, specifically for lying about his membership in the NSDAP, yet MG apparently never even considered removing him from office. The difference with the Altheim case appears to be the timing. MG apparently did not become aware of the falsification until late 1946, after the May 1946 city council elections and after this man[63] had been elected a department head (*berufs-mäßiger Stadtrat*) by the new city council. The MG investigation dragged out for over a year. Finally in January 1948, when OB Schar-nagl reported to the city council about MG's prosecution of the department head, he defended the man, a fellow CSU member, stating that he had included an addendum with his Fragebogen, which he

---

60. Memorandum from Dr. Karl Altheim to OB Kolb, 3 July 1947, Mag. 1090/103, Bd. 1, StA Ffm.
61. ICD Political Activities Report, 23 August 1946, p. 8f, OMGH, 8/194-2/6, 5 of 6, RG 260, IfZ.
62. "Ansprachen, die anlässlich der Feier des 60. Geburtstages von Herrn Stadtrat Dr. Karl Altheim am 19. Oktober 1959 im Magistratssitzungssaal gehalten wurden," StA Ffm.
63. This department head must remain unnamed because of personal privacy considerations and German data protection law.

had failed to make a copy of and which MG apparently had never received. The addendum claimed that the department head had indeed applied to join the party because he feared he would not otherwise be able to get a job, having been forced out of a state job for political reasons. It also stated he had never paid dues or received a party membership book, and thus had responded negatively to the question of Nazi party membership. Scharnagl elaborated further that the leader of the Nazi Party local branch (Ortsgruppenleiter) had testified in the department head's case, in late 1947, that he had never heard of this man having been a Nazi member. Scharnagl noted how when the accused had been arrested and interrogated by the Gestapo in 1938, he never mentioned a party membership to try to defend himself. The MG judge, however, felt that there was evidence of formal guilt and noted that persons in high positions who had falsified their Fragebogen could be punished for up to three years. However, because he was convinced of this official's anti-Fascist stance and his democratic views, his punishment was to be limited to either six months in jail or five thousand Reichsmarks. According to Scharnagl, the MG judge did not want the official to suffer any real liabilities. The accused official was appealing the sentence to the Americans, because the German Spruchkammer had decided that he did not fall at all under any of the categories of incrimination (vom Gesetz nicht betroffen). Citing this as a "discrepancy between American and German jurisprudence" [Rechtsempfinden], the OB appealed to the Munich council to retain its trust in the department head.[64]

The official representatives for the SPD, KPD and CSU factions responded by officially "taking note" (Kenntnis nehmen) of the information and "regarding it as taken care of " (betrachten die Angelegenheit von sich aus als erledigt).[65] Whether he had to pay the fine is not ascertainable, although the official never served any prison time. The case is interesting because MG never tried to remove him from office, either directly or by pressuring the OB or the council to do so. In addition, the German denazification tribunal was informed by the U.S. authorities that he had not only denied that he was ever a member of the Nazi party, which indeed could be explained by an application that never resulted in actual membership, but that he had also been a member of the SA since May 1933 (Rottenführer) and a member of the SS thereafter.[66] There were apparently quite a few people

64. Stadtratssitzungsprotokoll vom 13 Jan. 1948, p. 9ff, RP 721/1, StA Mü.
65. Ibid.
66. Ministerium für Sonderaufgaben(MSo) 6-356, Bayerisches Hauptstaatsarchiv. These memberships were discovered in the Nazi membership files the Ameri-

who applied for Nazi party membership, yet never joined, in order to avoid political discrimination, but these other memberships apparently went beyond merely applying. Yet the German tribunal did not find these noteworthy and, if he knew about them, OB Scharnagl chose not to mention them to the city council. There indeed could have been extenuating circumstances here, like in Altheim's case, but unlike the Frankfurt Social Democrat's case, this Munich CSU department head never had to resign or serve prison time, and did not get caught up in MG partisan machinations.[67] The later timing of the Munich case coincided with less stringent denazification policies (amnesties) and more lenient views on Nazi incrimination, as well as with the passage of months since the department head had been elected, all factors which made MG intervention less likely and which differed from the Frankfurt situation. However, probably just as important, this Munich case occurred in a city where the 1946 city council and OB elections had resulted in a conservative (CSU) victory, where the official involved was a conservative party member, and where there had been less partisan conflict and more cooperation among councilors in the advisory council. All of these factors also made MG less likely to pursue the case in the same way it had Altheim's.

In conclusion, MG influenced elections indirectly through its licensing procedures, its guidelines determining who could and who could not vote, and through its selection and/or approval of acting OB and advisory city councilors. More directly, although covertly, local MG intervened into the democratically elected city council's election of the OB in the case of Stuttgart and of the 2. Bürgermeister and department heads in the case of Frankfurt. Higher echelons of U.S. MG may or may not have known – let alone have approved – of these cases of direct intervention. Yet because the Hessian cabinet was aware of the Frankfurt case, and MG intelligence reports at the Land-level referred to aspects of the Altheim case and the Frankfurt SPD's anger, it would certainly seem that at least the Hessian Land-MG did know and approve.

---

cans found in Munich in 1945 and were confirmed by me via the Berlin Document Center (BDC), although the BDC noted that the NSDAP membership entry date of 1.5.1937 was "a collective date for all those who applied for party membership after the closing of the party membership in 1933, which was lifted in 1937." PKK material, BDC.

67. In my interview with this department head in 1983 he denied any of these affiliations, but rather led me to believe that he had skillfully managed to stay out of the Party and its affiliated organizations. He continued to play a leading role in Munich's government until his retirement in the late 1970s.

On the other hand, MG's zonal policy of anti-Communism, which more or less replaced its policy of neutrality toward German political parties, was a policy from above that had the express approval of U.S. MG headquarters and the State Department. This policy included various forms of intervention, including granting material aid and media access to the non-Communist parties, anti-Communist propaganda, discouraging non-Communist German officials from retaining Communists in positions of influence, and placing KPD members who were in important positions under intense surveillance, which often verged on intimidation. It had the result of discouraging the cooperation of non-Communists with KPD members and thus ghettoizing the Communists, restricting the rights of the KPD to freedom of assembly and speech and thus hurting their own efforts at campaigning and/or influencing the electorate, and dismissing their ideas and proposals as Soviet-directed and thus not even worthy of consideration.

Denazification, Reinstatements and Restitution

U.S. Military Government had, by far, the most stringent denazification guidelines, at least in quantitative terms, of all the Allies. Yet the stringency – 28 percent of all German adults in the U.S. Zone were included under its guidelines[68] – made the implementation literally impossible. After first focusing in on the elites known to have been implicated in the Holocaust and in the use of slave labor, the Americans introduced Law No. 8 in September 1945, which prohibited Germans, who had been members of the NSDAP or its affiliates prior to 1937, from working until they went through denazification proceedings. One of the primary reasons MG turned over denazification to the Germans, in the spring of 1946, was the fact that the sheer number of people involved made it impossible for MG to implement the policy itself. MG had a shortage of personnel and a lack of necessary administrative channels sufficiently familiar with the different levels of political incrimination. The OMGUS Denazification Branch increasingly became frustrated, as it received more and more complaints from Germans and other branches of MG that economic, governmental, and other professional services that were crucial to getting German administrations functioning smoothly again could not operate if there were so many dismissals due to Law No. 8.

68. Griffith, p. 71.

Another reason for placing the Germans in charge was that the Americans wanted, understandably, to share the responsibility and the onus for denazification with the Germans themselves.

Yet, while U.S. authorities were unable to implement their original comprehensive policies as planned, they would not allow the Germans on the Land level, who eventually were placed in charge of denazification, to make revisions that might have made the policy, in its basic principles, realizable. The German minister presidents had major disagreements with the practicability of the scope of the laws they were asked to administer in March 1946, but they feared that their reputation as anti-Nazis would be at stake if they tried to press the Americans too hard for change.[69] In fact, according to his special denazification advisor, Dr. Walter Dorn, Military Governor Clay did perceive of German efforts to revise the laws as attempts to bypass denazification,[70] rather than as ways to make it practicable and just. Of course, Germans did sometimes bypass normal denazification procedures, especially in the early stringent phase of dismissals. In Munich, a city councilor noted that two hundred city employees who were ordered dismissed by MG were actually pensioned instead,[71] although MG permitted this to happen.[72] In some cases, especially those involving technical and financial experts, MG made its own exceptions about dismissals. Years later, these individuals had more promotions and years accumulated for pensions than colleagues with other expertise who were reinstated in 1949 or later, having lost their jobs for several years due to denazification.[73]

To a large extent, industry and commerce were allowed to denazify themselves, exemplifying the fact that economic priorities were placed far ahead of political ones. As the historian, Diethelm Prowe, has pointed out: "The assumption of the American officials clearly was that the economy and its organizations were basically non-political."[74] Prior to the proclamation of Law No. 8, for example, MG allowed the Frankfurt Chamber of Commerce and Industry, which was run by leading businesspeople, to license all firms for business except for those owned by individuals who had joined the Nazi

69. Dorn, *Unfinished Purge*, p. 261 f. See also Griffith, p. 75.
70. Dorn, *Unfinished Purge*, p. 329.
71. Stadtratssitzung, 6 July 1948, p. 1637, RP 721/2, StA Mü.
72. Stadtratssitzung, 13 July 1948, p. 1776, RP 721/2, StA Mü.
73. Personalausschusssitzung, 5 May 1949, RP 722/9, p. 474 ff, StA Mü.
74. Diethelm Prowe, "Economic Democracy in Post-World War II Germany: Corporatist Crisis Response, 1945–1948," *Journal of Modern History*, 57/3 (Sept. 1985), p. 480.

Party prior to 1933.[75] Even after denazification was turned over to the Germans, the Frankfurt Chamber of Commerce and Industry was allowed to maintain a special liaison with the denazification tribunals. This liaison "monitored" tribunal decisions involving businesspeople, in order "to coordinate the interests of the economy with the effects of denazification on economic life."[76] In the case of the Bosch firm in Stuttgart, MG circumvented the city denazification committees, which were initially responsible for reviewing all the cases that fell under Law No. 8, and instead let Bosch have its own special committee that was not under city jurisdiction. Despite OB Klett's complaints about the undermining of the authority of the city committees and the unfair inconsistency of MG's decision, the local MG commander, Col. Jackson, informed Klett that it was not his place to judge, and that he should be glad that MG, which in this case was Land-MG, had taken responsibility for Bosch.[77] Once denazification came into German hands in the spring of 1946, the same OB Klett often supported the expediting of trials of friends and/or experienced technocrats, either officially through his office or through informal letters to friends working on the denazification tribunals.[78] In only one of these cases was it apparent that MG was aware, and approved of, the OB's intervention. Klett had apparently followed Jackson's example and decided that, once denazification was in German hands, it was not MG's place to judge. Thus, someone like OB Klett could make his own denazification exceptions rather than waiting on MG revisions.

The MG, however, did eventually revise denazification policies, but in ways that gave rise to even more dissatisfaction among Germans and Americans committed to the concept of a fundamental purge and democratization of society. As reflected in the amnesties and individual exceptions that were made from mid-1946 on, MG did not remain consistent with the stringency of its policies or with the principles behind the original concept of denazification. The first U.S. amnesty, the Youth Amnesty, came in July 1946 and absolved some 900,000 incriminated persons, born after 1 January 1919,

75. 2 May 1945 Protokoll über die Besprechung mit Lt. Worth am 30 April 1945, Mag 4511, Bd. 2, StA Ffm.
76. "Entstehung und Aufgaben der Arbeitsgemeinschaft der Industrie- und Handelskammern des Landes Hessen," 23 May 1947, Ungeordnete MS. von H. G. Heymann, Archiv des Industrie- und Handelskammers Frankfurt a. M., n.d.
77. OB meeting with MG, 17 Oct. 1945, Hauptaktei 0052-1, StA St.
78. See 4 Oct. 1946 letter from Klett to Paul Braun; 10 April 1947 memo; 29 April 1947 memo; 19 Sept. 1946 letter to Klett; 27 Nov. 1946 memo, Hauptaktei 0052-1, Entnazifizierung Gesetz Nr. 104, StA St.

from almost all responsibility and thus penalties. The Christmas Amnesty of that same year absolved a further 1,000,000 low-income and disabled persons, who had been charged as either Offenders or Lesser Offenders, as compared to Major Offenders (*Hauptverbrecher*). Of those 1,400,000 presumed offenders of all categories (all those presumed to have been guilty of more than just being Followers or *Mitläufer*), almost 80 percent were eventually charged as the more nominally incriminated Lesser Offenders, and were automatically demoted to the lowest category, that of Followers, because of an amendment promulgated in October 1947.[79] As Followers, these Germans no longer had to fear being penalized.

This amendment had been promulgated after a large group of congressional representatives visiting Germany became convinced that denazification was impeding German recovery and that its conclusion should be expedited. However, Congress was not satisfied with the results of the amendment, and in March 1948 the House Appropriations Committee refused to approve an Army deficiency appropriation bill unless denazification was halted. Under pressure from German denazification authorities not to close down the program, the zonal military governor, General Lucius D. Clay, managed to retain the most highly incriminated of the remaining Class I (Major) Offenders and Class II Offenders for trial, but this was only 10 percent of those still pending. The remaining 90 percent were simply reclassified downward at least two notches to the category of Followers. These amnesties and amendments worked to the benefit of those originally charged in the more incriminated categories, whereas those presumed originally to be the least incriminated had been tried prior to these changes, during the period when more stringency was exercised. Because of this sequence of prosecuting the "little fish" first, while eventually letting most of the "big fish" go, many of those who should have been removed from positions of authority in public administrations as well as in private industry never even came to trial. In fact, altogether, in 1949, after denazification had been stopped, only twenty-seven thousand individuals were considered still ineligible to hold public office.[80]

As might be expected, denazification came to be supported less and less by Germans, even among those who had been its most ardent supporters early on. Most German non-Nazi and anti-Nazi critiques of denazification were based on its unfairness: the Ger-

---

79. Korman, p. 127.
80. Griffith, p. 72ff.

mans who were tried first had been those suspected of the least degree of incrimination, yet because the denazification program was made more and more lenient by the Americans, through the introduction of amnesties, as they got more and more frustrated with it, those tried early on received the toughest sentences, while those guilty of much worse behavior often got much less severe punishments or never came to trial at all.[81]

Support of denazification – albeit more in its theory than in its actual practice – came to be more and more limited to a leftist ghetto of the SPD and KPD. Yet, even the parties of the Left began to distance themselves from strict denazification by the time of the 1948 elections, after seeing that their association with the policy was a political liability.[82] Not only were they critical of the effects of the initially all-encompassing program and later of the amnesties and amendments, but now fell prey to appeasing the majority of the German electorate whose support they wanted to win. Most of the electorate either wanted to dump the baby out with the bathwater because of the unfairness of the program as implemented, or had never supported the idea of this rather revolutionary purge in the first place.[83]

Denazification had started out partly as an MG policy to punish Germans who had actively supported the NSDAP. Initially the denazification plans also had implied "penetrating behind Nazism to revolutionize the authoritarian society which they [the Germans] still passively accepted." Over time, MG interpreted denazification more narrowly as a removal of Nazis from positions of influence. According to William Griffith, the denazification chief in Bavaria, some of the German officials assigned to the task of implementing denazification may have had too much in common, socioeconomically, with the Nazis who would appear before them in the tribunals, and may have been too fearful of the type of "social revolution that severe denazification would bring" to fully support the program.[84]

For a number of Germans, however, including some who worked in the tribunals, the concept of denazification encompassed the removal of Nazi privileges and its counterpart, restitution for victims of Nazism, including the rehiring of those fired during the Third

81. Korman, p. 140.
82. Ibid., p. 263. Some Germans certainly just wanted to put the whole chapter of Nazism behind them.
83. See Griffith, p. 74.
84. Griffith, p. 74.

Reich and the awarding of the appropriate promotions they would have achieved during that period of dismissal.[85] Other Germans, probably like those Griffith describes, tended to carry MG's narrower interpretation of denazification even further. They came to regard denazification as a temporary cleansing process that should have no real long-term effects on those who would go through it. As the political scientist, John Herz, said in 1948: "Nothing could be more revealing than the strange modification of meaning that that the term 'denazification' itself has undergone. While at first signifying the elimination of Nazis from public life, it has now in German everyday language come to mean the removal of the Nazi stigma from the individual concerned, that is, the procedure by which he gets rid of certain inhibitions or restrictions ('Mr. X was denazified yesterday' – he can now take up his former profession again)."[86]

This difference is crucial for understanding the German discussions and conflicts surrounding the practice of denazification. It was precisely long-term effects that were prerequisites to structural democratization, as well as a permanent denazification. But neither of the two occurred. As Griffith reported in 1950:

> The very top Nazis were – temporarily – immobilized, but otherwise, Nazis, militarists, industrialists, and bureaucrats were free to re-enter society. And they re-entered in thousands; the flood of "renazification" ran full tide. From 40 to 80 per cent of the officials in many branches of public administration are now reinstated former Nazis. More important, many of them are present-day authoritarians.
>
> Abandoned by the Americans and universally denounced by the disgusted Germans, denazification had failed – failed to come near achieving *any* objective ever set forth for it, by Americans or Germans. And the effort to construct democratic foundations for German society, and thus prevent a recrystallization of its traditional authoritarian social structure, had probably failed with it.[87]

85. In late 1948 the former Westphalian minister of justice published an article on denazification in the U.S. Zone, in which he criticized "the fact that nothing decisive has thus far been done in favor of indemnities for those persecuted by the Nazi regime, for the prisoners of the concentration camps, for the survivors of those murdered or deprived of their civil rights." Artur Sträter, "Denazification," *The Annals of the American Academy of Political and Social Science* (1948), p. 51.
86. John H. Herz, "The Fiasco of Denazification in Germany," *Political Science Quarterly*, 63, no. 4 (1948), p. 590.
87. Griffith, p. 74. Fortunately, a "traditional authoritarian social structure" did not recrystallize, as Griffin in 1950 feared it might. But more solid "democratic foundations for German society" might have been established earlier if denazification and de-authoritarianism had occurred more thoroughly.

In the three cities under examination in this study, there are numerous examples of city-council debates on how far-reaching denazification should go. The council members discussed whether its implications should be more narrowly defined to a temporary removal of those politically incriminated from influential posts, or more broadly defined to an almost revolutionary democratization of society. The municipality, as the earliest form of restored German administration, operated under the early guidelines that reflected a broader MG interpretation of denazification. However, when it later came to questions like the reinstatement of former Nazis who had either been through, or who had not yet had, their denazification trials, denazification guidelines were needed from the German Land governments, which actually received them from MG. Land policies were needed for the municipalities to have both consistent practices and the assurance that they would be backed up by higher authorities in the event of an appeal. Land guidelines were long in coming, and MG provided little guidance in the meantime. When state policies did come, they represented the new and narrower MG position that former Nazis could not be penalized in their employment. This was quite different from the policy that the city councils had anticipated, and varied considerably from most of the citywide practices up until that point. This provoked much debate within the city personnel committees, which had to make hiring and rehiring recommendations, and in the councils' plenary sessions where votes on these recommendations occurred.

In the first months of the occupation, the municipal governments in all three cities – usually at the suggestion of or under pressure from Antifas – had put NSDAP activists and officeholders to work. They were assigned to remove bombing debris, while party members, in particular, were forced to share or give up their housing to either generally nonincriminated individuals, or to victims of the Nazi regime.[88] Local MG, in the absence of any official MG policy, had allowed this practice and had even required it in some cases. In Stuttgart, for example, Lt. Col. Charles Jackson held OB Klett personally responsible, in late September 1945, for the procurement of Nazi labor for rubble removal and for overseeing the confiscation of Nazis' housing and the redistribution of it to nonincriminated Germans.[89] But MG was inconsistent in its discriminatory policies, even in this

88. Stadtarchiv Frankfurt a. M., S1/25 Nachlass B. Müller.
89. Verfügung des amtierenden Bürgermeisters an das Wohnungsamt, 20 June 1945 and Protokoll der Besprechung des OBs bei der Militärregierung, 25 Sept. 1945, Hauptaktei 0052-2, StA St. See also "Arbeitskräfte für die Trümmerbeseitigung,"

immediate postwar phase. In late July 1945, the Stuttgart MGO, Lt. Col. Jackson, under orders from his superiors, announced the prohibition of wage and salary cuts in the private and public sector, on the basis of political incrimination.[90] It would seem as if, at least in this early stage, both local government and local MG had broader conceptions of denazification than their Land-level superiors.

In late September 1946, the outspoken SPD city councilor in Munich, Rudolf Bössl, adamantly supported an SPD motion to remove politically incriminated civil servants (*Beamten* and *Angestellten*) from posts in the Housing Office and all other municipal offices which dealt with the public. His definition of political incrimination included all those classified within the top two categories of major incrimination, according to the 3 March 1946 Law for the Liberation from National Socialism and Militarism. This included anyone who had held an office in the SA, the SS, or the Nazi welfare organization (NSV), rather than just those who had been active NSDAP party members. Bössl's main concern was that those who were, themselves, being denazified should not be in the position of denazifying housing or other aspects of German life. The CSU head of the Housing Office, however, protested that there were limits even in denazification, and that one could not cross certain borders when it came to guaranteeing that certain crucial tasks of the city administration be covered by experienced personnel, especially those in the area of housing.[91] Ultimately, the department head's point of view, which by this time coincided with that of MG, triumphed.

The first elected city councils were forced to reconsider certain denazification practices after Land governments issued decrees – which apparently stemmed from MG[92] – that housing should be returned to incriminated persons and that nonincriminated and persecuted persons would have to vacate the premises. Whether the Land- governments fully supported MG in this narrowing of the conception of denazification or not, they certainly did not openly protest it. Not all Germans were willing to resign themselves to the abandonment of a broadly conceived denazification program that would revamp society. Munich City Councilor Bössl, in May 1948,

---

and "Tätigkeitsberichte der Stadtverwaltung an die Militärregierung, 10-16 Nov. 1945 and 19–24 Nov. 1945, Hauptaktei 6231-3, StA St.

90. OB Klett an Könekamp, 25 July 1945, Hauptaktei 0314-3, StA St.

91. Personal-Ausschusssitzung vom 26 Sept. 1946, RP 719/5, p. 870 ff, StA Mü.

92. Decrees such as this had to have MG approval in this early phase and, more often than not, they were MG decrees for which MG wanted the Germans to take public responsibility.

reiterated his position that those without political incrimination, as well as victims of the Nazis, should receive priority in employment, housing, etc., over former Nazi activists. Although the city council apparently had not yet systematically made changes consistent with the April 1947 Bavarian decree that required the return of housing to those from whom it had been removed, pressure to do so increased on the eve of new municipal elections in the spring of 1948. Bössl cited the role of "election psychosis" to explain certain (CSU) councilors' unwillingness to continue to bypass the governmental decree.[93] Bössl's position was in the minority by that time, and in Munich thereafter, any general preferential treatment of non-Nazis and anti-Nazis, as well as discriminatory treatment of former Nazis, ceased. Any measures associated with denazification were now, after the passage of amnesties and amendments, suspect to most Germans, who by this time were longing for a return to normalcy, especially since the revolutionary changes had not materialized.

In the same way that municipal administrations had to function for quite some time, without guidelines on the "discriminatory" denazification of housing by MG policymakers and Land governments, they were also left on their own to decide whether to rehire previously dismissed personnel who were considered politically incriminated. Before official guidelines were handed down, debates raged over whether administrations were "morally obligated" to rehire these people who often had put in many years as municipal officials or whether the moral issue was really restitution, i.e., training, hiring, or rehiring, for those who had been persecuted by the Nazis. By the time the higher echelons set up policies, they were much more lax than those practiced by the cities, and in fact required many people to be rehired. City administrations had often tried to avoid rehiring such people in favor of hiring new and nonincriminated individuals. This municipal practice had not been without controversy, however. Department heads, who were usually experienced bureaucrats and more often from the Right of the political spectrum if they professed any political allegiance at all, along with some city councilors – particularly those in the CDU/CSU and the FDP and some of the right-wing splinter parties – had been upset by the loss of expertise when these people had been dismissed in the first place, and since then, had pushed hard for their reinstatement.

Typical of the left – right divisions over hiring practices and reinstatements, were several city council committee votes in November

93. Stadtratssitzung, 25 May 1948, RP 721/1, StA Mü.

of 1947 in Munich. For example, a heated debate in the Munich city council's steering committee meeting broke out over whether the city should license someone for one of the municipal slaughter-houses who had fallen under the so-called Christmas Amnesties. Using the argument that there was no legal basis on which to reject the application, even though the applicant's Nazi attitudes were known, the department head moved that this particular man be licensed. In a 7 – 6 vote of the parties of the Right against the parties of the Left, the SPD and KPD members unsuccessfully voted against licensing this individual. They noted that in the recent past there had been several such close votes in which the narrow right-wing majority had managed to hire and/or license Nazis. One SPD city councilor noted in disgust that nowadays one could no longer do anything "against 100 percent Nazis."[94] On the same day, the Munich Personnel Committee debated postponing for three months the reinstatement of city employees who had been pre-1937 NSDAP members. This would enable POWs, who were expected back soon, and various "Followers" whose trials were coming up before the denazification tribunals, to receive priority for employment. In an eight to six vote, the SPD/KPD supporters of the postponement lost to the more conservative councilors. In several other similarly close votes, reinstatement decisions were passed by the same conservative voting block.[95]

The lack of hiring guidelines from MG and/or the Länder could be used as an argument that one had no legal grounds upon which not to reinstate former employees and others with experience acquired during the Third Reich. Without laws legitimizing the practice of not hiring amnestied and/or "denazified" individuals who were not specifically banned from their previous posts, discrimination against former Nazis was illegal. The experience of such individuals was likely to be more highly valued than that of other Germans who, during the Third Reich, had been unable to acquire the training and experience needed to put them on this same level. Thus, the latter were more likely to experience discrimination once again, but this time for their lack of experience, if not also for the persecution they may have suffered as anti-Nazis.

German legal decisions often worked against municipal govern-ments' desires to implement a denazification via the reversal of priv-ileges granted to Nazi elites. In Stuttgart in the spring of 1948, an

---

94. Hauptausschusssitzungsprotokoll, 6 Nov. 1947, RP 720/4, p. 1807f., StA Mü.
95. Personalausschusssitzung, 6 Nov. 1947, RP 720/6, p. 1650 ff, StA Mü.

administrative court judged that the former members of the SS who owned homes in a special SS settlement had the right to remain in that settlement because of the recognition of the legality of their purchases at the time they acquired the homes. City councilors from the CDU, the Neue Partei, the SPD, and the KPD joined forces in criticizing that court decision and trying to have it reconsidered. It was first pointed out by various councilors that it was dangerous for such people to continue to live together. It was also realized that even if some SS members were currently not living there due to incarceration or by choice, they were still the legal owners and thus the current residents were being forced to pay rent to them. The councilors then pointed out that the SS settlement had been built between 1937 and 1939 with municipal and private funds, and that the SS members themselves had had to pay almost nothing to own their own homes. Therefore, on the basis of their interpretation of the Allied Control Council (ACC) regulation that revoked any legal or economic privileges of members or families of members of militaristic or paramilitary organizations, the settlement was illegal. But the German court paid no heed to the ACC regulation and MG did not intervene to enforce it. Because the city had no authority over the court, it was powerless. A three-part motion, however, was passed in the city council, according to which it was recommended that either (1) the city was to revoke all the contracts and take over the ownership, or (2) the Landtag was to pass a law clarifying the legal status of such settlements, or (3) the mayor's office was to see to it that all legal and police means be used to protect the politically nonincriminated from being evicted in favor of someone (a former SS member) politically incriminated.[96]

These motions had no real power of enforcement behind them, because the court could take action against any city resolution it deemed in conflict with its decision, and the city council could not pressure the Landtag into passing anything. One of the councilors apparently realized the futility of their motion when he said: "The last months have clearly shown that it is not possible to retrieve a prevented or missed revolution through administrative measures."[97] By the end of the year, there was no legal basis according to which the homes of the SS owners could be taken away unless it was part of their denazification tribunal judgment or if they were delinquent in paying their special SS loans.[98]

96. Gemeinderatssitzungsprotokoll, 26 May 1948, p. 423 ff., StA St.
97. Ibid., p. 438. My translation of quote.
98. Ibid., 16 Dec. 1948, p. 670.

The lack of effective legislation directed at the denazification of private property or of public sector positions prevented any real socioeconomic and bureaucratic denazification of society. The fact that this legislation now had to come from above, rather than from the local level, meant that grassroots attempts at fundamental changes in society no longer had any chance in a system that had once again become a bureaucratic top-down structure.

The number of reinstatements in the three cities, as well as in the U.S. Zone as a whole, was probably highest in the late 1940s and early 1950s. The first two years of the occupation were characterized more by denazification dismissals than reinstatements, but 1947 marked the reversal of this trend. Interestingly enough, whereas statistics for reinstatements in Munich and Stuttgart were kept for 1947, a time when debate was still heated, they are not readily available for the following years. In the case of Frankfurt, the supposed model city for the U.S. Zone, they are not available even for 1947. Munich reported that 4,300 denazification-related dismissals from municipal jobs had occurred in 1945 and 1946, while 500 persons, or 12 percent of those dismissed, were reinstated. The prerequisites for reinstatement in Munich included a high level of expertise of the dismissed person, the availability of the post, a low level of political incrimination (only those amnestied or, at most, considered Followers), the provision that no politically nonincriminated person lose his or her position to make room for an incriminated one, and the approval of the works council.[99] In Stuttgart 1,708 city employees were dismissed in 1945[100] and 2,423 employees were dismissed in 1946,[101] while 319, or 10 percent of those dismissed were reinstated in 1947.[102]

There are frequent references, if not complaints, by city officials about the fact that the states' (Länder) denazification and reinstatement practices were much more lenient than that of the municipalities.[103] An increase in the number of reinstatements on all levels must have occurred after 1947 if the "renazification" figures given by the

---

99. Leistungsbericht des Personalamts für 1947, 23 March 1948, p. 3f, BuR 260/12/I, StA Mü.
100. Verwaltungsberichte 1945, Bericht des Personalamts für 1945, p.3, Hauptaktei 0622, StA St.
101. Verwaltungsberichte 1946, Bericht des Personalamts für 1946, p. 2, Hauptaktei 0622, StA St.
102. Verhandlung des Personalprüfungsausschusses, 22 Oct. 1947, Jahresbericht, Protokolle des Gemeinderats, StA St.
103. See in particular Personalausschusssitzung, 23 Jan. 1947, p. 108, statement by BM Wimmer, RP 720/5, StA Mü.

former head of the Bavarian Denazification Branch are to be taken seriously. In 1950 he maintained that, in the U.S. Zone, "from 40 to 80 percent of the officials in many branches of public administration (were) now reinstated former Nazis."[104] Whereas the municipal reinstatement figures included all employees, from workers to tenured civil servants, these zonal figures focused on "officials." This was clearly because of the growing legal pressure within all levels of German government to defend the rights of tenured civil servants (officials) through the restoration of employment and pensions, regardless of political incrimination. This trend was not without controversy.

The U.S. MG, in particular, was strongly against the restoration of the old-style German professional civil service (*Berufsbeamtentum*), but its personnel policy of relying so heavily on German expertise over political or democratic qualifications had fertilized the soil for such a tendency to grow. German experts in public administrations were generally civil servants and they used their clout to guarantee the continuation of their special privileges and elite status. As will be shown in the next section, this is one area where determined American attempts at democratization failed.

German Civil Service Reform

The debate over civil service reform was not unrelated to that of a sweeping structural versus a narrowly defined individual denazification process. Both involved issues of expediency versus reform, continuity versus change, and normalization versus democratization. Whereas U.S. MG, over time, had come to support the most expedient form of denazification that would least disturb economic reconstruction, it held on to hopes of democratizing Germany through civil service reform. Many of the same Germans who had supported a sweeping structural denazification also supported the concept of civil service reform, for fundamentally the same reasons. However, the American occupiers' tendency to place efficiency and experience above democratic alternatives in many of their German personnel decisions presented a model that some Germans used in order to avoid dismissing or permanently firing civil servants and, to some extent, to bypass fundamental structural reforms of the civil service.

But American plans for civil service reform included changes beyond the democratization agenda that was shared by some Ger-

104. Griffith, p. 74.

mans, who hoped to transform the civil service from a historically priveleged, authoritarian elite[105] to a group of responsible and democratic public sector employees. In its crusade for civil service reform, U.S. MG lost some potential German allies by insisting on imposing their own model for the German civil service. The association of certain MG reforms, like political neutrality for civil servants, with totally non-German traditions created a kind of nationalist defensiveness, even among some of the German Left. The imposition of such reforms from above, without real German impetus, struck some potential German supporters as cultural imperialism.

Another complicating factor was the fact that numerous members of the SPD, who had supported a broader denazification and democratization agenda, were themselves civil servants. Their status as such had provided many of them with their first entree into administrative and government positions. After decades as outcasts, the SPD, during the Weimar Republic, had managed finally to make inroads into the civil service. After the 1933 political dismissals by the Nazis, there were few Social Democrats left in the civil service. The end of World War II brought hopes to the SPD of restoring its gains from the 1920s; thus many Social Democrats were unwilling to abolish the civil service altogether. Although they may have supported more democratic social reforms than seemed to be occurring under the U.S. occupation, they were not prepared to give up their special rights and privileges.[106] The KPD was the only political party that uniformly supported MG's initiatives for civil service reform, including the proposal for a total abolition of a tenured civil service (*Berufsbeamtentum*).

The local level was not directly involved in German civil service reform, as neither local MG nor German municipal administrators had jurisdiction over such policies. But because the restoration of special privileges like guaranteed lifelong employment and very high pensions affected tight postwar budgets, and because the denazification of municipal employees involved large numbers of civil servants whose privileged status might make them immune to certain repercussions of denazification, lively discussion about the status of the civil service arose frequently in city council meetings. The ultimate restoration of the privileged status of civil servants, regardless

105. See Jürgen Kocka, "1945: Neubeginn oder Restauration?" in Carola Stern und Heinrich A. Winkler (eds.), *Wendepunkte deutscher Geschichte 1848–1945* (Frankfurt a. M., 1979), p. 153.

106. Rudolf Billerbeck, *Die Abgeordneten der ersten Landtage (1946–1951) und der Nationalsozialismus* (Düsseldorf, 1971), p. 192.

of political incrimination, placed the local-level denazification even more into question and made it even less defensible.

On the other hand, the reinstatement of civil servants allowed little opportunity for training or hiring individuals from outside the municipal bureaucracy and hierarchy for new posts. In addition, the early retirement of dismissed civil servants with full compensation restricted the availability of funds for any new personnel. This strengthened the tendency of the German administrations to rely on experienced bureaucrats and their old structures in which they had served like cogs in a wheel, rather than to take advantage of this opportunity for change and reform.[107] The reinstatement of dismissed public employees became the rule rather than the exception, and this was even more true for civil servants (*Beamten*) than for the other groups of employees: salaried employees (*Angestellten*) and wage-earning workers. Because of their position at the top of the hierarchy of the public sector, and the expense that was entailed for the cities, the issue of reinstating civil servants, or at least retaining their pension privileges, sparked frequent discussions in the various city councils.

In Stuttgart and Munich, in particular, heated debates on the reinstatement of civil servants and/or their pension privileges caused rifts within the councils, as well as within political parties. In Munich, two SPD city councilors, Gustav Schiefer, who headed the Munich trade unions, and Karl Bössl, a city director and thus a fairly high-level civil servant, argued in a meeting of the personnel committee in December 1946. While Bössl supported retaining all civil service privileges, Schiefer refused to vote for the early pensioning of civil servants on the basis that no one else in the public or private sector was even considered for early pensions. Schiefer felt that while the civil servants, as a group, had not suffered any disadvantages during or after the war, the working class was bearing the brunt of the hard times, as well as paying for the civil servants to have such early pension privileges.[108] Schiefer, unlike his other SPD colleague, the head of the Personnel Department (a civil servant), Dr. Otto Seemüller, felt that a more stringent standard for denazification should be used for civil servants than for those in the private sector, because the former

---

107. Jürgen Kocka has pointed out that the situation was different in the Soviet Zone. There, one preferred to accept administrative inefficiency for a few years, rather than to reinstate former Nazis and Nazi followers. Kocka, "1945," p. 154. Of course the Soviet Union's primary interest was in political control, rather than denazification, let alone, democratization.
108. Personalausschusssitzung, 5 Dec. 1946, RP 719/5, p. 1170 ff., StA Mü.

were "servants of the state."[109] In 1948, Bössl also made it clear that, while he supported retaining civil servants' privileges, he did not feel that politically incriminated, tenured civil servants had the right to be reinstated in their posts. He considered those with political incrimination no longer civil servants and therefore without claim to such privileges.[110] Schiefer and Bössl are representative of the conflict within the SPD over the German civil service. There was general consensus that politically incriminated civil servants should receive the same treatment as other Germans in the denazification process and should lose all privileges associated with their former civil service status, but there was disaccord on the issue of retaining the special privileges of the civil service as a whole.

On the part of those to the Right of the SPD, there was no desire to differentiate between the privileges of politically incriminated and nonincriminated civil servants. All civil servants, in their opinion, were to retain their special status and to be given priority for reinstatements, as well as full pensions if they retired. In Stuttgart, representatives of the CDU and FDP argued emotionally against demoting reinstated civil servants to Angestellten. They felt that this would be too much of "a moral demotion" and that, instead, they should be reinstated as at least civil servants on probation (auf Widerruf).[111]

In Munich, the single member of the so-called "partyless Catholic group" introduced a motion in the city council in September 1948 to pay full pensions to all civil servants with tenure who had been dismissed due to their Nazi political incrimination. The councilor, who was a lawyer, argued that, if one had legal rights prior to 1933, they could not be denied in this "Fourth Reich." The Social Democratic OB, Thomas Wimmer, countered this with the argument that there was no directive from MG that required the full rehabilitation of dismissed individuals through reinstatements or pensions. He also pointed out that he and the local MGO, as well as the head of the Special Branch for Denazification, had discussed the implications of the fact that approximately half of Munich's tenured civil servants had joined the Nazis, whereas the other had displayed backbone and continued their work without becoming NSDAP members. They felt that if half had resisted pressure to join without terrible consequences, the other half should not be rewarded for their cowardly or opportunistic behavior.[112] For the moment, while there was a ban on most munici-

109. Personalausschusssitzung, 9 Jan. 1947, RP 720/5, p. 19 ff., StA Mü.
110. Stadtratssitzung, 5 Oct. 1948, RP 721/3, p. 2568, StA Mü.
111. Personalprüfungsausschuss fürs Polizeipräsidium, 21 Feb. 1947, StA St.
112. Personalausschusssitzung, 30 Sept. 1948, RP 721/9, p. 1263 f., StA Mü.

pal hiring due to the budgetary belt-tightening required by the effects of the summer 1948 currency reform, OB Wimmer was able to maintain his position. However, once the new West German government eventually triumphed over MG in its passage of laws guaranteeing the rights of tenured civil servants to their jobs and pensions,[113] there were no legal grounds on which to reject reinstatement applications or refuse to pay the pensions of Nazi civil servants.

There are numerous instances in all three cities where various Germans, but especially those politically affiliated to the Right of the SPD, expressed concern that any reduction of civil servants' privileges, even if it involved denazification, would be too demoralizing a treatment. This was also the case on the Länder level. But there, since that was where the first MG civil service reform initiatives began, one was more likely to see a strong U.S. MG reaction to such attitudes. On the one hand, MG did not object to titular concessions, like allowing civil servants who had been removed from their posts to retain the designation of their former posts with the addition of "a.D." (außer Dienst), which implied they had simply retired.[114] On the other hand, when, in March 1949, the Württemberg-Baden Landtag passed pension laws discriminating in favor of the wives of German POWs who were civil servants over other POWs' wives, the head of the Land MG issued a press release expressing his shock over this biased treatment. He wrote: "We are quite different from you in resisting and not sharing in the glorification you give to the 'beamten' (civil servants)." The Landtag responded by urging "that MG should avoid hampering social legislation."[115]

The German civil service was viewed as being in need of reform because it was seen as one of the social structures that had been coopted into the Nazi regime and had performed as a compliant tool of the Nazis. The collaboration of the German civil service with National Socialism and its authoritarian nature were not seen as conducive to the formation of a new democratic order by either American[116] or Ger-

---

113. Art. 131 of the Basic Law restored the rights and privileges of the German civil servants and in this way provided for the almost complete rehiring and/or pensioning of civil servants dismissed during the occupation because of political incrimination during the Third Reich.

114. "Dienstenthebungen," Memo from OMGBY-CAD to the Bavarian Minister President, 2 Dec. 1946, Akt XXIII-107, Archiv des Industrie- und Handelskammer-München.

115. "Verwaltung durch die Militärregierung," 22 March 1949 Press Release, Hauptaktei 0310-3, StA St.

116. Letter from Edward Litchfield (OMGUS-CAD) to Chief of Staff, 18 July 1947, p. 1f., POLAD/460/4, 2 of 4, RG 84, IfZ. See also Kocka, "1945," p. 153. Kocka

man reformers. There was less consensus about how the civil servants were to be controlled politically, and how their loyalty to the new order was to be achieved while reeducating them to believe in and practice democracy. Although the most radical solution would have been to abolish the tenured civil service altogether,[117] most German critics were more interested in bringing it under democratic control.

The German civil service had peculiarities, even within the European context. The primary characteristics of the German civil service stemmed from an 1873 code that was modified in 1907, and then guaranteed in the Weimar constitution, as well as later in the 1937 German Civil Service Law. Some specific characteristics of the German civil service were: that only jurists could fill the highest administrative posts, that before the final examination (*Schlußprüfung*), civil service trainees had to go through several years of practical training within the administration, and that pensions would be eliminated altogether if the civil servant resigned prior to retirement. In addition, German civil servants had the right to run for office without resigning from the civil service, had no outside supervision or control by any independent commissions, and had lifelong tenure, with their service and loyalty relations determined by public sector law. These rights contrasted with those of Angestellten, whose nontenured employment was under the jurisdiction of private law.[118] These anomalies, in particular, upset the Allies.

All attempts at German civil service reform originated with the occupation powers. The concepts for reform varied according to the set-up of the civil service in each of the powers' home countries. The Soviets and the Americans involved themselves the most in civil service reform. The Soviets declared the German Civil Service Law of 1937 null and void, and abolished a tenured civil service altogether as part of their transformation of German society. The Americans were primarily concerned with the authoritarian nature of the civil service, which they wanted to transform to one known for serving the people. The Americans were also concerned with the civil ser-

---

notes that among the Allies, the Americans in particular tended to hold the authoritarian, bureaucratic tradition of Germany responsible for the "illiberal and undemocratic path" that German history had taken.

117. Billerbeck, p. 191. Civil servants in the United States also enjoy tenure rights and various other privileges, although not to the extent of the Germans, then or now.

118. Wolfgang Benz, "Die Auseinandersetzungen um das Berufsbeamtentum 1945-1952," Skripten der Sektion 9, "Deutsche Nachkriegsgeschichte nach 1945: Neuaufbau oder Restauration?" bei dem 33. deutschen Historikertag, 26. bis 30. März 1980 in Würzburg, p. 1.

vants' lack of accountability to the public,[119] and with the fact that civil servants had the right to charge any citizen who criticized them with the crime of insulting a civil servant (*Beamtenbeleidigung*).[120]

The Americans also felt that the life-long security of tenure for career civil servants led to an arbitrary treatment of the public, as well as a caste system; all privileges fell to the tenured civil servants while other salaried employees, or even wage workers, might perform the same tasks but had fewer rights and less security. Not only would this cause an isolation of the civil servants from the public, but also an antipathy on the part of the public toward the civil servants. The Americans also criticized the recruitment of civil servants for government jobs for being based more on social class characteristics and academic criteria than on principles of competition and achievement. This led to a discrimination based on sex, race, religion, and political beliefs.[121] Lastly, and the most problematic for Germans who otherwise agreed with the basic MG principles of German civil service reform, the participation of civil servants in political parties and parliaments, according to the Americans, made the separation of powers between the executive and legislative branches impossible.[122]

In order to initiate changes in the German civil service in the fall of 1946, U.S. MG first introduced laws via the minister presidents reforming the structure of the civil service in the three Länder of the U.S. Zone. These reforms, however, fundamentally remained only on paper. Once the Bizone was formed in 1947, plans were made for a separate, independent administration for government personnel that would implement MG's reform ideas and follow the Anglo-Saxon model of a Civil Service Commission. Although a law empowering this Personnel Office went into effect on 23 June 1948, German administrations and the Economic Council (Wirtschaftsrat), which opposed it, managed to bypass the office's authority by prolonging the procedure of adjusting this Bizonal law to the individual Länder.[123]

119. Cf. Munich Detachment Historical Report for 1947–48, p. 41, StA Mü.
120. Benz, p. 3f.
121. Of course the U.S. system also had its tradition of discrimination, especially against racial minorities.
122. Benz, p. 3f. Germans of all political persuasions feared that the prohibition of active political participation by civil servants would once again encourage political apathy on the part of the civil service, which would make it easier for them to continue to act as a compliant tool of any regime. See also CIC-Berichte, 7 Oct. 1946, p. 2, Hauptaktei 000-8/7, StA St.
123. Benz, p. 4f. See also Gerard Braunthal, "The Anglo-Saxon Model of Democracy in West Germany," *Archiv für Sozialgeschichte*, XVII, 1978, p. 267.

Hesse was the only Land in the U.S. Zone which genuinely seemed to want to reform the civil service. But Hesse's reform orientation ultimately worked against the success of civil service reform nationwide for two reasons. First, the Personnel Office for the Bizone was located in Frankfurt, which meant that a disproportionately high number of Hessians constituted its personnel. Since Hesse, alone among the three Länder of the U.S. Zone, had an SPD government and thus a large number of SPD-oriented officials, the SPD was considered by many to be overrepresented in the Personnel Office. Second, all Bizonal administration, including the Personnel Office, technically included only salaried employees and no civil servants in the traditional sense, because the British and Americans set up these structures from scratch and could put their civil service reforms into practice here. The combination of this large SPD presence and the lack of traditional civil servants in the Personnel Office set its representatives up for German accusations of being overly leftist and underqualified.[124] This provided more ammunition to the critics of the Personnel Office and the often conservative opponents of civil service reform.

One of the few substantive changes that MG was able to institute was requiring a minimum of three years before a reinstated civil servant, who would now be on probation, could be promoted to the status of a civil servant for life, and before any other promotion could occur. MG also prohibited German administrations from provisionally hiring or keeping waiting lists for civil servants they hoped to reinstate when there was not a position open at the time.[125] Although there were surely cases of Germans sidestepping these restrictions, they at least served to delay the process of reinstating some incriminated civil servants in their former posts at the same, or an even higher, status.

German Land-level attempts to avoid recognizing the authority of the Personnel Office provoked the British and American military governors, in February 1949, into imposing MG Law No. 15 on the administrators of the Bizone. By reducing states' rights, British and U.S. MG hoped to establish uniform civil service regulations, first at the Bizonal and thereafter at the federal level.[126] This MG decree went much further in achieving structural reforms than the version on which the Germans had been working. It abolished the category

124. Hans Hattenhauer, *Geschichte des Beamtentums*, Vol. 1: *Handbuch des Öffentlichen Dienstes* (Köln, 1980), p. 463 ff.
125. Personalausschusssitzung, 5 May 1948, p. 645 f., RP 721/8, StA Mü.
126. John Gimbel, *The American Occupation of Germany* (Stanford, 1968), p. 239.

of nontenured Angestellten, leaving two categories of civil servants, those with tenure and those without, along with general waged workers. It also established a political incompatibility rule whereby any civil servant would have to resign from his or her job prior to running for any legislative office. The Germans managed to revise this to exclude municipal council offices and the Parliamentary Council, as well as the first elected Bundestag in 1949. Although its restrictions were to be implemented in the elections for the Economic Council and the Länder parliaments, it was simply ignored by the Germans in the latter case. Law No. 15 also provided that civil servants could be disciplined by the next highest authority, although they would have the right to appeal to the Personnel Office. This independent Personnel Office was granted wider jurisdiction by the MG decree; besides handling appeals for disciplinary measures, it was also to serve as the mediator between the individual interests of the employees and the administrative apparatus of the Bizone, as well as between the public and the bureaucracy. It was also to be responsible for preventing discriminatory hiring practices and for overseeing the recruitment of the civil service. In this context, it was to administer aptitude and specialized knowledge tests, as well as set up the necessary classification system and process for advertising and filling open positions. The Personnel Office's final task was to smooth the transition for those who had been Angestellten and would now become Beamten, and to define the differences between tenured and nontenure-track civil servants and between civil servants and waged workers.[127] This extension of the powers of the Personnel Office only made its original German opponents more determined to bypass its authority.

Few of the changes included in Law No. 15 were liked by the Germans, but there was relative consensus on the issues of strengthening the individual responsibility and accountability of the civil servants by loosening up the practice of just following orders, improving the chances of promotion through achievement rather than education or other prepatory training, guaranteeing the equal treatment of men and women, removing the right to remain silent in court proceedings or toward the media, and allowing for the removal of a tenured civil servant on the basis of poor performance. There was also some German support for the provision that outsiders without civil service experience would now have the opportunity to enter the civil service without having to start from the bottom and work their way up within

127. Benz., p. 5f.

the bureaucracy. This would be possible via the imposition of quotas and the open advertising of available positions. Finally, various Germans agreed with the part of the MG law that restricted the monopoly of jurists in the higher echelons of the civil service.[128]

Despite the fact that the Western Allies imposed Law No. 15 on the Germans, the Parliamentary Council that was writing the Basic Law for the new Federal Republic of Germany managed to prolong the negotiations on how to incorporate this law into the Basic Law so long that it never was completely implemented. Almost two-thirds of the elected representatives to the Parliamentary Council were themselves civil servants, and they exerted major influence through their individual presence, as well as through the civil servant interest groups they represented (in particular the Deutscher Beamtenbund and various regional organizations). The Parliamentary Council ultimately came up with articles pertaining to the civil service that were vague enough in their wording to satisfy the interests of the organized civil servants and to appease the Allies.[129]

As soon as the Federal Republic was founded, a series of laws were passed that took advantage of the loopholes in the Basic Law, and basically restored the old traditional career civil service, as well as the category of Angestellten. Already in the summer of 1949, a minister president conference rejected the continued existence of the Bizonal Personnel Office as an alien body in an otherwise traditionally German administrative structure. Instead, the 1937 Civil Service Law was to be cleaned up and once again put into effect. The Bundestag passed a reformed law that did not contradict the Basic Law, but did conflict with the MG Law No. 15, which explicitly had not been suspended, as it was supposed to provide a model for the new regulations. The Allied High Commission initially vetoed the German law, but then withdrew the veto once it was assured that the law would be revised to conform to Law No. 15. The law which had been passed by the Bundestag was then declared provisional until 31 December 1950. This deadline was then repeatedly extended. In the meantime, Law No. 15 was suspended continually until the end of 1952. In the spring of 1952, the Allies decided to withdraw all pressure on the Germans to effect a reform of the civil service. They also had not protested the West German law of May 1951, which restored all civil service claims to anyone removed or retired due to denazification, or who had been expelled from the East or suffered any other

128. Ibid., p. 7.
129. Ibid., p. 7ff.

loss. The Federal Civil Service Law of 1953 did not reflect any wishes of MG that had not had the support of the German Parliamentary Council and, ultimately, of the civil servants themselves.[130]

A structural reform like that of the entire civil service would have had to have been either implemented on all administrative levels from the very beginning of the occupation, or made a prerequisite for the founding of the Federal Republic. The Western Allies did neither. U.S. MG did not pursue a course of reform until 1946, after the local and state level administrations, with their civil service foundations, were intact. At that point, it ordered the minister presidents to issue laws that reflected some of the Americans' wishes, but which – perhaps intentionally – lacked the necessary provisions for effective enforcement. The Personnel Office was never accepted by most Germans, as reflected in the numerous delaying tactics used to avoid accepting its jurisdiction. Even MG Law No. 15 needed to be converted into German laws and procedures in order to be implemented. By the time the Germans were called upon to implement it, they had begun the transformation from conquered enemy to ally, and therefore had enough political leverage to skirt the issue of the final form and thus the implementation of the reforms.[131] By 1952, the Allies had backed down completely and the German civil service, for the most part, had returned to its 1937 status.

The German tactic of constant postponements, combined with the growing political alliance between the Western Allies and the West German governing elites, allowed the German *Praxis* to triumph over the MG efforts at civil service reform. This was the opposite of the other pattern of the occupation, in which certain German reform initiatives – often grassroots – had been squelched by the alliance of German officials with U.S. MG personnel, thanks to their shared emphasis on expediency. In this case, a U.S. reform initiative was halted by the determination of German state, zonal, and federal-level bureaucrats to retain their elite status and ward off change. At the same time, there was a more general German resistance to those aspects of U.S. reforms which seemed "foreign" and "un-German." One of the few consistent and concerted U.S. MG efforts at democratization was compromised, and ultimately forsaken, due to German resistance. Because MG initiative was not seriously pursued until the latter phase of the occupation when German officials had reestablished a great deal of their autonomy, it was

130. Ibid.
131. See Hattenhauer, p. 469.

possible for the Germans to use postponements and political leverage to restore the majority of their old civil service privileges.

An initial implementation of MG's civil service reforms at the level
of the municipality would have found less German resistance and
would have shaped the formation of municipal government as well as
that of the higher-level bureaucracies. This would have been yet
another way to open up German government to fresh, new personnel and to realize more of a Stunde Null. But it also would have
meant less continuity, as some experienced civil servants would have
surely tried to enter the private sector if they no longer had their special privileges within the civil service. Also, not nearly as many of the
civil servants who had been dismissed for reasons of political incrimination would have sought reinstatement if they had not been able to
retain the high pensions and their old elite status. While this would
probably have opened the way more for change and reform, it would
also have affected, at least temporarily, the efficiency of the various
German bureaucracies. Thus, it is doubtful that MG would have pursued the reforms early on due to these consequences of slowing the
speed of recovery. The MG's reliance on German experience was
synonymous, whether it realized it or not, with its reliance on the
German civil service. By the time MG introduced its civil-service
reforms, the old civil service was once again intact and functioning
quite efficiently. Without aggressive coercion, the German civil service was not likely to support its own reform and the resulting loss of
privileges, let alone its own dissolution. Once again, the propitious
moment for reform had been lost, but in this case it was MG that,
consciously or not, let the moment slip by for its own reform.

Economic Reconstruction

It is not the purpose of this section to delineate the various details
of how MG affected economic developments in the U.S. Zone and
eventually West Germany. Much has been written by both Germans
and Americans, often in polemical terms, about General Clay's prevention of nationalization measures in Hesse and his opposition to
codetermination by the trade unions as well as his decision to stop
dismantling in the U.S. Zone and, as signalled by Secretary of State
James Byrnes's speech at Stuttgart in September 1946, the decision
to rebuild Germany economically along capitalist lines.[132] Historians

132. See in particular John H. Backer, *Winds of History: The German Years of Lucius
DuBignon Clay* (New York, 1983); Rolf Badstübner, *Restaurationsapologie und*

have also focused on how the German public, as a whole, and the political parties responded to these economic developments. In the immediate postwar period, the majority of Germans wanted some form of planned economy with a nationalization or socialization of at least those major industries that had been instrumental in the Nazi regime's pursuit of war. They also wanted to retain public control over utilities, communication, and transportation, so that all would continue to have equal and affordable access to them. The only political groups that still fully supported laissez-faire capitalism in 1945 were the remaining strands of the DVP, the DDP, and the Staatspartei which coalesced into the FDP. Even the CDU's 1945 Frankfurt Program (Leitsätze) stressed a planned economy along some sort of Christian socialist lines and thus reflected these general attitudes. MG's shaping of the economy in a more capitalist direction and its discouragement of any socialist orientation did have its impact upon the evolution of German political party platforms. This impact was mirrored in the CDU's policy transformation to a more traditionally liberal (in the nineteenth-century sense of the word) free-market economy with some welfare state provisions in its 1949 Düsseldorf Program.[133] The SPD did not abandon its hopes for a planned economy, although it did gradually retreat from its Marxist analysis of National Socialism, with its implicit condemnation of capitalism once German public opinion came to favor capitalism more and more. This evolution of public opinion occurred as the positive effects of the currency reform and Marshall Plan aid were felt and anti-Soviet and general Cold War tensions climaxed in the midst of the Berlin Blockade.[134]

Fortschrittsverteufelung (Frankfurt, 1978); Gimbel, *American Occupation*; Gulgowski; Jürgen Kocka, "Restauration oder Neubeginn? Deutschland 1945–1949," *Demokratie und Sozialismus*, Nr. 1 (1979), p. 112–119; Wolfgang Krieger; Plum; Eberhard Schmidt, *Die verhinderte Neuordnung 1945–1952* (Frankfurt, 1970); and Dörte Winkler, "Die amerikanische Sozialisierungspolitik in Deutschland 1945–1948," in Heinrich A. Winkler (ed.), *Politische Weichenstellungen in Nachkriegsdeutschland* (Göttingen, 1979). For an excellent overall analysis of the impact of American industrial culture on postwar West Germany, see Volker R. Berghahn: "West German Reconstruction and American Industrial Culture, 1945–1960," in *The American Impact on Postwar Germany*, ed. Reiner Pommerin (Providence, R.I. and Oxford, 1995), p. 65–81.

133. See for example Hans Georg Wieck: *Christliche und Freie Demokraten in Hessen, Rheinland-Pfalz, Baden und Württemberg 1945/46* (Düsseldorf, 1958). Cf. Billerbeck, p. 80f.

134. See John A. Maxwell, "Failed Social and Economic Policies: The German Social Democratic Programme, 1945–1949, " *Europa*, vol. 5, no. 2 (1982), p. 163–176. Cf. Billerbeck, p. 82f.

The U.S. MG actively encouraged German support of a free market economy and discouraged KPD, SPD, and union support for various degrees of nationalization and a planned economy, as well as a thorough denazification of the economy, and codetermination and an active role for the works councils in corporate decision making.[135] Although MG definitely showed a preference for those parties which supported its economic agenda, it did not need to work through the parties to achieve this particular agenda. However, military governor Clay did intervene at whatever level was necessary to keep the Germans on a capitalist course. Probably even more important than intervention was the apparent economic recovery U.S. MG's policies produced, as compared to the Soviet Zone of occupation. But when it did become directly involved in German economic decisions, it was on the zonal and bizonal levels; from there it had control over Länder developments, such as that involving the nationalization clause in the Hessian constitution.

The municipality was not autonomous enough to develop very much of its own economic program, but MG economic policy certainly affected the municipal level. City administrations were often given the task of overseeing the licensing of denazified businesses. They also oversaw the assignment of, and supervision over, trustees to manage those firms from which owners or managers had been removed for reasons of Nazi incrimination. City councilors represented their own political and economic interests and social concerns when they debated issues like the influential role the Chambers of Commerce and Industry were playing in rebuilding the economy as compared to the role of the workers in their organizations, such as the unions or the works councils. Because Germans on all levels of administration believed, at least for a time, that they would democratically decide their own economic development, appointed and elected municipal officials took their local decision-making roles very seriously, as they assumed that these would coincide with, or at least influence, developments on the higher levels. When zonal and bizonal developments did not necessarily mesh with some of their ideas of denazification and democratization of the economy, they let their frustrations be known. It is these municipal-level expressions of economic hopes and disillusionments with economic policies pursued by MG, as well as inter-German disagreements on economic developments and MG reactions to German expressions of discontent, that will concern us here.

135. Billerbeck, p. 111 ff.

Just as denazification discussions on the municipal level often involved questions of civil service reform, economic reforms also came up often in the context of denazification of the economy. The broader concept of denazification carried with it a transformation of the economy so that the propertied elite that had bolstered the Nazi regime would, at a minimum, lose its property (businesses), and nonincriminated individuals with business experience would be placed in charge of those firms, as trustees for the government. These trustees would remain in charge while it was decided whether to sell shares that had belonged to the incriminated individuals to the public, to convert them into cooperatively owned enterprises, or to completely nationalize them.[136] Other aspects of this broad denazification included a denazification of money. The deputy mayor of Munich, the Social Democrat Thomas Wimmer, argued vehemently in April of 1946 that in order for "denazification to have any real results, a denazification of money would first have to be initiated." He criticized the flourishing black market and felt that "everyone who had two healthy arms and legs" should have to work, and that no one had the right to live, let alone profit, from the work of someone else.[137]

A narrower conception of denazification of the economy would, on the other hand, simply mean the installation of temporary trustees for the time needed for the owner or manager to go through denazification proceedings, after which the old leadership would return and "business as usual" would resume. This latter interpretation generally conformed to that of MG, at least after mid-1946. Occasionally, as part of the denazification sentence or during the time before the individual owner or manager was tried, he or she might continue to work in the firm, but with the official status of a common laborer (*gewöhnlicher Arbeiter*). This usually resulted in the owner simply pulling the strings from behind the stage, with the

136. Bauunternehmen- und Entnazifizierungsunterausschuss, 27 Sept. 1945, p. 4f., RP 718/3, StA Mü. Although the experience of the Nazis' confiscation of property made some Germans wary of such tactics, most Germans on the Left, whether in the internal discussions of the Antifas or within works councils (Betriebsräte), the parties, or in the city council meetings, regarded policies such as dismantling war-related industries, and either nationalizing or cooperatively owning and running their remnants as peace time enterprises, as part of denazifying and democratizing the economy. See Michael Fichter, "Aufbau und Neuordnung: Betriebsräte zwischen Klassensolidarität und Betriebsloyalität," in Von Stalingrad zur Währungsreform, ed. Martin Broszat (Munich, 1988), p. 469–549.

137. Stadtratssitzung, 11 April 1946, RP 719/1, p. 238 f., StA Mü.

employees following his or her orders rather than those of the trustee. An indication that this was the norm rather than the exception can be found in the fears, expressed by the Chamber of Commerce and Industry in Frankfurt, that the unions and the KPD were trying to have those individuals who were demoted to ordinary labor actually be paid ordinary wages. Most unsettling to the Chamber was the fact that MG appeared to be allowing this to happen.[138] MG did not continue in that direction very long, however.

Local MG in Munich stated clearly, as early as September 1945, right after Law No. 8 had been issued to denazify the economy, that neither individual firms nor the economy as a whole were to suffer any losses as a result of denazification.[139] One way in which this was to be accomplished became clear in 1946, when MG there reversed its policy of not granting licenses to run firms to the spouses of incriminated individuals.[140] This covert return to the status quo ante can also be seen in the mixed messages the OB of Munich received in the spring of 1946 about how his Office for the Purification of the Economy (Wirtschaftsbereinigungsamt) was to respond to requests from the owners of firms, who had been prohibited from running their businesses, to return to their businesses and to have the trustees who had been running them in their absence be recalled. The owners were reacting to a 15 April 1946 memorandum from the Bavarian Economics Ministry, which referred to the fact that "the trustees had been recalled and the previous legal status of the firms was back in effect." This policy, according to the ministry document, was based on a decision made by the Bavarian MG. Yet when the city contacted the Property Control Division of the Munich MG to confirm it, it claimed to have had no information on this new policy. The OB ultimately decided that because trustees had only been placed in charge of firms where the owners had been removed by MG, the city would not return these firms to their original owners until it received explicit instructions from MG to do so.[141] In this case, the Land-level of both MG and the German government placed economic recovery above denazification, while

138. "Stand der Denazifizierung der Wirtschaft; Besondere Bemerkungen der Industrie- und Handelskammern, 5 Nov. 1945, Abt. 507, Nr. 386, Zug. 67/79, Hessisches Hauptstaatsarchiv.

139. Bauunternehmen- und Entnazifizierungsunterausschuss, 27 Sept. 1945, RP 718/3, p. 3, StA Mü.

140. Leistungsbericht des Gewerbeamtes für das Jahr 1946, p. 15, BuR 260/11, StA Mü.

141. Bericht des OB-Münchens an den Oberbayerischen Regierungspräsidenten, May 1946, MSo, AZ 1-64, Bd. 1, Bayerisches Hauptstaatsarchiv.

neither the local German government nor local MG, at least at this point, took advantage of the ambiguity of the situation in order to abandon denazification.

MG seemed to remain actively involved in economic developments longer than in any other aspect of German life. This involvement was not always to the liking of the Germans involved. For example, a committee of the Munich Chamber of Commerce and Industry complained to the Bavarian Economics Ministry in late October 1948 about MG officers requesting information from firms about their "internal affairs." The committee wanted to know to what extent MG had the right to do this, and asked for guidelines according to which the firms might deny MG information. Interestingly enough, the ministry avoided this somewhat sensitive aspect of MG-German relations by simply not responding to the Chamber committee at all.[142]

On the other hand, Germans sometimes found MG more willing to compromise on certain economic directives than their own government officials. In December 1946, in a Munich Chamber of Commerce and Industry discussion, the story was relayed of how MG personnel who were sent to oversee the dismantling of various companies, which had been designated for reparations, had been convinced to exempt certain workshops and equipment from the inventory list. This was regarded as "proof, that direct negotiations with MG could lead to a positive result, while no support could be found in the Economics Ministry."[143]

More leftist-oriented Germans were discontent with the large role they felt the Chambers of Commerce and Industry and the elite classes, as a whole, were playing alongside MG in directing the German economy. Gustav Schiefer, the head of the Munich trade unions, complained frequently, in his capacity as head of the SPD group in the Munich city council, that the workers and the unions were being excluded from economic planning, and that under those circumstances there could be no real democratization of the economy.[144] Schiefer also criticized the Bizonal Economics Office in Frankfurt, which had been formed by British and U.S. MG, for introducing a free market economy and for being made up of "represen-

142. 27 Oct. 1948 letter, Akt XXIII,-568 (II), Archiv des Industrie- und Handelskammers-München.
143. IHK-Sitzungsprotokoll, 10 Dec. 1946, p. 5, Archiv des Industrie- und Handelskammers-München. In 1946 MG's power far outweighed that of the German state ministry.
144. Stadtratssitzung, 8 July 1947, RP 720/2, StA Mü.

tatives from the propertied classes, industry and agriculture."[145] Schiefer condemned the hoarding that had been occurring as a symptom of a private free market economy. He pleaded for the institution of a planned economy prior to the equalization of burdens (*Lastenausgleich*), in order to prevent the occupation powers from playing into the hands of the German bourgeoisie. In that way, he felt that the hoarding would be stopped and that there would at least be a step toward more equal (re)distribution of goods.[146]

Anxiety was expressed in all three city councils over the idea that MG wanted to model the German economy along U.S. lines. In a Munich city council meeting in June 1948, the SPD department head responsible for the city's financial management complained about the Americans' insensitivity toward Germans' social welfare needs. He stressed that despite the need, after the currency reform, to tighten the city's budget, the top priority of the city, and of Germans in general, would be to make sure that no one would go hungry or be left to freeze.[147] In the more traditionally working class city of Stuttgart, Hans Stetter, the head of the local trade unions, who was also an SPD city councilor, warned of certain Germans' hopes that the Americans would get rid of the works councils altogether. He cited an applicant for a high-level city position, who, as deputy head of another municipal office, had a very bad reputation with the works council. This applicant told his own office's works council representatives that "in a few years there would not be any works council at all." He explained that there would be so much American capital in the German economy that Americans would control the majority interests and that "since there were no works councils in the U.S., the Americans certainly wouldn't tolerate them in Germany."[148]

Although the Americans did not abolish the works councils, MG was not always on the friendliest of terms with organized labor, especially in Stuttgart. Like Schiefer in Munich, Stetter in Stuttgart blamed the direction that the economy and the administration were taking for the hoarding that had taken place prior to the currency reform. He called upon the workers not to buy from those retailers who had been hiding their goods to sell until they could get more valuable currency for them. He was also critical of the effects of the currency reform on price levels. After the Württemberg-Baden trade union conference had unsuccessfully demanded, in their 3 July 1948

145. Stadtratssitzung, 6 July 1948, RP 721/2, p. 1597, StA Mü.
146. Ibid., p. 1597 ff.
147. Stadtratssitzung, 15 June 1948, RP 721/1, p. 1277, StA Mü.
148. Gemeinderatssitzungsprotokolle, 1948 (II), 16 Sept. 1948, p. 285 StA St.

meeting,that small savings accounts be converted on a one RM – one DM basis, they had requested an expedient social equalization of burdens. This would include legal protection against dismissals and a 15 percent wage increase to counterbalance the rise in prices. The former was passed by the Landtag, but nothing came of the hopes for a wage increase or of a Landtag discussion of worker – management codetermination because of the MG reaction against a vote on codetermination. Various industry groups of the unions and works councils committees also became more assertive and ultimately frustrated with their union leadership, whom they felt were not standing up to MG and the management representatives adequately. This led to the local Stuttgart union leadership, under Stetter, calling for a half-day work stoppage and rally in Stuttgart on 28 October 1948. Speaking before a large but disciplined crowd, Stetter criticized the economic policies of Ludwig Erhard in the Economic Council, the high costs of the occupation, and some of the dismantling plans, and called for price controls on nonluxury items and harsh punishment for profiteers and tax evaders.[149]

Although the crowd dispersed in a calm and orderly fashion, shortly therafter stones were thrown at a window of an upscale retail store and at the surrounding lights by a handful of men. Several instances of disturbing the peace and resisting arrests followed, although only one of the Germans who were eventually tried and found guilty by an MG court was even from Stuttgart. The unions immediately disassociated themselves from the rowdies and condemned their violent methods. General Clay, however, blamed Stetter personally as the instigator for having given such a provocative speech, which he considered a direct affront to MG. The city of Stuttgart was punished with a one-week curfew and the loss of the right of assembly for two and a half weeks, although there was no evidence that any of the events had been politically organized. The unions throughout the Bizone responded with a twenty-four-hour general strike on 12 November, during which demands – including the return of codetermination which MG had suspended and the end to the negative effects the currency reform had on the working class – were made that were very similar to those expressed by Stetter on 28 October in Stuttgart.[150]

This fall 1948 conflict in Stuttgart, and the way it was handled by Clay, only made antagonisms between labor and MG worse. To a

149. Vietzen, p. 135 ff. Cf. Fichter, p. 544f.
150. Ibid., p. 137 ff. A certain level of codetermination between workers and management had been established in a few firms.

certain extent, dealing with MG probably made the prospect of trying to negotiate with other Germans autonomously seem easy to the
unions. It probably also convinced some union leaders that they
were going to have an uphill battle in their attempts to achieve any
goals that MG directly opposed. Perhaps for this reason, the German unions – and within the individual firms, the works councils –
soon developed a reputation for compromising with management.
By the time the Federal Republic was autonomous, at least in its
domestic policies, the unions had dropped much of their political
program in the midst of increasing economic stability and harmony
in the workplace, and settled for[151] the economic measures of codetermination and a social-market economy (*soziale Marktwirtschaft*).
In some ways this union development was symbolic of the outcome
of the tension between an expedient economic recovery and social
stability to which MG and most German elites were giving highest
priority and the more complex and time-consuming political and
social democratization agenda that was being postponed, if not forsaken – even by some erstwhile reformers.

Conclusion

As compared to the first year of the occupation, MG did play much
more of a behind-the-scenes role in local-level German affairs after
the 1946 municipal elections. MG's early appointments of the OB
and Bürgermeister, and its approval of the department heads and
advisory city councilors had a long-term effect on the personnel continuity in those offices in Munich and Stuttgart, and in most other
municipalities in the U.S. Zone. Certain MG representatives tried to
influence the first postwar elections, especially in Stuttgart and
Frankfurt, where they feared the democratic process would not result
in the election of their preferred candidates. In those cases, the MG
interveners hoped that the autonomy that the elections would bring
to the Germans would be exercised by those individuals whom these
MG officials felt would best represent MG's perceived interests.

After 1946, MG continued to help shape German political developments, but by then local MG had fewer representatives and their
role had been decreased to that of liaison between the local Germans and the higher levels of MG. Its influence was exercised from

151. See Billerbeck, p. 115. For an analysis of the works councils' accomplishments,
see Fichter, p. 547 ff.

the zonal level, where it had direct contact with Land, zonal, and eventually bizonal and trizonal German officials. After 1946, MG's local political influence was most apparent in its anti-Communism campaign and its retreat from its initially stringent and broadly conceived denazification program. This retreat, in turn, had an effect on economic developments, because a thorough denazification of the economy would have gone beyond the removal, often temporary, of heads of commerce and industry. Personnel changes within the economic elite due to the use of trustees, and a significant reduction in the number of the old economic elites who had been implicated in the Nazi regime might have transformed the political complexion of the leaders of commerce and industry. This could have enhanced the role of the unions and workers in economic planning, and thus have paved the way for more viable prospects for more widespread codetermination, more decartellization, more cooperatively run businesses, and economic democratization in general.

This retreat from a thorough denazification also had an effect on civil service reform, which became less and less likely as dismissed civil servants, expecting to retain their traditional civil service privileges, returned to their posts. The MG's reliance on experienced German bureaucrats from the earliest days of the occupation also reinforced the status of the civil service and strengthened it to fight off denazification and democratization efforts as well as other aspects of its own reforms.

Thus, in conclusion, the retreat of MG from municipal affairs, and the return of self-government to the Germans in Frankfurt, Munich, and Stuttgart was a gradual process which began with the restoration of the democratic process in late May 1946, and was mostly concluded by the time of the founding of the Federal Republic in May 1949. The U.S. occupation authorities still exercised some influence over German developments, which also affected local German affairs, until 1955 when the Occupation Statute was signed. Their primary concern however, at least from 1946 on, was with economic recovery, and they found numerous German allies who shared this priority. How many of these allies recognized what this prioritization could cost in the long run is unclear. The prospects for the potential realization of numerous structural democratic reforms of German political and socioeconomic life had already been diminished considerably during the early days of the occupation, because of the MG appointment of non-Nazis, rather than activist anti-Nazis to top-level posts. The fact that many of these Germans remained in their posts once the democratic process was restored, and that MG and many German leaders gave top priority to economic recovery after 1946 further diminished the chances for the realization of a sweeping political and socioeconomic democratization of Germany. Once these patterns were established and the MG-sanctioned German personnel and representatives of parties licensed by MG ran for election, it was not easy for new political figures to run for office, let alone have a chance of winning.

The international context, in particular East – West tensions, also played a role in how these priorities were arranged. The following quote by the historian, Leonard Krieger, about the occupying powers in general is pertinent for an analysis of U.S. MG – German relations: "As international relations worsened and the German institutional net was, in its varying forms, knit or re-knit, the occupying powers insensibly scaled down their criteria of democratization to mean the practical cooperation of Germans with the respective occupying power and, especially in the west, to include an acknowledgment of the actual direction the Germans were taking."[152] Of course, "the actual direction the Germans were taking" had been greatly influenced by MG's priorities and by who these "Germans" were who had the power to be taking a course of direction in the first place.

---

152. Leonard Krieger, "The Potential for Democratization in Occupied Germany," in: John D. Montgomery and Albert O. Hirschman (eds.), *Public Policy*, 17 (1968), p. 57.

Chapter VII

CONCLUSION

The Legacy of the U.S. Occupation

*T*he end of the war, the collapse of the Third Reich, and the beginning of Allied military occupation in late 1944 and early 1945 represent a watershed in German history. For a short and highly specific moment, there seemed to be a *Nullpunkt*, one of those unique periods in history when a boundary could be drawn to demarcate the past from the future. The Allied powers determined how that line would be drawn in conjunction with the Germans, with whom or through whom they chose to work. No one, whether for political or for practical reasons, wanted to dispose of the entire German past. Allied advisors with expertise in German affairs recommended retaining and/or reforming certain German traditions, while they counseled that others should be transformed completely. These recommendations were grounded in a knowledge of German history and based on a particular perception of their governments' interests in the future political, social, and economic development of Germany. These advisors varied in their analyses, not just from occupation power to occupation power, but also among themselves. Some of the advisors to the U.S. occupation authorities, especially those who were emigrés and academic experts on Germany, had at least as much interest in Germany's future as in how Germany's future should fit into international developments or accommodate U.S. foreign policy interests.

Policymakers in the various departments of the executive branch of U.S. government, on the other hand, were primarily concerned with U.S. interests and international developments. Their concerns, however, varied according to how much of a threat they considered a post-war Germany to represent, and according to the kind of German future they considered to be in America's best interest. The Treasury Department, under Henry Morgenthau, placed an emphasis on demilitarization and deindustrialization in order to prevent future German aggressions, whereas the State Department stressed a policy of integrating a Western-oriented and denazified Germany – solidly grounded in capitalism – back into the international community of nations. The War Department's top priority, on the other hand, hinged on an expeditious withdrawal of U.S. troops after the quick completion of a military occupation, which would guarantee military security concerns, with as little political involvement in German affairs as possible.

The Treasury Department lost its voice in policy planning with the death of President Roosevelt and the transition to the Truman administration. The only place where its interests continued to be represented to any extent was in the official U.S. occupation directive, JCS 1067. Neither the State nor the War Departments felt particularly committed to JCS 1067, although it was the primary official directive for MG in Germany, and its implementation ultimately fell under the jurisdiction of those two departments. For a variety of reasons, including the fact that a military occupation is usually run by military men according to military rules and regulations, the War Department had the most influence on the implementation of the occupation policies. Even if some civilian experts were given temporary military status to work within the administration of MG, such as much of the ICD personnel, their rank was never considered to be on the same level as that of the regular military. Furthermore, the military governor of the U.S. Zone routed all the State Department instructions through the War Department, giving the latter significant control over the former. The only U.S. occupation agency which was not answerable to the War Department was POLAD in Germany, which reported directly to the State Department and represented its interests. It was the chief engineer of political policy in the U.S. Zone of occupied Germany.

Conflicts often arose between the military implementers and the civilian policymakers, as well as with the special – often academic and/or emigré – advisors, who were frequently caught in the middle. The advisors usually worked either for POLAD or for the military governor or his deputy. When it came to having an impact on MG policies and the implementation of decisions, their expertise in German affairs was often just as wasted as that of the OSS and other such intelligence analysts. Neither these advisors nor the reformist experts in specialized areas of MG, like ICD, had direct control over how, if at all, the actual MG leadership and its detachments employed their advice and information. Special political and socioeconomic advisors did not always agree with each other, or with the reformers in ICD or OSS, but unlike most regular military MG personnel or technical experts, they were committed to a long-term occupation with a strong political and socioeconomic agenda. Thus POLAD officials and other special experts gave advice predicated on plans for a long-term occupation, which articulated complex political goals; they counseled, however, an MG whose top priority was to restore order and security so that it could return its personnel to the States as soon as possible. This conflict in orientation resulted in many policies being implemented in their most expeditious form rather than in the way they were originally intended to be.

By mid-1946, U.S. priorities within the long-term political and socioeconomic agenda had changed from decartellization, industrial disarmament, denazification, and democratization to anti-Communism and capitalist economic reconstruction. POLAD pursued these new priorities with vigor. Until this point POLAD had been slow to provide clear instructions to MG in the midst of the State Department's qualms over JCS 1067. But once Secretary Byrnes gave his Stuttgart speech in September 1946, a direct path was cleared to economic reconstruction. Any other policies which did not directly enhance this goal would have to be postponed or adjusted so that they would not stand in the way. Most of the special advisors had returned home by this time, so they were not present to protest the repercussions of this taxonomy of priorities, while many of the reformist men in intelligence and information control services were now either purged or departing Germany in disillusionment. This left POLAD and MG to pursue these goals.

Meanwhile, Congress and U.S. business interests were putting pressure on the executive branch to bring American soldiers home, and to stop slowing German economic recovery with denazification. The Army, eager to accelerate its withdrawal, came to realize that a swift German economic recovery might allow just that. The State Department, on the other hand, could kill two birds with one stone: by fulfilling Germans' material needs in the Western Zones in the midst of a growing German awareness of the considerably direr conditions in the Soviet Zone, the first step toward German economic recovery, toward assured German support for capitalism and, indirectly, against the appeal of Communism, would be achieved. New priorities overshadowed the original occupation policies of denazification, demilitarization, and democratization, which receded to a back burner or were simply declared accomplished. In other words, whatever German political and socioeconomic reforms had not been achieved in that first year would probably have many fewer opportunities to be pursued seriously in the near future, at least unless they fit directly into the new agenda.

What had been accomplished fully in that first year was ultimately largely determined by the Germans whom MG had selected to help carry out the occupation directives. The particular people that MG detachments appointed initially in the various villages, towns, and cities in the U.S. Zone to implement the occupation policies and the decisions made by those appointees in that first year shaped the political, social, and economic developments throughout the entire occupation and, I would argue, in some ways throughout the next decades. Even before new priorities replaced the original occupation goals of demilitarization, denazification, and democratization, the MG detachments made pragmatic decisions in order to pursue their top priority of getting things in their community or region running again, rather than to restore or create a German civil society and to foster democratic progress. They chose Germans with administrative experience who seemed cooperative and respectful of their military authority rather than clear-cut democratic anti-Nazis. The former type of German seemed more pragmatic and apolitical, while the latter, who sometimes also had the prerequisite background and some experience for the position, usually had an overt political agenda of his/her own. The War Department wanted to avoid involvement in German politics and to suppress German political activity as much as possible. Moreover, the State Department had its own political agenda for the Germans. Hence, the selection of seemingly apolitical, if not malleable, efficient German administrators by MG rather than politicized, activist Germans on the political Left seemed to mesh well with both the War and State Departments' goals. However, this conformity was more coincidental than intentional. The ready availability of Germans, who would be both cooperative and efficient at getting the practical tasks of putting a municipal administration and a municipality back into working order, provided the rationale for the choice of initial appointees.

The fact that the appointed mayors selected their deputies, department heads, and advisory city councilors gave them a tremendous amount of autonomous power. This power went above and beyond the first year of the occupation, because of the personnel continuity that occurred in these administrative posts and elected bodies well into the 1950s. The appointed municipal elites shared a goal with their MG overseers, which was to endow German society with normalcy and order again, as quickly as possible. Given the damage, disorder, and material hardships at the end of the war, this was understandable and commendable. Any Germans interested in the fate of the community surrounding them would have a proclivity in this direction. This predilection, however, if pursued single-mindedly, carried with it the danger of losing the propitious immediate postwar moment that might have occasioned reforms, such as those articulated at Potsdam involving denazification, demilitarization, and, in particular, democratization.

Most of the German appointees had little interest in structural changes and often tried to sabotage those MG policies like denazification, which threatened to affect either bureaucratic efficiency[1] or the speed of material recovery. The appointed mayors were solely accountable to U.S. MG and thus could potentially forge autocratic regimes. If they fostered the appearance of cooperating with MG, they were often able to manipulate the detachment, sometimes even to bypass MG policies. For example, OB Blaum in Frankfurt, certainly the prototype of this kind of authoritarian leader, and OB Klett in Stuttgart both used MG support as a foil to avoid any accountability to their advisory councils. This lack of even informal accountability to the, albeit advisory, city councils, let alone the population at large, limited the impact that critics of the mayors' methods and other reformers normally would have had through the pressure of the democratic process.[2] In Frankfurt, the leftist-oriented *Frankfurter Rundschau* did step in to criticize Blaum, and although it was unable to stop his autocratic style, it did influence public opinion and surely made his bid for the 1946 election even less likely to succeed. In this particular case, MG could not protect Blaum against the ICD-supported German editorial board, although it had its revenge against some of Blaum's critics when it intervened in the department head elections.

1. Herbert Schnoor has pointed out that the priority the German administrators gave to bureaucratic efficiency over democratic reliability in their choice of personnel led to an acceptance of politically incriminated Germans who appeared all too easily to be indispensable. See Herbert Schnoor, "Gedanken zum Neuaufbau der Verwaltung nach 1945," in Friedrich Gerhard Schwegmann (ed.), *Die Wiederherstellung des Berufsbeamtentums nach 1945 : Geburtsfehler oder Stützpfeiler der Demokratiegründung in Westdeutschland?* (Düsseldorf, 1986), p. 21.
2. Here, I am referring to parts of this process that go beyond elections, such as accountability through public criticism, representative councils with powers of oversight, etc.

The diminished outlets for the voice of a democratic opposition exacerbated the effects of the early ban on political activity. The ban squelched Antifa activism and, whether intentionally or not, the reform potential that it represented. In addition, the top-down development of the local political parties brought with it a revival of both party hierarchies and political dogmas. This development, which preceded the lifting of the political ban, because of the reliance on the old Weimar local political party leaders for the lists of suggested advisory city councilors, further diminished the potential for a fresh political start. These Weimar political elites had a stake in the status quo ante and were, as a result, less likely to pursue major structural changes.

This outcome of MG practices contrasted with the original MG policy stipulating that German democratic forces should be encouraged. The failure to grant new, or at least significantly refurbished, democratic political parties an opportunity to introduce structural changes, as part of a broadly defined denazification and democratization program, reduced the potential for change in that first year. The MG's discouragement of various German democratic reformers undermined their capacity to organize, campaign, and gain support in the 1946 and 1948 elections. Any substantive changes, which such reformers might have introduced in that first year, could not have been simply reversed in the successive years. They would clearly have had an impact on elections and on the route German developments followed, both during and after the occupation. As it was, MG's support of those Germans it considered more apolitical, "expert," and pragmatically cooperative gave them an advantage in elections and a predominant role in the shaping of the Federal Republic. Equal support, if not encouragement, from MG for other, often more democratic, reformers would have increased the chances that their reform plans, which often coincided with the early official U.S. occupation goals, would come to fruition.

The MG's support of those seemingly apolitical, but actually often quite conservative, Germans privileged a trend toward continuity in German political and socioeconomic structures. Numerous pre-Depression mainstream Weimar elites were restored to power. The MG and those Germans it chose as allies represented the desire for normalization and material recovery. Given Germany's turbulent history during the twentieth century, this emphasis struck a resonant chord within the German population. But normalization and material recovery did not have to mean restricting the potential of real structural change. Although the achievement of normalization and material recovery may have been delayed, somewhat, by the transition to a more democratic society, the long-term goal might well have created more widespread "normalcy" and material well-being, as well as justice and equality for all. Structural changes, such as the socialization or redistribution of more fundamental components of the economy and more cooperatively run housing and business ventures, might have gone hand-in-hand with a thorough denazification of the economy; this would have affected the socioeconomic structure by purging and recasting the old economic elite, who were often tainted by collaboration with the Nazi regime. The way would have been opened for more egalitarianism and a genuine equalization of burdens (*Lastenausgleich*). A more enduring, cathartic effect on society – a confrontation and a reckoning with the Nazi past rather than a mere avoiding responsibility for the past (*Vergangenheitsbewältigung*), might also have resulted. If a thorough denazification of the civil service and general civil service reform had transpired during the earliest days of the occupation, it might have prevented the immediate resurrection of the bureaucratic barricades against change. A fundamental process of denazification would also have opened the door to more democratic access to government, not only because the civil service would have been more open to newcomers and more assertive in terminating civil servants who abused authority or performed poorly, but also because it would have displayed a more democratic responsiveness and accountability to the citizenry.

There is, of course, a more unequivocally positive side to the legacy of personnel continuity in postwar Western Germany. The political and social stability of the early decades of the Federal Republic can certainly be ascribed to the competence and achievements of administrators, who represented personnel continuity within the German civil service both before and after 1933. Such continuity helped to steer almost all administrative energies toward a pragmatic course in pursuit of economic reconstruction and the eventual so-called Economic Miracle. Economic prosperity resulted in social stability, which ensured the smooth functioning and acceptance of the Federal Republic's political system. But this occurred at the cost of a clean break with the past[3] and the actualization of a Stunde Null with all the potential it could have promised.

To what extent local-level developments in that first year might have changed larger scale developments, like the growing Cold War

---

3.   Ibid. See also Richard Löwenthal, "Prolog: Dauer und Verwandlung," in Richard Löwenthal and Hans-Peter Schwarz (eds.), *Die zweite Republik* (Stuttgart, 1974), p. 9–25.

tensions, or the abandonment of denazification and democratization in favor of anti-Communism and capitalism, is one of those hypothetical questions that both fascinate and mystify historians. In the U.S. Zone of occupation and ultimately in all three Western Zones – because of the predominant economic and therefore political influence of the United States – the inherent tension between the need to restore order versus the necessity to institute change in the immediate postwar period yielded a victory of the forces of restored order. If MG had encouraged changes by working with the Germans interested in introducing them, there would have been less polarization between the moderate Right, which initially was more reform-oriented and skeptical of a purely capitalist economy, and the Left. The early cooperation between Social Democrats and Communists and other leftist splinter groups, as well as some middle-of-the-road progressives and Catholics, could have resulted in new alignments and revised political programs. It could also have prompted a retreat from dogmatic ideologies or old rivalries and feuds; it might even have nurtured the successful development of new parties altogether. This could have lessened the tensions with the Soviet Zone. Developments like the formation of the SED were not merely reactions to political developments in the Western German Zones. They also mirrored the coerced development of a one-party system in Eastern Europe and the Soviet "satellite" policy as a whole. But it is possible that Soviet defense mechanisms would have been triggered less often by the frequently confrontational posture of the U.S. and its German allies.[4]

If the United States had supported Germans who had been reformist and perhaps less adamantly anti-Communist in the first place, while granting its own experts on Germany a more influential role in the occupation, the resulting changes might have conformed more closely to the Allied Yalta and Potsdam agreements. These, in turn, could have facilitated better quadripartite control and harmonious relations. Whether the Soviet walkout from Allied meetings or its decision to blockade Berlin might have been avoided if internal German political developments had been more reformist and democratic, and had allowed the Left a larger role is certainly open to debate. It is also unlikely that this would have prevented the West-

---

4. As we learn more about Stalin's behavior with new access to Russian archives, it seems that Soviet defensiveness may well have been just as strong. But whether German Communists would have followed the Soviet line as readily as they did in the Western Zones if the animus toward Communism had been cultivated less remains subject to debate.

ern decisions to bypass quadripartite decision making as displayed in the actions taken to stop the dismantling of Western German industry, to consolidate the British and U.S. Zones economically into the Bizone, to introduce a tripartite currency reform, or to form a Parliamentary Council charged with drafting a constitution for a Western Germany. Perhaps the tone in East – West relations would have remained more cooperative if there had been fewer polarized political relations within Germany. Would this have avoided or deferred the division of Germany, rendering Stalin's offer for a neutral one a more realistic possibility in Western eyes? However amorphous and obscure the connection between larger-scale international developments in the late 1940s and the local-level German ones in the mid-1940s may seem, there was undoubtedly some kind of relationship between the two.

I shall not speculate ad infinitum on this "what-if" topic; however we do need to ponder the alternative possibilities to what became the legacy of the American occupation for West German developments. The cental assertion of this book is that the most auspicious moment for democratic changes was in the first months of the occupation. Because the only functioning level of German administration that existed at that time was the local one, it was municipal politics that could reveal either the success or failure of democratic change. Democratic changes initiated at the local level in a *Nullpunkt* situation by grassroots groups like the Antifas and truly representative citizens' councils would have helped to solidify a tradition of genuinely participatory democracy from below. This trend, with the appropriate support from the occupation authorities, could have ascended and radiated to successively higher levels of German self-government. These grassroots democratic forces supported the stated Allied policies of a thorough denazification, demilitarization, decartellization, and democratization. No doubt such a grassroots democratic approach to change would have been more chaotic and time-consuming than a time-honored bureaucratic approach to restoring order, which relied on the administrative experience of mature civil servants. But the U.S. military, the German bureaucratic emphasis on the restoration of order, and the political primacy of capitalist economic recovery obstructed the depth and breadth of the process of genuine democratization that many Germans had hoped for after the defeat of Hitler. After all, this was the promise that the Allies had formulated in their occupation goals.

The result of this lack of democratization and the stress on economic recovery was a 1950s retreat, not only into the private sphere and consumerism, but also into a general skepticism toward political involvement and participatory democracy. This suspicion expressed itself in the reserved German reaction to HICOG attempts to introduce town meetings. It was similarly reflected in the somewhat sensationalized, but nonetheless real "renazification" of numerous medium and high-level government and private sector posts. Moreover, the growing intolerance toward any organizations to the Left of the SPD conveyed the lingering impact of MG's orientation and the stengthening of native German anti-Communism, which fostered the "red scare" and culminated in the 1956 ban on the KPD or on any organizations suspected of association with either Communism or the Soviet Union. The negative MG response to German and U.S. attempts to democratize Germany in the immediate postwar period yielded poor German – German relations and a passive general acceptance, however reticent, of rearmament. The anti-rearmament, anti-draft *"ohne mich"* movement of the 1950s, the re-emergence of a peace movement, and the attempt to hold a referendum on the issue of rearmament and West German entry into NATO did reflect some real grassroots democratic activism and opposition to the Cold War political developments of the 1950s. But these were all too easily dismissed by the government as subversive, while the government crackdowns on such expressions of protest were too passively accepted by a politically disillusioned and at times even submissive, but increasingly prosperous, society. Even the SPD decided to distance itself further from traditional Marxism in its 1959 Godesberg Program in an attempt to cast aside any doubts one might have had about its anti-Communism. Economic recovery did allow the trade unions more leverage to negotiate *Mitbestimmung* rights, but these went much less far than was hoped by the unions and the works councils in the early postwar period. The union participation in industrial decision making was limited primarily to bread-and-butter economic issues, and no longer spilled over into the larger socioeconomic and political realms.

The postwar social market economy raised the standard of living and provided a tighter social welfare net for most Germans by the mid- to late 1950s. This fostered a complacency in the majority of Germans who had lived through the short-lived Thousand-year Reich, the turmoil of the war, and the material and political uncertainty of the immediate postwar period. It made most Germans reluctant to concern themselves with either domestic or international political developments. It was not until the late 1960s that a growing number of voices calling for changes and governmental responsiveness to citizens' wishes made themselves heard. To a certain extent, it was a new postwar generation of West Germans, which began to assert its demands for democratic change, particularly in the area of educational reform. But the many environmentalist, antinuclear, pacifist, and feminist groups that emerged from below were not limited to a membership among the postwar generation alone. The 1970s saw a rapid increase in the number of citizens' action committees (*Bürgerinitiative*) and grassroots special-interest groups, as compared to formal lobbying groups. Particularly interesting is that these initiatives took place outside the traditional arena of party politics. These groups generally kept their distance from the parties, just as the parties made no major efforts to incorporate these activists and their concerns into their structures. This was indicative of the distrust of the traditionally hierarchical parties toward populist activists and vice versa, a distrust which had its roots in the immediate postwar period.[5] It was not until the formation of the Green Party that this distrust was transcended. The Green Party, as a very nontraditional political party, aspired to be and to remain more of a democratic grassroots or "alternative" movement than a traditionally hierarchical political party, although it entered the German electoral system on a par with old-line political parties.

Extraparliamentary populist activism continues to exist in Germany. The opposition movement that brought down the government of the German Democratic Republic was clearly a grassroots one. The fact that the New Forum and various other East German reformist political groups tried to remain part of a spontaneous movement, refusing to play traditional party politics while the other parties profited from support and material aid from West German political parties, was at least partly responsible for their poor showing in the 1990 elections. The West German support for the East German offshoots of the CDU, SPD, and FDP, like the U.S. support of those Western German political parties it felt ideologically closest to during the occupation period, significantly disadvantaged the burgeoning of any new East German parties or political movements. The citizens of the GDR, like their West German brothers and sisters some forty years ago, chose material prosperity and reliance on an economically successful Western power over more complex – and uncertain – internal democratic reforms. In both cases, a strong economic power offering a quick capitalist solution to pressing eco-

---

5. Parties had always distrusted activists whom they did not control and who might make inroads into their base of support.

nomic concerns in the midst of political upheaval found eager allies among the native leadership and, without too much difficulty, was able to gain the support of the general population. Even though East Germans, as the minority, have now merged their major political groupings into those of the larger West German parties[6] and, in the process, have acceded to their hierarchical structures and political platforms, those who sought grassroots reforms and structural democratization in the 1980s, provoking the fall of the Honecker regime, will probably not be satisfied with the top-down German political system and mere access to material comforts. In a way, this continued tension between economic recovery and sociopolitical democratization mirrors the early developments during the U.S. occupation of Germany. The immediate economic success that was anticipated – as we now know, an overly optimistic expectation in the case of a united Germany – overpowered the grassroots impetus for democratic transformation.

6. The exception here is the Party of Democratic Socialism (PDS), the successor to the Socialist Unity Party (SED).

BIBLIOGRAPHY

Archival Sources

Archiv der Industrie- und Handelskammer Frankfurt am Main:
Manuscript by H. G. Heymann.
Archiv der Industrie- und Handelskammer München:
Akt XXIII-107 (Dienstenthebungen).
Akt XXIII-568 (II).
Sitzungsprotokolle, 1945–1949.
Bayerisches Hauptstaatsarchiv:
Ministerium für Sonderaufgaben (MSo) files.
Office of Military Government-Bavaria files on microfiche:
Record Group (RG) 226, OMGBY.
Berlin Document Center (BDC):
NSDAP and SS and SA as well as some auxiliary organization files were
    checked for elected and appointed office holders in Munich, Frankfurt
    and Stuttgart, 1945–1948.
Hauptstaatsarchiv Stuttgart (Baden-Württemberg):
Office of Military Government-U.S. and Württemberg-Baden files on
    microfiche:
Record Group (RG) 260, OMGUS and OMGWB.
Hessisches Hauptstaatsarchiv:
Abteilung (Abt.) 501, 502, 503, 507.
Institut für Zeitgeschichte -Munich (IfZ):
Diaries and Papers:
ED 117: Fritz Eberhard
ED 120: Wilhelm Hoegner
ED 122: James K. Pollock Diaries
Du 005: Georg Fischer Nachlass
MA 1427/2: Walter J. Muller Nachlass.
Military Government Collections:
Fg 14.
Manuscripts:
Walter Dorn, "The Unfinished Purge," unfinished MS.

Office of Military Government-U.S. Zone files on microfiche:

RG 84, POLAD

RG 84, POLAD TS

RG 260, AG

RG 260, CAD

RG 260, ISD

RG 260, ODI

RG 260, OMGBY

RG 260, OMGH

RG 260, OMGWB

RG 260, OMGUS

RG 260, POLAD

RG 260, USGCC.

National Archives Record Administration (NARA)-Washington, D. C.

Modern Military Branch:

Record Group (RG) 59, OSS, Research and Analysis (R&A) reports.

RG 226, OSS, Field Intelligence Studies (FIS).

RG 226. OSS, XL files.

RG 226, OSS/SSU, Field Intelligence Studies (FIS).

State Department

RG 84, POLAD TS files.

Stadtarchiv Frankfurt am Main(StA Ffm):

Ansprachen.

Chroniken und Ortsgeschichte (S5).

Magistratsakten (Mag).

Mitteilungen der Stadtverwaltung Frankfurt a. M.

Nachlässe:

S1/38 Kurt Blaum

Wilhelm Hollbach

S1/25 B. Müller

S1/30 Peter Fischer

S1/98 T. Häbich.

Personensammlung (S2).

Personnel Records.

Protokolle:

Amtsleiterbesprechungen 1945

Bürgerratssitzungen 1945–1946, including Ausschusssitzungen

Magistratssitzungen 1945–1949

Stadtverordnetenversammlungssitzungen 1946–1949, including
    Ausschusssitzungen.

Stadtarchiv München(StA Mü):

Bürgermeister und Rat-Akten (BuR).

"Munich Detachment Historical Report for 1947–1948."

Ratskartei.

Ratssitzungsprotokolle (RP), 1945–1949, including Ausschusssitzungen.

Verzeichnis vom Direktorium A.

Stadtarchiv Stuttgart (StA St):
Hauptaktei.
Manuscripts:
Kc 248 Heinz Eschwege: "Vom Niedergang und Aufstieg der Stadt
    Stuttgart," 1962.
Personalamt files.
Personalprüfungsausschuss fürs Polizeipräsidium files.
Protokolle:
Gemeindebeiratssitzungen 1945–1946, including Ausschusssitzungen.
Gemeinderatssitzungen 1946–1949, including Ausschusssitzungen.
Innere Abteilungssitzungen 1945–1949.
Wirtschaftsarchiv-Baden-Würrtemberg, Stuttgart:
Sitzungsprotokolle des Vorläufigen Württembergischen Witschaftsrates.

Unpublished Primary Sources in Private Collections

Personal papers of Dr. Elgin Hollbach, Daughter of OB Wilhelm Hollbach,
    Frankfurt a. M.

Interviews

Professor James Aronson, chief of press, District Information Services
    Control Command (DISCC)-Western Military District; New York, 27
    Dec. 1985.
Emil Carlebach, KPD city councilor 1948–49 in Frankfurt and member of
    the original editorial board of the *Frankfurter Rundschau*; Frankfurt, 30
    May 1983.
Heinz Eschwege, member of "Rettet Stuttgart" and Radio Stuttgart,
    1945–1946; Stuttgart, 30 Nov. 1983.
Dr. Rupprecht Gerngross, leader of the Freiheits-Aktion-Bayern (FAB);
    Munich, 28 Feb. 1982.
Dr. Otto Gritschneder, city councilor (parteilose Katholiken) in Munich
    1948–52; Munich, 26 March 1982.
Dr. Erwin Hamm, CSU city councilor in Munich 1948–1956 and profes-
    sional Munich department head 1945–1974; Munich, 1 July 1983.
Dr Hildegard Hamm-Brücher, FDP city councilor in Munich, 1948–52;
    Munich, 1 July 1983.
Dr. Wolfgang Haußmann, *Bürgermeister* of Stuttgart, 1945–46; FDP city
    councilor in Stuttgart 1946–53; Stuttgart, 30 Nov. 1982.
Dr. Elgin Hollbach, daughter of OB Wilhelm Hollbach; Frankfurt a. M., 27
    July 1983.
Ernest Langendorf, DISCC Press Control officer in Munich; Munich,
    25 Feb. 1982.

Dr. Ottheinrich Leiling, FAB member; Munich, March 1982.

Adelheid Liessmann, KPD city councilor in Munich, 1946–1953; Munich, 20 April 1982.

Adolf Maislinger, KPD city councilor in Munich, 1945–46; Munich, 20 Oct. 1982.

Rudi Menzer, SPD city councilor in Frankfurt 1945–1946 and professional department head 1946–1960 and Bürgermeister 1960–66 and Hessian Landtag member 1966–70; Frankfurt a. M., 6 June 1983.

Oskar Neumann, KPD city councilor in Munich1948–52; Munich, 2 April 1982.

Kal Oravetz, legal advisor to G-5, USFET Headquarters; Plymouth, N. H., 18–19 Oct. 1986.

Gabriele Schiefer, daughter-in-law of Gustav Schiefer, SPD Munich city Councilor, 1945–52; Munich, 28 March 1982.

Dr. Ludwig Schmid, CSU city councilor in Munich 1945–52; Munich, 4 August 1982.

Henry Walter, deputy detachment commander in Stuttgart 1948–49; Plymouth, N.H., 17–19 Oct. 1986.

Georg Wulffius, German advisor and interpreter for the Historical Information and Political Intelligence Division of the Munich MG detachment, 1945–1946; 3 May 1982, Munich.

Correspondence with U.S. Military Government and Information Control Division Personnel

Cedric Belfrage, DISCC Press Control officer in Frankfurt 1945; letter of 22 Nov. 1984.

Lt. Col. (Ret.) Hugh G. Elbot, ICD censor in Stuttgart 1945, Civil Affairs officer, Stuttgart detachment 1945–1946; letter of 26 July 1986.

Marion B. Findlay, Political Intelligence officer in Stuttgart from July 1946 to Jan. 1947; letter of 17 Oct. 1986.

Col. (Ret.) Charles L. Jackson, Stuttgart detachment commander July 1945–1946; letters of 6 August 1986 and 20 September 1986.

Gerald C. Sola, Jr., deputy detachment commander 1946, Frankfurt, and detachment (L&S) commander1949, Frankfurt; letter of 20 July 1986.

Rolland H. Stimson, Trade and Industry officer in Stuttgart detachment in July 1945 and assistant detachment commander Sept. 1945–July 1946; letter of 22 September 1986.

Shepard Stone, ICD Press Licensing staff member, August–Dec. 1945; letter of 8 Nov. 1984.

Published Documents

Magistrat der Stadt Frankfurt a. M. (ed.). *Frankfurt am Main 1945–1965*: Ein 20-Jahresbericht. Frankfurt, n.d.

Notter, Harley A. *Postwar Foreign Policy Preparation 1939–1945*. Department of State Publication 3580. General Foreign Policy Series 15. Washington, 1950.

Operations Research Office. Johns Hopkins University. *A Survey of the Experience and Opinions of U.S. Military Government Officers in World War II*. Chevy Chase, Md., 1956.

Pollock, James K. et al.(eds.), *Germany under Occupation*. Ann Arbor, 1949.

"Protocol of the Proceedings of the Berlin Conference of 2 August 1945." *House of Commons, Accounts and Papers*. XXIV, 1946–47. London, 1947.

Provost Marshall General's School. *U.S. Military Government in Germany: Operations from late-March to mid-July 1945*. Training Packet No. 57. Frankfurt, 1950.

Raymond, Col. John M. "Military Government Regulations." In USFET, G-5, *Military Government Weekly Information Bulletin*. Military Government Conference Edition. August 27-28, 1945, p. 130.

Ruhm von Oppen, Beate (ed.). *Documents on Germany under Occupation 1945–54*. London, 1955.

Supreme Headquarters Allied Expeditionary Forces (SHAEF). *Handbook for Unit Commanders (Germany)*. 15 September 1944.

Starr, Joseph R. *U.S. Military Government in Germany: Operations during the Rhineland Campaign*. MG Training Packet No. 56. Karlsruhe, 1950.

United States Department of State. *Germany, 1947–1949: The Story in Documents*. Publication 3556. Washington, 1950.

_____. *Participation of the U.S. Government in International Conferences, 1 July 1945 – 30 June 1946*. Washington, 1946.

United States Forces, European Theater. *Occupation*. Washington, 1945.

Other Published Primary Sources

American Friends of German Freedom. *Germany Tomorrow*. New York, 1944.

Belfrage, Cedric. *Seeds of Destruction*. New York, 1954.

Blum, John Morton (ed.). *From the Morgenthau Diaries: Years of War, 1941–1945*. Boston, 1967.

Bolten, Seymour R. "Military Government and the German Political Parties." *Annals of the American Academy of Political and Social Sciences*, 267 (1950): 55–67.

Bruner, Jerome S. *Mandate from the People*. New York, 1944.

Cantril, Hadley and Mildred Strunk. *Public Opinion 1935–1946*. Princeton, N.J., 1951.

Carlebach, Emil. "Frankfurts Antifaschisten 1945." In *Als der Krieg zu Ende war: Hessen 1945* . Ed. Ulrich Schneider. Frankfurt a. M., 1980.

_____. *Zensur ohne Schere : Die Gründerjahre der "Frankfurter Rundschau" 1945/47*. Frankfurt, 1985.

Coles, Harry L. and Albert G. Weinberg. *Civil Affairs: Soldiers Become Governors*. Washington, 1964.

Dorn, Walter L. *Inspektionsreise in der US-Zone*. Trans. and Ed. Lutz Niethammer. Stuttgart, 1973.

Dunner, Joseph. "Information Control in the American Zone of Germany, 1945–1946." In *American Experiences in Military Government in World War II*. Ed. Carl J. Friedrich. New York, 1948: 276–291.

Engler, Robert. "The Individual Soldier and the Occupation." *Annals of the American Academy of Political and Social Sciences*, 267 (1950): 77–86.

Erinnerungsschrift zur Feier des 25. Jahrestages der FAB am 27. und 28. April 1945. Munich, 1970.

Fainsod, Merle. "The Development of American Military Government Policy During World War II." In *American Experiences in Military Government in World War II*. Ed. Carl J. Friedrich. New York, 1948: 23–51.

Friedrich, Carl J. (ed.), *American Experiences in Military Government in World War II*. New York, 1948.

Gillen, J. F. J. *State and Local Government in West Germany, 1945–53*. Ed. Historical Division of the Office of the U.S. High Commissioner for Germany. n.p., 1953.

Griffith, William E. "Denazification in the United States Zone of Germany." *Annals of the American Academy of Political and Social Sciences*, 267 (1950): 68–76.

Hagen, Paul. *Germany after Hitler*. New York, 1944.

Hale, William Harlan. "Our Failure in Germany." *Harper's Magazine*, 181, no. 1147 (December 1945): 515–523.

Kennan, George F. *Memoirs, 1925–50*. Boston, 1967.

Korman, John G. *U.S. Denazification Policy in Germany 1944–1950*. Historical Division, Office of the U.S. High Commissioner for Germany, 1952.

Leipner, Kurt (ed.). *Chronik der Stadt Stuttgart 1933–1945*. Stuttgart, 1982.

Lincoln, Charles. *Auf Befehl der Militärregierung*. Trans. Hans and Elsbeth Herlin. Munich, 1965.

Ludwig, Emil. *The Moral Conquest of Germany*. Garden City, N. Y., 1945.

Lumme, H. W. "Will America be Lost ... ? Military Government-Ecke Reuterweg." *MG-Information, Zeitschrift für die Mitarbeiter im Bereich der Metallgesellschaft AG*. Frankfurt a. M. (1981): H.1, 70–71.

Martin, James Stewart. *All Honorable Men*. Boston, 1950.

Mosely, Philip E. "The Occupation of Germany: New Light on How the Zones Were Drawn." *Foreign Affairs*, 28 (July 1950): 580–604.

Murphy, Robert. *Dipolmat Among Warriors*. New York, 1964.

Neumann, Sigmund. "Transition to Democracy in Germany." *Political Science Quarterly*, 59 (1944): 341–362.

Norman, Albert. *Our German Policy: Propaganda and Culture*. New York, 1951.

Penrose, Ernest F. *Economic Planning for the Peace*. Princeton, 1953.

Plischke, Elmer. "Denazifying the Reich." *The Review of Politics*, 9 (April 1947): 153–172.

Pollock, James K. *What Shall Be Done With Germany?* Northfield, Minn., 1944.

Richter, Hans Werner. "Ost und West— Die ausgleichende Aufgabe Mitteleuropas." *Der Ruf*, nr.12, 1 Sept. 1945: 2.

Schattenhofer, Michael (ed.). *Chronik der Stadt München 1945–1948*. Munich,1980.

Seger, Gerhart H. and Siegfried K. Marck. *Germany: To Be or Not To Be?* New York, 1943.

Shuster, George. *The Ground I Walked on: Reflections of a College President*. New York, 1961.

Starr, Joseph R. *Denazification, Occupation and Control of Germany*. Salisbury, N.C., 1977.

Stimson, Henry L. and McGeorge Bundy. *On Active Service in Peace and War*. New York, 1947.

Strölin, Karl. *Stuttgart im Endstadium des Krieges*. Stuttgart, 1950.

Swarm, William R. "The Impact of the Proconsular Experience on Civil Affairs Organization and Doctrine." In Robert Wolfe, ed. *Americans as Proconsuls: U.S. Military Government in Germany and Japan, 1944–52*. Carbondale, 1984.

Vietzen, Hermann. *Chronik der Stadt Stuttgart 1945–1948*. Stuttgart, 1972.

Warburg, James P. *The Long Road Home: The Autobiography of a Maverick*. Garden City, N.Y., 1964.

Newspapers and Magazines

Das andere Deutschland.

Bayerische Landeszeitung, Nachrichtenblatt der Allierten 12. Heeresgruppe für die deutsche Zivilbevölkerung, 1 June 1945.

Frankfurter Allgemeine Zeitung, 26 March 1955; 27 March 1967; 8 May 1970.

Frankfurter Presse, 6 July 1945.

Frankfurter Neue Presse, 15 August 1946.

Frankfurter Rundschau, 27 Nov. 1945; 31 Dec. 1945; 26 March 1970; 19 March 1974.

Münchner Merkur, 29 April 1949; 27 April 1955.

News Digest, 30 April 1945.

New Yorker, 13 May 1945.

New York Herald Tribune, 2 Nov. 1944.

New York Times, 10 July 1945.
Stuttgarter Zeitung, 17 August 1950; 3 July 1963.
Süddeutsche Zeitung, 26 April 1946.
Sunday Times, 29 April 1945

Secondary Sources (Published)

Abelshauser, Wilhelm. *Wirtschaft in Westdeutschland, 1945–1948. Rekonstruktion und Wachstumsbedingungen in der amerikanischen und britischen Zone.* Stuttgart, 1975.

Backer, John H. *Priming the German Economy. American Occupational Policies 1945–48.* Durham, N. C., 1971.

_____. *The Winds of History: The German Years of Lucius DuBignon Clay.* New York, 1983.

Badstübner, Rolf. *Restaurationsapologie und Fortschrittsverteufelung.* Frankfurt, 1978.

Balabkins, Nicholas. *Germany under Direct Controls. Economic Aspects of Industrial Disarmament 1945–48.* New Brunswick, 1964.

Balfour, Michael. *Four-Power Control in Germany and Austria 1945–1946.* Survey of International Affairs 1939–46. London, 1956.

Berghahn, Volker R. "West German Reconstruction and American Industrial Culture, 1945–1960." In *The American Impact on Postwar Germany.* Ed. Reiner Pommerin. Providence, R.I. and Oxford, 1995: 65–81.

Billerbeck, Rudolf. *Die Abgeordneten der ersten Landtage (1946–1951) und der Nationalsozialismus.* Düsseldorf, 1971.

Blumenstock, Friedrich. *Der Einmarsch der Amerikaner und Franzosen im nördlichen Württemberg im April 1945.* Stuttgart, 1957.

Boehling, Rebecca. "Grassroots Democracy and Military Government: Local German Politics in the United States Zone of Occupation, 1945–49." *Zeitschrift für Kulturaustausch.* 1987/2: 270–274.

_____. "Die politischen Lageberichte des Frankfurter Oberbürgermeisters Blaum an die amerikanische Militärregierung." In *Archiv für Frankfurts Geschichte und Kunst*, 59 (1985): 485–537.

Borsdorf, Ulrich and Lutz Niethammer, eds. *Zwischen Befreiung und Besatzung. Analysen des US-Geheimdienstes über Positionen und Strukturen deutscher Politik 1945.* Wuppertal, 1976.

Braunthal, Gerard. "The Anglo-Saxon Model of Democracy in West Germany." *Archiv für Sozialgeschichte*, 17 (1978): 245–277.

Bungenstab, Karl-Ernst. "Die Ausbildung der amerikanischen Offiziere für die Militärregierungen nach 1945." *Jahrbuch für Amerika-Studien*, 18 (1973): 195–212.

_____. *Umerziehung zur Demokratie? Re-education Politik im Bildungswesen der US-Zone 1945–49.* Düsseldorf, 1970.

Chamberlin, Brewster S. *Kultur auf Trümmern: Berliner Berichte der amerikanischen Information Control Section, Juli–Dezember 1945.* Stuttgart, 1979.

Conference of Scholars on the Administration of Occupied Areas, 1943–55.
10–11 April 1970. Independence, Missouri, 1970.

Dastrup, Boyd L. *Crusade in Nuremberg: Military Occupation, 1945–1949.*
Westport, Conn, 1985.

Daub, Richard. *Journalismus zwischen Zwang und Freiheit.* Frankfurt a. M.,
1981.

Davis, Franklin M., Jr. *Come as a Conqueror: The United States Army's
Occupation of Germany 1945–1945.* New York, 1967.

Debatin, Otto. *Der Vorläufige Württembergische Wirtschaftsrat des Jahres
1945: Eine Chronik.* Stuttgart, 1955.

Dorn, Walter L. "The Debate over American Occupation Policy in
Germany 1944–45." *Political Science Quarterly,* 72 (1957): 481–501.

Falter, Jürgen W. "Kontinuität und Neubeginn. Die Bundestagswahl 1949
zwischen Weimar und Bonn." *Politische Vierteljahresschrift* 22 (1981):
236–63.

Fichter, Michael. "Aufbau und Neuordnung: Betriebsräte zwischen
Klassensolidarität und Betriebsloyalität." In *Von Stalingrad zur
Währungsreform.* Munich 1990: 469–549.

Foschepoth, Josef, ed. *Kalter Krieg und deutsche Frage.* Deutschland im
Widerstreit der Mächte 1945–1952. Göttingen, 1985.

Frei, Norbert. *Amerikanische Lizenzpolitik und deutsche Pressetradition.*
Munich, 1986.

Friedmann, W. *The Allied Military Government of Germany.* London, 1947.

Gaddis, John Lewis. *The United States and the Origins of the Cold War.* New
York, 1972.

Gatzke, Hans W. *Germany and the United States: "A Special Relationship?"*
Cambridge, Mass., 1980.

Gietz, Axel. *Die neue Alte Welt: Roosevelt, Churchill und die europäische
Nachkriegsordnung.* Munich, 1986.

Gimbel, John. *The American Occupation of Germany. Politics and the Military,
1945–49.* Stanford, 1968.

――――. *A German Community under American Occupation.* Stanford, 1961.

Graml, Hermann. "Die Alliierten in Deutschland." In *Westdeutschlands Weg
zur Bundesrepublik 1945–1949.* Beiträge von Mitarbeitern des Instituts
für Zeitgeschichte. Munich, 1976: 25–52.

Gulgowski, Paul W. *The American Military Government of United States
Occupied Zones [sic] of Post World War II Germany.* Frankfurt a. M., 1983.

Hammond, Paul W. "Directives for the Occupation of Germany: The
Washington Controversy." In *American Civil-Military Decisions.* Ed.
Harold Stein. Birmingham, AL, 1963: 311–464.

Hattenhauer, Hans. *Geschichte des Beamtentums. Vol. I: Handbuch des
Öffentlichen Dienstes.* Köln, 1980.

Hencke, Klaus-Dietmar and Hans Woller, eds. *Lehrjahre der CSU: Eine
Nachkriegspartei im Spiegel vertraulicher Berichte an die amerikanische
Militärregierung.* Stuttgart, 1984.

Herz, John H. "The Fiasco of Denazification in Germany." *Political Science Quarterly*. Vol. LXII, No 4 (1948): 569–594.

Hofmann, Wolfgang. "Oberbürgermeister als politische Elite im Wilhelminischen Reich und in der Weimarer Republik." In *Oberbürgermeister. Deutsche Führungsschichten in der Neuzeit*. Ed. Klaus Schwabe. Vol. 13. Boppard am Rhein, 1979: 17–38.

Holborn, Hajo. *American Military Government. Its Organizations and Policies*. Washington, 1947.

Hurwitz, Harold. *Die Stunde Null der deutschen Presse: Die amerikanische Pressepolitik in Deutschland 1945–1949*. Köln, 1972.

Huster, Ernst Ulrich, et al. *Determinanten der westdeutschen Restauration 1945–1949*. Frankfurt a. M. 1972.

Kimball, Warren F. *Swords or Ploughshares? The Morgenthau Plan for Defeated Nazi Germany, 1943–46*. Philadelphia, 1976.

Kirn, Richard and Madlen Lorei. *Frankfurt und die drei wilden Jahre*. Frankfurt, 1962.

Kocka, Jürgen. "1945: Neubeginn oder Restauration?" In *Wendepunkte deutscher Geschichte 1848–1945* . Ed. Carola Stern und Heinrich A. Winkler. Frankfurt a. M., 1979: 141–168.

_____. "Restauration oder Neubeginn? Deutschland 1945–1949." *Demokratie und Sozialismus*, Nr. 1 (1979): 112–119.

Krieger, Leonard. "The Potential for Democratization in Occupied Germany: A Problem in Historical Projection," *Public Policy*, 17 (1968): 27–58.

Krieger, Wolfgang. *General Lucius D. Clay und die amerikanische Deutschlandpolitik 1945–1949*. Stuttgart, 1987.

Kropat, Wolf-Arno. *Hessen in der Stunde Null 1945/47*. Wiesbaden, 1979.

Kuklick, Bruce. *American Policy and the Division of Germany*. Ithaca, N.Y., 1972.

Lademacher, Horst. "Aufbruch oder Restauration – Einige Bemerkungen zur Interdependenz von Innen- und Aussenpolitik in der Gründungsphase der Bundesrepublik Deutschland." In *Deutschland in der Weltpolitik des 19. und 20. Jahrhunderts*. Ed. Immanuel Geiss and Bernd J. Wendt. Düsseldorf, 1973: 563–84.

Lange-Quassowski, Jutta-B. *Neuordnung oder Restauration. Das Demokratiekonzept der amerikanischen Besatzungsmacht und die politische Sozialisation der Westdeutschen*. Opladen, 1979.

Latour, Conrad F. and Thilo Vogelsang. *Okkupation und Wiederaufbau: Die Tätigkeit der Militärregierung in der amerikanischen Besatzungszone Deutschlands 1944–1947*. Stuttgart, 1973.

Loewenberg, Gerhard. "The Remaking of the German Party System." In *European Politics*. Eds. M. Dogan and R. Rose. Boston, 1971: 259–280.

Mauch, Berthold. *Die bayerische FDP, 1945–1949*. Munich, 1981.

Mausbach-Bromberger, Barbara. *Arbeiterwiderstand in Frankfurt am Main*. Frankfurt, 1976.

Maxwell, John A. "Failed Social and Economic Policies: The German Social Democratic Programme, 1945–1949." *Europa*, 5, no. 2 (1982): 163–176.

Merritt, Anna J. and Richard L., eds. *Public Opinion in Occupied Germany. The OMGUS Surveys 1945-1949.* Chicago, 1970.

Mick, Günter. *Den Frieden gewinnen: Das Beispiel Frankfurt 1945 bis 1951.* Frankfurt a. M., 1985.

Mintzel, Alf. "Besatzungspolitik und Entwicklung der bürgerlichen Parteien in den Westzonen." In *Das Parteiensystem der Bundesrepublik.* Ed. Dietrich Staritz. 2nd ed. Opladen, 1980: 73-89.

Moskowitz, Moses. "The Political Re-education of the Germans: The Emergence of Parties and Politics in Württemberg-Baden." *Political Science Quarterly,* 61, no. 4 (1946): 535-561.

Müller, Roland. *Stuttgart zur Zeit des Nationalsozialismus.* Stuttgart, 1988.

Napoli, Joseph F. "Denazification from an American's Viewpoint." *Annals of the American Academy of Political and Social Sciences.* 264 (1949): 115-123.

Neumann, Franz. *Behemoth. The Structure and Practice of National Socialism: 1933-1944.* 2nd ed. New York, 1944.

Niclauss, Karlheinz. *Restauration oder Renaissance der Demokratie? Die Entstehung der Bundesrepublik 1945-1949.* Berlin, 1982.

Niethammer, Lutz. "Aktivität und Grenzen der Antifa-Ausschüsse 1945: Das Beispiel Stuttgart." *Vierteljahrshefte für Zeitgeschichte* (1975), no. 3: 297-331.

_____. " Die amerikanische Besatzungspolitik zwischen Verwaltungstradition und politischen Parteien in Bayern 1945," *Vierteljahrshefte für Zeitgeschichte,* 15 (1967): 153-210.

_____, et al. *Arbeiterinitiative 1945: Antifaschistische Ausschüsse und Reorganisation der Arbeiterbewegung von Deutschland.* Wuppertal, 1976.

_____. *Entnazifizierung in Bayern.* Frankfurt, 1972.

Peterson, Edward N. *The American Occupation of Germany.* Detroit, 1978.

_____. *The Many Faces of Defeat: The German People's Experience in 1945.* New York, 1990.

Plum, Günther. "Versuche gesellschaftspolitischer Neuordnung. Ihr Scheitern in Kräftefeld deutscher und allierter Politik," In *Westdeuschlands Weg zur Bundesrepublik 1945-1949.* Beiträge von Mitarbeitern des Instituts für Zeitgeschichte. München, 1976: 90-117.

Pommerin, Reiner, ed. *The American Impact on Postwar Germany.* Providence, R.I. and Oxford, 1995.

Prowe, Diethelm. "Economic Democracy in Post-World War II Germany: Corporatist Crisis Response, 1945-1948." *Journal of Modern History.* 57/3 (Sept. 1985): 451-482.

Robinson, Donald B. "Why Denazification is Lagging." *American Mercury.* 62 (May 1946): 563-570.

Rogers, Daniel E. "Transforming the German Party System: The United States and the Origins of Political Moderation, 1945-1949." *Journal of Modern History,* 65/3 (Sept. 1993): 512-541.

Rudzio, Wolfgang. "Die ausgebliebene Sozialisierung an Rhein und Ruhr." *Archiv für Sozialgeschichte,* 18 (1978): 1-39.

Sauer, Paul. *25 Jahre Baden-Württemberg, Rückblick auf die Entstehung des Bundeslandes*. Ausstellungskatalog des Landtags in Zusammenarbeit mit dem Hauptstaatsarchiv Stuttgart. Stuttgart, 1977.

Schmidt, Eberhard. *Die verhinderte Neuordnung 1945-1952*. Frankfurt a. M.,1970.

Schmollinger, Horst and Dietrich Staritz. "Zur Entwicklung der Parteien in den Westzonen." In *Das Parteiensystem der Bundesrepublik*. Ed. Dietrich Staritz. 2nd ed. Opladen, 1980: 109-126.

Schnoor, Herbert. "Gedanken zum Neuaufbau der Verwaltung nach 1945," In *Die Wiederherstellung des Berufsbeamtentums nach 1945: Geburtsfehler oder Stützfehler der Demokratiegründung in Westdeutschland?* Ed. Friedrich Gerhard Schwegmann. Dusseldorf, 1986: 17-24.

Schott, Herbert. *Die Amerikaner als Besatzungsmacht in Würzburg (1945-1949)*. Mainfränkische Studien, Würzburg, 1985.

Schorske, Carl E. "The Dilemma in Germany." *Virginia Quarterly Review*, 24, no. 1 (Winter 1948): 29-42.

Schwarz, Hans-Peter. *Vom Reich zur Bundesrepublik. Deutschland im Widerstreit der aussenpolitischen Konzeptionen in den Jahren der Besatzungsherrschaft 1945-1949*. 2nd ed. Stuttgart, 1980.

Smith, Bradley F. *The Shadow Warriors: OSS and the Origins of the CIA*. New York, 1983.

Smith, Jean Edward. *Lucius D. Clay: An American Life*. New York, 1990.

Smith, Richard Harris. *OSS: The Secret History of America's First Central Intelligence Agency*. Berkeley, 1972.

Snell, John L. *Wartime Origins of the East-West Dilemma over Germany*. New Orleans, 1959.

Söllner, Alfons (ed.). *Zur Archäologie der Demokratie in Deutschland: Analysen politischer Emigranten im amerikanischen Geheimdienst*. 2 vol. Frankfurt, 1982.

Staritz, Dietrich, ed. *Das Parteiensystem der Bundesrepublik*. 2nd ed. Opladen, 1980.

Sträter, Artur. "Denazification." *Annals of the American Academy of Political and Social Science*, 260 (Nov. 1948): 43-52.

Timmermann, Johannes. "Anton Fingerle zum Gedächtnis." *Münchner Anzeiger*. 26 March 1982: 26.

Wehdeking, Volker Christian. *Der Nullpunkt. Über die Konstituierung der deutschen Nachkriegsliteratur (1945-48) in den amerikanischen Kriegsgefangenenlagern*. Stuttgart, 1971.

Wettig, Gerhard. *Entmiliarisierung und Wiederbewaffnung in Deutschland 1943-1955*. München, 1967.

Wieck, Hans Georg. *Christliche und Freie Demokraten in Hessen, Rheinland-Pfalz, Baden und Württemberg 1945/46*. Düsseldorf, 1958.

Willis, F. Roy. *The French in Germany, 1945-1949*. Stanford, 1962.

Winkler, Dörte. "Die amerikanische Sozialisierungspolitik in Deutschland 1945-1948." In *Politische Weichenstellungen in Nachkriegsdeutschland*. Ed. Heinrich A. Winkler. Göttingen, 1979: 88-100.

Winkler, Heinrich A. (ed.), *Politische Weichenstellungen im Nachkriegsdeutschland*. Göttingen, 1979.

Wolfe, Robert (ed.). *Americans as Proconsuls: U.S. Military Government in Germany and Japan, 1944–52*. Carbondale, Ill., 1984.

Woller, Hans. *Gesellschaft und Politik in der amerikanischen Besatzungszone: Die Region Ansbach und Fürth*. München, 1986.

Wuermeling, H. L. *Die Weisse Liste. Umbruch der politischen Kultur in Deutschland 1945*. Berlin, 1981.

Ziemke, Earl F. *The U.S. Army in the Occupation of Germany 1944–46*. Army Historical Series. Washington, 1975.

Zink, Harold. *American Military Government in Germany*. New York, 1947.

_____. *The United States in Germany, 1944–1955*. Princeton, 1957.

Unpublished Secondary Sources

Benz, Wolfgang. "Die Auseinandersetzungen um das Berufsbeamtentum 1945–1952." Skripten der Sektion 9: "Deutsche Nachkriegsgeschichte nach 1945: Neuaufbau oder Restauration?" bei dem 33. deutschen Historikertag, 26. bis 30. März 1980 in Würzburg.

Beyersdorf, Peter. "Militärregierung und Selbstverwaltung: Eine Studie zur amerikanischen Besatzungspolitik auf der Stufe einer Gemeinde in den Jahren 1945–1948, dargestellt an Beispiele aus dem Stadt- und Landkreis Coburg." Ph.D. dissertation. University of Erlangen-Nürnberg, 1966.

Boehling, Rebecca L. "The Effects of American Anti-German Sentiment on Planning and Policy-Making for Postwar Germany, 1943–1947." M.A. thesis. University of Wisconsin-Madison, 1980.

Diskant, James A. "German Reconstruction and Labor Activism: The Case Study of Dortmund, 1945–1955." Ph.D. dissertation. Boston College, 1988.

Eilks, Thomas. "Die Münchner SPD 1945–1948." Staatsexamenarbeit. University of Munich, 1983.

Gerstenberg, Günther. "Der Wiederaufbau der Münchner Gewerkschaftsbewegung und der Bayerische Gewerkschaftsbund 1945–1949." Magisterarbeit. University of Munich, 1984.

Höhn, Maria. "GIs, Veronikas, and Lucky Strikes: German Reactions to the American Military Presence in the Rhineland-Palatinate during the 1950s." Ph.D. dissertation. University of Pennsylvania, 1995.

Kock, Peter Jakob. "Die Grundlegung des bayerischen Nachkriegsföderalismus." Ph.D. dissertation. University of Munich, 1981.

Mensonides, Louis J. *United States Foreign Policy: Germany, 1945–1959*. Ph.D. dissertation. University of Kentucky 1964 (Ann Arbor, 1969).

Sturm, Hubert. "Thomas Wimmer." Hauptseminararbeit. University of
  Munich, 1980.
Wacker, Hans. "Kurze Lebensbeschreibung von Dr. h.c. Karl Scharnagl. "
  Part of then (1981) unfinished Ph.D. dissertation on Scharnagl.
  University of Munich.

Index